The Work of Teachers
in America:
A Social History
Through Stories

The Work of Teachers in America: A Social History Through Stories

Edited by

Rosetta Marantz Cohen
Samuel Scheer
Smith College

LEA   LAWRENCE ERLBAUM ASSOCIATES, PUBLISHERS
1997   Mahwah, New Jersey

Lawrence Erlbaum Associates, Inc., Publishers
10 Industrial Avenue
Mahwah, New Jersey 07430-2262

Cover design by Kathryn Houghtaling and Jessica LaPlaca

Library of Congress Cataloging-in-Publication-Data

Cohen, Rosetta Marantz.
  The work of teachers in America : a social history
through stories / Rosetta Marantz Cohen, Samuel Scheer.
   p. cm
  Includes biographical references and index.
  ISBN 0-8058-2690-4 (cloth : alk. paper). — ISBN
0-8058-2250-X (paper : alk. paper).
  1. Teachers—United States—History. 2. Teachers—United States—Social Conditions. 3. Teachers—United States—Biography.
  I. Scheer, Samuel. II. Title
  LB1775.2.C645 1996
  371.1'00973'09—dc20

Books published by Lawrence Erlbaum Associates are printed
on acid-free paper, and their bindings are chosen for strength
and durability.

Printed in the United States of America
10 9 8 7 6 5 4 3 2 1

To our families and to Elizabeth

Contents

ᘓ ◆ ങ

Preface

๛ ◆ ๙

This book is a social history of the teaching profession told through the medium of stories. The volume traces the evolution of the teacher and the teacher's work from the early republican period, when teaching was itinerant and short-term, to contemporary times, when the complexities of the teacher's job make it more than full-time work. We believe the volume fills a great void in the literature on teachers and teaching. Although there is considerable statistical research on the history of the profession, far less social history has been written, and no work before this one has documented the profession over time, and from the point of view of the teacher.

The stories in the volume are told through a great range of narrative forms. These include fiction and poetry, journal entries, letters, ethnographic descriptions, and excerpts from novels and autobiographies. As the introduction to the book makes clear, we have chosen to define "story" here in a broad sense, encompassing any narrative that draws the reader into its world in a vivid and emotionally compelling way. Stories of this sort allow the reader to experience firsthand the struggles and successes of many different kinds of teachers, over the course of 200 years. Included are the voices of men and women, Whites, Blacks, and Asian Americans. There are stories about gay teachers and teachers of disabled children. Stories are set in urban, inner-city classrooms, in remote areas of rural America, and in affluent suburbs. Many of the stories are written by the teachers themselves, and take the form of journals or letters. Others are written by former teachers, who have gone on to become professional writers. By viewing 200 years of the teaching profession through this colorful and varied lens, one gains a unique perspective on the field, its continuities and problems.

The Work of Teachers in America is directed to a wide audience. Certainly the book is intended for use in educational foundations courses, including the history of American education, and the sociology of teaching. The volume may be used alone, or along with a traditional textbook, as a collection of primary sources to supplement the students' understanding of a particular historical epic. We also see this work as a useful text in teacher education courses. The vivid focus on classroom life presented in these stories, and the timeless nature of the issues considered here make the volume a lively alternative to a book of case studies. Indeed, we believe that these stories have a richness and complexity unmatched by case studies. Problems of discipline, burnout, parental indifference, and other such subjects, are drawn with great subtlety in many of these works. Finally, because the book is composed of so many wonderful stories, we see an additional audience outside the confines of an education classroom—in any reader who is generally interested in the subject of teaching.

The book is divided into four historical sections. The first part deals with images of the teacher during the Colonial and Early Republican period (1780–1830), when teaching was neither a career nor a profession, and the teacher's ability to wield a cudgel took priority over other pedagogical skills. The second part considers early reforms in the field, and the feminization of teaching during the Common School era (1835–1875). Stories in this section document the courageous work of pioneer teachers and teachers who ventured south in the early aftermath of the Civil War. Part III deals with the Progressive Period (1880–1945). These stories document the development of urban schools and the education of immigrant America. Many of the pieces in this section show the tension between the new and the old, between reform and the stubborn traditions of the past. The final part of the volume looks at the "modern" teacher, and the radical transformation of the profession from the 1950s to the present. In this final part of the book, stories consider a range of issues, including multiculturalism, class conflict, and the ambiguous line that teachers must walk between the personal and the public.

Each section of the book closes with a series of questions, activities, and suggested readings. We have designed the questions both to help readers reflect on individual stories and to make connections between stories and across time periods. For better or worse, there are continuities in the profession that span centuries. The questions and activities are designed to help the reader recognize these continuities, and to consider, perhaps, how the more troubling and persistent characteristics of the teaching profession might ultimately be changed.

ACKNOWLEDGMENTS

We would like to thank the many people who assisted us in writing and compiling this volume. Bruce Sajack, the research librarian at Smith College; Georgia Barnhill of the American Antiquarian Society; Gail Farr of the Balch Institute for Ethnic Studies; and Ellen Sulser of the State Historical Society of Iowa.

We would like to thank Linda Henigin, at Erlbaum, for her help with the project, as well as the following reviewers who offered suggestions in revising the manuscript: Deborah Anders, University of Arizona; Betty A. Sichel, University of Houston; and Thomas V. O'Brien, Millersville University.

We would also like to thank Paula Marantz Cohen, Murray S. Cohen, Bruce Murphree, and Richard Millington for their editorial suggestions and other helpful input.

Finally, we are deeply indebted to our editor at Lawrence Erlbaum Associates, Naomi Silverman, who championed this project and provided invaluable assistance.

—Rosetta Marantz Cohen
—Samuel Scheer

Introduction

The pieces collected in this volume trace the evolution of the teacher and the profession from the late 18th century to the present day. Although they represent a range of narrative forms, including letters, memoirs, short fiction, and ethnographies, all the selections included here are "stories"; they draw us both intellectually and emotionally into another world where different classrooms and different eras can be felt with great immediacy. Each piece in this volume, whether written in the past or in contemporary America, is a rich source for instructing the reader in the nature of the teaching act and in the reality of the teacher's life over time.

In the past several years, many educational theorists have come to embrace the idea of "story" as a legitimate vehicle for understanding the complex act of teaching. For Kathy Carter (1993), Michael Connelly and Jean Clandinin (1992), Robert Coles (1989), and many other investigator–practitioners, the knowledge gleaned from stories about teaching is perceived to be as valuable or even more valuable than the knowledge derived from other kinds of research approaches. These scholars have produced a body of work that has stretched the literature of educational research, and caused something of a crisis in a field long wedded to the quantitative and the empirical. The new interest in story knowledge, combined with a growing literature on constructivism and subjective sense-making in the classroom, truly seems to be revolutionizing teacher education. In many teacher education classes, case studies, ethnographies, and teacher autobiographies stand on level ground with traditional, quantitatively based textbooks. The personal, subjective experience of practitioners—whether told through their own voices, or secondhand—has gained an authority and a utility that it never was considered to possess before. Now a far greater range of sources and subjects become available for scrutiny, and the work of teaching opens itself up to study in even more rich and complex ways.

How does story knowledge differ from other ways of knowing? Anyone who has become engrossed in a powerful autobiography or a work of fiction knows well the inherent appeal of the story. Stories can delight and instruct us. A great story draws the reader into its own world, allowing for a kind of vicarious experience that often demands a reassessment of reality in light of its disclosures. Although "paradigmatic or scientific explanation requires

1

consistency and noncontradiction," story, as Kathy Carter noted, "accom-modates ambiguity and dilemma as central figures or themes" (Carter, 1993, p. 6). Stories, in other words, present life with all its unpredictability and subjectively understood motivations. Although most stories ultimately im-pose an order and coherence on the events being described, that order, in the best writing, is nuanced and complex and subject to a multiplicity of interpretations.

The particular way in which stories describe and define reality make them well suited to the illumination of the work of the teacher. The subjectivity of classroom experience, and the overlapping and contradictory forces that continuously play themselves out there make classrooms apt subjects for stories. The educational philosopher Maxine Greene has for decades inte-grated fictional allusions in her critical writing to illustrate obscure or abstract ideas about teaching. Indeed, more than 20 years ago, Greene defended the place of literature, with all of its capacity to evoke felt experience, in the education of teachers. "Literary experiences," wrote Greene, "are the most accessible experiences for educators remote from themselves." For teachers, "the evocation of literary works ... summons up possibilities" (Greene, 1978, p. 3).

This volume of teacher stories, then, falls in with a literature and methodological approach that has already existed in our field for many years, but has only recently gained a more formal and widespread acceptance. Like case studies and other qualitative material recently integrated into teacher education classes, this collection offers a window into the teacher's work and world. However, the volume attempts to extend that qualitative mate-rial in two important ways. In the first place, it adds the rich material provided by fiction to the story literature now used in education courses. Novels and short stories written by and about teachers and teaching have long provided a vivid and instructive picture of the profession. Like other forms of story narrative, fiction elevates and synthesizes experience in a wonderfully immediate way. Indeed, fiction often surpasses other narrative forms because of the imaginative and rhetorical skills of the author. We believe it is an important and long-neglected addition to preservice literature.

A second way in which this volume differs from other new preservice literature is in its historical perspective. The stories here offer readers not only a glimpse into a diverse range of contemporary classrooms, but also into the classrooms of the past. Teaching is one of the few professions that seems to systematically repudiate its own history, to discard as useless many of the ideas and understandings that preceded the present day. And yet there is clearly much to be learned about the profession—and about the society in general—by viewing teachers' work and lives from earlier decades or even earlier centuries. In terms of teachers' work in the classroom, historical stories offer surprisingly rich and useful material. In stories written 50, 100, or 200 years ago are keen insights into working with disaffected children, dealing with heterogeneous grouping, and resolving conflicts with parents. Teacher stories from the past also offer a unique perspective on the larger forces that influenced our culture throughout time: America's preoccupations and prejudices are reflected in the voices of teachers, and in their particular challenges in each era. Finally, in reading these stories from the past, one comes to see even more clearly how personal uncertainties and interior conflicts about the profession itself—conditions we tend to associate with contemporary practitioners—are experienced by even the earliest teachers in this volume. As human nature does not change, neither it seems, does the teacher's tenuous relationship to the craft. It is both constructive and consoling to recognize this enduring characteristic of the profession.

Indeed, one of the striking things you will note when reading through 200 years of stories about teachers is how consistently difficult the job of teacher has always been. In virtually every piece one can see the extent to which this is so. Teachers have always been called on to do more than transmit knowledge. In the 18th century, along with the many menial duties associated with the job, teachers were expected to act as moral exemplars, to ensure the safekeeping of children's souls. Later, during the Common School period and again, with the rise of Progressivism, the teacher was still expected to be a moral paradigm, but also to Americanize the students, to inculcate democratic values, and to prepare the charges for the world of work. By the second half of the 20th century, the teacher's role had, of course, grown still more complex and problematic. With the breakdown of traditional systems of support, teachers now were expected to act *in loco parentis*, to take on many of the caregiving responsibilities traditionally ascribed to the family.

Low pay and low status also emerge as timeless characteristics of the profession. The vulnerability and powerlessness of the teacher is as palpably manifest in the 18th-century figure of Ichabod Crane as it is in the late 19th-century hero of W. E. B. Du Bois' "The Coming of John," or in Jonathan Kozol's description of his own experience as a teacher in "Death at an Early Age" (1967). The isolation of the teacher is felt as strongly in Philip Freneau's "The Private Tutor" (1788) as in Richard Dokey's "Teacher" (1980).

Reading through two centuries of stories about the profession, one inevitably comes to ask why it is that teachers, so often selfless and over-worked, are so consistently maligned and unappreciated. Part of the reason is due, no doubt, to the fact that teachers spend their careers with children. In a country that emphasizes commerce and trade, teaching has often been seen as "women's work," and a refuge for those who cannot make it in the business world. Another reason for the low regard of the teacher may be explained by his ongoing role as transmitter of one generations' values to the next. In doing so, the teacher, it seems, often comes to represent tensions and ambiguities associated with those values. As spokesperson for all the choices—good or bad—that we have made about our culture and ourselves, the teacher is necessarily an easy target for hostility and resentment. Today, as in the past, whenever confidence in our own prevailing ideals and institutions comes into question, it is understandable that we would feel discontentment toward those charged with perpetuating those institutions.

In many of the stories in this volume you find protagonists who are situated in just the position just described. They have become the brunt, if not of outright hostility, then of a kind of vague social scorn. Many of these protagonists, both past and present, manage to transcend that scorn, triumphing both professionally and personally against difficult odds. Others do not, succumbing to the kind of malaise and indifference that we have come to associate with "burnout." Those who succeed offer interesting, useful lessons in survival. The failures are instructive as well.

The fiction, letters, memoirs, and other forms of narrative presented here focus a wide lens on the evolving work of the teacher. The teachers in these stories are mainstream and marginalized, from urban, suburban, and rural communities, male and female, gay and straight, and from a range of ethnic backgrounds. They work with elite students and disadvantaged ones, those with learning disabilities and physical disabilities. Indeed, there is no collection we know of that presents so broad an array of voices as this one. In hearing those voices together, one gains a unique perspective on this remarkably inclusive profession.

The stories in this collection are organized chronologically, in four sections that trace the evolution of the teaching profession from the post-Revolutionary years to the late 20th century. The first section, "The Teacher in the Early Republic," considers portraits of teachers and tutors well before the establishment of the public school. In these years, before teaching was in any sense a codified profession, teachers tended to be literate, but nomadic individuals for whom the work of the classroom was done out of default. The voices in this section are mostly those of young, White men, because the profile of the teacher in these years almost always included those characteristics. Without community support or a professional identity to gird them, most teachers of the period describe their jobs as demeaning and difficult—a kind of impoverished servitude from which one only hopes to escape. Interestingly, the exceptions to this view are found in the experience of Emma Hart Willard and Daniel Payne, a woman and a Black man whose writings are excerpted here. As teachers and founders of their own schools, these individuals became empowered and liberated at a time when there were virtually no other career options open to them. When the majority of teachers wrote of their work in disparaging terms, Willard and Payne championed the profession.

The second section of the volume focuses on the impact of the Common School Movement on the teacher. The period between 1835 and 1875 sees the formal and systematic entrance of women into the field, sanctioned by common school reformers like Horace Mann and James Carter. Part II presents the voices of a range of women teachers, both Black and White, who worked both in New England cities and in more rugged and dangerous venues. The pioneer letters of Cynthia Bishop and Martha Rogers describe the hardships of teaching in pioneer communities, and Charlotte Forten vividly recreates her work with freedmen in South Carolina. The section also considers other kinds of reforms that gained ground during the period, including reforms in school curriculum and in the uses of corporal punishment in the classroom.

Part III focuses on the years of the Progressive Movement both in urban America, in the South, and in the Midwest. Many of the teachers presented in this section work with students who are in some way "marginal." They are either poor immigrants, newly arrived in the city; African Americans, long denied access to adequately funded schools; or, as in the case of Helen Keller, they are physically disabled. The voices in this section highlight both the struggles and the rewards of working with these "new" kinds of students. The stories also begin to suggest the extent to which public school teaching is fast becoming a highly organized and stratified profession, vulnerable to the ills of other large, bureaucratic systems.

The final section of this volume begins at the middle of this century and brings the reader to the present day. The stories in Part IV highlight both the diversity of students and teachers today, and the ongoing hardships associated with the work. In the 50 years that are represented in Part IV, dramatic shifts take place in the demographics of schoolchildren; unions alter the power and status of teachers; and strong social movements impact the nature of the teaching force as well as relationships between students and teachers. These realities are vividly illustrated in a range of story narratives that take the reader from the "old-fashioned" classrooms of the 1950s to the multicultural and complex world of contemporary urban schools.

Each of the four sections opens with an introduction setting the pieces in a more detailed historical context. These preliminary remarks offer a social backdrop for the stories that follow, and consider the changing social characteristics of those who entered the profession during each period. At the end of each section, there are a series of questions and activities intended to provoke thought and debate. The questions deal with specific stories, with the larger themes that link each section together, and with issues that emerge across sections of the book. For better or worse, although much has changed in our profession since the early years of the republic, much has also stayed the same.

Part I

*"…This Wretched State
of Meanness and Servility":
The Teacher in the Early Republic*

In fiction, poetry, and personal memoir, the image of the teacher as it emerges in the Early Republic is frequently less than flattering. Whether in dame schools, district schoolrooms, or in private homes, the teacher is often depicted in the literature of the period as a person of little learning and great pretension—a bully, a braggard, and a boor. Many of the nation's most eminent intellectuals and statesmen allude in their letters and journals to the problematic nature of their early instructors, suggesting that their own intellectual flowering took place in spite of the influence and teachings of these first pedagogues.

But in defense of the teachers in this period, the job of imparting knowledge to young Americans during the post-Revolutionary era was very difficult. Until the rise of the common school movement in the second decade of the 19th century, little public support existed either for schools or for those who taught in them. Although it is true that as early as the middle of the 17th century, colonies were mandating the establishment of community schools, that schooling was neither entirely tax supported nor compulsory. Indeed, many Americans seem to have maintained a long and abiding suspicion of formal education—and particularly of publicly supported education outside the home. Scholars have attributed that suspicion to a number of causes. Many new Americans understandably feared the taxation that was needed to support public schools. Pervasive too was a general unease about the imposition of outside values and cultures. Communities in the Early Republican years still tended to be powerfully connected to their European roots; in many, English was not yet spoken, and old world customs were best preserved not in the public schoolroom, but in the home. Finally, many families saw little use in formal education, because the agrarian lifestyle of the overwhelming majority of Americans called for little book knowledge beyond basic literacy. At the time of the framing of the Constitution and in the first years of the Republic, Thomas Jefferson had built a powerful argument concerning the inextricable connection between democracy and education. Knowledge of history, political philosophy, and government, he argued, would safeguard the country against the rise of despots, as individual citizens could draw on the lessons of the past to recognize tyranny when it inevitably arose. Benjamin Rush added to the argument for public education with a warning that the unraveling of the Republic would more likely come from the masses than from the ruling elite: Crime, moral dissolution, and a general breakdown of established order could be anticipated if schooling was not mandated in communities. Neither one of these arguments seemed to hold powerful sway with the new American citizenry.

So it was that the job of teacher, from this early point in our nation's history, was often a bitter and demeaning business. Although the profile of the teacher differs a bit from region to region (often because of religious and economic factors that defined the various cultures of these regions) records indicate that throughout the 18th century, schoolteachers were almost always White, male, and young. Teaching paid too poorly to be perceived as a profession in itself. Instead, educated young men would frequently choose the job of teaching as a temporary way station to some other profession—most often the ministry—or as a means for raising capital for a journey westward. Although women teachers certainly existed, they presided over "dame" schools in their kitchens and parlors, where their work was less as formal instructors than as caregivers. Women were also conscripted to teach during the summer months, when any able-bodied man would necessarily be preoccupied with the farm. The overwhelming consensus among communities was that a man was needed to run the schoolhouse.

Long-term commitment to a school or community was rare among teachers in the young republic. And the commitment of the community to the teacher was similarly tentative. Teachers were expected to "board around," living for brief periods with a succession of families in a particular town, taking their meals with these families and suffering the indignities of being neither relative nor friend in the houses in which they resided. In addition to their work in the schoolhouse, teachers were required to perform a range of chores such as weeding the local cemetery and sweeping out the church. In many communities, teachers were often friendless and isolated, perceived as public and/or private servants whose book knowledge was only minimally valued by the constituency they served. That loneliness and social deprivation is poignantly illustrated in some of the passages that follow, including the famous segment from "The Legend of Sleepy Hollow" in which the sycophantish schoolmaster, Ichabod Crane, attempts to endear himself to the local ladies.

Within the classroom itself, the district teacher encountered the greatest challenge. Most schools were ungraded, and teachers often dealt with a vast range of ages and levels in a single classroom. Children were sent to school at extraordinarily young ages, not from a family's love of learning so much as from a desire to get the child out from under a mother's feet. Two- and three-year-old toddlers sat on long backless benches beside their teenage classmates, barely capable of even staying awake. In a much quoted passage from the memoirs of John Burroughs (1922), the writer remembers a singular moment as a toddler in his own district school education when, having fallen backward off a bench in the schoolroom he awoke to find himself in a neighbor's bed—happily relieved of the day's dreary schoolwork. Attendance for pupils was sporadic at best. Before the rise of the Common Schools, most students attended formal schooling for only several weeks out of the year, when they could be spared from household duties. What is more, students had no standard texts; generally pupils came to school with whatever book or primer the family happened to own, and it was common for each student in a classroom to have a different book.

All of these factors served to make the teacher's job extraordinarily trying. From the stories and memoirs of teachers that come to us from the period, it is clear that the vast majority of the schoolday was occupied in frustrated attempts by the teacher to maintain discipline. Often the success of a teacher was gauged merely by this one criteria, and certainly in the majority of passages that follow, "moral 'suasion" seems to be a central and unpleasant preoccupation. The endless attempts at restoring order amidst the general chaos of the schoolroom seem to have led many teachers to a liberal use of the rod. Some unfortunate students speak of even worse punishments, depicting their tutors as nothing short of sadists whose sole purpose in the classroom appears to be the infliction of outlandish physical torments.

The depictions of teachers in these early, post-Revolutionary narratives emerge in interesting contrast to the stories that follow in the next section. Here is an educational scene largely uninfluenced by either private reformers or state and federal regulations. Both the teachers and the communities who hire them are essentially on their own in terms of standards and expectations. With the rise of the Common School movement—marked not only by its compulsory education laws, but also by a new civic-mindedness and concern for the education of the underclass—characters like Ichabod Crane, Updike Underhill, and Warren Burton's "Particular Master" show themselves far less frequently in the literature. Indeed, Burton's final recollection of the gifted Mr. Ellis already points the way to a new kind of education, grounded in a gentler and more humane approach to learning.

"The Rare Adventures of Tom Brainless" From *The Progress of Dulness*

ఴ ◆ చ

John Trumbull, 1773

This deeply satiric poem mocks both teacher and student alike. In its cynical description of the grammar school curriculum, and in the way Trumbull ridicules the shoddy standards for college entrance, the poem echoes the sentiments of Benjamin Franklin, who also used satire to attack the school system of the day.

Throughout *The Progress of Dulness*, we follow the exploits of three unsavory students, Tom Brainless, Dick Hairbrain, and Miss Harriet Simper as they make their tentative way through school and into the various professions. In "Tom Brainless," the dull and lazy protagonist is sent by his parents to the local priest to be tutored in the classical curriculum that will prepare him for a life of ease. Under the master's tutelage, Tom sleeps through most of his lessons or parrots Greek or Latin phrases without the slightest understanding of their meaning (the Priest himself doesn't understand them), and then is packed off to college where he proceeds to use a succession of pretended illnesses to avoid any work. Ultimately cast out of school, the boy finds refuge in the one occupation that "will always take a fool"—teaching—where he teaches his students "not to read, but to fear and tremble." Tom bides his time in the classroom with "threats and blows," until he can achieve his ultimate goal—to become a priest.

Trumbull's complaint, in "The Rare Adventures of Tom Brainless," is with all the levels of hypocrisy that surround classical education; that is, the kind of education pursued by the middle and upper classes in the post-Revolutionary period. Like Franklin, Trumbull believed that a more useful education would be one in which English and other modern languages were taught. The new middle class of businessmen and professionals, he believed, would find little value in a solid curriculum of dead languages. In Trumbull's poem, all par-

ties—teachers, parents, clergy, and college officials alike—serve in a conspiracy to perpetuate the ignorance of the young. And the conspiracy
continues, it is suggested here, into the next generation as Tom is himself
heralded as an excellent teacher by the parents of his unfortunate scholars.

John Trumbull (1750–1831) was himself the product of an elite education.
Born in 1750 into a wealthy Connecticut family, Trumbull showed extraordinary intellectual ability at a very young age, passing the entrance examination for Yale College (an examination that demanded extensive knowledge
of Greek and Latin) at the age of 7. Trumbull waited 6 years to matriculate
at Yale, however, and then spent 9 years there as a student and a tutor.

Throughout his career, John Trumbull affiliated himself with the Connecticut Wits, a group of conservative intellectuals who tended to eschew the Deist
and egalitarian ideas popularized by American thinkers during the Enlightenment. It is all the more interesting then that his educational ideas should be so
forward-looking. That interest in education led to several other projects of note:
Trumbull assisted Noah Webster in editing his dictionary, and devoted several
years to the overhauling of the Connecticut state curriculum.

"THE RARE ADVENTURES OF TOM BRAINLESS" FROM *THE PROGRESS OF DULNESS*

John Trumbull, 1773

"Our *Tom* is grown a sturdy boy;
His progress fills my heart with joy;
A steady soul that yields to rule,
And quite ingenious too at school.
Our master says, (I'm sure he's right)
There's not a lad in town so bright.
He'll cypher bravely, write and read,
And say his catechism and creed,
And scorns to hesitate or faulter
In primmer, spelling-book or psalter.
Hard work indeed—he does not love it;
His genius is too much above it.
Give him a good substantial teacher,
I'll lay he makes a special preacher.
I've lov'd good learning all my life:
We'll send the lad to college, wife."
    Thus sway'd by fond and sightless passion,
His parents hold a consultation:
If on their couch, or round their fire,
I need not tell, or you enquire.

The point's agreed; the boy well pleas'd,
From country cares and labours eas'd;
No more to rise by break of day
To drive home cows, or deal out hay;
To work no more in snow and hail,
And blow his fingers o'er the flail,
Or mid the toils of harvest sweat
Beneath the summer's sultry heat.
Serene, he bids the farm good-bye,
And quits the plow without a sigh.
Propitious to their constant friend,
The pow'rs of idleness attend.
 So to the priest in form he goes,
Prepar'd to study and to doze.
The parson in his youth before,
Had run the same dull progress o'er:
His sole concern to see with care
His church, and farm in good repair.
His skill in tongues, that once he knew,
Had bid him long, a last adieu;
Away his latin rules had fled,
And Greek had vanish'd from his head.
 Then view our youth with grammar teazing,
Untaught in meaning, sense or reason;
Of knowledge e'er he gain his fill, he
Must diet long on husks of *Lillie*
Drudge on for weary months in vain;
By mem'ry's strength, and dint of brain;
From thence to murd'ring *Virgil's* verse,
And construing *Tully*, into farce,
Or lab'ring with his grave preceptor,
In Greek to blunder o'er a chapter.
The latin testament affords
The needy help, and ready words;
At hand the dictionary laid,
Gives up it's page in frequent aid;
Hard by the lexicon and grammar,
Those helps for mem'ry when they stammer;
The lesson's short; the priest contented;
His task to hear is sooner ended.
He lets him mind his own concerns,
Then tells his parents how he learns.
 A year thus spent in gathering knowledge,

The lad sets forth t' unlade at college,
While down his sire and priest attend him,
To introduce and recommend him:
Or if detain'd, a letter's sent
Of much apocryphal content,
To set him forth, (how dull soever)
As very learn'd and very clever;
A genius of the first emission,
With burning love for erudition;
So studious he'll outwatch the moon
And think the planets set too soon;
He had but little time to fit in;
Examination too must frighten;
Depend upon't he must do well,
He knows much more than he can tell;
Admit him, and in little space
He'll beat his rivals in the race;
His father's incomes are but small,
He comes now, if he comes at all.
    So said, so done, at college now
He enters well—no matter how—
New scenes awhile his fancy please,
But all must yield to love of ease.
In the same round condemn'd each day,
To study, read, recite and pray;
To make his hours of business double—
He can't endure th' increasing trouble:
And finds at length, as times grow pressing,
All plagues are easier than his lesson.
With sleepy eyes and count'nance heavy,
With much excuse of *non paravi*,[1]
Much absence, *tardes* and *egresses*,
The college-evil on him siezes.
Then ev'ry book, which ought to please,
Stirs up the seeds of dire disease:
Greek spoils his eyes (the print's so fine)
Grown dim with study—and with wine;
Of *Tully's* latin much afraid,
Each page, he calls the doctor's aid;
While geometry, with lines so crooked,
Sprains all his wits to overlook it.
His sickness puts on every name,

---

[1] *Non pavari*: I have not prepared for recitation; an excuse commonly given.

It's cause and uses still the same;
'Tis tooth-ach, cholic, gout or stone,
With phases various as the moon:
But though through all the body spread,
Still makes its cap'tal seat, the head.
In all diseases, 'tis expected,
The weakest parts be most infected.
    Kind headach hail! thou blest disease,
The friend of idleness and ease;
Who mid the still and dreary bound,
Where college-walls her sons surround,
In spite of fears, in justice' spight,
Assum'st o'er laws dispensing right,
Set'st from his talk the blunderer free,
Excus'd by dulness and by thee.
Thy vot'ries bid a bold defiance
To all the calls and threats of science,
Slight learning human and divine,
And hear no prayers, and fear no fine.
    And yet how oft the studious gain,
The dulness of a letter'd brain;
Despising such low things the while
As English grammar, phrase and style;
Despising ev'ry nicer art,
That aids the tongue, or mends the heart:
Read antient authors o'er in vain,
Nor taste one beauty they contain;
Humbly on trust accept the sense,
But deal for words at vast expence;
Search well how ev'ry term must vary
From lexicon to dictionary;
And plodding on in one dull tone,
Gain antient tongues, and lose their own,
Bid every graceful charm defiance,
And woo the skeleton of science.
    Come ye who finer arts despise,
And scoff at verse as heathen lies;
In all the pride of dulness rage
At *Pope*, or *Milton's* deathless page;
Or stung by truth's deep-searching line,
Rave ev'n at rhymes as low as mine:
Say ye who boast the name of wise,
Wherein substantial learning lies.

Is it, superb in classic lore,
To speak what *Homer* spoke before,
To write the language *Tully* wrote,
The style, the cadence and the note?
Is there a charm in sounds of Greek,
No language else can learn to speak;
That cures distemper'd brains at once,
Like *Pliny's* rhymes for broken bones?
Is there a spirit found in latin,
That must evap'rate in translating?
And say, are sense and genius bound
To any vehicles of sound?
   Is it by mathematic's aid
To count the worlds in light array'd,
To know each star, that lights it's eye,
To sparkle in the midnight sky?
Say ye, who draw the curious line
Between the useful and the fine,
How little can this noble art
It's aid in human things impart,
Or give to life a chearful ray,
And force our pains, and cares away.
   Is it to know whate'er was done
Above the circle of the sun?
Is it to lift the active mind
Beyond the bounds by heav'n design'd;
And leave our little world at home,
Through realms of entity to roam;
Attempt the secrets dark to scan,
Eternal wisdom hid from man;
For sense, deal loads of definitions,
And fritter truth in sub-divisions,
And make religion but the sign
In din of battle when to join?
Vain man, to madness still a prey,
Thy space a point, thy life a day,
A feeble worm, that aim'st to stride
In all the foppery of pride!
The glimmering lamp of reason's ray
Was giv'n to guide thy darksome way.
Why wilt thou spread thine insect-wings,
And strive to reach sublimer things?
Thy doubts confess, thy blindness own,

Nor vex thy thoughts with scenes unknown.
Indulgent heav'n to man below,
Hath all explain'd we need to know;
Hath clearly taught enough to prove
Content below, and bliss above.
Thy boastful wish how proud and vain,
While heav'n forbids the vaunting strain!
For metaphysics rightly shown
But teach how little can be known:
Though quibbles still maintain their station,
Conjecture serves for demonstration,
Armies of pens drawn forth to fight,
And ****** and ****** write.
   Oh! might I live to see that day,
When sense shall point to youths their way;
Through every maze of science guide;
O'er education's laws preside;
The good retain; with just discerning
Explode the fopperies of learning;
Give antient arts their real due,
Explain their faults, and beauties too;
Teach where to imitate, and mend,
And point their uses and their end.
Then bright philosophy would shine,
And ethics teach the laws divine;
Our youths might reach each nobler art,
That shews a passage to the heart;
From antient languages well known
Transfuse new beauties to our own;
With taste and fancy well refin'd,
Where moral rapture warms the mind,
From schools dismiss'd, with lib'ral hand,
Spread useful learning o'er the land;
And bid the eastern world admire
Our rising worth, and bright'ning fire.
   But while through fancy's realms we roam,
The main concern is left at home;
Return'd, our hero still we find
The same, as blundering and as blind.
  Four years at college doz'd away
In sleep, and slothfulness and play,
Too dull for vice, with clearest conscience,
Charg'd with no fault, but that of nonsense,

(And nonsense long, with serious air
Has wander'd unmolested there)
He passes trial fair, and free,
And takes in form his first degree.
    A scholar see him now commence
Without the aid of books or sense:
For passing college cures the brain,
Like mills to grind men young again.
The scholar-dress, that once array'd him,
The charm, *Admitto te ad gradum*,[2]
With touch of parchment can refine,
And make the veriest coxcomb shine,
Confer the gift of tongues at once,
And fill with sense the vacant dunce.
So kingly crowns contain quintessence
Of worship, dignity and presence;
Give learning, genius, virtue, worth,
Wit, valor, wisdom and so forth;
Hide the bald pate, and cover o'er
The cap of folly worn before.
    Our hero's wit and learning now may
Be prov'd by token of *Diploma*,
Of that *Diploma*, which with speed
He learns to construe and to read;
And stalks abroad with conscious stride,
In all the airs of pedant-pride,
With passport sign'd for wit and knowledge,
And current under seal of college.
    Few months now past, he sees with pain
His purse as empty as his brain;
His father leaves him then to fate,
And throws him off, as useless weight;
But gives him good advice, to teach
A school at first, and then to preach.
    Thou reason'st well; it must be so;
For nothing else thy son can do.
As thieves of old, t'avoid the halter,
Took refuge in the holy altar:
Oft dulness flying from disgrace
Finds safety in that sacred place;
There boldly rears his head, or rests
Secure from ridicule or jests;

---

[2]*Admitto te ad gradum*: I admit you to a degree; words used in conferring the honors of college.

Where dreaded satire may not dare
Offend his wig's extremest hair;
Where scripture sanctifies his strains,
And rev'rence hides the want of brains.
    Next see our youth at school appear,
Procur'd for forty pounds a year,
His ragged regiment round assemble,
Taught, not to read, but fear and tremble.
Before him, rods prepare his way,
Those dreaded antidotes to play.
Then thron'd aloft in elbow-chair,
With solemn face and awful air,
He tries with ease and unconcern,
To teach what ne'er himself could learn;
Gives law and punishment alone,
Judge, jury, bailiff, all in one;
Holds all good learning must depend
Upon his rod's extremest end,
Whose great electric virtue's such,
Each genius brightens at the touch;
With threats and blows (incitements pressing)
Drives on his lads to learn each lesson;
Thinks flogging cures all moral ills,
And breaks their heads to break their wills.
    The year is done; he takes his leave;
The children smile; the parents grieve;
And seek again, their school to keep,
One just as good, and just as cheap.
    Now to some priest, that's fam'd for teaching,
He goes to learn the art of preaching;
And settles down with earnest zeal
Sermons to study, and to steal:
Six months from all the world retires
To kindle up his cover'd fires;
Learns the nice art, to make with ease
The scriptures speak whate'er he please;
With judgment unperceiv'd to quote
What *Poole* explain'd, or *Henry* wrote;
To give the gospel new editions,
Split doctrines into propositions,
Draw motives, uses, inferences,
And torture words in thousand senses;
Learn the grave style and goodly phrase,

Safe-handed down from *Cromwell's* days,
And shun with anxious care, the while
Th' infection of a modern style:
Or on the wings of folly fly
Aloft in metaphysic sky;
The system of the world explain,
Till night and chaos come again;
Deride what old divines can say,
Point out to heav'n a nearer way:
Explode all known, establish'd rules,
Affirm our fathers all were fools:
The present age is growing wise,
But wisdom in her cradle lies;
Late, like *Minerva*, born and bred;
Not from a *Joves's*, but scribler's head,
While thousand youths their homage lend her,
And nursing fathers rock and tend her.
  Round him much manuscript is spread,
Extracts from living works, and dead,
Themes, sermons, plans of controversy,
That hack and mangle without mercy,
And whence, to glad the reader's eyes,
The future dialogue shall rise.
  At length matur'd the grand design,
He stalks abroad, a grave divine.
  Mean while, from ev'ry distant seat
At stated time the clergy meet.
Our hero comes, his sermon reads,
Explains the doctrine of his creeds,
A licence gains to preach and pray,
And makes his bow, and goes his way.
  What though his wits could ne'er dispense
One page of grammar, or of sense;
What though his learning be so slight,
He scarcely knows to spell or write;
What though his skull be cudgel-proof!
He's orthodox, and that's enough.
  Perhaps with genius we'd dispense;
But sure we look at least for sense.
  Ye fathers of our Church, attend
The serious counsels of a friend,
Whose utmost wish, in nobler ways,
Your sacred dignity to raise.

"The Private Tutor"

ⅎ ◆ ⅓

Philip Freneau, 1788

Philip Freneau's (1752–1832) devastating portrait of the private tutor demonstrates that the plight of the young scholar, employed by a wealthy family, was often no better than that of the district teacher.

Like other protagonists described in this section of the book, Freneau's unfortunate subject enters into his employment with naive enthusiasm, responding to a call for a highly erudite individual and to the promise of a "handsome salary." What he finds at the home of his employer are stupid, recalcitrant children, and a household that holds him in complete contempt. Even his salary is denied him in the end, when the family's examiners discover that the children have learned nothing over the course of the year.

Philip Freneau is clearly drawing in this piece on his own miserable experience as a teacher. After graduating from Princeton in 1771, where he was a classmate of James Madison and Aaron Burr, Freneau began his career teaching at a rural district school on Long Island. He lasted at the job only 13 days. Upon beating his hasty retreat, Freneau wrote to his friend James Madison, "Long Island I have bid adieu, with all its brutish brainless crew, The youth of that detested place, are void of reason and of grace, From Flushing hills to Flatbush plains, Deep ignorance unrivall'd reigns" (Leary, 1941, p. 38). As in his satiric prose, the tutor Freneau evidently had serious problems with his employers: "After I forsook them," he wrote, "they pursued me for four days and swore that if I was caught in New York they would either Trounce or maim me" (Leary, p. 39). Freneau went on to teach with greater success in Maryland, and to become a successful poet and journalist. His early interest in the plight of the teacher reflects a lifelong concern for the downtrodden. Much of Freneau's writing dealt with the treatment of slaves, Indians, and the poor.

"THE PRIVATE TUTOR"

Philip Freneau, 1788

THIS is an animal that would be truly worthy of pity, if there were any reason to believe that he himself was at all sensible of the misery of his condition. Insensibility, or a want of the finer feelings, is generally allowed to be a true characteristic of the lower orders of the human species. It was, nevertheless, undoubtedly meant for a blessing by the power that form'd the mind, and resembles the divine spirit of the poppy, that friendly plant, which by exerting its charming sleepy influence over the mortal frame, benumbs the senses, and gives ease to the soul when Nature is inflicting her most excruciating torments.

THE PRIVATE TUTOR is absolutely a slave in every respect, except that he has not, like other slaves, the privilege and pleasure of keeping company with, and enjoying the conversation of his equals, without incurring disgrace thereby. Bred up in the habits and pursuits of a liberal mind, he has, we will suppose, taken his degrees at a college, can boast of a general acquaintance with books; and has imbibed high ideas of liberty and independence. What then can alleviate his vexation and anguish, when he finds himself compelled by want of fortune to sink into this pitiful situation?—Nothing but that friendly, yet fatal insensibility (whether natural or acquired) which I mentioned above.

To prevent as much as possible any young man of spirit and abilities from degrading himself into this wretched state of meanness and servility, I will endeavour to give an idea of the usage a private tutor may generally expect from the *Bashaws* that most commonly employ them.

THE first step you take when you find yourself driven to embrace this miserable occupation, is, to look carefully over the newspapers of the day. By and by you see an advertisement to the following purport:

WANTED: A person capable of teaching not only the languages, but Philosophy, Geography, Pneumatology, Metaphysics, Chemistry, Meteorology, Bell-Letters, and other polite arts and sciences. He will be employed as private tutor in a family of consequence, and, if approved, may expect a handsome salary.

YOU immediately determine within yourself to take advantage of Fortune while she is in a favourable mood, and strike boldly for the place. Upon application to the printer, you are informed that the advertiser is a country gentleman of immense fortune, by the name of Adrian Van der Bunscooten, Esquire, who resides, with his family, at his seat about a dozen miles from the city.

HAVING dressed yourself in the best manner you are able, you set out on foot, without loss of time, and towards noon arrive very weary at the desired port.

THE first person you see is a servant, who wishes to know your business in that place?—After having enquired whether the master of the house be at home or not, and being answered in the affirmative, you send word up by the servant, that "a man has come to accept the place of private tutor in the family, as offered in the public papers."

THE gentleman of the house, upon hearing this, instantly comes down to take a view of you: ten to one but he looks at you through a magnifying glass. If he has penetration enough to discover (or thinks he discovers) that you are at once possessed of education and servility of soul, and the place is not engaged, he intimates that you may possibly suit his purpose.—You then naturally enquire what the yearly income is to be?—He tells you it is no less than <u>thirty pounds</u>, lawful currency of the State; to be paid either quarterly, or at the end of the year, as may best suit!

RATHER than wander again in the disconsolate mood of a <u>Man out of business</u>, you accept the terms, without daring to intimate that the salary is by no means adequate to the trouble you expect to be at: Nay, you even venture to tell him, that you would prefer receiving it in a lump at the end of the year!

YOU are then informed that your pupils are to be three young gentleman and two young ladies—that it is expected the young gentlemen will be at <u>all times</u> under your eye, and that whenever they think proper to go a shooting, swimming, or elsewhere, you must attend them for fear of accidents.

HAVING nodded with your head by way of assent to this proposition, the great man informs you, with an eye of ineffable good nature and condescension, that you will have the honour to breakfast, dine, and sup with himself and family, except when the governor, the controuler of the finance, or some other great gentleman or lady from the city, pays a visit <u>to the house</u>, in which case it will be expected that you descend to your proper element, the kitchen.

A GREAT man's kitchen naturally gives you an idea of plenty; you therefore shrug up your shoulders, by way of telling him that you agree to his terms.

YOU are next informed by the lady of the house, Madam Catarina Van der Bunscooten, that her beloved offspring, and her dear lambs, <u>may be led, but not drove</u>—that the art and mystery of teaching is to play them into knowledge with marbles, nine-pins, shuttle cocks, and whirligigs—that many children, from her own knowledge, have been taught to read merely by playing cards and dice, and that constraint of any kind has nothing to do with education.

STRUCK with the admirable beauty and fine apparel of this great lady, you bow your head, in token of being thoroughly convinced of the truth of what she has asserted.

AFTER being settled in the family, you soon perceive that the servants pay less attention to you than your knowledge of Greek would seem to demand. If wine is handed to the guests, you are the very last that is noticed, if not sometimes wholly neglected.—Your shoes are either not blacked in the morning at all, or it is left for yourself to do. Yet, if you are once known to perform this menial office with your own hands, farewell to all ideas of consequence with, or respect from, the sable brotherhood of the kitchen.

THE coachman, however, still condescends to acknowledge himself to be upon a level with you; but if you will not converse freely, drink punch, and smoke a pipe with him in his hovel; or teach the footman to read, write, cypher, and play tricks in winter evenings, you are a lost man—and will be treated with little else than abuse and contempt by all the inferior part of the household.

THE young ladies are averse to learning geography; as they tell the gentleman, their father, that your method of teaching is rather obscure and unintelligible.—Adrian van der Bunscooten gives you a friendly hint of this, in the presence of the young junto; and intimates also that "neither the girls nor the boys are defective in point of genius—the fault of not learning cannot therefore be imputed to them."

YOU now put your earnest prayers to him that is author of all plainness, common sense, clear reasoning, and perspicuity of thought and language, "that he would be graciously inclined to enable you so to express your ideas of things, that they may be conveyed without obscurity, let, or hindrance into the minds of your dear young pupils."

A LUCKY thought then strikes you: your scholars have not been studious or attentive enough to gain a rational idea of the globe of the earth from a plane surface on paper; you therefore procure a large round pippin or an orange, and mark thereon the equator, the tropics, the polar circles, with the parallells [sic] of latitude and longitude. You, further, represent the different cities of the world and their situations, by *pins* stuck into the apple or the orange.— While you are explaining matters in this manner, your pupils are constantly endeavouring to stifle a loud laugh.—The farce ends with one of the young ladies stealing away the apple when the lecture is finished, and soon after eating it up for her own edification and amusement.

THE first year of your servitude at length comes to a conclusion: the great man sends for the physician, the county lawyer, and the clergyman; they are desired to examine the young students, male and female, and give an account of the proficiency that has been made by them in their education.—They are unanimously of opinion (upon examination) that the young ladies and gentlemen have learned "little, or nothing worth mentioning."

IT cannot be my fault, says the great man of the house; my own father, <u>Dederick van der Bunscooten</u> was never looked upon as defective in genius: My wife is allowed, on all hands, to be descended from the great lawyer <u>Shadrach O'Possum</u>, the oracle of his age and nation; how can it be then, that <u>these here young youths</u> have not made more proficiency?—my thirty pounds salary cannot be thrown away in this manner!

<u>BUT, are you sure</u>, says the private tutor, <u>that you yourself are not a swine, sir?</u>

HERE the conversation ends: You lose your whole salary, curse the trade of a PRIVATE TUTOR, and spend the remainder of your life in basket-making.

"Ichabod Crane" From "The Legend of Sleepy Hollow" (set c. 1790)

ଚ୍ଚ ◆ ଔ

Washington Irving, 1820

"The Legend of Sleepy Hollow" is part of *The Sketchbook of Geoffrey Crayon, Gent*, that was published serially in America and England between 1819 and 1820, and reprinted in book form in 1820. The teacher Irving depicts in this tale, however, is clearly of an even earlier vintage, probably from the first decade after the American Revolution. Like other teachers of the period, Ichabod Crane teaches in an ill-kempt and decrepit one-room schoolhouse, where the windows are patched by copybooks. In fact, in virtually every respect, Crane himself is a caricature of the period peda-gogue. A great believer in the virtues of the rod, he flogs his pupils energetically, while presenting himself to their parents as an elegant scholar and an esthete. Painfully poor, Crane supplements his meager salary by cutting hay, driving cows, and instructing local residents in the parish psalmody. Like other unflatteringly portrayed pedagogues of his day, Crane is shown as less than manly in a number of ways, including his great preference for parlor talk and the company of ladies. He dreams of escaping the detested life of teaching by marrying a rich woman, but his fate, of course, is less happy—undone at last by the headless horse-man.

Washington Irving's (1783–1859) vituperative portrait of Crane may have been inspired by his own earliest experiences as a student. Irving's first teacher failed to recognize his gift with language and brandished him a dunce. The dunce went on to found the literary journal *Salamagundi*, and to write a series of extraordinarily successful books. Indeed, Irving was the first American to gain an international reputation as a man of letters and to make writing his full-time profession.

"ICHABOD CRANE" FROM
"THE LEGEND OF SLEEPY HOLLOW"
(SET C. 1790)

Washington Irving, 1820

In the bosom of one of those spacious coves which indent the eastern shore of the Hudson, at that broad expansion of the river denominated by the ancient Dutch navigators the Tappan Zee, and where they always prudently shortened sail, and implored the protection of Saint Nicholas when they crossed, there lies a small market-town or rural port, which by some is called Greensburgh, but which is more generally and properly known by the name of Tarry Town. This name was given, we are told, in former days, by the good housewives of the adjacent country, from the inveterate propensity of their husbands to linger about the village tavern on market-days. Be that as it may, I do not vouch for the fact, but merely advert to it, for the sake of being precise and authentic. Not far from this village, perhaps about two miles, there is a little valley, or rather lap of land, among high hills, which is one of the quietest places in the whole world. A small brook glides through it, with just a murmur enough to lull one to repose; and the occasional whistle of a quail, or tapping of a woodpecker, is almost the only sound that ever breaks in upon the uniform tranquillity.

I recollect that, when a stripling, my first exploit in squirrel shooting was in a grove of tall walnut trees that shades one side of the valley. I had wandered into it at noon-time, when all nature is peculiarly quiet, and was startled by the roar of my own gun as it broke the Sabbath stillness around, and was prolonged and reverberated by the angry echoes. If ever I should wish for a retreat, whither I might steal from the world and its distractions, and dream quietly away the remnant of a troubled life, I know none more promising than this little valley.

From the listless repose of the place, and the peculiar character of its inhabitants, who are descendants from the original Dutch settlers, this seques-tered glen has long been known by the name of SLEEPY HOLLOW, and its rustic lads are called the Sleepy Hollow Boys throughout the neighboring country. A drowsy, dreamy influence seems to hang over the land, and to pervade the very atmosphere. Some say that the place was bewitched by a high German doctor, during the early days of the settlement; others, that an old Indian chief, the prophet or wizard of his tribe, held his powwows there before the country was discovered by Master Hendrick Hudson. Certain it is, the place still continues under the sway of some witching power, that holds a spell over the minds of the good people, causing them to walk in a continual revery. They are given to all kinds of marvelous beliefs; are subject to trances and visions; and frequently see strange sights, and hear music and voices in the air. The whole neighborhood abounds with local tales, haunted spots, and twilight superstitions; stars shoot and meteors glare oftener across the valley than in any other part of the country, and the nightmare, with her whole nine fold, seems to make it the favorite scene of her gambols.

The dominant spirit, however, that haunts this enchanted region, and seems to be commander-in-chief of all the powers of the air, is the apparition of a figure on horseback without a head. It is said by some to be the ghost of a Hessian trooper, whose head had been carried away by a cannon-ball, in some nameless battle during the Revolutionary War; and who is ever and anon seen by the country folk, hurrying along in the gloom of the night, as if on the wings of the wind. His haunts are not confined to the valley, but extend at times to the adjacent roads, and especially to the vicinity of a church at no great distance. Indeed, certain of the most authentic historians of those parts, who have been careful in collecting and collating the floating facts concerning this specter, allege that, the body of the trooper having been buried in the church-yard, the ghost rides forth to the scene of battle in nightly quest of his head; and that the rushing speed with which he sometimes passes along the Hollow, like a midnight blast, is owing to his being belated, and in a hurry to get back to the church-yard before daybreak.

Such is the general purport of this legendary superstition, which has furnished materials for many a wild story in that region of shadows; and the specter is known, at all the country firesides, by the name of the Headless Horseman of Sleepy Hollow.

It is remarkable that the visionary propensity I have mentioned is not confined to the native inhabitants of the valley, but is unconsciously imbibed by every one who resides there for a time. However wide-awake they may have been before they entered that sleepy region, they are sure, in a little time, to inhale the witching influence of the air, and begin to grow imaginative,—to dream dreams and see apparitions.

I mention this peaceful spot with all possible laud; for it is in such little retired Dutch valleys, found here and there embosomed in the great state of New York, that population, manners, and customs remain fixed; while the great torrent of migration and improvement which is making such incessant changes in other parts of this restless country sweeps by them unobserved. They are like those little nooks of still water which border a rapid stream; where we may see the straw and bubble riding quietly at anchor, or slowly revolving in their mimic harbor, undisturbed by the rush of the passing current. Though many years have elapsed since I trod the drowsy shades of Sleepy Hollow, yet I question whether I should not still find the same trees and the same families vegetating in its sheltered bosom.

In this by-place of Nature there abode, in a remote period of American history, that is to say, some thirty years since, a worthy wight of the name of Ichabod Crane; who sojourned, or, as he expressed it, "tarried," in Sleepy Hollow, for the purpose of instructing the children of the vicinity. He was a native of Connecticut—a state which supplies the Union with pioneers for the mind as well as for the forest, and sends forth yearly its legions of frontier woodsmen and country schoolmasters. The cognomen of Crane was not inapplicable to his person. He was tall, but exceedingly lank, with narrow shoulders, long arms and legs, hands that dangled a mile out of his sleeves, feet tht might have served for shovels, and his whole frame most loosely hung together. His head was small, and flat at top, with huge ears, large green glassy eyes, and a long snipe nose, so that it looked like a weather-cock perched upon his spindle neck to tell which way the wind blew. To see him striding along the profile of a hill on a windy day, with his clothes bagging and fluttering about him, one might have mistaken him for the genius of famine descending upon the earth, or some scarecrow eloped from a cornfield.

His schoolhouse was a low building of one large room, rudely constructed of logs; the windows partly glazed, and partly patched with leaves of old copy-books. It was most ingeniously secured at vacant hours by a withe twisted in the handle of the door, and stakes set against the window-shutters; so that, though a thief might get in with perfect ease, he would find some embarrassment in getting out—an idea most probably borrowed by the architect, Yost Van Houten, from the mystery of an eel-pot. The schoolhouse stood in a rather lonely but pleasant situation, just at the foot of a woody hill, with a brook running close by, and a formidable birch-tree growing at one end of it. From hence the low murmur of his pupils' voices, conning over their lessons, might be heard in a drowsy summer's day, like the hum of a beehive, interrupted now and then by the authoritative voice of the master, in the tone of menace or command; or peradventure, by the appalling sound of the birch, as he urged some tardy loiterer along the flowery path of knowledge. Truth to say, he was a conscientious man, and ever bore in mind the golden maxim, "Spare the rod, and spoil the child." Ichabod Crane's scholars certainly were not spoiled.

I would not have it imagined, however, that he was one of those cruel potentates of the school who joy in the smart of their subjects; on the contrary, he administered justice with discrimination rather than severity; taking the burden off the backs of the weak, and laying it on those of the strong. Your mere puny stripling that winced at the least flourish of the rod, was passed by with indulgence; but the claims of justice were satisfied by inflicting a double portion on some little tough, wrong-headed, broad-skirted Dutch urchin, who sulked and swelled and grew dogged and sullen beneath the birch. All this he called "doing his duty by their parents;" and he never inflicted a chastisement without following it by the assurance, so consolatory to the smarting urchin, that "he would remember it, and thank him for it, the longest day he had to live."

When school-hours were over he was even the companion and playmate of the larger boys; and on holiday afternoons would convoy some of the smaller ones home who happened to have pretty sisters, or good housewives for mothers, noted for the comforts of the cupboard. Indeed, it behooved him to keep on good terms with his pupils. The revenue arising from his school was small, and would have been scarcely sufficient to furnish him with daily bread, for he was a huge feeder, and, though lank, had the dilating powers of an anaconda; but to help out his maintenance, he was, according to country custom in those parts, boarded and lodged at the houses of the farmers whose children he instructed. With these he lived successively a week at a time; thus going the rounds of the neighborhood, with all his worldly effects tied up in a cotton handkerchief.

That all this might not be too onerous on the purses of his rustic patrons, who are apt to consider the costs of schooling a grievous burden, and schoolmasters as mere drones, he had various ways of rendering himself both useful and agreeable. He assisted the farmers occasionally in the lighter labors of their farms; helped to make hay; mended the fences; took the horses to water; drove the cows from pasture; cut wood for winter fire. He laid aside, too, all the dominant dignity and absolute sway with which he lorded it in his little empire, the school, and became wonderfully gentle and ingratiating. He found favor in the eyes of the mothers by petting the children, particularly the youngest; and like the lion bold, which whilom so magnanimously the lamb did hold, he would sit with a child on one knee, and rock a cradle with his foot for whole hours together.

In addition to his other vocations, he was the singing-master of the neighborhood, and picked up many bright shillings by instructing the young folks in psalmody. It was a matter of no little vanity to him, on Sundays, to take his station in front of the church gallery, with a band of chosen singers; where, in his own mind, he completely carried away the palm from the parson. Certain it is, his voice resounded far above all the rest of the congregation; and there are peculiar quavers still to be heard in that church, and which may even be heard half a mile off, quite to the opposite side of the mill-pond, on a still Sunday morning, which are said to be legitimately descended from the nose of Ichabod Crane. Thus by divers little make-shifts in that ingenious way which is commonly denominated "by hook and by crook," the worthy pedagogue got on tolerably enough, and was thought, by all who understood nothing of the labor of head-work, to have a wonderfully easy life of it.

The schoolmaster is generally a man of some importance in the female circle of a rural neighborhood, being considered a kind of idle gentleman-like personage, of vastly superior taste and accomplishments to the rough country swains, and, indeed, inferior in learning only to the parson. His appearance, therefore, is apt to occasion some little stir at the tea-table of a farm-house, and the addition of a supernumerary dish of cakes or sweet-meats, or, peradventure, the parade of a silver tea-pot. Our man of letters, therefore, was peculiarly happy in the smiles of all the country damsels. How he would figure among them in the church-yard, between services on Sundays! gathering grapes for them from the wild vines that overran the surrounding trees; reciting for their amusement all the epitaphs on the tombstones; or sauntering, with a whole bevy of them, along the banks of the adjacent mill-pond; while the more bashful country bumpkins hung sheepishly back, envying his superior elegance and address.

From his half itinerant life, also, he was kind of traveling gazette, carrying the whole budget of local gossip from house to house; so that his appearance was always greeted with satisfaction. He was, moreover, esteemed by the women as a man of great erudition, for he had read several books quite through, and was a perfect master of Cotton Mather's "History of New England Witch-craft"—in which, by the way, he most firmly and potently believed.

He was, in fact, a mixture of small shrewdness and simple credulity. His appetite for the marvelous, and his powers of digesting it, were equally extraor-dinary; and both had been increased by his residence in this spell-bound region. No tale was too gross or monstrous for his capacious swallow. It was often his delight, after his school was dismissed in the afternoon, to stretch himself on the rich bed of clover bordering the little brook that whimpered by his schoolhouse, and there con over old Mather's direful tales until the gathering dusk of the evening made the printed page a mere mist before his eyes. Then, as he wended his way, by swamp and stream and awful woodland, to the farm-house where he happened to be quartered, every sound of nature, at that witching hour, fluttered his excited imagination,—the moan of the whippoor-will from the hill-side; the boding cry of the tree-toad, that harbinger of storm; the dreary hooting of the screech-owl, or the sudden rustling in the thicket of birds frightened from their roost. The fire-flies, too, which sparkled most vividly in the darkest places, now and then startled him, as one of uncommon brightness would stream across his path; and if, by chance, a huge blockhead of a beetle came winging his blundering flight against him, the poor varlet was ready to give up the ghost, with the idea that he was struck with a witch's token. His only resource on such occasions, either to drown thought or drive away evil spirits, was to sing psalm-tunes; and the good people of Sleepy Hollow, as they sat by their doors of an evening, were often filled with awe at hearing his nasal melody, in "linked sweetness long drawn out," floating from the distant hill, or along the dusky road.

Another of his sources of fearful pleasure was, to pass long winter evenings with the old Dutch wives as they sat spinning by the fire, with a row of apples roasting and spluttering along the hearth, and listen to their marvelous tales of ghosts and goblins, and haunted fields, and haunted brooks, and haunted bridges, and haunted houses, and particularly of the headless horseman, or Galloping Hessian of the Hollow, as they sometimes called him. He would delight them equally by his anecdotes of witchcraft, and of the direful omens and portentous sights and sounds in the air which prevailed in the earlier times of Connecticut; and would frighten them wofully with speculations upon comets and shooting stars; and with the alarming fact that the world did absolutely turn round; and that they were half the time topsy-turvy!

From
The Algerine Captive

ℬ ◆ ℭ

Royall Tyler, 1797

Poverty, social isolation, unswerving disrespect—these are the conditions of life for Royall Tyler's unfortunate hero, Updike Underhill. The themes developed in this lively picaresque novel echo once again the ones found in other "education" literature of the day. Whereas Tyler's novel begins with the hero's receiving respectable schooling at the hands of the town's minister, the pretension and hypocrisy of the college admission system is again introduced here. Like the college examiners in John Trumbull's poem, Underhill's Harvard examiners are obsessed with the value of the classics:

> With them dead languages were more estimable than living, and nothing more necessary to accomplish a young man for all that is profitable and honourable in life than a profound knowledge of Homer. One gravely observed, that he was sure General Washington read Greek, and that he never would have captured the Hessians at Trenton, if he had not taken his plan of operation from that of Ulysses and Diomede seising the horses of Rhesus, as described in the tenth book of the Iliad. (Tyler, 1967, p. 34)

In the section of the novel excerpted here, Underhill himself turns to schoolteaching. The hero's experience is an exercise in dashed hopes. This American Candide imagines his pupils engaged in long, serious study, during which time he will read his favorite Greek. He also expects to be overwhelmed with the gratitude of their parents, to be financially solvent, to be surrounded by doting friends, and stimulated by the erudition of the local minister. Needless to say, these expectations go unmet. Underhill's resolution to spare the rod is almost immediately overturned, as are virtually every positive image he associates with the whole process of education. Having weathered every conceivable humiliation, Underhill is finally denied even payment in cash for his work: "My request for present payment," he recounts, "was received with astonishment. I found I was not to expect it until the next autumn, and then not in cash, but produce" (Tyler, p. 52).

Underhill's experience with compensation was not uncommon in the Colonial and early district schools, where teachers were often given payment in grain or other local crop—whether they wanted it or not!

This two-volume novel is a kind of early investigation of the ways in which democracy was practiced and not practiced in the New Republic: After visiting Franklin in America and cavorting with Tom Paine in London, Underhill books a passage on a slave ship ironically called "Sympathy." The ship's captain deals for 250 slaves as if they were "so many head of cattle." Underhill denounces the barbaric treatment of the slaves that are crammed together, beaten, and raped.

The picaresque design of the novel moves the hero through a number of different professions, with a particular focus on medicine, but teaching is a recurrent theme. Indeed, later in the novel, Underhill again finds himself employed as a tutor, but this time in the South. Here, the hero assumes in advance that he will receive a paltry wage, given the generally "low estate of teachers in that region." Underhill learns that "the school masters, before the war, had been usually collected from unfortunate European youth, of some school learning, sold for their passage into America: so that to purchase a school-master and a negro was almost synonymous" (Tyler, 1967, p. 144).

Royall Tyler (1757–1826) was a Harvard graduate whose play, "The Contrast," was the first American comedy to be produced by a professional American company. Dramatist, novelist, and judge (he was chief justice of the Vermont Supreme Court), Tyler resembled other intellectuals of his day in the far-reaching nature of his interests and his talents.

FROM *THE ALGERINE CAPTIVE*

Royall Tyler, 1797

Delightful task! to rear the tender thought,
To teach the young idea how to shoot,
To pour the fresh instruction o'er the mind,
To breathe th' enliv'ning spirit, and to fix
The gen'rous purpose in the glowing breast.

Thomson.

ARGUMENT.

The Author keepeth a Country School—The Anticipations, Pleasures, and Profits of a Pedagogue.

By our minister's recommendation, I was engaged to keep a school in a neighbouring town, so soon as our fall's work was over.

How my heart dilated with the prospect, in the tedious interval previous to my entering upon my school! How often have I stood suspended over my dungfork, and anticipated my scholars, seated in awful silence around me, my arm-chair, and birchen sceptre of authority! There was an echo in my father's sheep pasture. More than once I have repaired there alone, and exclaimed, with a loud voice, Is *master* Updike Underhill at home? I would speak with *master* Underhill! for the pleasure of hearing how my title sounded. Dost thou smile, indignant reader? pause, and recollect if these sensations have not been familiar to thee, at some time in thy life. If thou answerest disdainfully—no—then I aver thou hast never been a corporal in the militia, nor a sophimore at college.

At times I however entertained less pleasing, but more rational, contemplations on my prospects. As I had been once unmercifully whipped, for detecting my master in false concord, I resolved to be mild in my government, to avoid all manual correction, and doubted not by these means to secure the love and respect of my pupils.

In the interim of school hours, and in those peaceful intervals when my pupils were engaged in study, I hoped to indulge myself with my favourite Greek. I expected to be overwhelmed with the gratitude of their parents, for pouring the fresh instruction over the minds of their children, and teaching their young ideas how to shoot. I anticipated independence from my salary, which was to be equal to four dollars, hard money, per month, and my boarding; and expected to find amusement and pleasure among the circles of the young, and to derive information and delight from the classic converse of the minister.

In due time my ambition was gratified, and I placed at the head of a school, consisting of about sixty scholars. Excepting three or four overgrown boys of eighteen, the generality of them were under the age of seven years. Perhaps a more ragged, ill-bred, ignorant set, never were collected, for the punishment of a poor pedagogue. To study in school was impossible. Instead of the silence I anticipated, there was an incessant clamour. Predominant among the jarring sounds were—Sir, may I read? May I spell? Master, may I go out? Will master mend my pen?—What with the pouting of the small children, sent to school not to learn, but to keep them out of *harm's way*, and the gruff surly complaints of the larger ones, I was nearly distracted. Homer's *poluphloisboio thalasses*, roaring sea, was a whisper to it. My resolution to avoid beating them made me invent small punishments, which often have a salutary impression on delicate minds; but they were insensible to shame. The putting of a paper fool's-cap on one, and ordering another under my great chair, only excited mirth in the school; which the very delinquents themselves often increased by loud peals of laughter. Going, one frosty morning, into my school, I found one of the larger boys sitting by the fire in my arm-chair. I gently requested him to remove. He replied that he would, when he had warmed himself:—"father finds wood, and not you." To have my throne usurped, in the face of the school, shook my government to the centre. I immediately snatched my two-foot rule, and laid it pretty smartly across his back. He quitted the chair, muttering that he would tell father. I found his threats of more consequence than I apprehended. The same afternoon, a tall raw-boned man called me to the door: immediately collaring me with one hand, and holding a cart-whip over my head with the other, with fury in his face, he vowed he would whip the skin from my bones if ever I struck Jotham again: ay, he would do it that very moment, if he was not afraid I would take the law of him. This was the only instance of the overwhelming gratitude of parents I received. The next day it was reported all over town what a cruel man the master was. "Poor Jotham came into school, half frozen and near fainting; master had been sitting a whole hour by the warm fire; he only begged him to let him warm himself a little, when the master rose in a rage, and cut open his head with the tongs, and his life was despaired of."

Fatigued with the vexations of my school, I one evening repaired to the tavern, and mixed with some of the young men of the town. Their conversation I could not relish; mine they could not comprehend. The subject of race-horses being introduced, I ventured to descant upon Xanthus, the immortal courser of Achilles. They had never heard of 'squire Achilles or his horse; but they offered to bet two to one that Bajazet, the Old Roan, or the deacon's mare, Pumpkin and Milk, would beat him and challenged me to appoint time and place.

Nor was I more acceptable among the young women. Being invited to spend an evening, after a quilting, I thought this a happy opportunity to introduce Andromache, the wife of the great Hector, at her loom; and Penelope, the faithful wife of Ulysses, weaving her seven years' web. This was received with a stupid stare, until I mentioned the long time the queen of Ulysses was weaving; when a smart young woman observed, that she supposed miss Penelope's yarn was rotted in whitening, that made her so long: and then told a tedious story of a piece of cotton and linen she had herself woven, under the same circumstances. She had no sooner finished, than, to enforce my observations, I recited above forty lines of Greek from the Odyssey, and began a dissertation on the cæsura. In the midst of my harangue, a florid-faced young man at the further end of the room, with two large prominent foreteeth, remarkably white, began to sing,

"Fire upon the mountain! run, boys run!"—and immediately the whole company rushed forward to see who should get a chance in the reel of six.

I was about retiring, fatigued and disgusted, when it was hinted to me, that I might wait on miss Mima home; but as I could recollect no word in the Greek which would construe into *bundling*, or any of Homer's heroes who *got the bag*, I declined. In the Latin, it is true, that Æneas and Dido, in the cave, seem something like a precedent. It was reported all over the town the next day, that master was a *papish*, as he had talked French two hours.

Disappointed of recreation among the young, my next object was the minister. Here I expected pleasure and profit. He had spent many years in preaching for the edification of private families, and was settled in the town in a fit of enthusiasm; when the people drove away a clergyman, respectable for his years and learning. This he was pleased to call an awakening. He lectured me at the first onset for not attending the conference and night meetings; talked much of gifts, and decried human learning as carnal and devilish; and well he might, he certainly was under no obligations to it; for a new singing master coming into town, the young people, by their master's advice, were for introducing Dr. Watts's version of the Psalms. Although I argued with the minister an hour, he remains firmly convinced to this day, that the version of Sternhold and Hopkins is the same in language, letter, and metre, with those psalms king David chanted in the city of Jerusalem.

As for the independence I had founded on my wages, it vanished like the rest of my scholastic prospects. I had contracted some debts. My request for present payment was received with astonishment. I found I was not to expect it until the next autumn, and then not in cash, but produce; to become my own collector, and pick up my dues, half a peck of corn or rye in a place.

I was almost distracted, and yearned for the expiration of my contract, when an unexpected period was put to my distress. News was brought, that, by the carelessness of the boys, the school-house was burnt down. The common cry now was, that I ought in justice to pay for it, as to my want of proper government the carelessness of the boys ought to be imputed. The beating of Jotham was forgotten, and a thousand stories of my want of proper spirit circulated. These reports, and even the loss of a valuable *Gradus ad Parnassum*, did not damp my joy. I am sometimes led to believe, that my emancipation from real slavery in Algiers did not afford me sincerer joy than I experienced at that moment.

I returned to my father, who received me with kindness. My mother heard the story of my discomfitures with transport; as she said she had no doubt that her dream about my falling into the hands of savages was now out.

"Memoirs of a Woman Teacher" From *Educational Biographies, Memoirs of Teachers, Educators, and Promoters and Benefactors of Education, Literature, and Science, Part I: Teachers and Educators* (c. 1804–1816)

ಇಂ ◆ ಚಚ

Emma Hart Willard, 1861

Both in her sensibility and in her achievements, Emma Hart Willard (1787–1870) was remarkably ahead of her time. This pioneer in women's education not only established the Troy Female Seminary—the first college-level institution for women in the United States, she also went on to write history and geography textbooks, to train teachers, and to improve the curriculum in the new common schools. Indeed, to read Willard's memoirs in the context of other passages in this section is to encounter a voice that seems decidedly ahead of her time. During the years of Emma Hart's childhood, few women pursued formal education of any kind. Certainly no colleges admitted women, and there were few high schools for girls either. Female boarding schools existed in New England in the late 18th century, but these refined institutions were not academic in their orientation. Girls who matriculated at such schools studied mainly the womanly arts of embroidery, painting, and music.

Even before Willard put forth her pioneering proposals for female education, other women were campaigning for change. Susanna Rowson, a popular novelist of the period, published in 1794, *Mentora, Or Young Lady's Friend*, which presents an argument very similar to Willard's: that young ladies need lessons in English grammar and in home economics, not in "bad

French…how to work fillagre, make wafer-work, daub sattin, and work ill-proportioned figures in cloth … " (Winslow, 1927, p. 211). Like Rowson, Willard acted upon her discontentment by opening her own school.

The passage excerpted here opens with the start of Willard's formal education in the school of Dr. Thomas Miner. Her success as a student and teaching assistant led her, by the age of 21, to assume control of another institution in Middlebury, Vermont. Less than 10 years later, Willard's appeal to Governor DeWitt Clinton for a charter to open a unique institution for girls led to the start of the Troy Seminary. Willard's efforts on behalf of women's education sparked an energetic movement that continued from that point on.

"MEMOIRS OF A WOMAN TEACHER" FROM *EDUCATIONAL BIOGRAPHIES, MEMOIRS OF TEACHERS, EDUCATORS, AND PROMOTERS AND BENEFACTORS OF EDUCATION, LITERATURE, AND SCIENCE, PART I: TEACHERS AND EDUCATORS* (1804–1816)

Emma Hart Willard, 1861

In my childhood I attended the district school, but mostly from causes already related, none of my teachers so understood me as to awaken my powers or gain much influence over me. My father, happily for his children, left to his own family, used to teach us of evenings, and read aloud to us; and in this way I became interested in books and a voracious reader. A village library supplied me with such books as Plutarch's Lives, Rollins' Ancient History, Gibbon's Rome, many books of travels, and the most celebrated of the British poets and essayists.

Near the close of my fifteenth year, a new academy was opened about three-quarters of a mile from my father's house, of which Thomas Miner, a graduate, and once a tutor of Yale College, was the Principal, afterwards well known as an eminent physician president of the State Medical Society, and one of the most learned men of our country. Before the opening of the Academy, my mother's children had each received a small dividend from the estate of a deceased brother. My sister Nancy determined, as our parents approved, to spend this in being taught at the new school; but having at that time a special desire to make a visit among my married brothers and sisters in Kensington, (whose children were of my own age), I stood one evening, candle in hand, and made to my parents, who had retired for the night, what they considered a most sensible oration, on the folly of people's seeking to be educated above their means and prescribed duties in life. So Nancy went to school, and I to Kensington. A fortnight after, one Friday evening, I returned. Nancy showed me her books and told me of her lessons. "Mother," said I, "I am going to school to-morrow." "Why, I thought you had made up your mind not to be educated, and besides, your clothes are not in order, and it will appear odd for you to enter school Saturday." But Saturday morning I went, and received my lessons in Webster's Grammar and Morse's Geography. Mr. Miner was to hear me recite by myself until I overtook the class, in which were a dozen fine girls, including my elder sister. Monday, Mr. Miner called on me to recite. He began with Webster's Grammar, went on and on, and still as he questioned received from me a ready answer, until he said, "I will hear the remainder of your lesson tomorrow." The same thing occurred with the Geography lesson. I was pleased, and thought, "you never shall get to the end of my lesson." That hard chapter on the planets, with their diameters, distances, and periodic revolutions, was among the first of Morse's Geography. The evening I wished to learn it, my sister Lydia had a party. The house was full of bustle, and above all rose the song-singing, which always fascinated me. The moon was at the full, and snow was on the ground. I wrapt my cloak around me, and out of doors of a cold winter evening, seated on a horseblock, I learned that lesson. Lessons so learnt are not easily forgotten. The third day Mr. Miner admitted me to my sister's class. He used to require daily compositions. I never failed, the only one of my class who did not; but I also improved the opportunities which these afforded, to pay him off for any criticism by which he had (intentionally though indirectly) hit me,—with some parody or rhyme, at which, though sometimes pointed enough, Mr. Miner would heartily laugh—never forgetting, however, at some time or other, to retort with interest. Thus my mind was stimulated, and my progress rapid. For two successive years, 1802-3, I enjoyed the advantages of Dr. Miner's school, and I believe that no better instruction was given to girls in any school, at that time, in our country.

My life at this time was much influenced by an attachment I formed with Mrs. Peck, a lady of forty, although I was only fifteen. When we were first thrown together, it was for several days, and she treated me not as a child, but an equal—confiding to me much of that secret history which every heart sacredly cherishes; and I, on my part, opened to her my whole inner life, my secret feelings, anxieties and aspirations. Early in the spring of 1804 when I had just passed seventeen, Mrs. Peck proposed that a children's school in the village should be put into my hands.

The school-house was situated in Worthington street, on the great Hartford and New Haven turnpike; and was surrounded on the other three sides by a mulberry grove, towards which the windows were in summer kept open.

At nine o'clock, on that first morning, I seated myself among the children to begin a profession which I little thought was to last with slight interruption for forty years. That morning was the longest of my life. I began my work by trying to discover the several capacities and degrees of advancement of the children, so as to arrange them in classes; but they having been, under my predecessor, accustomed to the greatest license, would, at their option, go to the street door to look at a passing carriage, or stepping on to a bench in the rear, dash out of a window, and take a lively turn in the mulberry grove. Talking did no good. Reasoning and pathetic appeals were alike unavailing. Thus the morning slowly wore away. At noon I explained this first great perplexity of my teacher-life to my friend Mrs. Peck, who decidedly advised sound and summary chastisement. "I cannot," I replied; "I never struck a child in my life." "It is," she said, "the only way, and you must." I left her for the afternoon school with a heavy heart, still hoping I might find some way of avoiding what I could not deliberately resolve to do. I found the school a scene of uproar and confusion, which I vainly endeavored to quell. Just then, Jesse Peck, my friend's little son, entered with a bundle of five nice rods. As he laid them on the table before me, my courage rose; and, in the temporary silence which ensued, I laid down a few laws, the breaking of which would be followed with immediate chastisement. For a few moments the children were silent; but they had been used to threatening, and soon a boy rose from his seat, and as he was stepping to the door, I took one of the sticks and gave him a moderate flogging; then with a grip upon his arm which made him feel that I was in earnest, put him into his seat. Hoping to make this chastisement answer for the whole school, I then told them in the most endearing manner I could command, that I was there to do them good—to make them such fine boys and girls that their parents and friends would be delighted with them, and they be growing up happy and useful; but in order to [do] this I must and would have their obedience. If I had occasion to punish again it would be more and more severely, until they yielded, and were trying to be good. But the children still lacked faith in my words, and if my recollection serves me, I spent most of the afternoon in alternate whippings and exhortations, the former always increasing in intensity, until at last, finding the difference between capricious anger and steadfast determination, they submitted. This was the first and last of corporeal punishment in that school. The next morning, and every after, I had docile and orderly scholars. I was careful duly to send them out for recreation, to make their studies pleasant and interesting, and to praise them when they did well, and mention to their parents their good behavior.

Our school was soon the admiration of the neighborhood. Some of the literati of the region heard of the marvelous progress the children made, and of classes formed and instruction given in higher branches; and coming to visit us, they encouraged me in my school, and gave me valuable commendation.

At the close of this summer school, I determined to seek abroad advantages, especially in drawing and painting, with reference to future teaching. The two only remaining sons of my mother had become merchants in

Petersburg, Virginia, and were able and willing to furnish assistance to their younger sisters, and also to relieve our parents from the dread of indebtedness, which at one time their utmost exertions could scarcely keep from crossing the domestic threshold....

When I began my boarding school in Middlebury, in 1814, my leading motive was to relieve my husband from financial difficulties. I had also the further object of keeping a better school than those about me; but it was not until a year or two after, that I formed the design of effecting an important change in education, by the introduction of a grade of schools for women, higher than heretofore known. My neighborhood to Middlebury College, made me bitterly feel the disparity in educational facilities between the two sexes; and I hoped that if the matter was once set before the men as legislators, they would be ready to correct the error. The idea that such a thing might possibly be effected by my means, seemed so presumptuous that I hesitated to entertain it, and for a short time concealed it even from my husband, although I knew that he sympathized in my general views. I began to write (because I could thus best arrange my ideas) "an address to the — Legislature, proposing a plan for improving Female Education." It was not till two years after that I filled up the blank. No one knew of my writing it, except my husband, until a year after it was completed (1816), for I knew that I should be regarded as visionary, almost to insanity, should I utter the expectations which I secretly entertained in connection with it. But it was not merely on the strength of my arguments that I relied. I determined to inform myself, and increase my personal influence and fame as a teacher; calculating that in this way I might be sought for in other places, where influential men would carry my project before some legislature, for the sake of obtaining a good school.

My exertions meanwhile, became unremitted and intense. My school grew to seventy pupils. I spent from ten to twelve hours a day in teaching, and on extraordinary occasions, as preparing for examination, fifteen; besides, always having under investigation some one new subject which, as I studied, I simultaneously taught to a class of my ablest pupils. Hence every new term some new study was introduced; and in all their studies, my pupils were very thoroughly trained. In classing my school for the term of study, which was then about three months, I gave to each her course, (being careful not to give too much) with the certain expectation, that she must be examined on it at the close of the term. Then I was wont to consider that my first duty as a teacher, required of me that I should labor to make my pupils by explanation and illustration *understand* their subject, and get them warmed into it, by making them see its beauties and its advantages. During this first part of the process, I talked much more than the pupils were required to do, keeping their attention awake by frequent questions, requiring short answers from the whole class—for it was ever my maxim, if attention fails, the teacher fails. Then in the *second* stage of my teaching, I made each scholar recite, in order that she might *remember*—paying special attention to the meaning of words, and to discern whether the subject was indeed understood without mistake. Then the *third* process was to make the pupil capable of *communicating*.[1] And doing this in a right manner, was to prepare her for examination. At this time I personally examined all my classes.

This thorough teaching added rapidly to my reputation. Another important feature of a system, thus requiring careful drill and correct enunciation, was manifested by the examinations. The pupils, there acquired character and confidence. Scholars thus instructed were soon capable of teaching; and here were now forming my future teachers; and some were soon capable of aiding me in arranging the new studies, which I was constantly engaged in introducing.

Here I began a series of improvements in geography—separating and first teaching what could be learned from maps—then treating the various subjects of population, extent, length of rivers &c., by comparing country with country, river with river, and city with city,—making out with the assistance of my pupils, those tables which afterwards appeared in Woodbridge and Willard's Geographies. Here also began improvements in educational history. Moral Philosophy came next, with Paley for the author, and Miss Hemingway for the first scholar; and then the Philosophy of the Mind—Locke the author, and the first scholars, Eliza Henshaw, Katharine Battey, and Minerva Shiperd.

The professors of the college attended my examinations; although I was by the President advised, that it would not be becoming in me, nor be a safe precedent, if I should attend theirs. So, as I had no teacher in learning my new studies, I had no model in teaching, or examining them. But I had full faith in the clear conclusions of my own mind. I knew that nothing could be truer than truth; and hence I fearlessly brought to examination, before the learned, the classes, to which had been taught the studies I had just acquired.

---

[1]Communicating: "This threefold process, in some studies, as the Philosophy of Mind, of which an entire view should be taken, requires the whole term; in others, as in geography and history, parts may be taken, and the pupils made thorough in each as they go along. In mathematics, the three steps of the process are to be gone through with, as the teacher proceeds with every distinct proposition. But still, there will, in every well-instructed class, be this three-fold order prevailing, and during the term, requiring a beginning, a middle, and an end; the first of the term being mostly devoted to teaching, and the middle to reciting, and the last to acquiring a correct manner of communicating" [Editor's note in the 1861 publication].

From *The District School As It Was* (set c. 1810)

֍ ◆ ֎

Warren Burton, 1833

If Emma Willard's memoirs point the way to a more enlightened period in *women's* education, Warren Burton's writing seems to summarize and encapsulate the era in which *he* grew up. Burton's vivid description of a district school embodies all the idiosyncracies of the early republican era in schooling, and particularly the range of teacher types to be found there. The narrator traces his experiences over a succession of grades in a school that stands as a living caricature of the American district schoolhouse. From the opening pages of his book, Burton's writing underscores the odd compromises and community tensions that invariably surrounded the district school:

> The Old School-House in District No. 5, stood on the top of a very high hill, on the north side of what was called the County road. The house of Capt. Clark, about ten rods off, was the only human dwelling within a quarter of a mile. The reason why this seminary of letters was perched so high in the air, and so far from the homes of those who resorted to it, was this:—Here was the centre of the district, as near as surveyor's chain could designate. The people east would not permit the building to be carried one rod further west, and those of the opposite quarter were as obstinate on their side. (p. 18)

The two passages excerpted here represent the worst and best of a district school education. The first section describes Burton's experiences with a man he calls only "the Particular Master," a brute and a sadist cut from the same cloth as so many other literary pedagogues of the day. Burton's torturer contrives a number of unique punishments, including "standing in a stooping posture, with the finger on the head of a nail in the floor" (p. 54).

Luckily, however, Burton's district school education ends on a very high note. In a chapter that clearly suggests the coming of a new age in schooling, the author presents "reform" in the person of Mr. Ellis. All of the traits that emerged as sycophantish and insincere in other pedagogues seem genuine and winning in Mr. Ellis: He is cordial and kind to the ladies, informed and interested with the men; his love of children is apparent, and his knowledge is presented as genuine, unpretentious, and good-humored. Most impressive of all, Mr. Ellis does not resort to the rigid, rote methods of the traditional schoolmaster. To the astonishment and consternation of his pupils, this teacher requires composition and letter-writing instead of catechisms of grammatical terms. Burton's description of the class' gradual liberation, and their subsequent feelings of love and indebtedness to the schoolmaster are poignant testimony to the fact that Common School reform was long overdue.

Although written in first person from the point of view of the author, the book is actually a fictional memoir. Warren Burton (1800–1866) was home-educated by his grandparents, and prepared on his own to enter Harvard College where he graduated with distinction in 1821. After an apprenticeship as a teacher, Burton entered a theological seminary in Cambridge and became a Unitarian minister. Burton followed many educated men of his period in devoting himself to a range of reform efforts. He was strongly attracted to the mystical currents of his day, notably Transcendentalism, phrenology, and Pestalozzianism. He was also a member of the Brook Farm experiment from 1841–1844. Of his many works, *The District School As It Was* has been the most popular and the most enduring.

FROM *THE DISTRICT SCHOOL AS IT WAS* (SET C. 1810)

Warren Burton, 1833

THE PARTICULAR MASTER— VARIOUS METHODS OF PUNISHMENT.

I have given some account of my first winter at school. Of my second, third, and fourth, I have nothing of importance to say. The routine was the same in each. The teachers were remarkable for nothing in particular: if they were, I have too indistinct a remembrance of their characters to portray them now; so I will pass them by, and describe the teacher of my fifth.

He was called the *particular* master. The scholars in speaking of him, would say, "He is so particular." The first morning of the school, he read us a long list of regulations to be observed in school, and out. "There are more rules than you could shake a stick at before your arm would ache," said some one. "And if the master should shake a stick at every one who should disobey them, he would not find time to do much else," said another. Indeed, it proved to be so. Half the time was spent in calling up scholars for little misdemeanors, trying to make them confess their faults, and promise stricter obedience, or in devising punishments and inflicting them. Almost every method was tried that was ever suggested to the brain of pedagogue. Some were feruled on the hand; some were whipped with a rod on the back; some were compelled to hold out, at arm's length, the largest book which could be found, or a great leaden inkstand, till muscle and nerve, bone and marrow, were tortured with the continued exertion. If the arm bent or inclined from the horizontal level, it was forced back again by a knock of the ruler on the elbow. I well recollect that one poor fellow forgot his suffering by fainting quite away. This lingering punishment was more befitting the vengeance of a savage, than the corrective efforts of a teacher of the young in civilized life.

He had recourse to another method, almost, perhaps quite, as barbarous. It was standing in a stooping posture, with the finger on the head of a nail in the floor. It was a position not particularly favorable to health of body or soundness of mind; the head being brought about as low as the knees, the blood rushing to it, and pressing unnaturally on the veins, often caused a dull pain, and a staggering dizziness. That man's judgment or mercy must have been topsy-turvy also, who first set the example of such an infliction on those whose progress in knowledge depended somewhat on their being kept right end upward.

The above punishments were sometimes rendered doubly painful by their taking place directly in front of the enormous fire, so that the pitiable culprit was roasted as well as racked. Another mode of punishment—an anti-whispering process—was setting the jaws at a painful distance apart, by inserting a chip perpendicularly between the teeth. Then we occasionally had our hair pulled, our noses tweaked, our ears pinched and boxed, or snapped, perhaps, with India-rubber; this last the perfection of ear-tingling operations. There were minor penalties, moreover, for minor faults. The uneasy urchins were clapped into the closet, thrust under the desk, or perched on its top. Boys were made to sit in the girls' seats, amusing the school with their grinning awkwardness; and girls were obliged to sit on the masculine side of the aisle, with crimsoned necks, and faces buried in their aprons.

But I have dwelt long enough on the various penalties of the numerous violations of Master Particular's many orders. After all, he did not keep an orderly school. The cause of the mischief was, he was variable. He wanted that perservering firmness and uniformity which alone can insure success. He had so many regulations, that he could not stop at all times to notice the transgressions of them. The scholars, not knowing with certainty what to expect, dared to run the risk of disobedience. The consequence of this procedure on the part of the ruler and the ruled was, that the school became uncommonly riotous before the close of the season. The larger scholars soon broke over all restraint; but the little ones were narrowly watched and restricted somewhat longer. But these gradually grew unmindful of the unstable authority, and finally condemned it with almost insolent effrontery, unless the master's temper-kindled eye was fixed directly and menacingly upon them. Thus the many regulations were like so many cobwebs, through which the great flies would break at once, and so tear and disorder the net that it would not hold even the little ones, or at all answer the purpose for which it was spun.

I would not have it understood that this master was singular in his punishments; for such methods of correcting offenders have been in use time out of mind. He was distinguished only for resorting to them more frequently than any other instructor within my own observation. The truth is, that it seemed to be the prevailing opinion both among teachers and parents, that boys and girls *would* play and be mischievous at any rate, and that consequently masters *must* punish in some way or other. It was a matter of course; nothing better was expected.

AUGUSTUS STARR, THE PRIVATEER WHO TURNED PEDAGOGUE—HIS NEW CREW MUTINY, AND PERFORM A SINGULAR EXPLOIT.

My tenth winter, our school was put under the instruction of a person named Augustus Starr. He was a native of a neighboring town, and had before been acquainted with the committee. He had taught school some years before, but, for the last few years, had been engaged in a business not particularly conducive to improvement in the art of teaching. He had been an inferior officer aboard a privateer in the late war, which terminated only the winter before. At the return of peace, he betook himself to land again; and, till something more suitable to his tastes and habits should offer, he concluded to resume school-keeping, at least for one winter. He came to our town; and, finding an old acquaintance seeking for a teacher, he offered himself, and was accepted. He was rather genteelly dressed, and gentlemanly in his manners.

Mr. Starr soon manifested that stern command, rather than mild persuasion, had been his method of preserving order, and was to be, still. This would have been put up with; but he soon showed that he could deal in blows as well as words, and these not merely with the customary ferule, or supple and tingling stick, but with whatever came to hand. He knocked one lad down with his fist, hurled a stick of wood at another, which missed breaking his head because it struck the ceiling, making a dent which fearfully indicated what would have been the consequence had the skull been hit. The scholars were terrified, parents were alarmed, and some kept their younger children at home. There was an uproar in the district. A school-meeting was threatened for the purpose of dismissing the captain, as he began to be called, in reference to the station he had lately filled, although it was not a captaincy. But he commanded the school-house crew: so, in speaking of him, they gave him a corresponding title. In consequence of these indications, our officer became less dangerous in his modes of punishment, and was permitted to continue still in command. But he was terribly severe, nevertheless; and in his words of menace, he manifested no particular respect for that one of the ten commandments which forbids profanity. But he took pains with his pupils, and they made considerable progress according to the prevailing notions of education.

Toward the close of the school, however, Starr's fractious temper, his cuffs, thumps, and cudgelings, waxed dangerous again. There were signs of mutiny among the large scholars, and there were provocations and loud talk among parents. The man of violence, even at this late period, would have been dismissed by the authority of the district, had not a sudden and less formal ejection overtaken him.

The captain had been outrageously severe, and even cruel, to some of the smaller boys. The older brothers of the sufferers, with others of the back seat, declared among themselves, that they would put him by force out of the school-house, if any thing of the like should happen again. The very afternoon succeeding this resolution, an opportunity offered to put it to the test. John Howe, for some trifling misdemeanor, received a cut with the edge of the ruler on his head, which drew blood. The dripping wound and scream of the boy were a signal for action, as if a murderer were at his fell deed before their eyes. Thomas Howe, one of the oldest in the school and the brother of the abused, and Mark Martin, were at the side of our privateer in an instant. Two others followed. His ruler was wrested from his hand, and he was seized by his legs and shoulders, before he could scarcely think into what hands he had fallen. He was carried, kicking and swearing, out of doors. But this was not the end of his headlong and horizontal career. "To the side-hill, to the side-hill," cried Mark, who had him by the head. Now it so happened that the hill-side opposite the school-house door was crusted, and as smooth and slippery as pure ice, from a recent rain. To this pitch, then, he was borne, and in all the haste that his violent struggles would permit. Over he was thrust, as if he were a log; and down he went, giving one of his bearers a kick as he was shoved from their hands, which action of the foot sent him more swiftly on his way from the rebound. There was no bush or stone to catch by in his descent, and he clawed the unyielding crust with his nails, for the want of anything more prominent on which to lay hold. Down, down he went. Oh for a pile of stones or a thicket of thorns to cling to, even at the expense of a torn apparel or scratched fingers! Down, down he went, until he fairly came to the climax, or rather anti-climax, of his pedagogical career. Mark Martin, who retained singular self-possession, cried out, "There goes a shooting *star.*"

When our master had come to a "period or full stop," to quote from the spelling book, he lay a moment as if he had left his breath behind him, or as if querying whether he should consider himself alive or not; perhaps whether it were really his own honorable self who had been voyaging in this unseamanlike fashion, or somebody else. Perhaps he was at a loss for the points of compass, as is often the case in tumbles and topsy-turvies. He at length arose and stood upright, facing the ship of literature which he had lately commanded; and his mutinous crew, great and small, male and female, now lining the side of the road next to the declivity, from which most of them had witnessed his expedition. The movement had been so sudden, and the ejection so unanticipated by the school in general, that they were stupefied with amazement. And the bold performers of the exploit were almost as much amazed as the rest, excepting Mark, who still retained coolness enough for his joke. "What think of the *coasting* trade, captain?" shouted Mark; "is it as profitable as privateering?" Our coaster made no reply, but turned in pursuit of a convenient footing to get up into the road, and to the school-house again. While he was at a distance approaching his late station of command, Mark Martin stepped forward to hold a parley with him. "We have a word to say to you, sir, before you come much farther. If you will come back peaceably, you may come; but as sure as you meddle with any of us, we will make you acquainted with the *heft* and the hardness of our fists, and of stones and clubs too, if we must. The ship is no longer yours; so look out, for we are our own men now." Starr replied, "I do not wish to have anything more to do with the school; but there is another law besides club law, and that you have got to take." But when he came up and saw John Howe's face stained with blood, and his head bound up as if it had received the stroke of a cutlass, he began to look rather blank. Our spokesman reminded him of what he had done, and inquired, "which is the worst, a ride and a slide, or a gashed head?" "I rather guess that you are the one to look out for the law," said Thomas Howe, with a threatening tone and look. Whether this hint had effect, I know not, but he never commenced a prosecution. He gathered up his goods and chattels, and left the school-house. The scholars gathered up their implements of learning, and left likewise, after the boys had taken one more glorious slide down the hill.

There were both gladness and regret in that dispersion;—gladness that they had no more broken heads, shattered hands, and skinned backs to fear; and regret that the season of schooling, and of social and delightful play, had been cut short by a week.

The news reached most of the district in the course of the next day, that our "man of war," as he was sometimes called, had sailed out of port the night before.

A COLLEGE MASTER AGAIN—HIS CHARACTER IN SCHOOL AND OUT—OUR FIRST ATTEMPTS AT COMPOSITION—BRIEF SKETCH OF ANOTHER TEACHER.

My twelfth winter has arrived. It was thought best to try a teacher from college again, as the committee had been assured that there were teachers to be found there of the first order, and well worth the high price they demanded for their services. A Mr. Ellis was engaged at twenty dollars per month, from the same institution mentioned before. Particular pains were taken to ascertain the college character, and the school-keeping experience of the gentleman, before his engagement, and they were such as to warrant the highest expectations.

The instructor was to board round in the several families of the district, who gave the board in order to lengthen the school to the usual term. It happened that he was to be at our house the first week. On Saturday Mr. Ellis arrived. It was a great event to us children for the master to stop at our house, and one from college too. We were smitten with bashfulness, and stiffened into an awkwardness unusual with us, even among strangers. But this did not last long. Our guest put us all at ease very soon. He seemed just like one of us, or like some unpuffed-up uncle from a genteeler life, who had dropped in upon us for a night, with cordial heart, chatty tongue, and merry laugh. He seemed perfectly acquainted with our prevailing thoughts and feelings, and let his conversation slide into the current they flowed in, as easily as if he had never been nearer college than we ourselves. With my father he talked about the price of produce, the various processes and improvements in agriculture, and the politics of the day, and such other topics as would be likely to interest a farmer so far in the country. And those topics, indeed, were not a few. Some students would have sat in dignified or rather dumpish silence, and have gone to bed by mid-evening, simply because those who sat with them could not discourse on those deep things of science, and lofty matters of literature, which were particularly interesting to themselves. With my mother Mr. Ellis talked at first about her children. He patted a little brother on his cheek, took a sister on his knee, and inquired the baby's name. Then he drew forth a housewifely strain concerning various matters in country domestic life. Of me he inquired respecting my studies at school years past; and even condescended to speak of his own boyhood and youth, and of the sports as well as the duties of school. The fact is, that Mr. Ellis had always lived in the country till three years past; his mind was full of rural remembrances; and he knew just how to take us to be agreeable himself, and to elicit entertainment in return.

Mr. Ellis showed himself at home in school, as well as at the domestic fireside. He was perfectly familiar with his duties, as custom had prescribed them, but he did not abide altogether by the old usages. He spent much time in explaining those rules in arithmetic and grammar, and those passages in the spelling-book, with which we had hitherto lumbered our memories.

This teacher introduced a new exercise into our school, that we had never thought of before as being possible to ourselves. It was composition. We hardly knew what to make of it. To write—to put sentence after sentence like a newspaper, a book, or a sermon—oh! we could not do this; we could not think of such a thing; indeed, it was an impossibility. But we must try, at any rate. The subject given out for this novel use of thought and pen was friendship. Friendship—what had we to say on this subject? We could feel on it, perhaps, especially those of us who had read a novel or two, and had dreamed of eternal friendship. But we had not a single idea. Friendship! oh! it is a delightful thing! This, or something similar, was about all we poor creatures could think of. What a spectacle of wretchedness did we present! A stranger would have supposed us all smitten with the toothache, by the agony expressed in the face. One poor girl put her head down into a corner, and cried till the master excused her. And, finally, finding that neither smiles nor frowns would put ideas into our heads, he let us go for that week.

In about a fortnight, to our horror, the exercise was proposed again. But it was only to write a letter. Any one could do as much as this, the master said; for almost every one had occasion to do it in the course of life. Indeed, we thought, on the whole, that we *could* write a letter, so at it we went with considerable alacrity. But our attempts at the epistolary were nothing like those spirited, and even witty, products of thought which used ever to be flying from seat to seat in the shape of billets. The sprightly fancy and the gushing heart seemed to have been chilled and deadened by the reflection that a letter *must* be written, and the master *must* see it. These epistolary compositions generally began, continued, and closed all in the same way, as if all had got the same recipe from their grandmothers for letter writing. They mostly commenced in this manner: "Dear friend, I take my pen in hand to inform you that I am well, and hope you are enjoying the same blessing." Then there would be added, perhaps, "We have a very good schoolmaster; have you a good one? How long has your school got to keep? We have had a terrible stormy time on't," &c. Mark Martin addressed the master in his epistle. What its contents were I could not find out; but I saw Mr. Ellis read it. At first he looked grave, as at the assurance of the youth; then a little severe, as if his dignity was outraged; but in a moment he smiled, and finally he almost burst out with laughter at some closing witticism.

Mark's was the only composition that had any nature and soul in it. He wrote what he thought, instead of thinking what to write, like the rest of us, who, in the effort, thought just nothing at all; for we wrote words which we had seen written a hundred times before.

Mr. Ellis succeeded in delivering us from our stale and flat formalities before he had done. He gave us no more such abstract and lack-idea subjects as friendship. He learned better how to accommodate the theme to the youthful mind. We were set to describe what we had seen with our eyes, heard with our ears, and what had particularly interested our feelings at one time and another. One boy described the process of cider-making. Another gave an account of a squirrel-hunt; another of a great husking; each of which had been witnessed the autumn before. The girls described certain domestic operations. One, I remember, gave quite an amusing account of the coming and going, and final tarrying, of her mother's soap. Another penned a sprightly dialogue, supposed to have taken place between two sisters on the question, which should go a visiting with mother, and which should stay at home and "take care of the things."

The second winter (for he taught two), Mr. Ellis occasionally proposed more abstract subjects, and such as required more thinking and reasoning, but still, such as were likely to be interesting, and on which he knew his scholars to possess at least a few ideas.

I need not say how popular Mr. Ellis was in the district. He was decidedly the best schoolmaster I ever went to, and he was the last.

"The School-Master in the Dark South" From *Recollections of Seventy Years* (c. 1830)

☙ ◆ ❧

Daniel Alexander Payne, 1888

This excerpt from Daniel Alexander Payne's autobiography *Recollections of Seventy Years*, presents a brief but telling picture of an extraordinary Black educator. Payne was born in Charleston, South Carolina in 1811 to free parents with deep religious convictions. A passionate scholar from an early age, Payne opened his own school for free Black children when he was 19 years old. After the Nat Turner Rebellion, however, Payne's school was closed, and the young teacher went north to enroll in the Lutheran Theological Seminary in Gettysburg. The next years of Payne's life were spent working as a reformer and crusader for the African Methodist Episcopal Church. After 11 years of service, Payne was made a bishop. Payne ended his career in the position of President of Wilberforce University. He was the first Black college president in the United States.

The passage excerpted here deals with Payne's early experiences with self-education and the opening of his school. The passage stands in powerful contrast to many of the other pieces in this section, largely because of its joyful and optimistic tone. The young Payne speaking here is clearly in love with both learning and teaching. He relishes not only the subject matter he is to impart, but also the pedagogy; his techniques for introducing biology and other natural sciences to his students are decidedly modern, and a far cry from the loathsome rote recitations described in other passages in Part I.

Frederick Douglass wrote of Daniel Payne that his was a "life without flaw, and a name without blemish." Payne's profoundly moral character and ingenuous good humor come through in the voice of this passage. Teaching and learning is clearly this man's deepest calling.

"THE SCHOOL-MASTER IN THE DARK SOUTH" FROM
RECOLLECTIONS OF SEVENTY YEARS (C. 1830)

Daniel Alexander Payne, 1888

I resolved to devote every moment of leisure to the study of books, and every cent to the purchase of them. I raised money by making tables, benches, clothes-horses, and "corset-bones," which I sold on Saturday night in the public market. During my apprenticeship I would eat my meals in a few minutes and spend the remainder of the hour allowed me at breakfast and dinner in reading. After the day's work was done I perused my books till nearly twelve o'clock; and then, keeping a tinder-box, flint, steel, and candle at my bedside, I would awake at four, strike a light, and study till six, when my daily labors began. Thus I went on reading book after book, drawing pictures with crayon, and now and then composing verses. In my nineteenth year I forsook the carpenter's trade for the life of an educator.

* * *

My first school was opened in 1829 in a house on Tradd Street occupied by one Caesar Wright. It consisted of his three children, for each of whom he paid me fifty cents a month. I also taught three adult slaves at night, at the same price, thus making my monthly income from teaching only three dollars. This was not sufficient to feed me, but a slave-woman, Mrs. Eleanor Parker, supplied many of my wants. I was happy in my humble employment, but at the end of the year I was so discouraged at the financial result, and by the remarks expressed by envious persons, that I decided to seek some other employment which would yield better pay.

At this juncture a wealthy slave-holder arrived in Charleston, *en route* to the West Indies for his health. Knowing that British law emancipated every slave that put his foot on British soil, he desired to obtain the services of a free young man of color sufficiently intelligent to do his out-of-door business. I was commended to him, and called upon him at the Planters' Hotel. Among the inducements he offered he said: "If you will go with me, the knowledge that you will acquire of men and things will be of far more value to you than the wages I will pay you. Do you know what makes the difference between the master and the slave? *Nothing but superior knowledge.*"

This statement was fatal to his desire to obtain my services, for I instantly said to myself: "If it is true that there is nothing but superior knowledge between the master and the slave, I will not go with you, but will rather go and obtain that knowledge which constitutes the master." As I politely took my leave these words passed through my mind:

> He that flies his Saviour's cross
> Shall meet his Maker's frown.

Then these reflections followed. "In abandoning the school-room am I not fleeing from the cross which the Saviour has imposed upon me? Is not the abandonment of the teacher's work in my case a sin?" The answer was easily found, and I resolved to re-open my school and inform my patrons to that effect.

On the first of the year 1830 I re-opened my school, which continued to increase in numbers until the room became too small, and I was constrained to procure a more commodious place. This in turn became too small, and one was built for me on Anson Street, by Mr. Robert Howard, in the rear of his yard. This house is still standing (1886). Here I continued to teach until April, 1835.

During the three years of my attendance at the school of Mr. Thomas S. Bonneau I learned how to read, write, and spell; also arithmetic as far as the "Rule of Three." Spelling was a delightful exercise of my boyhood. In this I excelled. Seldom did I lose my place at the head of my class, and he who won it did not occupy it long. History was my great delight. Of geography and map-drawing, English grammar and composition I knew nothing, because they were not taught in any of the schools for colored children. I therefore felt the need of knowledge in these directions; but how was I to obtain it?

I had a geography, but had never seen an atlas, and, what was more, I knew not how or where to get one. Fortunately for me, one day as I was sitting on the piazza endeavoring to learn some lesson, a woman entered the gate and approached me with a book in her hand. Said she: "Don't you want to buy this book?" Taking it, I opened it, and to my great joy I beheld the colored maps of an atlas—the very thing I needed. Said I: "What will you take for it?" The woman had found it on the street, and replied: "Whatever you choose to give." All that I could command at the time was a York shilling (twelve and one-half cents in silver coin), so I gave it to her, and rejoiced over my prize. Immediately I went to work with my geography and atlas, and in about six months was able to construct maps on the Mercator's and globular projection. After I had acquired this ability I introduced geography and map-drawing into my school. At the same time with geography I studied and mastered English grammar. I began with "Murray's Primary Grammar," and committed the entire book to memory, but did not understand it; so I reviewed it. Then light sprung up; still I felt like one in a dungeon who beheld a glimmer of light at a distance, and with steady but cautious footsteps moved toward it, inspired by the hope that I would soon find its source and come out into the full blaze of animated day. I then made a second review of it, and felt conscious of my power to teach it. I therefore added that to my curriculum.

Having now the groundwork, I began to build the superstructure. I commenced with "Playfair's Euclid," and proceeded as far as the first five books. The next thing which arrested my attention was botany. The author and her specimens enchanted me; my progress was rapid, and the study became to me a source of great happiness and an instrument of great usefulness. Descriptive chemistry, natural philosophy, and descriptive astronomy followed in rapid succession.

"Burret's Geography of the Heavens" was my text-book in the last-named science. Stimulated by this interesting guide, I watched the total eclipse of 1832 from its commencement to its completion with my *naked eye*; but I paid dear for my rash experiment. The immediate result was a partial loss of sight. No book could be read for about three weeks. Whenever I opened a book the pages had the appearance of *black sheets*. From this injury I have never fully recovered. Up to that time my eyes were like those of the eagle; ever since they have been growing weaker and weaker.

Then, on a Thursday morning, I bought a Greek grammar, a lexicon, and a Greek Testament. On the same day I mastered the Greek alphabet; on Friday I learned to write them; on Saturday morning I translated the first chapter of Matthew's Gospel from Greek into English. My very soul rejoiced and exulted in this glorious triumph. Next came the Latin and the French. Meanwhile I was pushing my studies in drawing and coloring till I was able to produce a respectable flower, fruit, or animal on paper and on velvet.

My researches in botany gave me a relish for zoology; but as I could never get hold of any work on this science I had to *make books* for myself. This I did by killing such insects, toads, snakes, young alligators, fishes, and young sharks as I could catch. I then cleaned and stuffed those that I could, and hung them upon the walls of my school-room. The following fact will give the index of my methods. I bought a live alligator, made one of my pupils provoke him to bite, and whenever he opened his mouth I discharged a load of shot from a small pistol down his throat. As soon as he was stunned I threw him on his back, cut his throat, ripped open his chest, hung him up and studied his viscera till they ceased to move. The flesh of all that I killed I cooked and tasted. I excepted nothing but the toad and snake. My detestation for these was too intense to allow me to put their flesh into my mouth.

My enthusiasm was the inspiration of my pupils. I used to take my first class of boys into the woods every Saturday in search of insects, reptiles, and plants, and at the end of five years I had accumulated some fine specimens of each of these. I had also taken a fatherless boy to educate gratuitously. This lad's sister one day found a large caterpillar on an elderberry-tree. This worm she sent to me. It was the length and thickness of a large laboring-man's middle finger. It had four rows of horns running the whole length of its body; these horns were made up of golden and ebony-like points; its head was also encircled with a crown of these horns.

Not being able to determine the species or genus of this worm, I took it to Mrs. Ferguson, the sister of Judge Colcox, who was unable to give me any information in regard to it; but she advised me to take it to Dr. Bachman, who was then the most distinguished naturalist in South Carolina. I little knew what that visit was to bring about ultimately.

The Doctor received me kindly, and gave its classification. He also instructed me in its nature and habits, and how to carry it through its different stages of existence. This, however, I preferred him to do, allowing me at the same time to visit his studio and observe the transformations. This request was kindly complied with by the learned divine and naturalist. On my second visit he took me into his garden and showed me his fine collections of flowers. He also exhibited to me his herbarium and his valuable collection of insects from different parts of the world. On my last visit he took me into his parlor and introduced me to his wife and daughters as "the young philosopher." There I sat and conversed with his family as freely as though all were of the same color and equal rank; and by my request his daughter skillfully performed several pieces upon the piano. A remark of his at that visit has occurred to me many times through life. There was upon the center-table, protected by a large glass globe, an artificial tree bearing a collection of beautifully-mounted birds. My attention was drawn to them, and I expressed myself to the effect that he had about him everything to make his home pleasant. His reply was substantially this: "Yes; I feel it my duty to throw around my home every possible attraction for my daughters, so that they may never have occasion to seek elsewhere for forbidden pleasures."

My school increased in popularity, and became the most popular of five which then existed. It numbered about sixty children from most of the leading families of Charleston. But I was not without enemies who endeavored to arrest the progress of my school and destroy my usefulness by such remarks as these: "He is an impostor." "Who ever heard of any one learning such things—such things as he teaches—but men trained in a college." "He must deal with the devil."

Such imputations and slanders availed nothing. They seemed to render me more popular, and at last two of the other school-masters came to me to be taught such sciences as they knew not. It was a happiness for me to assist them, which I did, directing them to the authors and the methods which I had employed. It was also one of my methods in order to interest my pupils to erect several gymnastic instruments, that they might develop their muscular systems and find amusement to break the monotony of the school-room; but in all their sports I led them in person.

Part I
Questions and Activities

ᴆ ◆ ৪

1. What is the common image of the Colonial teacher that emerges in the works of Irving, Trumbull, Freneau, and Tyler? To what extent do you think this image is shaped by individual character, and to what extent is it a response to community imperatives and other forces outside the teachers' control?

2. What factors suggested in the reading may explain Emma Hart Willard's unusual success as a woman teacher and educator?

3. Compare the teaching style of Daniel Alexander Payne with the style of Warren Burton's Mr. Ellis. What do they appear to have in common, both in terms of pedagogy and philosophy? How do they differ from other teachers in the section?

4. Given the way teaching and teachers are depicted in this section, what reforms would be necessary to improve the profession?

5. Write a letter from a late 18th-century teacher describing the circumstances of your employment to a friend.

6. Read Benjamin Franklin's famous essay "Silence Dogood, On The Higher Learning," and compare his view of Harvard College and classical education with the description of the classically trained pedagogue in Trumbull's "The Rare Adventures of Tom Brainless" and Tyler's "*The Algerine Captive.*"

7. Read Benjamin Rush's "Thoughts Upon Female Education," and compare it to Willard's philosophy on female education.

SUGGESTED READINGS

Cremin, L. A. *American Education: The National Experience 1783–1876* (New York: Harper Colophon Books, 1980).

Curti, M. *The Growth of American Thought* (3rd ed.; Harper and Row, 1964). Chapter 5 deals with the period of the American Enlightenment.

Franklin, B. "Silence Dogood, On the Higher Learning" from *Benjamin Franklin on Education*, John Hardin Best, ed. (New York: Teachers College Press, 1962).

Rush, B. "Thoughts Upon Female Education," from *Essays on Education in the Early Republic*, Frederick Rudolph, ed. (Cambridge: Belknap Press, 1965).

Part II

*"As to the Moral Condition
of the People…": The Teacher
and The Common School*

By the second decade of the 19th century, the liabilities of the old district system of schooling were increasingly apparent. Gross disparities in funding existed from one district to another, and over the previous decades district school teachers were held to no common performance standard, nor were there any accepted criteria for judging such individuals. Communities tended increasingly to opt for the cheapest schools, the lowest paid teachers, and the minimum in materials they could get away with, relying on rate bills to supplement the teacher's wages. Rate bills—a system of charging parents for the specific number of days their child attended school—inexorably worked to reduce attendance and to increase parental hostility toward the teachers who were pressured to justify their wage on a daily basis.

The deteriorating condition of the district schools and the use of rate bills tended to create a sharp division between the schooling of wealthy and poor citizens. Anyone with means turned to the independent pay schools that proliferated in cities around the country. Edward Everett Hale, in recalling his own grammar school education at the private Boston Latin School, summarized the feelings of the middle class with regard to the more "public" educational options:

> ...there was no public school of any lower grade, to which my father would have sent me, any more than he would have sent me to jail. Since that time I have heard my contemporaries talk of the common school training of the day, and I do not wonder at my father's decision. The masters, so far as I know, were all inferior men; there was constant talk of "hiding" and "cow-hides" and "ferules" and "thrashing," and I should say, indeed, that the only recollections of my contemporaries about those school-days are of one constant low conflict with men of a very low type. (Hale, 1927 p. 17)

For the growing number of those unable or unwilling to pay even the most modest amount for schooling, there existed the option of the pauper school. These institutions, generally church-run, had difficulty attracting students, largely due to the exigencies of the pauper laws that governed their use. According to the law, parents were obliged to publically declare themselves as paupers prior to enrolling their children in the schools; most impoverished families preferred illiteracy over any kind of public education that required such mortification. Statistics indicate that by 1828, over half the estimated 400,000 children between the ages of 5 and 15—the overwhelming majority of them poor—were not enrolled in any school at all.

The problematic state of public education was a subject of increasing concern among intellectuals, workers' organizations, and reformers. Indeed, for vastly contrasting reasons, a wide range of constituencies began, in the first decades of the century, to rally support for tax-supported public schools. Labor leaders saw a free, adequate system of education as the only reasonable strategy for ameliorating the abuses of the factory system—a system where children were pressed into the workforce and routinely exploited, and where workers saw no opportunity for advancement. Free public schooling became a recurring theme in labor literature in the 1820s, and a major plank on workers' political platforms after 1828.

Many citizens were drawn into the crusade for public schooling through newly created *lyceums*, local learned societies where ordinary people met to discuss new scientific discoveries and exchange practical knowledge. Early on, the cause of public education became a favorite topic of intellectual debate among lyceum members, particularly when linked with discussion of new educational trends from abroad. The educational ideas of the Swiss teacher Peztalozzi found a rapt audience in the lyceum as did innovative methodologies from Prussia and Italy. When, in 1831, the various state lyceums merged into a national organization, free common schooling was high on their platform of concerns.

Certainly the most vocal supporters of free public schools were the new reformers who came on the American scene at the start of the 19th century. As at no point before in American history, a spirit of humanitarian zeal swept the middle and upper classes of the day, inspired in part by a deepening economic depression in the 1830s. These reformers, many of them Transcendentalists, embraced a sweeping array of causes at once. Antislavery, temperance, women's rights, and public education were among the many issues they supported.

That the new reformers were drawn from outside the ranks of the poor and working class is clearly apparent from the educational reform agenda they passionately espoused. Crusaders by and large allied themselves not with the poor and disenfranchised adults, but with their children. To the American-born, Protestant reformers, the children of the immigrant poor, in particular, were innocent victims not only of inhumane social policies, but of their own parents' ignorance and vice. The parents, they reasoned, could be considered unsalvagable; the children were not. What is more, to educate these children was a matter of public urgency. Without schooling they would certainly grow up to become a massive burden on the system—the ultimate threat to Jefferson's great republican experiment.

The thrust of curriculum reform of the period, then, is far less intellectual than it is moralistic and assimilationist. A strong Protestant (and some would say, elitist) ideology infiltrated the common school agenda, drawing in the critically needed support of the monied classes. Horace Mann, the movement's most tireless advocate, campaigned for public schools by playing on this theme of moral and Christian virtue: To the propertied classes, Mann described the common school as the cheapest means of self-protection and insurance. "Where else," he asked, could you "find any police so vigilant and effective, for the protection of all the rights of person, property and character?" (Mann, 1841/1957, p. 53). Mann's arguments eventually worked. By midcentury, many states were moving toward centralized, tax-supported elementary schools; compulsory education laws were being enacted, and attention was turning finally and in a systematic way to the training and preparation of teachers.

The shift toward mass education with a focus on morality and virtue necessarily affected the nature of the teaching force. In the first place, the need for teachers rose exponentially. If education was to be compulsory, and if all manner of child was to attend the school, then the ranks within the profession would have to swell. Already, before the common school movement had formally begun, urban reformers were grappling with strategies to cope with the sheer numbers of children interested in schooling. The Lancastrian System, imported to America in the first years of the 19th century, seemed for a while like an ideal solution to the problem. Through an elaborate system of students teaching students, up to 1,000 students could be accommodated in basic catechisms of spelling and arithmetic by a single paid teacher. Such schools were highly organized, operating with a kind of mechanical efficiency that was impressive to many an onlooker. But from the perspective of many common school reformers, Lancastrian schools were not the solution. Massive amphitheaters were not places where virtue and civility could be taught. Pestalozzian ideas about object lessons required a more intimate forum, with a teacher who loved and understood children. Although it was critical to keep costs at a minimum, it was also critical to effectively assimilate and civilize youth. Both of these needs could be met by the hiring of women. Indeed, the feminization of the teaching force, which begins in this period and persists for more than 150 years, long resolved the competing interests of cost and quality. The ranks of young, educated women were rapidly growing in the first decades of the 19th century. Women from middle-class families, well schooled and devout, were eager for meaningful work to fill those years between school and marriage. Catherine Beecher, a powerful social reformer and an advocate for women's education, exhorted the monied classes to teach. Beecher knew that the mental idleness that accompanied a traditional privileged life for women was deadening to the soul. Teaching, she argued, was ideal preparation for marriage and childrearing. As for widows and women who would never marry (including many who lost husbands and fiancees in the Civil War), teaching emerged as a profession that often offered distraction and comfort. Unlike many of their male predecessors, this second category of women saw schoolteaching as a career—a life-long commitment that carried with it a spiritual dimension. The Protestant reform ideology infused deeper significance to the work, and prompted many to look toward the most challenging and needy students in America. The passages in this section present the stories of both Black and White women who taught the freedmen in the South, and women who went West to work with pioneers and settlers. The extraordinary difficulty of the work and its profound fulfillment come through vividly in these stories.

In summary, then, the common school period brought dramatic change to the teaching force. The feminization, the new moral curricular imperative, the humanistic ideas of European educators—these changes were written about and disseminated in educational journals and in the normal schools, institutions especially designed for teacher training, which also began to proliferate by midcentury. Teaching was clearly becoming a profession, with its own culture, its own knowledge base, and its own standards.

"Bronson Alcott's Method" From *Record of a School:* *Exemplifying the General Principles of Spiritual Culture*

ဆ ◆ ଓଷ

Elizabeth Palmer Peabody, 1835

In this passage, Elizabeth Palmer Peabody (1804–1861) records for us the daily work of her mentor, Amos Bronson Alcott (1799–1888). The story of Alcott's school, the Temple School in Boston, is a testament to the ideas and preoccupations of the Common School Reform Movement, taken to a particularly colorful extreme. Alcott, the father of Louisa May and close friend to Emerson and other Transcendentalists, came to teaching with a deeply felt and elaborated ideology: He abhorred the traditional rote approach to education, and focused his energies on developing a technique that would liberate the spiritual life of the child. As the excerpt included in this collection demonstrates, that technique was an inductive and Socratic one, built on a series of religiously oriented questions, which the teacher would proffer in the kindest and most gentle way possible. It was a technique, Alcott believed, that could be used with children of all ages and intellectual levels, as demonstrated by Peabody's description of a lesson in Wordsworth that Alcott is directing to pupils as young as 4 and 5. Whereas the curriculum of the post-Revolutionary school was rigidly circumscribed, the curriculum of the Temple School was as broad as life itself. No topic should be excluded from classroom discussion, Alcott contended, including speculations on religion and sex.

Alcott's radically idealistic approach found support among intellectuals of his day—including Emerson who gave cash gifts for the upkeep of the Temple School. But, ultimately, it proved too innovative even for the common school reformers. When, in 1839, Alcott decided to integrate the Temple School, all but two children were permanently withdrawn. At that point, the great educational reformer gave up teaching and took up farming.

Alcott's Transcendalist approach to the education of young children embodies many of the ideas that emerge in less dramatic fashion throughout the common school period. His focus on Christian values and the importance of personal integrity were themes in many common school classrooms. Certainly, his view of the child as an essentially good and delicate being finds resonance in the work of other "new" educators. Pestalozzi and Froebel—the German founder of the kindergarten whose ideas were increasingly popular during this period—share aspects of their ideology with Alcott.

Elizabeth Peabody, who served as both a teacher in the school and as Alcott's amanuensis for 2 years, eventually chose to embrace the more moderate teachings of Froebel, opening her own school and becoming herself an expert in the kindergarten curriculum. Her book on the subject, *Lectures in Training School for Kindergarten* (1888), was widely read. Judging from the friends and associates she wrote about in her memoirs, Peabody was a woman who knew most of the great intellectuals of her day. As the owner of the West Street Bookshop in Boston, she gathered around her writers and well-known Transcendalist thinkers. Her sister Mary married Horace Mann; her sister Sophia married Nathaniel Hawthorne. With such connections—and having had a young Emerson as her own Greek instructor—she was clearly well situated for documenting the intellectual world of America at mid-century.

"BRONSON ALCOTT'S METHOD" FROM *RECORD OF A SCHOOL: EXEMPLIFYING THE GENERAL PRINCIPLES OF SPIRITUAL CULTURE*

Elizabeth Palmer Peabody, 1835

Mr. Alcott re-commenced his school in Boston, after four years interval, September, 1834, at the Masonic Temple, No. 7.

Considering that the objects which meet the senses every day for years, must necessarily mould the mind, he felt it necessary to choose a spacious room, and ornament it, not with such furniture as only an upholsterer can appreciate, but with such forms as might address and cultivate the imagination and heart.

In the four corners of the room, therefore, Mr. Alcott placed upon pedestals, fine busts of Socrates, Shakespeare, Milton, and Sir Walter Scott. And on a table, before the large gothic window by which the room is lighted, the God of Silence, "with his finger up, as though he said, beware." Opposite this gothic window, is his own table, about ten feet long, whose front is the arc of a circle, and which is prepared with little desks for the convenience of scholars. On this table he placed a small figure of a child aspiring. Behind him is a very large bookcase, with closets below, a black tablet above, and two shelves filled with books. A fine cast of Christ, in basso-relievo, is fixed into this bookcase, so as to appear to the scholars just over Mr. Alcott's head. The bookcase itself is surmounted with a bust of Plato. On the northern side of the room, opposite the door, is the table of the assistant, with a small figure of Atlas, bending under the weight of the world. On a small bookcase behind the assistant's chair, are the figures of a child reading, and a child drawing. Two old pictures; one of Harding's portraits; and some maps hang on the walls. The desks for the scholars, with conveniences for placing all their books in sight, and with black tablets hung over them, which swing forward, when they wish to use them, are placed against the wall round the room, that when in their seats for study, no scholar need look at another. On the right hand of Mr. Alcott, is a sofa for the accommodation of visitors, and a small table, with a pitcher and bowl; and underneath the "table of sense," as this cold water table is called, is a small figure of Bacchus, riding on a barrel. Great advantages have been found to arise from this room; every part of which speaks the thoughts of Genius. It is a silent reproach upon rudeness.

About twenty children came the first day. They were all under ten years of age, excepting two or three girls. I became his assistant, to teach Latin to such as might desire to learn.

Mr. Alcott sat behind his table, and the children were placed in chairs, in a large arc around him; the chairs so far apart, that they could not easily touch each other. He then asked each one separately, what idea she or he had of the object of coming to school? To learn; was the first answer. To learn what? By pursuing this question, all the common exercises of school were brought up—successively—even philosophy. Still Mr. Alcott intimated that this was not all; and at last some one said, "to behave well," and in pursuing this expression into its meanings, they at last decided that they came to learn to feel rightly, to think rightly, and to act rightly. A boy of seven years old suggested, and all agreed, that right actions were the most important of these three.

Simple as all this seems, it would hardly be believed what an evident exercise it was to these children, to be led of themselves to form and express these conceptions and few steps of reasoning. Every face was eager and interested. From right actions, the conversation naturally led into the means of bringing them out. And the necessity of feeling in earnest, of thinking clearly, and of school discipline, was talked over. School discipline was very carefully considered; Mr. Alcott's duty, and the children's individual duties, and the various means of producing attention, self-control, perserverence, faithfulness. Among these means, punishment was mentioned; and after a consideration of its nature and issues, they all very cheerfully agreed, that it was necessary, and that they preferred Mr. Alcott should punish them, rather than leave them in their faults, and that it was his duty to do so. Various punishments were mentioned, and hurting the body was decided upon, as necessary and desirable in some instances. It was universally admitted that it was desirable whenever words were found insufficient to command the memory of conscience. After this conversation, which involved many anecdotes, many supposed cases, and many judgments, Mr. Alcott read from Krummacher's fables, a story which involved the free action of three boys of different characters, and questioned them respecting their opinion of these boys, and the principles on which it was seen by analysis that they acted. Nearly three hours passed away in this conversation and reading; and then they were asked, how long they had been sitting? None of them guessed more than an hour. After recess Mr. Alcott heard them read; and after that, spell. All present could read in such a book as Miss Edgeworth's Frank. Then each was asked what he had learned, and having told, they were dismissed one by one. The whole effect of the day seemed to be a combination of quieting influences, with an awakening effect upon the heart and mind.

The next day, a conversation somewhat like the former was commenced; but Mr. Alcott showed that he intended to have profound attention. When any one's eyes wandered, he waited to have them return to him, and he required that they should sit very still in their comfortable chairs. The questions, however, by interesting them very much, aided them in this effort. After recalling the conclusions of the day before, he read them more fables from Krummacher, paraphrasing, and interrupting himself constantly, to enforce what he was saying, by addressing it particularly to individuals; and requiring them now to guess what was coming next, and now to tell what they thought of things said and done. They then all read, and spelled, and, after recess, were placed in their seats, where each found a ruled blank-book and a lead pencil; with a printed volume, from which he directed them to copy a passage. Only half a dozen could write. He told the rest, even the youngest, to copy in printed letters, and this occupied them very diligently until school was done.

I will here speak somewhat at large of Mr. Alcott's mode of teaching the art of writing; as it is the result of a good deal of thought; and has grown out of his own experience as a teacher. For he early discovered how to obtain a remarkable command of his pen without instruction from others; and, having reasoned on the methods which necessity suggested to himself, he has reduced them very happily to their principles and constructed them into a natural system, whose results have perfectly satisfied him.

When children are committed to his charge very young, the first discipline to which he puts them, is of the eye; by making them familiar with pictures. The art of drawing has been well called the art of learning to see; and perhaps no person ever began to learn to draw, without astonishment at finding how imperfectly he had always been seeing. He finds that the most common forms are not only very falsely defined on his sense, but a vast deal that is before the eyes, is entirely overlooked. The human mind seems very gradually to descend from its own infinity into the details of the finite; and the senses give but little help when unaided by a developed mind. It has been demonstrated, not only by the acute reasonings of philosophers, but by observations made on persons, who have begun to see at late periods of life, that the eye sees scarcely any thing but what the mind has suggested beforehand. Yet by a reciprocal influence of the mind and the organ, this "avenue of wisdom," may become very broad. By a little attention to children's habits, and by exercise, their minds may very early attain great perfection in the use of this instrument, than which none is finer of all that are given to us; and none more effective in bringing to our fixed point in the universe that variety of the Almighty's manifestation of himself, to which it is necessary for us to have access, in order to be able to clothe our inward life with forms, by which it may manifest itself to kindred beings; carrying them and ourselves on, into harmony with the Divine intellect, and sympathy with his spirit. The Phrenologists say it was their first discovery, that persons who had prominent eyes were remarkable for their powers of learning and using language. Now, as all language is founded on imagery, it follows that fine and perfect organs of sight, giving to the mind vivid impressions of the forms of things, would make the language of the individual picturesque and lifely, and thus, even without resorting to the theory of Phrenology, the fact of prominent or fine eyes, connected with great powers of language, has an explanation. But without reference to the influence of clear vision upon expression in this way, there can be no doubt of its effect upon thought. The forms of things are God's address to the human soul; they are the first incitement to activity of mind; or, to speak more accurately, they are the first supporters of that activity which is the nature of mind, and which can only be checked by the soul's being starved of nature.

It is from considerations of this kind, that Mr. Alcott very early presents to children pictured forms of things; and he selects them in the confidence that the general character of these forms will do much towards setting the direction of the current of activity, especially if we attend to and favor those primal sympathies, with which nature seems to wed different minds to different portions of the universe.

To aid the practice of the eye, in looking at forms, the practice of the hand in imitating them should soon follow. Mr. Alcott thinks the slate and pencil, or the chalk and blackboard, can hardly be given too early. The latter is even better than the former; for children should have free scope, as we find that their first shapings are always gigantic. And is it not best that they should be so? Miniature, when it appears first in the order of development, seems to be always the effect of checked spirit or some artificial influence.

With such education of the eye, as a preliminary, reading and writing may begin simultaneously; and the former will be very much facilitated, and the latter come to perfection in a much shorter time, than by the usual mode. By copying print, which does not require such a sweep of the hand as the script letter, a clear image of each letter is gradually fixed in the mind; and while the graceful curves of the script letter are not attained till afterwards, yet they are attained quite as early as by the common method of beginning with them; and the clearness and distinctness of print, is retained in the script, which, from being left to form itself so freely, becomes also characteristic of each individual's particular mind.

When the pages were presented to Mr. Alcott after their first trial, the hieroglyphics were sufficiently unintelligible it must be confessed. But, (what is another proof of how slowly the mind appreciates the arbitrary and finite,) the serious looks of the children, especially of the younger ones, as they exhibited their strange copies, betrayed no misgiving as to the want of resemblance; nor did Mr. Alcott rudely pointed it out. He took the writing for what it was meant to be; knowing that practice would at once mend the eye and the hand; but that criticism would check the desirable courage and self-confidence.

In the course of a few days, cards were placed at the desk of each child, on which were very large forms of the letters; and they were encouraged to imitate them. It soon became a regular arrangement for the children to pass their first school hour at this employment, and to return to it after the recess. After some weeks spent in this way, Mr. Alcott taught them the small script letter, but not to supersede the exercises in printing. Indeed, throughout the whole teaching, he recommends that this system of printing should be retained, especially in all those written exercises, which children are tempted to slight; for it prevents the habit of indistinct writing, by keeping the imagination wonted to the original forms of the letters. The ultimate and sure result of this plan, is a simple unflourishing chirography, whose great and characteristic merit is intelligibleness; and constant practice in writing the script, gradually adds to this merit the grace of beauty. When a child begins on this plan of writing at five years of age, by the time he is seven or eight, he has much of the ease of a practised penman, combining considerable rapidity with perfect intelligibleness, and a fair degree of beauty. Mr. Alcott has verified this in many hundreds of instances in his own schools, within ten years. There is a vast deal of difference, however, in the improvement of individuals; and the matter cannot be hurried. Time will accomplish it, in all instances.

It was soon found that Mr. Alcott, with all his mildness, was very strict. When sitting at their desks, at their writing, he would not allow the least inter-communication, and every whisper was taken notice of. When they sat in the semi-circle around him, they were not only requested to be silent, but to appear attentive to him; and any infringement of the spirit of this rule, would arrest his reading, and he would wait, however long it might be, until attention was restored. For some time the acquirement of this habit of stillness and attention was the most prominent subject, for it was found that many of the children had very little self-control, very weak attention, very self-indulgent habits. Some had no humility, and defended themselves in the wrong; a good deal of punishment was necessary, and some impressions upon the body (on the hand;) but still, in every individual instance, it was granted as necessary, not *only* by the whole school, but I believe, no bodily punishment was given without the assent of the individual himself; and they were never given in the room. In many of the punishments,—in the pauses of his reading, for instance, the innocent were obliged to suffer with the guilty. Mr. Alcott wished both parties to feel that this was the inevitable consequence of moral evil in this world; and that the good, in proportion to the depth of their principle, always feel it to be worth while to share the suffering, in order to bring the guilty to rectitude and moral sensibility.

On all these occasions, he conversed with them; and, by a series of questions, led them to come to conclusions for themselves upon moral conduct in various particulars; teaching them how to examine themselves, and to discriminate their animal and spiritual natures, their outward and inward life; and also how the inward moulds the outward. They were deeply interested in these conversations, and would constantly declare this; although, at first, some, who were very often revealing to themselves and others their hitherto unrecognized weaknesses and faults, were so deeply mortified, that it was constantly painful. The youngest scholars were as much interested as the oldest, and although it was necessary to explain language to them rather more, it was found less necessary to reason on moral subjects. They did not so often inquire the history of an idea, or feeling; but they analysed the feelings which prompted action better. It was very striking to see how much nearer the kingdom of heaven were the little children, than were those who had begun to pride themselves on knowing something. We could not but often remark to each other, how unworthy the name of knowledge was that superficial acquirement, which has nothing to do with self-knowledge; and how much more susceptible to the impressions of genius, and how much more apprehensive of general truths were those, who had not been hackneyed by a false education....

...Wednesday, 4th.—I arrived at quarter past nine, and found them all writing their journals, or their spelling lessons. At quarter of ten, Mr. Alcott began to read to the youngest division of the spelling class, and those of the youngest class who were present. He read a parable of Krummacher to illustrate *indolence*, which not only awakened their attention very strongly, but attracted the notice of many of the rest; and he talked a little with a boy of the larger class, to enforce the lesson upon him.

At ten o'clock, the class turned to spell. They all spelled well, until it came to one little boy, who missed. Mr. Alcott said, do you know why you do not spell the words right? The child looked enquiringly. It is because you do not use your eyes, to see how the letters are placed; and so you have no picture of the word in your mind. And he went on describing how he should look at the letters, picture them out, lay up the picture in his mind; and when he heard the word, should think how one letter came after the other. He talked a great while; and not only the one addressed, but all the little boys, seemed much interested and edified. The words were defined to these children, and then Mr. Alcott called the rest of the class to turn and spell.

Birth was the first word. Mr. Alcott remarked that we had once before talked of birth, and their ideas had been brought out. Now I am going to speak of it again, and we shall read Mr. Wordsworth's Ode. He then asked the youngest child present, how old he was, and found he was four. He then asked the oldest, and she was twelve years old. He said, that little boy, in four years, had not had time to make much comparison of thoughts and feelings; this comparison makes up *conscious life*. He asked those who understood him, to hold up their hands. Several held up their hands. Those who do not understand these words, may hold up their hands. A great many of the younger ones held up their hands.

Mr. Alcott said he was not surprised that they did not understand; but perhaps they would understand some things he was going to say. Life is a kind of memory—conscious life is *memory*. Now, said he to the oldest, do you feel that any change has taken place in you, in twelve years; do things seem the same to you as they did six years ago? She recognised a change. A boy of ten, also said, that he did also. Mr. Alcott said, that Mr. Wordsworth had lived, when he wrote this ode, about thirty years, and consequently he had felt changes, and he had expressed this in the lines he was about to read. He then began and read the first stanza of the Ode of Immortality, up to the line: "The things which I have seen, I now can see no more." He here stopped, and asked why Mr. Wordsworth could not see the things which he had seen before; had they changed, or had he changed? He had changed, said a boy of ten. Have you had any degree of this change? Yes, and more in this last year, than in all my life before. Mr. Alcott said he thought that there were periods in life, when great changes took place: he had experienced it himself.

He then said: but let us all look back six months; how many of you look at things, and feel about them differently from what you did six months ago? How many of you feel that this school-room is a different place from what it was the first week you were here? Almost every one, immediately, with great animation, held up his hand. He then asked those who knew why this was, to hold up their hands. Many did. And when called on to answer, they severally said, because we know more; because we think more; because we understand you; because you know us; because you have looked inside of us. Mr. Alcott said, the place is very different to me; and why? They gave similar answers; but he said they had not hit it. At last one said: because we behave better. Yes, said he, you have it now; knowledge is chaff of itself; but you have taken the knowledge and used it to govern yourselves, and to make yourselves better. Why, if I thought I only gave you knowledge, and could not lead you to use it to make yourselves better, I would never enter this school-room again!

He then went on and read the next stanzas of the Ode; stopping to ask them about the effects of the rainbow, the rose, the waters on a starry night, on themselves. He then stopped and said, there are some minds which live in the world, and yet are insensible; which do not see any beauty in the rainbow, the moon, the waters on a starry night. As he went on through the next stanza, so descriptive of the animation and beauty of spring, he paused on every line, and asked questions. Why are "the cataracts said to blow their trumpets?" A little girl said, because the waters dash against the rocks. "The echoes thronging through the woods," led out to recollections of the sound in the woods in spring; to echoes which they had severally heard. As the animating pictures of "children pulling flowers on May day;" the "child springing up on the mother's arm," &c. came up, every countenance expressed the most vivid delight; and one girl exclaimed, what a succession of beautiful pictures! All full of life, said Mr. Alcott; and he went on to the lines, "but there's a tree;" and when he had read these lines, he said: was that a thought of life? No, a thought of death, said several. Yes, said Mr. Alcott, Mr. Wordsworth had lived long enough to feel changes; he had known death, as well as life.

When he came to the line: "Our birth is but a sleep, and a forgetting," he stopped and asked how that was? After a pause, one of the most intelligent boys, eight years old, said, he could not imagine. The two oldest girls said, they understood it, but could not explain it in words. Mr. Alcott then observed that the little boy whose attention to the spelling, and reading, and arithmetic, he is so often obliged to spur up, was holding up his hand. Do you understand it? said Mr. Alcott. Yes. Well, what does it mean? Why, you know, said he very deliberately, that, for all that our life seems so long to us, it is a very short time to God; and so when we die it seems all a sleep to God. He repeated this, at Mr. Alcott's request; and I said to him: so Mr. Wordsworth was thinking of God; and how God felt on seeing that a child was born into this world? He paused, looked a little distressed, and repeated the word forgetting. I said, wait and tell me your thought. Why, you know, said he, *God knows us, but we don't.* He looked at me with a look of doubt whether I should understand him. And our knowledge of ourselves, in comparison with what God knows about us, said I, seems like *forgetfulness* itself? Yes, said he, that is it, (with a cleared up countenance.) All the rest listened with interest and an expression of great pleasure; and then one girl said, the soul comes from heaven; it goes to sleep in that world, and wakes up in this.

Mr. Alcott then read on to the line: "Heaven lies about us in our infancy;" when he shut up the book, and asked every child separately, what he understood by birth. They all answered, and many repeated the definitions which they gave the other day.

Mr. Alcott said, that he observed one striking difference in their answers; some expressed the idea that the soul shaped and made the body; others that the body was made and the soul put into it. Which is right? said one boy. That is more than I can tell, but I incline to the first opinion; that is my opinion. You are all nearly right, however; you all have the important ideas, birth is not the beginning of the spirit; life is the memory, or a waking up of spirit. All the life of knowledge is the remembrance, or waking up of what is already within; "the rising of life's star, that hath elsewhere is setting." What is life's star? The soul, said they. But birth is sometimes the prelude to the death of the soul, said Mr. Alcott. How? said one boy. Because the soul becomes the slave of the body; is governed, darkened, shut up and buried in it; and it is necessary that is should be born again, born out of the body, do you understand that? Yes. Some of you have needed to be born again; and have begun your new life, said Mr. Alcott.

*   *   *   *   *   *

One morning when he was opening Pilgrim's Progress to read, he said, that those who whispered, or broken any rule since they came to school, might rise to be punished. They expected punishment with the ferule. About a dozen rose. He told them to go to the ante-room, and stay there while he was reading. They did so. The reading was very interesting; for though it had been read before, every new reading brings new associations, and peculiar conversation. Those in the ante-room, could hear the occasional outbursts of feeling which the reading and conversation elicited. A lady visitor, who was present, went out just before the reading closed, and found those who had been sent out, sitting in the ante-room, looking very disconsolate; and perfectly quiet, though no directions had been given to them. She expressed regret at their losing the interesting reading. Oh yes, we know! said they. We have heard them shout. Nothing is so interesting as Pilgrim's Progress, and the conversations, said one. We had rather have been punished any other way, said another.—When they were called in, they said the same thing to Mr. Alcott. He asked why? Because it would have been over in a minute, said one boy; but this conversation can never be another time, said another.

Having brought the whole school to this point, Mr. Alcott introduced a new mode. He talked with them, on the Monday before this last analysis; and having again adverted to the necessity of pain and punishment, in a general point of view, and brought them to acknowledge the uses of this *hurting of the body*, as he always phrased it, in concentrating attention, &c., he said, that he now intended to have it administered upon his own hand, instead of theirs; but that the guilty person must do it. They declared that they would never do it. But he soon made them understand that he was serious. They said they preferred being punished themselves. But he was determined that they should not escape the shame and pain of themselves administering the stroke upon him, except by being themselves blameless.

The effect was a profound and deep stillness. Boys who had never been affected before, and to whom bodily punishment was a very small affair, as far as its pain was concerned, were completely sobered. There was a more complete silence, and attention, and obedience, than there had ever been. And the only exceptions, which were experiments, were rigidly noticed. Mr. Alcott, in two instances, took the boys out in the course of the forenoon, and made them give it to him. They were very unwilling, and when they did it first, they did it very lightly. He then asked them, if they thought they deserved no more punishment than that? And so they were obliged to give it hard:—but it was not without tears, which they had never shed when punished themselves. This is the most complete punishment that a master ever invented,—was the observation of one of the boys, at home; Mr. Alcott has secured obedience now,—there is not a boy in school, but what would a great deal rather be punished himself, than punish him.

"Death in the School-Room (A FACT)"

ଚେ ◆ ଓଃ

Walt Whitman, 1841

Whitman's story, first published in *The United States Magazine and Democratic Review*, can actually be viewed as a piece of muckraker journalism. Whitman was a fervent believer in abolishing corporal punishment, an "ignorant, cruel doctrine" that was tantamount to "torture." In this story, which would have found a wide readership among the intellectual middle class, Whitman paints a persona of almost caricatured evil in the schoolmaster—a man insensible to the inner life and needs of his charges. Indeed, in virtually every respect Whitman's teacher is an inverse of Bronson Alcott. The story is interesting not only as a vivid piece of fiction, but as an example of the kinds of successful public relations ploys used by enlightened reformers to turn public support away from old educational practices.

Walt Whitman (1819–1892) himself spent 5 years as a public school teacher. Beginning shortly after his 18th year, the poet began his career "boarding round" in the homes of his students, a practice that Whitman found to be a good source of literary inspiration: Boarding was "one of my best experiences," he wrote, "and deepest lessons in human nature behind the scenes, and in the masses" (Stovall, 1963, p. 15). From 1836 to 1841, Whitman taught in a variety of country schools where he seems to have been treated much like other school masters in the early common school days. In addition to teaching ungraded classes 6 days a week without any vacations, he was required to perform a series of odd community functions including sitting up with corpses prior to burial.

Despite the constraints of curriculum and method imposed on him by the various communities in which he worked, Whitman evidently still managed to be an unorthodox teacher. He avoided textbooks, taught the new subject of mental arithmetic to stimulate quick thinking, and used new motivational games to encourage his students to like their classroom labor. Whitman, of course, also shunned the rod. His disciplinary technique was to narrate tales of their crimes, anonymously, to the assembled students, turning each infraction into a moral lesson. Like other Transcendentalist educators, Whitman was an advocate of normal schools and believed that teachers should attend these institutions throughout their professional lives to improve and enhance their teaching (Brasher, 1963).

"DEATH IN THE SCHOOL-ROOM (A FACT)"

Walt Whitman, 1841

TING-A-LING-LING-LING! went the little bell on the teacher's desk of a village-school one morning, when the studies of the earlier part of the day were about half completed. It was well understood that this was a command for silence and attention; and when these had been obtain'd, the master spoke. He was a low thick-set man, and his name was Lugare.

"Boys," said he, "I have had a complaint enter'd, that last night some of you were stealing fruit from Mr. Nichols's garden. I rather think I know the thief. Tim Barker, step up here, sir."

The one to whom he spoke came forward. He was a slight, fair-looking boy of about thirteen; and his face had a laughing, good-humor'd expression, which even the charge now preferr'd against him, and the stern tone and threatening look of the teacher, had not entirely dissipated. The counte- nance of the boy, however, was too unearthly fair for health; it had, notwithstanding its fleshy, cheerful look, a singular cast as if some inward disease, and that a fearful one, were seated within. As the stripling stood before that place of judgment—that place so often made the scene of heartless and coarse brutality, of timid innocence confused, helpless child- hood outraged, and gentle feelings crush'd—Lugare looked on him with a frown which plainly told that he felt in no very pleasant mood. (Happily a worthier and more philosophical system is proving to men that schools can be better govern'd than by lashes and tears and sighs. We are waxing toward that consummation when one of the old-fashion'd school-masters, with his cowhide, his heavy birch-rod, and his many ingenious methods of child-tor- ture, will be gazed upon as a scorn'd memento of an ignorant, cruel, and exploded doctrine. May propitious gales speed that day!)

"Were you by Mr. Nichols's garden-fence last night?" said Lugare.

"Yes, sir," answer'd the boy, "I was."

"Well, sir, I'm glad to find you so ready with your confession. And so you thought you could do a little robbing, and enjoy yourself in a manner you ought to be ashamed to own, without being punish'd, did you?"

"I have not been robbing," replied the boy quickly. His face was suffused, whether with resentment or fright, it was difficult to tell. "And I didn't do anything last night, that I am ashamed to own."

"No impudence!" exclaim'd the teacher, passionately, as he grasp'd a long and heavy ratan: "give me none of your sharp speeches, or I'll thrash you till you beg like a dog."

The youngster's face paled a little; his lip quiver'd, but he did not speak.

"And pray, sir," continued Lugare, as the outward signs of wrath disappear'd from his features; "what were you about the garden for? Perhaps you only receiv'd the plunder, and had an accomplice to do the more dangerous part of the job?"

"I went that way because it is on my road home. I was there again afterwards to meet an acquaintance; and—and—But I did not go into the garden, nor take anything away from it. I would not steal,—hardly to save myself from starving."

"You had better have stuck to that last evening. You were seen, Tim Barker, to come from under Mr. Nichols's garden-fence, a little after nine o'clock, with a bag full of something or other over your shoulders. The bag had every appearance of being filled with fruit, and this morning the melon-beds are found to have been completely clear'd. Now, sir, what was there in that bag?"

Like fire itself glow'd the face of the detected lad. He spoke not a word. All the school had their eyes directed at him. The perspiration ran down his white forehead like rain-drops.

"Speak, sir!" exclaimed Lugare, with a loud strike of his ratan on the desk.

The boy look'd as though he would faint. But the unmerciful teacher, confident of having brought to light a criminal, and exulting in the idea of the severe chastisement he should now be justified in inflicting, kept working himself up to a still greater and greater degree of passion. In the meantime, the child seem'd hardly to know what to do with himself. His tongue cleav'd to the roof of his mouth. Either he was very much frighten'd, or he was actually unwell.

"Speak, I say!" again thunder'd Lugare; and his hand, grasping his ratan, tower'd above his head in a very significant manner.

"I hardly can, sir," said the poor fellow faintly. His voice was husky and thick. "I will tell you some—some other time. Please let me go to my seat—I a'n't well."

"Oh yes; that's very likely;" and Mr. Lugare bulged out his nose and cheeks with contempt. "Do you think to make me believe your lies? I've found you out, sir, plainly enough; and I am satisfied that you are as precious a little villain as there is in the State. But I will postpone settling with you for an hour yet. I shall then call you up again; and if you don't tell the whole truth then, I will give you something that'll make you remember Mr. Nichols's melons for many a month to come:—go to your seat."

Glad enough of ungracious permission, and answering not a sound, the child crept tremblingly to his bench. He felt very strangely, dizzily—more as if he was in a dream than in real life; and laying his arms on his desk, bow'd down his face between them. The pupils turn'd to their accustom'd studies, for during the reign of Lugare in the village-school, they had been so used to scenes of violence and severe chastisement, that such things made but little interruption in the tenor of their way.

Now, while the intervening hour is passing, we will clear up the mystery of the bag, and of young Barker being under the garden fence on the preceding night. The boy's mother was a widow, and they both had to live in the very narrowest limits. His father had died when he was six years old, and little Tim was left a sickly emaciated infant whom no one expected to live many months. To the surprise of all, however, the poor child kept alive, and seem'd to recover his health, as he certainly did his size and good looks. This was owing to the kind offices of an eminent physician who had a country-seat in the neighborhood, and who had been interested in the widow's little family. Tim, the physician said, might possibly outgrow his disease; but everything was uncertain. It was a mysterious and baffling malady; and it would not be wonderful if he should in some moment of apparent health be suddenly taken away. The poor widow was at first in a continual state of uneasiness; but several years had now pass'd, and none of the impending evils had fallen upon the boy's head. His mother seem'd to feel confident that he would live, and be a help and an honor to her old age; and the two struggled on together, mutually happy in each other, and enduring much of poverty and discomfort without repining, each for the other's sake.

Tim's pleasant disposition had made him many friends in the village, and among the rest a young farmer named Jones, who, with his elder brother, work'd a large farm in the neighborhood on shares. Jones very frequently made Tim a present of a bag of potatoes or corn, or some garden vegetables, which he took from his own stock; but as his partner was a parsimonious, high-tempered man, and had often said that Tim was an idle fellow, and ought not to be help'd because he did not work, Jones generally made his gifts in such a manner that no one knew anything about them, except himself and the grateful objects of his kindness. It might be, too, that the widow was loth to have it understood by the neighbors that she received food from anyone; for there is often an excusable pride in people of her condition which makes them shrink from being consider'd as objects of "charity" as they would from the severest pains. On the night in question, Tim had been told that Jones would send them a bag of potatoes, and the place at which they were to be waiting for him was fixed at Mr. Nichols's garden-fence. It was this bag that Tim had been seen staggering under, and which caused the unlucky boy to be accused and convicted by his teacher as a thief. That teacher was one little fitted for his important and responsible office. Hasty to decide, and inflexibly severe, he was the terror of the little world he ruled so despotically. Punishment he seemed to delight in. Knowing little of those sweet fountains which in children's breasts ever open quickly at the call of gentleness and kind words, he was fear'd by all for his sternness, and loved by none. I would that he were an isolated instance in his profession.

The hour of grace had drawn to its close, and the time approach'd at which it was usual for Lugare to give his school a joyfully-receiv'd dismission. Now and then one of the scholars would direct a furtive glance at Tim, sometimes in pity, sometimes in indifference or inquiry. They knew that he would have no mercy shown him, and though most of them loved him, whipping was too common there to exact much sympathy. Every inquiring glance, however, remain'd unsatisfied, for at the end of the hour, Tim remain'd with his face completely hidden, and his head bow'd in his arms, precisely as he had lean'd himself when he first went to his seat. Lugare look'd at the boy occasionally with a scowl which seem'd to bode vengeance for his sullenness. At length the last class had been heard, and the last lesson recited, and Lugare seated himself behind his desk on the platform, with his longest and stoutest ratan before him.

"Now, Barker," he said, "we'll settle that little business of yours. Just step up here."

Tim did not move. The school-room was as still as the grave. Not a sound was to be heard, except occasionally a long-drawn breath.

"Mind me, sir, or it will be the worse for you. Step up here, and take off your jacket!"

The boy did not stir any more than if he had been of wood. Lugare shook with passion. He sat still a minute, as if considering the best way to wreak his vengeance. That minute, passed in death-like silence, was a fearful one to some of the children, for their faces whiten'd with fright. It seem'd, as it slowly dropp'd away, like the minute which precedes the climax of an exquisitely-performed tragedy, when some mighty master of the histrionic art is treading the stage, and you and the multitude around you are waiting, with stretch'd nerves and suspended breath, in expectation of the terrible catastrophe.

"Tim is asleep, sir," at length said one of the boys who sat near him.

Lugare, at this intelligence, allow'd his features to relax from their expression of savage anger into a smile, but that smile look'd more malignant if possible, than his former scowls. It might be that he felt amused at the horror depicted on the faces of those around him; or it might be that he was gloating in pleasure on the way in which he intended to wake the slumberer.

"Asleep! are you, my young gentleman!" said he; "let us see if we can't find something to tickle your eyes open. There's nothing like making the best of a bad case, boys. Tim, here, is determin'd not to be worried in his mind about a little flogging, for the thought of it can't even keep the little scoundrel awake."

Lugare smiled again as he made the last observation. He grasp'd his ratan firmly, and descended from his seat. With light and stealthy steps he cross'd the room, and stood by the unlucky sleeper. The boy was still as unconscious of his impending punishment as ever. He might be dreaming some golden dream of youth and pleasure; perhaps he was far away in the world of fancy, seeing scenes, and feeling delights, which cold reality never can bestow. Lugare lifted his ratan high over his head, and with the true and expert aim which he had acquired by long practice, brought it down on Tim's back with a force and a whacking sound which seem'd sufficient to awake a freezing man in his last lethargy. Quick and fast, blow follow'd blow. Without waiting to see the effect of the first cut, the brutal wretch plied his instrument of torture first on one side of the boy's back, and then on the other, and only stopped at the end of two or three minutes from very weariness. But still Tim show'd no signs of motion; and as Lugare, provoked at his torpiditiy, jerk'd away one of the child's arms, on which he had been leaning over the desk, his head dropp'd down on the board with a dull sound, and his face lay turn'd up and exposed to view. When Lugare saw it, he stood like one transfix'd by a basilisk. His countenance turn'd to a leaden whiteness; the ratan dropp'd from his grasp; and his eyes, stretch'd wide open, glared as at some monstrous spectacle of horror and death. The sweat started in great globules seemingly from every pore in his face; his skinny lips contracted, and show'd his teeth; and when he at length stretch'd forth his arm, and with the end of one of his fingers touch'd the child's cheek, each limb quiver'd like the tongue of a snake; and his strength seemed as though it would momentarily fail him. The boy was dead. He had probably been so for some time, for his eyes were turn'd up, and his body was quite cold. Death was in the school-room, and Lugare had been flogging A CORPSE.

From *Locke Amsden*
or The Schoolmaster: A Tale

ಬ ◆ ಛ

Daniel Pierce Thompson, 1847

Daniel Pierce Thompson's (1795–1868) novel about a common school teacher again stands in dramatic contrast to earlier literary depictions of the pedagogue. Thompson's hero, Locke Amsden, is a kind, mild-mannered, and intelligent young man, whose judgments in the classroom vividly illustrate many of the principles of common school reform. Here, as elsewhere, the central themes of education are less intellectual than moral and social. In the chapter excerpted here, Locke is hired by an illiterate father to serve as schoolmaster in a rural community in New England. As in other stories of early schooling, discipline is the first and most central concern of teacher and student alike. Locke's brother Ben has attempted to ease his transition into the community school by spreading word of the schoolmaster's "fiery and ungovernable temper." Such scare tactics represent the old-fashioned technique for maintaining control. They work for a while in keeping Locke's charges in check. But ultimately a more rational and humane approach to discipline has the more profound and lasting effect. At the end of the chapter, Locke Amsden demonstrates for the reader of his day how the "new teacher" interprets the work of the disciplinarian. In a powerful passage on the question of corporal punishment, the author wonders aloud why public flogging for adults has long been outlawed in our civil code, and yet is retained in the society of the schoolroom.

Locke Amsden's method of punishment is interesting on another level as well. It is one of the earliest examples of a teacher soliciting the support and active involvement of a parent in the educative process. Although the offending student's father is somewhat confused by the teacher's request for his participation in his son's upbraiding, the father willingly obliges him. The punishment then gains more significance: It is no longer a conflict between one youth and an arbitrary authority, but rather a larger and more meaningful attempt at socialization.

Like so many authors of fiction on schooling, Daniel Pierce Thompson
was himself a teacher. After an extended tenure as a private tutor to a
wealthy southern family, however, Thompson turned to law, ending his
career as Secretary of State in Vermont.

FROM *LOCKE AMSDEN OR THE SCHOOLMASTER: A TALE*

Daniel Pierce Thompson, 1847

"Delightful task to rear the tender thought—
To teach the young idea how to shoot!"

Thomson.

Those who have had much experience in the business of school-keeping,
before yielding their unqualified assent to the oft-quoted sentiment of the
great rural poet which we have placed over this chapter, would generally,
we apprehend, wish to offer, as legislators say, an amendment to the
proposition, in the shape of a proviso, something like the following: —
Provided always, that the teacher can have the privilege of selecting his
pupils. Such, at all events, were the feelings of our hero, as, with many
misgivings, he set out, on the appointed day, for the place where he was to
establish a government, in which (since the understood failure of Mr.
Jefferson's experiment of introducing self-government, on the principles of
a republic, into the college of which he was the founder) the golden mean
between absolute monarchy and anarchy is wholly wanting—a government
over what, he had reason to believe, would prove, in the present instance,
as rebellious a set of subjects as were ever brought to order beneath the
birchen sceptre of a pedagogue. But however mild his disposition, or
unassuming his general demeanor, Locke Amsden was by no means wanting
in resolution. He possessed, indeed, one of those seemingly paradoxical
characters, so often to be found in the world, and yet almost as often
misunderstood, in which great diffidence of manner is united with great
firmness of purpose, and a full confidence in the ability to execute. And,
consequently, whatever his fears and misgivings, he bravely combated them,
and endeavored to fortify his mind against the approaching hour of trial. In
this, he was much aided by his resolute little brother, Ben; who, for some
secret reason, had contrived to defeat a previously-made different arrangement for the present journey, that he might himself attend the former, in
whose success his pride and interest seemed to be wonderfully awakened.

On reaching the district where he had been engaged, Locke repaired at
once to the residence of his employer, at whose house, it had been before
arranged, he should first take up his lodgings, as the beginning of that round

of boarding through the district, which here, as in many other places, was made to add variety, to say the least of it, to the monotonous life of the schoolmaster. He was received with much rough cordiality by Bunker, and with some show of respect by his mastiff-mannered boys. The good dame of the house soon began to bestir herself in preparation for a meal for the "new master" and his brother, the latter of whom, it was understood, after obtaining refreshment for himself and horse, was to return home that evening.

While the dinner was preparing, Ben, having departed for the stables, to see to his horse, in company with the boys, with whom he seemed determined to scrape acquaintance, Locke and his host soon became engaged in conversation on those topics in which they had previously discovered themselves to feel a mutual interest.

"I have felt considerable curiosity, since I became acquainted with you, the other day," observed our hero, at a point in the conversation when the remark might seem appropriately introduced, "to know how it could have happened, that so thinking a man as yourself had never learned to read?"

"Are you quite certain I should have been so much of a thinker as I am, if I had received a book-education?" said Bunker, in reply.

"Your knowledge would have been more extensive, in that case, doubtless, sir; and if you had been the worse thinker for it, the fault would have been your own, I imagine," replied the other.

"All that may be," remarked Bunker, musingly, "and perhaps it is so—perhaps it is with learning, as it is with property, which we never keep and improve so well when given to us, or get easily, as when it is obtained by our own exertions—by hard knocks and long digging. But whether this is so or not, one thing to my mind is certain, and that is, that more than half of your great book-men are, after all, but very shallow thinkers; though the way they dress up a subject with language, generally procures them with the credit of being otherwise; for it is curious enough to see what a deal of real ignorance a few long words and learned terms are made to conceal."

"Ay," said Locke, "but does not your argument run against the abuse of learning, rather than its use?"

"Possibly," replied Bunker; "but, at any rate, I have often thought, that if I had received an education equal to some of your great scholars, I should have found out rather more than most of them appear to have done."

"Your impressions," rejoined Locke, "are, I suspect, by no means uncommon. I formerly thought so myself; but the more I study, the more I am convinced, that the unlearned are accustomed to expect much more from the learned than they should do. Scholars, however profound, can never discover what God has purposely hidden from the human mind."

"There may be something in your remarks," observed the other, "and I will think over the subject again. But now, to return to your first question - What was the reason I had never learned to read, was it?"

"It was."

"Well, I will tell you honestly: it was, first, total want of opportunity, and then pride, till I had got to be so old a dog, that I thought I would not attempt to learn any new tricks."

"Those are rather unusual reasons, for this country, at least, are they not?"

"They are the true ones, in my case, nevertheless. My father was a trapper, and pitched his cabin at the very outskirts of civilization, on one of the great rivers in Canada, where schools were wholly out of the question; —even books were so rare, that I don't recollect of ever seeing but one during the whole of my boyhood. That one was my mother's old worn and torn bible, which, at last, a gray squirrel, that came in through the roof of our cabin, one day when we were all out, knocked down from a shelf into the fire, as we concluded, because we saw him escaping with a leaf in his mouth, to help make his nest. This, as I said, was the only book I remember to have seen; and this I should not recollect, probably, but for the singular manner in which it was destroyed, and the fact also that my mother, when she discovered her loss, sat down and cried like a child—God bless her memory! —if she had lived, she would have got another, and most likely have taught me to read it. But she died soon after, leaving me, at the age of about five, to the care of an ignorant hussy, that my father, in due time, married. Well, there I remained till I was twenty; when I left, and found my way into this part of the country, among people, who, to my surprise, could all read and write. I was not long, however, in discovering, that I was about as ignorant a heathen as ever came out of the bush. But, instead of going to school as I might and should have done, I felt ashamed to let people know my condition, and so let pride deprive me of a blessing which I could have easily obtained. And so it continued with me, till I married and settled down here on a new farm; when, if the pride I spoke of died away, its place was soon supplied by business cares and a lot of little squallers, that took away all chance or thought of learning to read. But, though not able to read myself, I can easily get others to do this for me. And, late years, having bought a good many books of different kinds for my wife or boys to read to me, I have got, in this way, and by talking with book-men both round home and abroad, a pretty tolerable good run of most that has been printed. And the result has been, that I have been sadly disappointed in what I used to suppose the mighty wisdom of books. To be sure, there are many books that are full of information and true philosophy; but let me tell you,sir, there is a prodigious sight of nonsense bound up together in the shape of books."

The dinner being now announced as in readiness, Locke went out to call in his brother, whom he at length espied in the yard of a grist-mill belonging to Bunker, and situated at no great distance from his house. Ben had here collected round him not only the young Bunkers, but several other boys who had come to mill from different parts of the district; and he was apparently making some communications to them, to which they were very evidently listening with considerable interest and surprise. What might be the nature of his communication, however, Locke, at that time, neither suspected nor ascertained, as he did not go near enough to hear what was said, and as Ben, when questioned on the subject, after joining the other, refused or evaded any direct answer.

As soon as the brothers had finished the repast which had been prepared for them, Ben got up his team, and bidding his brother "to remember to put on a stiff upper lip when he went into his school," cracked his whip and started off for home.

The next morning, after breakfast, as Locke was about to leave for the school-house, for the commencement of his task, Bunker took him aside:—

"I should like to ask you one question, master," he said; "and if you answer it at all, which you can do as you like about, I hope you will do it candidly."

"Certainly, I will, Mr. Bunker," replied the other, in some surprise.

"Well, I overheard my boys saying last night, that your brother, who came with you, told them and some others down at the mill, that you had such a fiery and ungovernable temper, that your family, as well as all the boys in your neighborhood, always run from you, when you get offended (as you often do at almost nothing), lest you should seize an axe and split their brains out; and he begged of them, with tears in his eyes, not to cross you in school, or break any of your orders; for if they did, you would be almost certain to seize the shovel or a cleft of wood, and kill one of them on the spot; and then he should have to see his brother hung for doing only what was natural to him, and what he could n't help. Now, though I have said nothing, yet I think I see through the object of this story; and I want to ask you, not whether it is true—for I think it must be all humbug—but whether you put your brother up to this little plot, or whether it was one of his own hatching?"

"It was one solely of his own contriving, and used without my knowledge or consent," replied Locke, promptly.

"I am glad of it," rejoined Bunker; "for, though there would have been nothing very criminal in such a course, yet, I confess, it would have lowered you in my opinion. It was well enough in such a chick as I suspect your brother to be; and I have concluded to have it go, for the present, just as he left it; for there is no knowing how much it may help you in keeping the boys under. So I advise you to keep your own counsel, go to your school, be decided, but treat your scholars like men and women, and not like slaves or senseless puppets, as some of our masters have done, to their own sorrow, I think. Do this, and I presume you will have no trouble in managing them. But whatever method you may take to govern them, be sure that you make them good thinkers."

On reaching the school-house, where he found most of the pupils assembled, Locke soon saw indications, which convinced him, that Ben's bugbear representations, which had been made with so much address and apparent honesty that the truth of them seems not to have been doubted, were already known to every individual in school; and that, in consequence, he had become, with the younger portion of them especially, the object of a terror which he little thought it would ever be his lot to inspire. This, indeed, was plainly discoverable the first moment he entered the house; for coming among them somewhat unexpectedly, while his fancied traits of character were under discussion, they scattered for their seats with nearly as much haste and trepidation, as they would have shown had a dangerous wild beast walked into the room. And, in two minutes, all was so still, that not a sound, unless it was the beating of the hearts of the more timid, could be heard in the apartment. Nor did the vivid impressions of their new master's severity, which had thus oddly been received by the scholars, and which had fairly frightened them into such unwonted stillness, prove of so temporary a character as he expected. And often during the day, while arranging his classes or attending to the ordinary duties of the school, he scarcely knew whether he felt most secret amusement or pity at the evident sensations of many around him, as he observed with what trembling anxiety his movements were watched, and saw how many furtive and expressive glances were cast at his face, in which, as their excited imaginations then pictured him, they appeared to read that which put all thoughts of roguery or misbehavior to instant flight. All this, to be sure, had reference mainly to the younger portion of the pupils. The older part, it is true, though their demeanor was marked by a respectful quietness, appeared rather to be debating in their minds the expediency of taking their former courses, than entertaining any particular alarms for themselves, while their behavior should be, to a decent degree, orderly. And during the intermissions of the first two or three days, little groups of the usually insubordinate might have been seen engaged in discussing the momentous question, how far it might be safe or feasible to attempt to subjugate the master, in the same way they had several of his predecessors. In all these consultations, however, Tom Bunker, whom his father had secretly engaged to take Locke's part in case of trouble, unexpectedly hung back, telling them they could do as they pleased; but perhaps they would find out, that they had better let the man alone. This coming, as it did, from their acknowledged champion, and one who had generally acted as ringleader in their former outbreaks against their teachers, not a little dampened the ardor of the advocates of rebellion. And after a few idle threats and expressions of defiance, thrown out by the way of warding off any imputations which might be made on their courage for retreating from their position, they finally relinquished their designs on the master, and concluded to submit to his authority, at least till he became the aggressor, in those acts of tyranny that they expected he would ere long exhibit towards them. The movements of the latter, therefore, were watched with no less silent suspicion by the larger, than with fear by the smaller pupils, during the first week of his school. Perceiving all this, he very wisely shaped his course for establishing his authority on a more permanent foundation than can ever be raised in feelings where fear alone is the governing principle. While dignity and decision of manner marked his conduct in enforcing good order in school, he yet made kindness and courtesy to characterize his general demeanor towards all his scholars. This course he adopted no less from the suggestions of his own mind, drawn from the remembrance of the effect which kindness and respect in a teacher always produced on his feelings when he himself was a pupil, than from the recommendation of Bunker, "to treat his scholars like men and women."

The sentiment of the last-named person on this subject is indeed one well deserving of the consideration of all instructors of youth. Few teachers seem to be aware what a just estimate children put upon manners—how quickly they pass a sentence of condemnation on all that is coarse, contemptuous, or unfeeling, and how soon they appreciate every thing that denotes respect and kindness towards them. If teachers would properly consider this, they would find less difficulty, perhaps, in accounting for the little influence which they often find themselves capable of exercising over the minds of their pupils: for almost as certain as one pursues the first-named course of conduct towards them, will his precepts be rejected; while the precepts of him who exhibits the last-mentioned conduct will be readily received, and treasured up for improvement.

And such was the effect of the kind and judicious manner which Locke displayed among the rough and uncultured pupils he had undertaken to control. When they saw, that, instead of turning out the cruel and capricious tyrant they had expected, he wanted nothing of them but what their own consciences told them was just and reasonable, and especially when they found themselves uniformly treated with such respectful courtesy, when their behavior was not exceptionable, all the mingled feelings of hatred, fear, and suspicion, with which they had armed themselves in anticipation of an opposite treatment, rapidly melted into an affectionate reverence, that not only destroyed, in most of them, all inclination for insubordinate conduct, but made them anxious to gain his approbation; the more particularly so, doubtless, from the belief they still entertained, that his displeasure would be attended with fearful consequences to themselves.

The first object of our instructor, that of gaining willing ears for what he wished to impart, was now to a good degree, accomplished. And no sooner had he made sure of this important point, than he began to redouble his exertions to rouse their minds from that cold and listless intellectual condition in which they were unconsciously sunk, and which caused them to look upon learning and all attempts at mental excellence as a mere matter of secondary concern. This he did, not so much by general exhortation (for he well knew that scholars generally hate preaching masters), as by what logicians call arguments *ad hominem*, addressing the self-love of one, the vanity of another, the curiosity of a third, and so on; the dispositions of each having been previously studied for the purpose. In fine, he adopted almost as many expedients as he had pupils, in inciting them to push forward in their particular studies, and in awakening in their bosoms a love of learning. And, in doing this, he also labored incessantly, with argument, ridicule, and such familiar illustrations as they could best understand and appreciate, in showing them the superiority of mind over matter, or mere physical powers; and in setting up the true standard of excellence among them, instead of the false one, to attain to which seemed hitherto to have been the only object of their emulation. The happy results of these well-directed exertions were soon apparent. The exploits of the wrestling ring, the leaping match, and other of the rough athletics, in which it had been their chief pride to excel, were no longer the main topic of conversation; and the feats of bullies and hectoring blades, exercised upon school-masters, ministers, and deacons, were no longer considered a matter of boasting. The keen interest formerly manifested on all these subjects, indeed, had so sensibly declined, that they were now seldom mentioned. But in their place were heard, both during the intermissions of school, and the evenings spent at home, almost nothing but talk of studies, anecdotes of the school, or the discussion of the arithmetical puzzles, and the various interesting and curious questions relative to the phenomena of nature, which the teacher was in the habit of putting out, with which to exercise the minds of his pupils. The parents of the district witnessed this change in their children with no less surprise than pleasure, and wondered by what magic it could have been effected. Bunker, the committee-man, daily grew proud of his selection of a teacher, and declared he had already done more towards making good thinkers of his scholars than any of their former instructors had done in a whole winter. In short, before two weeks had elapsed, the whole Horn-of-the-Moon was ringing with praises of the new master.

But although young Amsden's school was fast becoming what he had so sedulously labored to make it, and although his pupils had generally, since the expiration of the first half week of their attendance, so far shown themselves disposed to obedience and propriety of behavior, as led him to believe that no attempt would now be made to resist his orders, yet it was not long before he found he should not be permitted to avoid the test to which a master's firmness and discretion are almost invariably put, in maintaining his authority, at some period or other of his school.

This period, which forms a sort of crisis in the teacher's government, resulting either in its overthrow, or in its establishment on a permanent basis, generally occurs about the third week of the school. After the first few days of the school, during which the restraints which scholars feel under a new master, or the fears they may entertain of his yet untried spirit and promptitude in administering punishment, usually keep them quiet and orderly, they begin to take liberties; though at first of so trivial a character, that a teacher, not finding in them any particular cause of complaint, suffers them to pass unnoticed. From this, the more evil-disposed go on crowding,

crowding a little, and a little more, upon his authority, till they get so bold that he finds the most decisive measures will alone save his dominion from a total overthrow.

Something like this was the process which Locke had perceived going on in his school, without knowing exactly where to interpose his authority; when one, a boy of about fourteen, who had been more forward than others in the course, one day grew so bold as to place his orders at absolute defiance. Perceiving at once that his government was at an end, unless the offender was conquered, and indignant at his unexpected audacity, our hero, under the impulse of the moment, was about to chastise him on the spot. A second thought, however, told him that he was too much irritated to do this now with the best effect on the offender, or on others inclined to become so; and he accordingly apprised the boy of the reason for deferring his punishment, but promised him, at the same time, that punishment would certainly follow. Although this act of disobedience was not instigated by any one, even by those from whom he had most reason to apprehend difficulties, yet either that, or the threatened chastisement, seemed to produce considerable sensation among them, by awakening, perhaps, remembrances of their old fracases in resisting their teachers on similar occasions, and in exciting in some degree their sleeping inclinations to take some such part when the punishment of the present offender should be inflicted. In addition to these suspicious appearances, he noticed, after his school was dismissed for the day, considerable mysterious whispering among two or three of those just mentioned, and overheard one of them, a relative of the offender, trying to excite the others to join him in preventing the threatened punishment, which they supposed would take place on the opening of the school the next morning. But our hero, unmoved by these unexpected and somewhat ominous demonstrations, resolved to go resolutely forward and do his duty, whatever might be the consequences to himself. On his way homeward, however, while reflecting upon the subject of school-punishment, its object, and the most effective manner of administering it to obtain that object, he began seriously to doubt the wisdom and expediency of the custom which he had always witnessed, and which he had proposed to follow in the present case, —that of inflicting chastisements in open school. He reasoned, and from a just notion of the human heart too, that the presence of companions, whom the delinquent knew to be looking on to see with what spirit he bore up under the operation, that they might afterwards praise him for the *spunk* he exhibited, or taunt him for his weakness if he was seen to succumb, would in most instances have a tendency to arm him with feelings of pride and obstinacy, which would not only destroy all the beneficial effects to be gained from the punishment, but often make him more obdurate than before. So strongly, indeed, did these considerations weigh on the mind of Locke, that he at length determined to adopt a different mode of punishing the boy in question; and after trying to judge of his own feelings, were he placed in the offender's situation, as to what course would most conduce to that penitence and humility best calculated for amendment, and calling to mind all he had ever observed of the effects of punishment on others, he at last hit on a plan which he determined to carry into immediate execution. Accordingly, after obtaining his supper, he repaired at once to the culprit's residence, and, taking his father aside, made known the boy's conduct, the absolute necessity of his punishment, and gave his reasons for wishing to inflict that punishment in private; ending with a request, that the other should call out his boy, and that they all three should repair together to the school-house for the purpose he had mentioned.

"Why, the boy deserves a basting richly enough, no doubt," observed the father; "yes, and a good one too. And, if I was you, I would give it to him. But what on earth do you want my help in flogging him for? Why, that is part of what we are paying you for, I take it, master."

"I wish for no help in the mere chastisement," replied Locke; "but I think your presence would add much to its beneficial effects, and it is only for your son's good that I request you to go."

"Well, well," rejoined the former, "if you think it will do the boy any good,—and I don't know but you are half right about it; for I think if I was a boy, I should dislike most confoundedly to be licked by a schoolmaster before my father—if you think this, why, I will go with you; but I kinder hate to, that's a fact."

His reluctance having been thus widely overcome, the father promptly called out his boy, who not daring to disobey the command which was then given him, followed the two others, in dogged silence, to the school-house. On reaching the house, which as expected and desired, was entirely solitary, Locke raised a light, and proceeded to the painful task before him. He first kindly addressed the offender; and, in a manner calculated to humble without irritating, set forth the probable consequences, both to him and the school, of suffering his offence to pass without punishment, which he had been called there to receive, and then administered a chastisement of adequate severity. After this, he was again addressed by his teacher, the father occasionally putting in a word, for nearly an hour, before the expiration of which he gave unequivocal evidence of not only being deeply penitent for the past, but resolved on good behavior for the future.

While so many alterations and improvements have been made in the education and management of children and youth at school, it is somewhat remarkable, that so little variation has taken place in the mode and character of school punishments, which, with some slight abatement, perhaps, in degree and frequency, have remained nearly the same since the days of King Solomon, who had a wondrous high opinion, it will be recollected, of the virtues of the rod. From nearly all our civil codes, instituted for the government of men, whipping, for the punishment of offences, has been repudiated, as not only barbarous, but calculated to harden rather than amend; and confinement in prison, or other punishment, substituted. Is the distinction which is thus kept up between the government of men and children, made because the young are more obdurate than the old? Certainly not; for the reverse of this is acknowledged to be the fact. Is it, then, because a similar change in the government of schools is impracticable? We understand not why this should be; since, if expulsions or degradations would not effect the object, rooms for solitary confinement might easily be provided for every school-house, and the delinquent imprisoned till he would be glad to purchase liberty by amendment. There may be sound reasons for the distinction we have mentioned, but we confess we are unable to discover them.

But suppose we admit, that the punishment of whipping is sometimes indispensable for insuring obedience and order in school, is there not room for improvement both in the frequency and manner of its application? Nothing has a greater tendency to brutalize the feelings, to deaden all the best sensibilities of the heart, than frequent repetitions of this questionable practice. If it must be resorted to, let it be seldom; and then, for reasons before suggested, let it be done in private, and, if possible in the presence of a parent. If thus done, unless we have read in vain the young heart, its restraining fears, and its keen and overpowering sense of guilt and shame, when conscious that there is no one present to uphold and countenance it in error, rare indeed will be the cases in which a repetition of the punishment will ever be found necessary.

The scholars, the next morning, assembled under the expectation that the business of the day would be opened by the promised punishment of the culprit of yesterday. But when they perceived that no movement of the kind was likely to be made, and especially when they noticed the altered demeanor of the boy, whose whole appearance, instead of the brazen looks which he wore on leaving school the preceding evening, now indicated the deepest humility, their disappointment was equalled only by their surprise. It was evident enough to them, that something had occurred to effect this unexpected alteration of circumstances. But what this was, they were wholly at a loss to conjecture. And, as the boy, when they went out, either avoided them or evaded their questions, the mystery was not solved till one of the boys, who had been home for his dinner, accidentally got hold of the truth, and hastened back to impart the important news to his companions.

"Hurra! boys," he exclaimed, as he came puffing up to a group assembled in the school-house yard to discuss the subject anew before entering the school for the afternoon, "hurra! boys, I have found out all about it, now."

"How was it, —how was it?" asked a dozen eager voices at once.

"I'll tell ye," replied the boy, lowering his voice, and assuming a look of awe, as he thought of what he was going to relate. "They took him—that is, his father and the master—they took him last night here to the school-house

—only think of that, all alone in the night!—and then the master gave him, I do spose, one of the terriblest hidings that ever was heard of."

"What! right afore his father?" exclaimed several of the older boys, evidently surprised and disconcerted to hear of this new mode of punishment, which might soon be adopted in their own cases.

"Yes," replied the former, "and then kept him half the night, forzino, talking to him like a minister, till he most cried himself to death, they said. How awful! wa'nt it, now?"

"Why, I rather he'd a killed me," responded one of the former, in which he seemed to be joined by both old and young; all of whom, for different reasons, saw much to dislike and dread in the picture.

"Well, I give in beat," observed the young bully, who, as before intimated, was meditating resistance to the punishment in question; "somehow, I can't get the hang of this new master. He does everything so different from what a fellow is looking for; and I have about concluded we may as well mind our own business, and let him alone."

"So, Mike, you have come to my opinion at last, have you?" said Tom Bunker, who had been listening in silence. "Now I have said but little about this affair, from first to last; and if you had had a chance to go on with the shine you was thinking of, I can't say what part I should have taken, if the master had needed help; but I want to tell you I think he has used us all like a gentleman, and I would fight for him. And now, Mike, what do you say to backing him up in keeping order, and using him as he wants to use us, for the rest of the winter?"

"That is what I have been thinking of myself—I am agreed," answered Mike.

"Well, then, boys," rejoined Tom, "let us all hands now into the house for our books; and the one that learns the most, and behaves the best, shall be the best fellow."

The crisis had passed. In the defeat of this last and impotent attempt to break down the authority of our schoolmaster, his triumph was completed. All seemed to understand this; and, for the remainder of the season, no school could have been more distinguished for good order and obedience.

All troubles in regard to government being now at an end, and no others being anticipated by Locke, he urged his pupils forward in their studies with all the incitements he could command. But even this may sometimes, perhaps, be carried too far. At all events, he was accused of so doing, in connection with an event which soon occurred, and which came near breaking up his school. But the relation of this unexpected and painful incident, we will reserve for a new chapter.

"A Struggle for the Mastery"
From *The Hoosier Schoolmaster: A Story of Backwoods Life in Indiana* (set c. 1850)

⁖ ◆ ⁗

Edward Eggleston, 1871

This excerpt from Edward Eggleston's famous novel *The Hoosier Schoolmaster* offers another view of schoolteaching in the rural Midwest during the early days of the common school. The novel, which was based loosely on his brother's experiences as a teacher in Riker's Ridge, Indiana, affords the author an opportunity to show off the idiosyncratic dialects that proliferated in rural communities at the time. Mr. Ralph Hartsook must contend not only with the predictable disorder and recalcitrance of his pupils, but also with a speech pattern so opaque as to be almost unintelligible.

Like Locke Amsden, Ralph Hartsook is a clever and amiable hero, a virtuous spirit whose commitment to the school and his students has a rather romantic caste. The chapter that follows deals with the ubiquitous question of discipline, and shows once again how the spirit of ingenuity and restraint can have a more powerful effect than the rod. The conflict here involves the issue of a school vacation: The students want a day off and assume the teacher will not grant it to them. A minor mutiny ensues, with the teacher prevailing—both physically and psychologically. By the end, a clear moral lesson has been learned.

Until writing *The Hoosier Schoolmaster*, Eggleston had been struggling in a career as a magazine journalist. The novel began as a three-part serialized work in *Hearth and Home* magazine in 1871. When early installments proved to be immensely popular, Eggleston went on to write more, enlarging the short story into a novel. Fifty thousand copies were sold in a few months, and the book was translated into many languages.

The fact that the work began as mass magazine fiction may explain the rather stereotypical nature of the characters and the town: The primary villain has the surname Means, the local preacher is named Brother Sodom, and the kind hero is Hartsook. The story has an enduring place in American fiction largely due to its depiction of a part of our country, its dialect, and an era hitherto undocumented in literature. It also offers a view of country school life in 19th-century America that is probably quite realistic.

"A STRUGGLE FOR THE MASTERY" FROM *THE HOOSIER SCHOOLMASTER: A STORY OF BACKWOODS LIFE IN INDIANA* (SET C. 1850)

Edward Eggleston, 1871

The school had closed on Monday evening as usual. The boys had been talking in knots all day. Nothing but the bulldog in the slender, resolute young master had kept down the rising storm. A teacher who has lost moral support at home, can not long govern a school. Ralph had effectually lost his popularity in the district, and the worst of it was that he could not divine from just what quarter the ill wind came, except that he felt sure of Small's agency in it somewhere. Even Hannah had slighted him, when he called at Means's on Monday morning to draw the pittance of pay that was due him.

He had expected a petition for a holiday on Christmas day. Such holidays are deducted from the teacher's time, and it is customary for the boys to "turn out" the teacher who refuses to grant them, by barring him out of the schoolhouse on Christmas and New Year's morning. Ralph had intended to grant a holiday if it should be asked, but it was not asked. Hank Banta was the ringleader in the disaffection, and he had managed to draw the surly Bud, who was present this morning, into it. It is but fair to say that Bud was in favor of making a request before resorting to extreme measures, but he was overruled. He gave it as his solemn opinion that the master was mighty peart, and they would be beat anyhow some way, but he would lick the master fer two cents ef he warn't so slim that he'd feel like he was fighting a baby.

And all that day things looked black. Ralph's countenance was cold and hard as stone, and Shocky trembled where he sat. Betsey Short tittered rather more than usual. A riot or a murder would have seemed amusing to her.

School was dismissed, and Ralph, instead of returning to the Squire's, set out for the village of Clifty, a few miles away. No one knew what he went for, and some suggested that he had "sloped."

But Bud said, "he warn't that air kind. He was one of them air sort as died in their tracks, was Mr. Hartsook. They'd find him on the ground nex' morning, and he 'lowed the master war made of that air sort of stuff as would burn the dog-on'd ole schoolhouse to ashes, or blow it into splinters, but what he'd beat. Howsumdever he'd said he was a-goin' to help, and help he would; but all the sinno in Golier wouldn't be no account again the cute they was in the head of the master."

But Bud, discouraged as he was with the fear of Ralph's "cute", went like a martyr to the stake and took his place with the rest in the schoolhouse at nine o'clock at night. It may have been Ralph's intention to preoccupy the schoolhouse, for at ten o'clock Hank Banta was set shaking from head to foot at seeing a face that looked like the master's at the window. He waked up Bud and told him about it.

"Well, what are you a-tremblin' about, you coward?" growled Bud. "He won't shoot you; but he'll beat you at this game, I'll bet a hoss, and me, too, and make us both as 'shamed of ourselves as dogs with tin-kittles to their tails. You don't know the master, though he did duck you. But he'll larn you a good lesson this time, and me too, like as not." And Bud soon snored again, but Hank shook with fear every time he looked at the blackness outside the windows. He was sure he heard footfalls. He would have given anything to have been at home.

When morning came, the pupils began to gather early. A few boys who were likely to prove of service in the coming siege were admitted through the window, and then everything was made fast, and a "snack" was eaten.

"How do you 'low he'll get in?" said Hank, trying to hide his fear.

"How do I 'low?" said Bud. "I don't 'low nothin' about it. You might as well ax me where I 'low the nex' shootin' star is a-goin' to drap. Mr. Hartsook's mighty onsartin. But he'll git in, though, and tan your hide fer you, you see ef he don't. *Ef* he don't blow up the schoolhouse with gunpowder!" This last was thrown in by way of alleviating the fears of the cowardly Hank, for whom Bud had a great contempt.

The time for school had almost come. The boys inside were demoralized by waiting. They began to hope that the master had "sloped." They dreaded to see him coming.

"I don't believe he'll come," said Hank, with a cold shiver. "It's past school-time."

"Yes, he will come, too," said Bud. "And he 'lows to come in here mighty quick. I don't know how. But he'll be a-standin' at that air desk when it's nine o'clock. I'll bet a thousand dollars on that. *Ef* he don't take it into his head to blow us up!" Hank was now white.

Some of the parents came along, accidentally of course, and stopped to see the fun, sure that Bud would thrash the master if he tried to break in. Small, on the way to see a patient perhaps, reined up in front of the door. Still no Ralph. It was just five minutes before nine. A rumor now gained currency that he had been seen going to Clifty the evening before, and that he had not come back though in fact Ralph had come back, and had slept at Squire Hawkins's.

"There's the master," cried Betsey Short, who stood out in the road shivering and giggling alternately. For Ralph at that moment emerged from the sugar-camp by the schoolhouse, carrying a board.

"Ho! ho!" laughed Hank, "he thinks he'll smoke us out. I guess he'll find us ready." The boys had let the fire burn down, and there was now nothing but hot hickory coals on the hearth.

"I tell you he'll come in. He didn't go to Clifty fer nothin'," said Bud, who sat still on one of the benches which leaned against the door. "I don't know how, but they's lots of ways of killing a cat besides chokin' her with butter. He'll come in—*ef* he don't blow us all sky-high!"

Ralph's voice was now heard, demanding that the door be opened.

"Let's open her," said Hank, turning livid with fear at the firm, confident tone of the master.

Bud straightened himself up. "Hank, you're a coward. I've got a mind to kick you. You got me into this blamed mess, and now you want to crawfish. You jest tech one of these 'ere fastenin's, and I'll lay you out flat of your back afore you say Jack Robinson."

The teacher was climbing to the roof with the board in hand.

"That air won't win," laughed Pete Jones outside. He saw that there was no smoke. Even Bud began to hope that Ralph would fail for once. The master was now on the ridge-pole of the schoolhouse. He took a paper from his pocket, and deliberately poured the contents down the chimney.

Mr. Pete Jones shouted, "Gunpowder!" and set off down the road to be out of the way of the explosion. Dr. Small remembered, probably, that his patient might die while he sat there, and started on.

But Ralph emptied the paper, and laid the board over the chimney. What a row there was inside! The benches that were braced against the door were thrown down, and Hank Banta rushed out, rubbing his eyes, coughing frantically, and sure that he had been blown up. All the rest followed, Bud bringing up the rear sulkily, but coughing and sneezing for dear life. Such a smell of sulphur as came from that schoolhouse.

Betsey had to lean against the fence to giggle.

As soon as all were out, Ralph threw the board off the chimney, leaped to the ground, entered the schoolhouse, and opened the windows. The school soon followed him, and all was still.

"Would he thrash?" This was the important question in Hank Banta's mind. And the rest looked for a battle with Bud.

"It is just nine o'clock," said Ralph, consulting his watch, "and I'm glad to see you all here promptly. I should have given you a holiday if you had asked me like gentlemen yesterday. On the whole, I think I shall give you a holiday, anyhow. The school is dismissed."

And Hank felt foolish.

And Bud secretly resolved to thrash Hank or the master, he didn't care which.

And Mirandy looked the love she could not utter.

And Betsey giggled.

"Letters From Pioneer Women Teachers"[1]

❧ ◆ ☙

Cynthia M. Bishop and Martha M. Rogers, 1850–1853

The schoolteaching women who chose to abandon friends and family in the East and make the solitary journey westward were of a unique breed. Their evangelical passion and physical toughness come through vividly in the many letters and journals that were left by them.

The physical and psychological hardships of teaching rough pioneer families required not only a special kind of character but also specialized training. Many teachers in the West received their preliminary education at an institute specially created for the purpose of preparing young ladies to work in these difficult environments. The National Popular Education Board in Hartford operated out of an orphan asylum, and served as an early normal school for district school teachers in New England who hoped to extend the reach of their influence beyond the tame Northeast. One of the goals of the National Board was to disseminate to the rustic West new ideas about education, including the notion that women were superior role models in the classroom. The common school reformer's concern for morality and Christian virtue were central preoccupations at the Hartford school, and techniques like the use of blackboards were considered innovations of real importance. Clearly, the majority of women who responded to the call for westward crusaders were individuals with strong Protestant beliefs. They also tended to be economically insecure, orphans, or in some comparable state of uncertainty and distress. Though the teachers were asked to commit to 2 years in the West, many—including the women in these passages—stayed longer. The freedom and autonomy of a working life in the West was often too compelling to abandon.

---

[1]The letters of Cynthia M. Bishop and Martha M. Rogers were first edited and published by Polly Welts Kaufman in her landmark book *Women Teachers on the Frontier* (New Haven: Yale University Press, 1984). The notes that follow have been taken directly from Ms. Kaufman's work.

Cynthia Bishop and Martha Rogers were both in their late 20s when they left the Hartford Institute and made their journeys westward. Both women write in these letters, directed to their teacher back East, of social and religious conflicts they experience in their new communities. For Bishop, the conflict concerns the use of the Protestant Bible in her classes. As an evangelical Protestant it is galling for her to compromise on this issue, and yet she does: She chooses to teach Christian lessons, precepts from the Bible, without bringing the book into the classroom. Her discussion of the Catholic resistance to sectarian study in schools prefigures the massive rejection of public education by Catholic families that would happen later in the century.

Mary Rogers' letter from Cassville, Missouri describes a scene of public drunkenness and violence that seems straight out of a Hollywood western. Rogers, who taught in a number of rough towns throughout the Ozarks, conjures up a world that stands in dramatic contrast to the genteel manners of the Northeast. Her letter underscores the distance that pioneer teachers had to travel—both geographically and socially—in their efforts to educate the western settlers.

CYNTHIA M. BISHOP FROM GEORGIA, VERMONT, AND LOWELL, MASSACHUSETTS, TO NEW DURHAM AND LAFAYETTE, INDIANA

New Durham, Laporte Co., Ind., July 23, 1853

My dear Miss Swift,

Considering the very kind interest you have taken in my welfare and usefulness I fear I have done wrong in not writing sooner; but trust you will excuse me.

I arrived at this place, Thurs., May 5th & was met by Miss Flynt, with whom I spent one week[2]. During this time I had the offer of two schools, one of which I could not refuse if I had tried. They were so importunate in their application. They had heard accidentally last fall from Miss Flynt that she expected a teacher friend from the East, & ever since had watched for my advent. I was amused by their confidence that they would have a good school if they obtained my services, though it made me fear lest I should, in the result, lower their estimate of eastern teachers. The principal actor in engaging me was the Hon. C. H. Cathcart, late a member of Congress. I board at his house which with its furniture & arrangements is that of a plain,

---

[2]Elizabeth E. Flynt was from Tewksbury, Massachusetts, and went out to teach in New Durham during the spring of 1850, where she started the first school. She later joined Bishop in teaching in the first public school in Lafayette.

respectable farmer. He sends four children to me—the oldest a girl of 15. I have two other girls of similar age & the rest of my pupils are of all ages from five to thirteen.

I find them rather backwards on account of seldom or never having a well qualified teacher. It is only seven years since the first school was taught in the district & they have been taught only part of each year.

I hope you will pardon my saying I was amused, but I really suppose I am the best qualified teacher they have had & I believe not a word of fault is found with me, at least I hear of none.

I do not know *how* to write about the school at present, so that you can, as it were, see it, but I shall have to put down my thoughts as they occur to me.

I open the school in the morning suggested by yourself, though I have practiced nearly the same before. I stated to Mr. Cathcart & Mr. Flood, the trustee, when they came after me, that I would use some religious means in school, & stated, briefly, my own sentiments. This I did with perfect frankness, & before I knew anything of the sentiments of these gentlemen, I found them perfectly willing I should do as I pleased, though it seems that neither of them usually attend public worship. I was glad when I found this to be the case, that I gave them my views at first.

None of the Cathcart family are professors, & I believe none of Mr. Flood's. There are several professors in the district, however, all of whom belong to the Methodists. Many of the children attend a Sabbath School, some three miles distant, & in order to give some Spiritual instruction to those who cannot go, I proposed to meet all who chose to come at six o'clock p.m. on each Sabbath, & I spend an hour in appropriate exercises....

I believe you wished to hear about our daily labors in the school. Before commencing it, I called on every family accompanied by Mrs. Cathcart, & the peple seemed pleased with the proceeding. I think the influence of it good.

I have not adopted your plan for the exercise *fully*, but I have a particular time for every class & in *much* the same order as you proposed. I have the children read first after prayers, & then hear two classes in Arithmetic before recess. After recess the little ones read again, & then the two largest classes, & then a half hour for writing closes the forenoon session.

I have an hour & a half intermission, then the little ones read, classes in Peter Parley's & Mitchell's Geograph[3] recite, the older scholars spell, & we have a few minutes to devote to miscellaneous exercises, which have excited so much interest that they have been willing to shorten the recess as a means of *prolonging* them. This I do not do, except occasionally.

After recess little ones again, then Grammar, which my three largest girls study, then I give some assistance in Arithmetic, hear Tables & sing to close.

---

[3]Peter Parley's tales and readers ranged from primers to story tours of the world. Peter Parley was the pen name of Samuel G. Goodrich.

One of the most important events which take place in school (i.e. in the estimation of the pupils) is the opening of our Post Office—a box in which they drop written questions on any subject which interests their minds. The questions are various, & sometimes require preparation in order to answer them. They have sponge to wipe their slates with—& the question is deposited "where does it come from," &c. We are about to have a new schoolhouse built, & they ask (& I cannot tell them, though I *guess* the Puritans, at Plymouth) "who built the *first schoolhouse* in the New World?" And the last time I opened it, I found the query, "what do men get drunk for?" I told them I would talk about it sometime—I hardly knew what to say, lest I should not make as strong an impression as I wished in favor of temperance, so I have borrowed Miss Flynt's drawings of the drunkard's stomach, & shall show & speak about them next Monday.

What can I do to help this cause? Would that I knew, for the father of one of my large girls, who *has* pretended (it must have been pretence) to preach the gospel, sometimes loses the dignity of *man*, by the use of alcohol. If I could receive any light upon my duty to an interesting family in their circumstances, I should be glad. The man received five thousand dollars, it is said, with his wife, some eighteen years since, & with the advantages then offered here, might have been worth ten times that amount or more, yet they are now so poor that people wonder how they manage to appear respectably. It is thought that they could not if none but honest means were ever used. I say this trusting that it is not too much to *whisper* to you if I could, & ask you how I could save the children,—a son of fourteen, who will enter my school bye & bye, if I stay,—from dishonestly getting what is not his own—for it is said he will pilfer orchards—& perhaps other places—& it is believed is secretly allowed in it. The oldest girl is an interesting one. I want to see her qualified to teach, but I have some misgivings about the family. I have written freely, but it is to Miss Swift, so I know all will be as it should be.

Mr. Cathcart has sent & bought a ten dollar set of maps for the use of his children & the school; they are beautiful & the pupils are much pleased. The scholars noticed that the *largest* countries on each maps were colored *yellow* & the query *why* was put in the P.O.

I think I have improved as a teacher in consequence of the instruction received at Hartford. I feel the need of more of the same high order, when, as I often do, I find it difficult to make my large girls *love* Grammar. They were put into it by unskillful teachers at nine and eleven years of age, & have *learned* it by rote enough to disgust them, & that is all the *good*, but not all the evil it has done. I think we are gaining slowly...[4] I have governed the school without using the rod thus far, though I sometimes think it would

---

[4]Kaufman notes that the paper on which the last part of the sentence appears seems to be

do one or two rogues good, who *forget* quite too often what they admit to be *right*.

I do not know whether I had better remain here some time, or go into a larger school. I have only twenty scholars, but shall have more soon. I engaged only for one term, but I believe they are intending to keep me as long as they can. They are able to pay me well, & I do not know as I shall be exacting, if I stay, in asking the $150 per year. I suppose I should have had that if you had given me a location. I like the country, & enjoy good health, though my eyes have been sore, & are quite weak now. It is almost mail time & my only chance to send this for three days.

Yours affectionately,

Miss Nancy Swift   Cynthia M. Bishop

****

Lafayette, Ind., May 16, 1854

My dear Miss Swift,

In much haste I snatch a moment to write you. I want a word of advice, & wish I had written a day or two sooner.—

The long-looked-for day for the opening of the public schools in this city is now near at hand; probably will be two weeks from yesterday, May 29. Myself & Miss Flynt are expecting to teach in the grammar schools.—We, as you know are Baptists, two or three others of the ten lady teachers engaged are Congregationalists or Presbyterians, & two more are members of the Methodist church. How many of these are impressed with a sense of obligation in regard to religious influences in school, I cannot say.—Other teachers are Universalist or—*nothingarian* perhaps; our Superintendent is a Pennsylvanian—was brought up a Quaker, his wife still says "thee & thou" & I have no evidence that he will *desire* even if he tolerates the use of the Bible & prayer in the schools. He *may* not oppose—the directors would not, probably, but the impression seems to be that in order not to exclude the Catholic children from the schools, it will be considered *not best to use the Bible at all there.* You know, my dear Miss S., that it must be a hard question for me to decide how I ought to act under these circumstances, especially as I am to conduct a grammar school in a quarter of the city where Catholics are most plenty. I think that if the superintendent & directors were all pious and prudent men, who felt the need of Christian influence in this city, that we could carry out our wishes without any serious trouble with either parents or children. But they (the directors) seem to fear to stand firm, &, as near as I can learn, the superintendent cares nothing about it.

I did not waver in my design to read the Bible at the opening of school until a day or two since, when I talked with one of the teachers, a Presbyterian, & one of the very *best* of the teachers elect, & she said she thought we could accomplish more good by giving way in *appearance*—not reading the Bible, &c., so as not to frighten the numerous foreign children away—but we could give oral & apparently accidental religious instruction in such times & ways as to excite no tempest.—If she, who is a resident of this city & a very pious, well-educated lady, thinks so, do you wonder I hesitate as to my duty?—Some say to me, Ask the superintendent if he will approve it, but if it is duty I dislike to ask *permission* of man—Another, the wife of a returned missionary tells me to open my school as I wish, making no allusion to the fact that I am *aware* of any difference of opinion in others, & as though considered it a matter of course.

Now, if I know my own heart at all, I wish to do what God would have me in this matter, that which, in the end, will result in the greatest good.—If you were within a short distance, so that I could visit you, it would be a *comfort* to go to your feet & sit down to be instructed.

If this letter reaches you in the time it ought, will you not sit down & answer it briefly, so that I may know your mind before Sun. May 28; & please write some suggestions how I had better *vary* or *carry* out my forms of proceeding, if I should have *commenced* before I receive it, either *with* or without my customary religious exercises, I *hope* I may get it *before* the schools *begin*.

The opening session will be very short, perhaps seven or eight weeks, & in Sept. the school year will commence.

We are in tolerable health of body, but do not, especially myself, enjoy that spiritual health so desirable in our station.

We have got to meet the superintendent within an hour, & spend most of the day in school exercises which is my reason for writing so hastily. I *must* put it in the next mail.

I will write again more deliberately soon so that the Committee can know how we are situated.

If you cannot consistently answer this—so be it, but offer one prayer that I may not make false steps. I will try to do my duty as far as I know it.

I shall teach the scholars the golden rule *& many other Bible precepts, whether I tell them where I found them or not. This I can* do at all events.

Yours with affectionate respect,

Miss N. Swift   Cynthia M. Bishop

****

Lafayette, Ind., Aug. 21, '54

Dear Miss Swift & Ladies of the Committee,

I will now, after some delay, report myself to you, but as I am spending my vacation at the sick & probably dying bed of an esteemed Christian friend, a clergyman, you will excuse the hasty & informal manner in which I write. Miss Swift will pardon my repetition in this letter, of what I may have communicated to her in a private note.

I came to this city last fall to take charge of a select school for girls, which had been established two or three years, intending if it pleased me & seemed best, to continue it. It was to remain during the winter term under the nominal control of its founder, & I was encouraged to think he would make some effort to assist me in finding rooms for it to occupy after that time, or such assistance as he might be able to render; but I found that it was of little use to look for aid from that quarter, & my compensation being very small, with much difficulty in governing, (which I find has ever attended private schools in this place), I at once concluded to enter the public schools where I could *depend* upon being supported in having order, &c. The Trustees told me the school houses which they were building would be finished in May, so I thought I would wait six or eight weeks for them. But the builders were so negligent my "tarrying time" was prolonged until June 27th, when the graded schools, the first of the kind in this city of 9,000 inhabitants, were opened, creating quite a pleasant interest among some of the citizens. The schoolrooms are ten in number, in three buildings, & into them are crowded from seventy to one hundred and four seats apiece. The houses are of brick & well built, but the rooms are not large enough for the seats put into them by one fifth.

The schools were suspended at the end of four weeks on account of very hot weather & the alarming prevalence of sickness, some cases of cholera, &c. We expect to open the fall session Sept. 4th. So you see I have had only one month's regular employment in five. If I had known that the houses would be so long in preparing I would have tried to find a *place* for a school to occupy, & taught. *Scholars* enough were ready for me, but a place a *decent* school-room was almost impossible to be found, therefore I hope I shall not be considered censurable.—I love the Society whose agents you are, & would fain help on its objects, & carry out its designs in my little sphere.

The schools are classed as primary, intermediate & grammar departments; one of the latter is under my charge. I had about forty pupils enter during the short session, but expect seventy five this fall, of ages ranging from ten to twenty, male & female, many of whom have never had a good school to attend before. *Do pray* that I may have grace & wisdom equal to this arduous responsibility. Is it not a great work to *begin* a *systematic* course in such a school? How *can* I succeed? The superintendent is not a religious man, & though he inculcates *good morals*, does not *wish* to have us use the Bible in school. He seems to fear that sectarian prejudices, of the Catholics principally, may be aroused & the Trustees are about of the same opinion. A part of the latter are men who "care for none of these things" either way, & two of them are evangelical professors, but are so *timid* or something else that they fall in with the rest.—I was determined never to *ask* permission *of man* to read the word of God, so I spoke to the Supt. (Mr. Naylor from Penn.) just before the schools opened, & told him my views of duty & asked him if it was *his intention to use any means to prevent* the *teachers* from *acting their own judgement & pleasure in this matter,* saying that I inquired for the sake of knowing what to depend upon; that my course had been & would be the same, in substance, wherever I went; & that if the performance of what I deemed a sacred duty was to be the means of trouble with those who employed me, I wished to know it *then,* as there was other situations to be had & I must go where I could act freely in the matter. I addressed him with perfect good nature, but with decision, in presence of another teacher & he replied, "Miss Bishop I do not wish you to leave, you may do as you think you ought to, I will make you no trouble."

But in my school are *some* Catholics, & there are *many* in the neighborhood who would attend if the priest would let them alone; so in view of all circumstances, instead of taking the Bible directly into school, I wrote off selections on the natural & moral attributes of God & our most prominent social duties as well as the great duty to love & worship Diety, & read them, offering a short extemporaneous prayer. I get the pupils to sing a verse or two when I can, but they are backward in this as in every thing, & being an inefficient singer myself, I find it hard to get along. Yet I am determined to perservere & we shall soon do better....

Last winter I did not feel that I had so good an opportunity to *do* as I now have. I have not received a saucy word from my pupils in the public school yet, not has any one *persisted* in disobeying. They have never been accustomed to strict *order* & I did not "draw the reins" *very* tight as the weather was so warm & they were not used to confinement, but we hope to improve this fall so much that we should not be ashamed to have you visit us any day. I can truly say that I never loved any school as I do this at present & I think most of the pupils are well pleased with me. I have never spoken a cross word in my new school room & hope & pray that I never may, yet I expect to be a tolerable disciplinarian. "Who is sufficient for these things?" May I feel that you all pray for me? If I fail it will do more than to injure *me.* My pupils will suffer & many others.

I do not, cannot say that I enjoy religion personally—I have no pastor this summer to counsel or encourage me in the little trials & vexations which have continually beset me; it has been difficult to find comfortable rooms or accomodations for myself, most of the time, without paying an extravagant price; I have been dealt rather unfairly with & cut short for means; & have given way to hard & repining feelings. But our church expect a pastor soon, & if things brighten up I shall probably try to make myself contented here, if the school prospers. I must say that I have been lonely & homesick owing to the above circumstances, but hope is now in the ascendant. I think if I were situated in a smaller place—a small village perhaps—that I should enjoy *society* better than in a city of the peculiar character which this possesses.

The Ladies of the Committee may be pleased with a word of explanation in relation to the last remark, therefore I will tell how the place appears to me. *Backward in intelligence*, as may be seen by the fact of its reaching the present size before building a public school house or supporting schools; *nothing to boast* of in *refinement*—*money*, which is the great object of pursuit, seeming to be the main passport into the "first circles," in which many persons move who are any thing but well-educated; & the continual coming & going of strangers rendering the newcomer an object of cold criticism to stated residents here, rather than of friendly interest. I do not love the place, but as I do love my school, I think I may become better pleased after a time.

My salary is $300 per annum, which I think *too low*, while board is higher here than in Chicago or Cincinnati, but I shall not accept so small a remuneration for so hard a place next year. The people, no doubt, really think it good wages.

I should be very happy to receive suggestions from any of the Committee, or of other intelligent Christians respecting my past or future course in relation to the *use of the Bible* & religious influence in school. If *truth* prevails I am content.

Yours affectionately,

Cynthia M. Bishop

Martha M. Rogers from Champlain, New York, to Cassville, Waldo, and Erie, Missouri

Cassville Barry Co. Mo. July 5th–50

Dear Miss Swift

Considering the length of time that letters occupy in going from here & also the change in my location, I have concluded to write. It may perhaps be too soon to tell definitely as to my *continuance* here—but not too soon to tell the past & present....

At Buffalo we parted with our northern division the last day of Apr. amid tears, good byes & such things. Gov. Slade took thirteen of us to the boat about seven at night after having paid our fare to Cin[cinnati] & given us our allowance for the remainder of our route as he was to leave us that night & go on to Chicago with the others. And after much kind affectionate advice, not forgetting his voluminous motto "Modest pretentions and Great works," left us alone, as Mr. Maltby had taken boat the night before with Misses Plimpton & Washburn for Cleavland & would join us next day.[5]

The lake [Erie] was so rough that we did not stir till morning. It was still rough & short seas & the consequence was that every body were sick & all our company excepting Miss Ladd some more, some less. Misses Kilgore, Brooks, Taylor & myself were among the worst[6] So we all lay all day groaning. It was a clear bright *May Day*, but not very 'joyous' to us. Miss Kilgore laugh & cry by turns to say if she "had only know this she never would have been caught on that *dreadful* lake." Miss Brooks, & Miss Taylor—"O, if they could only see home again they would never be seen on that lake" but poor I was too sick to even wish to get well. Indeed I had but one thought all day & that was "O how sick." We got to Cleavland about seven O'Clock at night when Mr. Maltby came on board & began to doctor us with brandy & some of his spicy jokes which latter in connection with the Lake becoming less boisterous proved highly beneficial & the next morning with the exception of a light head & very empty stomach I was well but not so Misses Brooks & Taylor. They were sick two or three days after.

We got into Sandusky about 8 O'Clock in the morning & took the cars at five for Cin. At about seven we left the Wilkinsons at Belvue[7] The Rev. Mr. Waldo was there to receive them. We than rode on till after eight before we got any breakfast & we were *right* hungry to be sure. It was ten O'Clock at night when we reached Cin. the night of the opening of Burnet House. The next day Mr. Maltby distributed us on three different boats. The four going to Ind. left at noon. Misses Brooks, Grosvenor, Ela Taylor & self took

[5]The Reverend Benjamin K. Maltby of Cleveland was a National Popular Education Board (NPEB) agent who escorted teachers across Ohio. Charlotte Plimpton of Hopkinson, Massachusetts, went to teach in a girls' school in western Pennsylvania and Mary Washburn from Burlington, Vermont, was going to teach in Henrietta, Ohio. *Third NPEB Report*, 1850, p. 17.

[6]Abby D. Killgore of Topsham, Maine, was headed for Mooresville, Indiana, where she became the second wife of James S. Kelly, a successful merchant. Harriet N. Brooks of Dalton, New Hampshire, married Ranselaer Winchell in LaHarpe, Illinois, in a few years. Emily Taylor not only joined Martha Rogers's class in 1850, but went out again in the fall of 1853 to Boonville, Missouri. She apparently went with her sister to Missouri the first time. She eventually returned to Hinsdale, New Hampshire, where in 1857 she married the Reverend Moses H. Wells. Mary Jane Ladd from Meredith, New Hampshire, married in the West. An alumna of Mount Holyoke, she married William T. Hatch within the year in Henry County, Indiana, and died in 1861 at the age of forty-six.

[7]The Wilkinson sisters, who first went together to teach in Bellevue, Ohio, eventually went separate ways. They were in their early twenties and were probably the oldest daughters of a Brandon, Vermont, physician. Mary married Emerson Covel within the year and Caroline went on to teach in Tennessee.

boat for St. Louis—And poor Miss June like the "Lone Star" to which she was hieing took boat by herself[8]

I would say here in explanation of our being out on the Sabbath—we found that we must be out one Sabbath either on this river [Ohio] or the Mo. And after looking it all over & considering how far some of us had yet to go Mr. Maltby concluded that it was best for us to go. Misses Brooks & Grosvenor were very reluctant to go & took care to remind us all along the route that we must bear Gov. Slade's displeasure for they were innocent to which we humbly acquiesced probably feeling that Gov. S. was too good a man to let his wrath continue after sundown, &, that it could not reach us so soon in this far off land....

Our boat kept us *waiting* one day & after taking on a cargo of babies (twelve in all), they left about nine o'clock in the evening. The next morning about seven, we left Miss Ela. We had a pleasant time & got to St.Louis the next Wednesday about three P.M. I sent my letter up to Dr. Ballard & about an hour or so Mr. Emerson came & said he found there was no boat going up the Mo. that night & we must wait till next evening[9] Misses Brooks & Grosvenor stepped off of our boat on to another just started for the upper Miss[issippi] so that they were not detained at all. We went to the the City Hotel & next evening took boat for [because] Mr. Emerson was going up the Miss. & would not be back till the next week so we came on alone. When we got into the Mo. we had a "right smart chance of snags, sawyers & sandbars" & we also had the pleasure of getting on the sandbars several times. We reached Jefferson about one P.M. Sat 11*th*. There parted with Miss Taylor who went to Boonville.

There I waited two days for the stage. Tuesday morning took the Stage at one in company with three gentlemen.... I was three days coming from Jeff City to Springfield rising at one in the morning & riding till seven & eight one night. I rode one day in company with a gentleman who was in the Stage last fall when Miss Sawyer came out & showed me the spot where they upset & he remarked that she was a woman of a strong mind for she made no fuss atall when they upset[10] The last day of the trip was performed in a rough lumber wagon 45 miles & I was tired out when I got to Springfield.

Mrs. Emerson received me very kindly and did all She could to make me comfortable. Soon after tea she told me not to feel bad but that Col. Love had engaged a teacher for the summer session but that she doubted not that I could soon get a School & that I was very welcome to a home with them

---

[8]No information is available about either Miss June or E.C. Grosvenor.

[9]The Reverend Mr. Emerson of Springfield, Missouri, was part of Govenor Slade's network. He had requested a teacher for Colonel Love's school from the board and apparently offered his home as a way station for teachers coming to Missouri.

[10]Ann E. Sawyer from Franklin, New Hampshire, went out to teach in an academy operated by R. D. Smith in Pleasant Retreat, Polk County, Missouri, in the class immediately preceding Martha Rogers's. She was twenty years old and had recently attended Mount Holyoke Seminary for two years.

till I found a Situation. But it all could not quell the rising of tumultuous feeling in my heart so far from home & friends, the people all strangers & everything so strange & different from all that I had been accustomed to that my heart died within me & when I went to bed that night tired weary & sad, I felt that there were some very rugged paths in this journey of life that we are travelling. I arose next morning sick in body & mind & I finally had to give up & be sick three days.

But my case soon excited the sympathy of the people & all were ready to assist me in any way & gentlemen would call & offer to write wherever they were acquainted & showed me every attention. When I had been there a week Col. Love sent me word that he was sorry he had engaged a teacher since I had come & that he would feel under obligation to employ me in the fall. He pretended that it was because he had not heard from the East & thought that he would not get a teacher before fall.... But I suspected that was not the real objection & I got it out of his son in law [Mr. Lee]. Mr. Emerson became obnoxious to them last Feb. through a letter of his that was published in that Jan. No. of the "Home Missionary" not intended for publication. This came to Springfield just about the time of the Benton excitement & the cry was instantly raised that he [Emerson] was a Abolitionist & of course ought not to be suffered to live[11]. So they stopped him from preaching & then they said he was distributing Abolition Tracts & then the old Col. [Love] got it into his head that he [Emerson] wanted to get Abolition teachers in the country to poison the minds of the young so he would have none of them. They might all go together for they were all alike.

I told Mr. Lee after he had told me this that he could tell Col. Love that the Society did not mean to send teachers here or anywhere else that did not *know enough* to mind their own business & that if he should want a teacher in the fall he had better send to the Society for one. Mr. Emerson laughed after the man was gone & said he thought the old gentleman would feel bad when he found what a "peert" teacher he had lost....

Miss Sawyer's Mr. Smith came ten miles out of his way to see me & give me any assistance in his power & wrote to this place for me & offered me his home if I should not find a situation. He felt very bad because he said he feared the Society would perhaps refuse to send any more to be so located.... Mr. Emerson left S[pringfield] on Friday May 7th & I stayed till Monday to take the Wagon not stage for this place...I found very kind friends in one of the two Pres[byterian] families in S. & stayed with them from Thursday to Monday May 10*th*. I left that morning at one & rode all day in

---

[11]Thomas Hart Benton (1782–1858), senator from Missouri since its entrance as a state in 1821, opposed the Compromise of 1850 because he believed it would give southern secessionists too many concessions. He was also opposed to Abolitionists and supported the gradual elimination of slavery. Because of his stand on the Compromise of 1850, he was defeated for reelection as a senator that same year.

the hot sun 55 miles to this place. It is on the Stage route & twelve miles from the Ark. line, and 100 to Van Buren Ark. The mail comes here three miles a week.

And now after so long a story what shall I say? I wish you could *see* for I can not picture the place to you as it is. The Courthouse is a two-story frame house with a chimney at one end outside.... The Hotel is made of three log houses—one has two glass windows, the other one, & the kitchen none.... We have three stores here—one of which is a log building without any windows—one grocery—three Blacksmiths—two Doctors & two Lawyers. As to preaching we have none of any sort. There [are] two Cumberland Presbyterian preachers living in town but one has lost the confidence of the people by his mercantile & other speculations & the other has other appointments. He is a fine man & came last Sabbath to help me organize a Sabbath School....[12]

And I must not forget the Schoolhouse which is a log house thirty-five by thirty with four windows & two doors, the south are boarded up & in the four windows of twelve panes each there are ten panes of glass. The cracks are filled with mud plaster & there is no "loft" & the shingles are very holey so that when it rains we take the books up & stand in one place till it begins to drop down & then we move to an other spot & then an other....

For a week after I came here I thought I would have to quit because I could not find a spot to put myself till I hit upon this place.... I have the best room in town. It's lathed & one coat of plaster put on about as well as I could put it on I should think. There is a fireplace in it two windows with curtains a closet on one side of the chimney & shelves on the other for books. The lower one being broader serves for wash stand & toilet stand. There is a door that opens on to a piazza 70 feet long & it faces the court house, grocery & one of the stores.

I commenced School Monday the 7th of May with sixteen scholars. At the end of the week I had twenty two & the next Monday I had twenty five & this week I have twenty-nine & they say that more are coming. But the difficulty now is a schoolhouse. Some want to build one but the majority are so inert that they come for nothing & I am now telling them that I will stay if they build such a House as I want but in that thing I will not Stay....

There is no congenial society in this place, not one. The doctor with the school board is intelligent but a Cambelite. The lawyers are *smart* but one is the greatest drunkard out.... There is a vast field for usefulness & I only hope & pray that I may make myself acceptable to them & so be useful to them. There is a great need of female culture here. I have young ladies 22, 19, 18 & so on that can hardly read & some whose parents cannot read....

[12]The Cumberland Presbyterians waived traditional educational requirements for the ministry in order to meet the religious needs of the West more quickly and depended on camp meetings to produce converts. They tended to reject the traditional Presbyterian tenet of predestination.

I shall probably have my trials here for I expect that wherever I may go I shall certainly be very lonely—but still I think I could have chosen, I could not have selected a place more in need of one of your teachers & I only wish there was one here better qualified for the work. I have not yet visited much as I have written about twelve letters—none of the length of this one & much shorter. They go altogether on horseback here as there is not a buggy in town. I have not received a letter since I came to Mo. & I suppose it will [be] August before I get one. My dear Miss S. I should like to hear from you & know what you think of my acts. I endeavored to do as well as I could. As to the books I have sold about three dolls worth. There is no paper currency in this state and coppers but as soon as I can get some paper I will send you the five dolls.

Affectionately Yours,

M. M. Rogers

****

Cassville, Sept. 18th—50

My dear Miss Swift

Precious, very precious is the sympathy of christian friends though they be afar off. Your letter of remembrance & sympathy was to my perplexed feelings what oil is to the troubled waters. I thanked God for it & took courage: but I will explain. I told you I think the condition of the School-house here & that I could not stay unless they built an other & in the Spring they talked as if they would.

A few weeks after I came here I received two letters from Col. Love offering me his school in the fall & all that I could make from it. Well I thought I would be in no hurry to answer him; this was a good location better than his for a permanent School & it was a dark region & if I could be useful here I would use these letters to stimulate the people to exertion for a permanent School. If I could not make a permanency here then I would go there as the next best thing I could do. When I showed the letters here some said they would give $50, others $25 towards the erection of a new house & I must not leave &c. But from their general liberality I did not put much faith in all their says and thought I would wait & see what they would *do*....

The school averaged 24 all the quarter; only six boys the oldest 13 had never seen a school. [He] did not know a letter when he commenced. I had some tall girls with corresponding (southern) tempers but it has been the pleasantest & most easily governed school that I ever had. The only punishment inflicted during the three months was slightly pinching a little fellows ear for laughing. They were never tardy always respectful, & always obeyed cheerfully. They were happy in school & loved to come & I attribute my success to the reading of the scriptures & prayers at the opening of the school mornings....

I have also gained the respect & confidence of the people generally & the warm esteem of the religious part of the Community. The married ladies all come to hear my instructions to their children on the Sabbath & I would not mind if they would not bring their nursing babies. They are very dear little things in the nursery—but in the S[abbath] S[chool] O how annoying to old maids! Mr. [Charles] Beecher did not tell what to do in such a case. I would like to ask him[13].

About three weeks before the close of the school I told the people that they must tell me decidedly what they would do for I must let Col. Love know. so three persons—one a Cumberland Presbyterian "Parson" another an elder & the third a Campbellite went round to ask assistance, about a house, & could raise *nothing*—as I anticipated but they came to me & said if I would stay—they would pledge themselves to make the house comfortable for me this winter & they thought by next spring there could be a new one built. I asked if there were objections to me. They said none to me nor to my teaching. It was only the fear of expense but they could not give me up. This place would never be any thing till there was a good permanent school besides they wanted me in the S.S. & it is a fact that there is not a female in this place competant to teach in the S.S. & but two men & they wanted my influence in the community. The Parson said since God had sent me to them they ought to keep me & they would do what they could to make my stay comfortable....

That Saturday the Whigs who are weak in this country assembled from all parts & had an illumination of feu de joie—and when they began to light up the courthouse, the Dr.'s wife [Mrs. Means] came along and says Miss Rogers let's illuminate the house for sport. I said yes, & I put three lights in my window & the other boarder put three in hers & Mrs. M[eans] lighted up her part of the house[14] These ladies husbands are Whigs & their parents are Bentonites but they side with their husbands so that we were all Whigs here. Just then Mrs. M's father "Parson" Burton & his wife came in—who are Benton—and went to blowing out the lights. I saw them coming so locked my door & put the key in my pocket so when they got to me they tried to raise the window. I held it & kept

---

[13]The Reverend Charles Beecher, Catharine Beecher's youngest brother, addressed Martha Rogers's class at Hartford.

[14]The household Martha Rogers lived in consisted of A. H. Burton, whose occupation was listed as "speculator," his wife, and four children; Jean Means, a physician, and his wife, who was Burton's daughter; and a single male lawyer and a single male merchant. U.S. Manuscript Census, 1850, Barry County, MO, p. 230.

my lights burning. This was all observed from the courthouse & applauded but I did not know it. The Parson said laughing "You can never leave Cassville after this, the Whigs will never let you go. A Whigwoman is such a rare thing here that they will keep you as a curiosity" &c. & so he joked me.

We then went & stood under the windows to hear the speeches. Then the resolutions & proceedings of the meeting, & you may fancy my consternation when I heard it resolved "to fire three salutes for that lady who illuminated her window." They did, shouting at each fire "for Miss Rogers for illuminating her window." It raised a great excitement among them & one man said he would come and throw mud in the cracks of the school ten days before he would let me go, & he would sign one scholar if he sent none. An other said that was worth a "thousand dollars." And Monday morning they got out an article and all the Whigs signed or promised to send children or [had] no children. It was not confined to the Whigs of course & the prospect before Wednesday was fair for as large a school as the summer session[15].

But I thought I would wait till after Examination before I made any new decisions. I made no extra preparation for examination. Tuesday & Wednesday morning was spent in reviewing & the parents & others were asked to come in the afternoon. There was a very good attendance (babies included). The girls were very much dressed—some of them in comical taste to be sure but that we will remedy in time. They all appeared unembarrassed & easy. They sang three songs "Try try again" "Sparkling & bright" "Up the Hills on a bright sunny morn" for the close. This is something new here & takes well. At the close I told them we had no writing to exhibit as we had no desks to write on. I had tried to do what I could with slates. I then said I would be glad to have every one present offer an opinion & make any suggestions on any thing. My friend the "Parson" then rose & complimented both teacher & pupils & spoke of the inconvenience of the house and called upon all present to unite in making the House comfortable & keeping me among them &c. Then brought our exercises to a close. It was five O'Clock & I was so exhausted that I feared I could not get through. I closed the 4th of Sept. to commence again the 1st of Oct for five months....

My dear Miss Swift I am ashamed to trespass upon your time with such long letters, & yet I do not know how I could make you understand my position otherwise.... As to the moral conditions of the people—there has been preaching twice in this place since I came here..... There is a grocery just across the square & there every day the sound of revelry, debach, &

---

[15]The Whigs did defeat Benton in 1850. However, the Whig Party Martha Rogers knew in New York did not support slavery. In Missouri in 1850, the Whigs were strong only because they united against Benton, a Democrat, and his opposition to the Compromise of 1850.

cursing is heard—& I have more than one scholar whose father is a sot. Rev. Mr. Cook of Auburn sends me the "Youth's Temperance Advocate" which I distribute very gladly.

A shocking circumstance took place here the 30th of Aug. Some four weeks before that, a Lawyer named Smythe, who got drunk every day & always carried knives & pistols fell out with a neighbor of his & brother drunkard both being drunk at the time. S. fired a pistol at the other [B.] but the cap burst. He [Smythe] then struck at him with it. The other's wife got between them & wrenched it from him. He [Smythe] then got his knife and wounded the other [B.] in five or six places. B. got on his horse & rode up here a mile & a half to have his wounds sewed when he swore that he would not kill S.

He [B.] had kept sober since that till the 30th Aug. when he had been drinking some; but was not intoxicated. That morning S. was seen riding into town with a bowie knife unsheathed in his hand. About 3 in the afternoon B. was sitting in front of one of the stores, when S. rode up very drunk & offered his hand to the merchant first. He refused & went inside. S. then offered his left hand to B. who put his hand in his [own] hand & said "no, you tried to kill me & I'll not shake hands with you."

On this S. brought over his right hand & aimed a pistol just between his eyes. Again the cap burst & B. escaped but on the instant he [B.] drew a knife twelve inches long & three wide & thrust it through [Smythe]. The first thrust cut through both lungs & would have been enough but he [B.] dug at him till he had inflicted eleven wounds each of which would have been mortal. It was in the square where all saw it. S. never uttered a word after he was hit but the last words heard from him were curses upon B. He slid from his horse & lay there. He groaned heavily two or three times but no one went near him till a brother lawyer came up—urged them to come & help take him some where for he was a human being. They then took him to the Doctor's office. The tailor made his shroud, all the women refusing to do it & but two men were willing to touch him any way. B. was tried that night & acquitted on the plea of self defence, it being the third time that S. had tried to shoot him.

I was horrified & could not sleep that night atall and I wondered that people did not exterminate that grocery at once. The next day his butchered, bloated body was taken to its last resting place, his wife & three children riding in the same wagon. This is a picture of Cassville. S. was a man of superior talents & education & the only thoroughly educated man in the place. He had formerly been a class leader & Methodist exhorter. He was also a "Son of Temperance" some two years ago. B. is also a man of good education & sense & would be a fine man but for this demon rum. He has not drunk since & says he will not. May God help him keep his resolution.

I have read Mary Carrow's School to my scholars with very good effect
& also some of the stories [in] the book which Mrs. Sigourney gave me.[16]
They all love to have me read to them & I [am] trying to excite curiosity &
and a desire to read themselves but the parents are no readers, have no
books nor papers—& there is not a woman in this town who is a fluent easy
reader & there are more than one who cannot read at all. I have thought
that I would like to have a few books for a sort of circulating Library to excite
a desire & taste for reading—such as "Miss Ellis's works," "Charlotte
Elisabeth Tales for the People" & "Temperance Tales."[17]. I think such would
be read & would create a taste for reading. I intend to write to Mr. Myers
for a S.S. Library. I would have done so before only that I was so unsettled
all summer not knowing if I should stay. What I next want is one of
Winchester's Charts; and Canvas & posters for working worsted with. I
could sell all such things if I had them, for the parents are very desirous that
their daughters should learn needlework. I could not obtain the materials
& therefore could not teach it. I would like very much to have this coming
session a class in Physiology & one in United States History, but cannot
obtain the books. A box directed to me to the care of J. & W. McDowell St.
Louis would be forwarded to me as they have a brother here selling goods
& he sends wagons there every two or three months, but the freight is four
cents a pound from there here so that it would cost more from St. L. here
than all the rest of the road.

You say "mention any little personal comfort you may need." If I had a
pound of Spermaciti candles & a rocking chair I should feel quite comfortable—as it is I think I shall live but they have nothing but the most inferior
kind of tallow candles, which are sometime green, & sometimes black, &
so debilitated by the heat that they cannot stand alone when put in
candlesticks—so that like the Coffee they have to be laid by to rest. I have
dispensed with lights all summer but can not any longer. I have been
accomodated all summer with a table a foot square—so since vacation I
have had one of larger dimensions—made a rough pine table without paint
or anything for which I had to pay $2.50. I got the cheapest thing I could
find for a cover for which I gave $1.50—making just $4 so that is the way
with everything. I am allowed two chairs—those straight backed kitchen
chairs—(they have no others in this place) which feel hard enough when I
come home tired & exhausted as I used in the hot weather, hardly able to

---

[16]Lydia Sigourney, a well-known Hartford author, wrote poems and stories with strong moral themes.
She was president of the Female Beneficent Society and met with several classes of teachers before they
went West.

[17]A collection of these books is in the Connecticut Historical Society. Sarah (Stickney) Ellis wrote
such works as *First Impressions; or, Hints to Those Who Would Make Home Happy* (New York: D. Appleton
& Co., 1846). The Charlotte Elizabeth Tales were written by Charlotte Elizabeth Tonna and published
by the American Tract Society. Like the Temperance Tales, published in Boston by Ford & Damrell, they
were little paperback tracts teaching morals in story form.

hold my head up & then I would have given any thing for an arm chair to hold me up, for I was often as drooping as the candles.

It is the Season of Camp meetings now. There was one two weeks since some 30 miles from this where two of my pupils went & one a young lady of 18 who has been a very rude, dancing, trifling girl, returned home rejoicing in a new found Saviour. I have not seen her since but they say she is a bright christian & that her very countenance is changed. Last week there was one some 8 miles from here where four more of my pupils came out bright—the daughter of the Parson with whom I board, two daughters of the elder I before mentioned, & the fact that a bright whole souled girl is cousin of the first young lady mentioned, has a deist father, careless mother, and a wicked sister who was so enraged at her when she returned that she cursed her & abused her cruelly. She is but 13 & will require much grace & encouragement to be able to endure the persecutions of such a home. I was not well enough to attend those meetings & I can not tell you how I felt when I heard that my pupils were the only converts at those meetings....

Miss Sawyer & I have opened a correspondence which I hope will prove as profitable to me as it is pleasant. Her school numbers between 60 & 70 this session & Mr. Smith has charge of the male department. He is a dear good man I often wish I had such an ally here. With the exception of Misses Taylor & June, I have not heard from one of our stars. I have received a letter from Miss T. and Miss June sent me word by one of the gentlemen who went to Texas from here that she had sent me a letter the week before they got there but I have not received it. The account you gave of those teachers heard from was so characteristic of each that I could not help smiling when reading it. We all anticipated difficulties for Sister Lord for she was always full of them even in Hartford. Miss Arnold's combativeness was rather too large not to excite opposition. Miss Warner would doubtless be as easy with her pupils as she was with her *hair.* And Miss Carpenter has such a truely Christjanly amiable disposition that she will be pleasantly situated any where.[18]

My compensation for the past quarter was seventy dolls. Paid for board & washing for eleven weeks—eighteen dolls fifty cts. I have on the list 32 different scholars—but the average attendance was twenty four & they pay only for the actual attendance of each pupil. Was not able to teach writing the last quarter as there were no desks & I deducted something in my charges lest they should say I had not taught all I agreed to but I shall do so no more.

---

[18]Susan A. Lord, who was living in Boston when she applied to the NPEB, first taught in Wisconsin in 1852. She was one of three teachers who went to San Francisco, where she taught at the Benicia Young Ladies Seminary before marrying a judge. Mary S. Arnold from Monmouth, Maine, was teaching in St. Charles, Illinois. Fanny A. Warner, who came from Sunderland, Massachusetts, taught in Aztalan, Wisconsin, until her marriage in 1851 to Alonzo M. Morrison, a lumber dealer in various parts of Wisconsin. S. Augusta Carpenter, who was only nineteen when she went West, returned to her native Greenfield, Massachusetts, sometime before 1854, when she married James Averill.

An other class will have been assembled in H[artford] & scattered before this reaches you. The Oregon class will also be on the boisterous Ocean[19]— busy & anxious hearts those would wish & hope that none would meet with such rebuffs as I did but I dare not for though it was trying to the flesh, yet if God could & would be best glorified in it it was all *right*, & I thank him that it is as well with me as it is. I shall look with some solitude to know if you censure the course which I took with regard to my breach of promise to Col. Love. Be not too severe for my inclination was to go, feeling that I would have more personal comfort & better society.

Throwing myself upon your mercy for sending such a long & illly written letter I will close with my many thanks for your dear letter, & may God spare you long to be a comfort to your friends & us, poor isolated ones so far away from home & friends is the prayer of M. M. Rogers.

[19]Arozina Perkins was in the fall class Martha Rogers mentioned, but the group for Oregon did not

From "Life On the Sea Islands"

ཨ྅ ◆ ོ

Charlotte Forten, 1864

First printed as a two part article in *The Atlantic Monthly,* Charlotte Forten's
(1837–1914) account of teaching recently freed slaves in Port Royal, South
Carolina is both moving and dramatic. Forten was one of a minute number
of northern Black women who made their way southward to teach during
the Civil War. Her observations about the conditions of the former slaves,
their readiness to learn, and the dangers that plague her work as a teacher
are poignant and deeply affecting.

Born to a prosperous and intellectual Black family in Philadelphia, Forten
led an early life of unusual privilege. Her grandfather and father were active in
the abolitionist movement and members of William Lloyd Garrison's Anti-
Slavery Society. Charlotte's father insisted that she be educated at home rather
than in the segregated schools of Philadelphia. For grammar school, Charlotte
Forten was sent to the Higginson Grammar School in Salem, Massachusetts,
and then to the Salem Normal School for a year of teacher training.

Forten found her way to Port Royal in 1862 at the urging of the poet John
Greenleaf Whittier. In 1861, these small sea islands had become the center
of dramatic conflict. President Lincoln had decided to close Southern coasts
from Virginia to Texas in an effort to prevent supplies from reaching
Confederate troops. Union soldiers captured Port Royal first, pushing the
Southern plantation owners off their land, and leaving the Port Royal
district in Northern hands. The 10,000 slaves who were left behind by
retreating Southerners were automatically converted into freedmen.

The education of these new citizens evolved into what came to be called
the Port Royal experiment. Abolitionist groups, in conjunction with the
United States War Department set out to prove that freedmen could be

educated and self-sufficient...and could ultimately fight for the Union cause. Forten spent 2 years working with these men and women in South Carolina, writing letters and journal entries about her experiences with the Island people. A number of those letters were published in *The Liberator*, an abolitionist magazine that had been started in 1831 by William Lloyd Garrison. Others were turned into more formal pieces of journalism, like the story presented here.

Charlotte Forten shared the responsibility of teaching on Port Royal with two other women, Ellen Murray of Milton, Massachusetts and Laura Towne from Shoemaker, Pennsylvania, who Forten described as "the most indispensible person on the place." Forten's journals are filled with descriptions and anecdotes of the lives and culture of the people on the island as well as an interesting account of her meeting with Harriet Tubman, the famous escaped slave who made several daring trips into the South to help other slaves escape on the Underground Railroad.

Forten returned to Philadelphia after her stint in the South. There she spent 12 years as a teacher, and eventually married Francis Grimke, who had been born a slave. Her one child died before the age of one. Forten devoted the rest of her life to writing, missionary work, and to her family.

FROM "LIFE ON THE SEA ISLANDS"

Charlotte Forten, 1864

It was on the afternoon of a warm, murky day late in October that our steamer, the United States, touched the landing at Hilton Head. A motley assemblage had collected on the wharf,—officers, soldiers, and "contrabands" of every size and hue: black was, however, the prevailing color. The first view of Hilton Head is desolate enough,—a long, low, sandy point, stretching out into the sea, with no visible dwellings upon it, except the rows of small white-roofed houses which have lately been built for the freed people....

...From Hilton Head to Beaufort the same long, low line of sandy coast, bordered by trees; formidable gunboats in the distance, and the gray ruins of an old fort, said to have been built by the Huguenots more than two hundred years ago. Arrived at Beaufort, we found that we had not yet reached our journey's end. While waiting for the boat which was to take us to our island of St. Helena, we had a little time to observe the ancient town....

...Little colored children of every hue were playing about the streets, looking as merry and happy as children ought to look,—now that the evil shadow of Slavery no longer hangs over them. Some of the officers we met did not impress us favorably. They talked flippantly, and sneeringly of the negroes, whom they found we had come down to teach, using an epithet more offensive than gentlemanly. They assured us that there was great danger of Rebel attacks, that the yellow fever prevailed to an alarming extent, and that, indeed, the manufacture of coffins was the only business that was at all flourishing at present. Although by no means daunted by these alarming stories, we were glad when the announcement of our boat relieved us from their edifying conversation.

We rowed across to Ladies Island, which adjoins St. Helena, through the splendors of a grand Southern sunset. The gorgeous clouds of crimson and gold were reflected as in a mirror in the smooth, clear waters below. As we glided along, the rich tones of the negro boatmen broke upon the evening stillness,—sweet, strange, and solemn:—

"Jesus make de blind to see,
Jesus make de cripple walk,
Jesus make de deaf to hear.
   Walk in, kind Jesus!
   No man can hender me."

It was nearly dark when we reached the island, and then we had a three-miles' drive through the lonely roads to the house of the superintendent. We thought how easy it would be for a band of guerillas, had they chanced that way, to seize and hang us; but we were in that excited, jubilant state of mind which makes fear impossible, and sang "John Brown" with a will, as we drove through the pines and palmettos. Oh, it was good to sing that song in the very heart of Rebeldom!

...The next morning L. and I were awakened by the cheerful voices of men and women, children and chickens, in the yard below. We ran to the window, and looked out. Women in bright-colored handkerchiefs, some carrying pails on their heads, were crossing the yard, busy with their morning work; children were playing and tumbling around them. On every face there was a look of serenity and cheerfulness. My heart gave a great throb of happiness as I looked at them, and thought, "They are free! so long down-trodden, so long crushed to the earth, but now in their old homes, forever free!" And I thanked God that I had lived to see this day.

After breakfast Miss T. drove us to Oaklands, our future home. The road leading to the house was nearly choked with weeds. The house itself was in a dilapidated condition, and the yard and garden had a sadly neglected look. But there were roses in bloom; we plucked handfuls of feathery, fragrant acacia-blossoms; ivy crept along the ground and under the house. The freed people on the place seemed glad to see us. After talking with them, and giving some directions for cleaning the house, we drove to the school, in which I was to teach. It is kept in the Baptist Church,—a brick building, beautifully situated in a grove of live-oaks. These trees are the first objects that attract one's attention here: not that they are finer than our Northern oaks, but because of the singular gray moss with which every branch is heavily draped. This hanging moss grows on nearly all the trees, but on none so luxuriantly as on the live-oak. The pendants are often four or five feet long, very graceful and beautiful, but giving the trees a solemn, almost funereal look. The school was opened in September. Many of the children had, however, received instruction during the summer. It was evident that they had made very rapid improvement, and we noticed with pleasure how bright and eager to learn many of them seemed....

...The first day at school was rather trying. Most of my children were very small, and consequently restless. Some were too young to learn the alphabet. These little ones were brought to school because the older children—in whose care their parents leave them while at work—could not come without them. We were therefore willing to have them come, although they seemed to have discovered the secret of perpetual motion, and tried one's patience sadly. But after some days of positive, though not severe treatment, order was brought out of chaos, and I found but little difficulty in managing and quieting the tiniest and most restless spirits. I never before saw children so eager to learn, although I had had several years' experience in New-England schools. Coming to school is a constant delight and recreation to them. They come here as other children go to play. The older ones, during the summer, work in the fields from early morning until eleven or twelve o'clock, and then come into school, after their hard toil in the hot sun, as bright and as anxious to learn as ever.

Of course there were some stupid ones, but these are the minority. The majority learn with wonderful rapidity. Many of the grown people are desirous of learning to read. It is wonderful how a people who have been so long crushed to the earth, so imbruted as these have been,—and they are said to be among the most degraded negroes of the South,—can have so great a desire for knowledge, and such a capability for attaining it. One cannot believe that the haughty Anglo-Saxon race, after centuries of such an experience as these people have had, would be very much superior to them. And one's indignation increases against those who, North as well as South, taunt the colored race with inferiority while they themselves use every means in their power to crush and degrade them, denying them every right and privilege, closing against them every avenue of elevation and improvement. Were they, under such circumstances, intellectual and re-fined, they would certainly be vastly superior to any other race that ever existed.

After the lessons, we used to talk freely to the children, often giving them slight sketches of some of the great and good men. Before teaching them the "John Brown" song, which they learned to sing with great spirit, Miss T. told them the story of the brave old man who had died for them. I told them about Toussaint, thinking it well they should know what one of their own color had done for his race. They listened attentively, and seemed to understand. We found it rather hard to keep their attention in school. It is not strange, as they have been so entirely unused to intellectual concentration. It is necessary to interest them every moment, in order to keep their thoughts from wandering. Teaching here is consequently far more fatiguing than at the North. In the church, we had of course but one room in which to hear all the children; and to make one's self heard, when there were often as many as a hundred and forty reciting at once, it was necessary to tax the lungs very severely....

...In the evenings, the children frequently came in to sing and shout for us. These "shouts" are very strange,—in truth, almost indescribable. It is necessary to hear and see in order to have any clear idea of them. The children form a ring, and move around in a kind of shuffling dance, singing all the time. Four or five stand apart, and sing very energetically, clapping their hands, stamping their feet, and rocking their bodies to and fro. These are the musicians, to whose performance the shouters keep perfect time. The grown people on this plantation did not shout, but they do on some of the other plantations. It is very comical to see little children, not more than three or four years old, entering into the performance with all their might. But the shouting of the grown people is rather solemn and impressive than otherwise. We cannot determine whether it has a religious character or not. Some of the people tell us that it has, others that it has not. But as the shouts of the grown people are always in connection with their religious meetings, it is probable that they are the barbarous expression of religion, handed down to them from their African ancestors, and destined to pass away under the influence of Christian teachings. The people on this island have no songs. They sing only hymns, and most of these are sad....

A few days before Christmas, we were delighted at receiving a beautiful Christmas Hymn from Whittier, written by request, especially for our children. They learned it very easily, and enjoyed singing it. We showed them the writer's picture, and told them he was a very good friend of theirs, who felt the deepest interest in them, and had written this hymn expressly for them to sing,—which made them very proud and happy. Early Christmas morning, we were wakened by the people knocking at the doors and windows, and shouting, "Merry Christmas!" After distributing some little presents among them, we went to the church, which had been decorated with holly, pine, cassena, mistletoe, and the hanging moss, and had a very Christmas-like look. The children of our school assembled there, and we gave them the nice, comfortable clothing, and the picture-books, which had been kindly sent by some Philadelphia ladies. There were at least a hundred and fifty children present. It was very pleasant to see their happy, expectant little faces. To them, it was a wonderful Christmas Day,—such as they had never dreamed of before. There was cheerful sunshine without, lighting up the beautiful moss-drapery of the oaks, and looking in joyously through the open windows; and there were bright faces and glad hearts within. The long, dark night of the Past, with all its sorrows and its fears, was forgotten; and for the Future,—the eyes of these freed children see no clouds in it. It is full of sunlight, they think, and they trust in it, perfectly.

After the distribution of gifts, the children were addressed by some of the gentlemen present. They then sang Whittier's Hymn, the "John Brown" song, and several of their own hymns, among them a very singular one, commencing,—

> "I wonder where my mudder gone;
>   Sing, O graveyard!
> Graveyard ought to know me;
>   Ring, Jerusalem!
> Grass grow in de graveyard;
>   Sing, O graveyard!
> Graveyard ought to know me;
>   Ring, Jerusalem!"

They improvise many more words as they sing. It is one of the strangest, most mournful things I ever heard. It is impossible to give any idea of the deep pathos of the refrain—

"Sing, O graveyard!"

In this, and many other hymns, the words seem to have but little meaning; but the tones,—a whole lifetime of despairing sadness is concentrated in them....

...Christmas night, the children came in and had several grand shouts. They were too happy to keep still.

"Oh, Miss, all I want to do is to sing and shout!" said our little pet, Amaretta. And sing and shout she did, to her heart's content.

She read nicely, and was very fond of books. The tiniest children are delighted to get a book in their hands. Many of them already know their letters. The parents are eager to have them learn. They sometimes said to me,—

"Do, Miss, let de chil'en learn eberyting dey can. We nebber hab no chance to learn nuttin', but we wants de chil'en to learn."

They are willing to make sacrifices that their children may attend school. One old woman, who had a large family of children and grandchildren, came regularly to school in the winter, and took her seat among the little ones. She was at least sixty years olds. Another woman—who had one of the best faces I ever saw—came daily, and brought her baby in her arms. It happened to be one of the best babies in the world, a perfect little "model of deportment," and allowed its mother to pursue her studies without interruption....

...Daily the long-oppressed people of these islands are demonstrating their capacity for improvement in learning and labor. What they have accomplished in one short year exceeds our utmost expectations. Still the sky is dark; but through the darkness we can discern a brighter future. We cannot but feel that the day of final and entire deliverance, so long and often so hopelessly prayed for, has at length begun to dawn upon this much-en-during race. An old freedman said to me one day, "De Lord make me suffer long time, Miss. 'Peared like we nebber was gwine to git troo. But now we's free. He bring us all out right at las'." In their darkest hours they have clung to Him, and we know He will not forsake them.

"The poor among men shall rejoice,
For the terrible one is brought to nought."

While writing these pages I am once more nearing Port Royal. The Fortunate Isles of Freedom are before me. I shall again tread the flower-skirted woodpaths of St. Helena, and the sombre pines and bearded oaks shall whisper in the sea-wind their grave welcome. I shall dwell again among "mine own people." I shall gather my scholars about me, and see smiles of greeting break over their dusk faces. My heart sings a song of thanksgiving, at the thought that even I am permitted to do something for a long-abused race, and aid in promoting a higher, holier, and happier life on the Sea Islands.

From "The March of Progress" (set c. 1878)

℘ ◆ ℘

Charles W. Chesnutt, 1901

The conflict presented in this short story by the most well-known Black fiction writer of his generation is one that dramatically underscores the changing profile of the teaching force in the decades following the Civil War. "The March of Progress" illustrates the dilemma of a Black community as it is torn between supporting its elderly White teacher—one who has devoted her life to the education of the freedmen's children—and her young Black pupil, who returns to town after college to educate his own people. It is a realistic dilemma, and one that powerfully illustrates the uniqueness of the teaching profession: No other profession opened its doors so early and so completely to such a range of disenfranchised constituencies. That a woman and a Black man are competing for the same "professional" job in this post-Civil War story is in itself remarkable.

Chesnutt (1858–1932) was born in Cleveland, Ohio, but grew up in Fayetteville, North Carolina, where his family moved in 1866. Early on, Chesnutt's exceptional abilities were recognized by the principal of his local school, a White educator named Robert Harris. When, after the death of Chesnutt's mother, family finances necessitated that he drop out, Harris suggested that the boy instead become a salaried "pupil–teacher." From that point on, Chesnutt spent more time teaching than being taught, and his rise in the profession follows a predictable course: From grammar school instructor, Chesnutt moved on to work in Fayetteville's new normal school; next, he became principal of the normal school. By the mid-1880s, Chesnutt had left the field altogether, moving first to New York City to become a reporter, then to Cleveland to study law. As his writing became more popular and successful, Chesnutt was able to support himself as a novelist and lecturer. He served as a member of Booker T. Washington's Committee of Twelve and as a member of the General Committee of the NAACP.

Much of Chesnutt's journalistic work centered on the theme of racism. His articles helped to remove several racist texts from circulation, and his written protest of A Birth of A Nation was successful in banning that film from the city of Cleveland. In Chesnutt's fiction (particularly in the stories "The Bouquet" and "Cicely's Dream," and the novels The House Behind the Cedars and The Colonel's Dream) ex-slaves, freedmen, and their children are desperate for education. Yet the schools they attend are invariably under-funded and inferior. School terms are necessarily brief and staff and facilities are paltry at best. Chesnutt's writing exposed the ways in which most public funds were redirected to private institutions, leaving Blacks and poor Whites with scant resources. For Black communities, the best alternative was often to find ways to support their own separate schools. Chesnutt's writing shows that although resources were almost nonexistent, the drive and determination of the Black community for education was extraordinary.

FROM "THE MARCH OF PROGRESS" (SET C. 1878)

Charles W. Chesnutt, 1901

The colored people of Patesville had at length gained the object they had for a long time been seeking—the appointment of a committee of themselves to manage the colored schools of the town. They had argued, with some show of reason, that they were most interested in the education of their own children, and in a position to know, bettter than any committee of white men could, what was best for their children's needs. The appointments had been made by the county commissioners during the latter part of the summer, and a week later a meeting was called for the purpose of electing a teacher to take charge of the grammar school at the beginning of the fall term.

The committee consisted of Frank Gillespie, or "Glaspy," a barber, who took an active part in local politics; Bob Cotten, a blacksmith, who owned several houses and was looked upon as a substantial citizen; and Abe Johnson, commonly called "Ole Abe" or "Uncle Abe," who had a large family, and drove a dray, and did odd jobs of hauling; he was also a class-leader in the Methodist church. The committee had been chosen from among a number of candidates—Gillespie on account of his political stand-ing, Cotten as representing the solid element of the colored population, and Old Abe, with democratic impartiality, as likely to satisfy the humbler class of a humble people. While the choice had not pleased everybody,—for instance, some of the other applicants,—it was acquiesced in with general satisfaction. The first meeting of the new committee was of great public interest, partly by reason of its novelty, but chiefly because there were two candidates for the position of teacher of the grammar school.

The former teacher, Miss Henrietta Noble, had applied for the school. She had taught the colored children of Patesville for fifteen years. When the Freedman's Bureau, after the military occupation of North Carolina, had called for volunteers to teach the children of the freedmen, Henrietta Noble had offered her services. Brought up in a New England household by parents who taught her to fear God and love her fellowmen, she had seen her father's body brought home from a Southern battle-field and laid to rest in the village cemetary; and a short six months later she had buried her mother by his side. Henrietta had no brothers or sisters, and her nearest relatives were cousins living in the far West. The only human being in whom she felt any special personal interest was a certain captain in her father's regiment, who had paid her some attention. She had loved this man deeply, in a maidenly, modest way; but he had gone away without speaking, and had not since written. He had escaped the fate of many others, and at the close of the war was alive and well, stationed in some Southern garrison.

When her mother died, Henrietta had found herself possessed only of the house where she lived and the furniture it contained, neither being of much value, and she was thrown upon her own resources for a livelihood. She had a fair education and had read many good books. It was not easy to find employment such as she desired. She wrote to her Western cousins, and they advised her to come to them, as they thought they could do something for her if she went there. She had almost decided to accept their offer, when the demand arose for teachers in the South. Whether impelled by some strain of adventurous blood from a Pilgrim ancestry, or by a sensitive pride that shrank from dependence, or by some dim and unacknowledged hope that she might sometime, somewhere, somehow meet Captain Carey—whether from one of these motives or a combination of them all, joined to something of the missionary spirit, she decided to go South, and wrote to her cousins declining their friendly offer.

She had come to Patesville when the children were mostly a mob of dirty little beggars. She had distributed among them the cast-off clothing that came from their friends in the North; she had taught them to wash their faces and to comb their hair; and patiently, year after year, she had labored to instruct them in the rudiments of learning and the first principles of religion and morality. And she had not wrought in vain. Other agencies, it is true, had in time cooperated with her efforts, but any one who had watched the current of events must have been compelled to admit that the very fair progress of the colored people of Patesville in the fifteen years following emancipation had been due chiefly to the unselfish labors of Henrietta Noble, and that her nature did not belie her name.

Fifteen years is a long time. Miss Noble had never met Captain Carey; and when she learned later that he had married a Southern girl in the neighborhood of his post, she had shed her tears in secret and banished his image from her heart. She had lived a lonely life. The white people of the town, though they learned in time to respect her and to value her work, had never recognized her existence by more than the mere external courtesy shown by any community to one who lives in the midst of it. The situation was at first, of course, so strained that she did not expect sympathy from the white people; and later when time had smoothed over some of the asperities of war, her work had so engaged her that she had not had time to pine over her social exclusion. Once or twice nature had asserted itself, and she had longed for her own kind, and had visited her New England home. But her circle of friends was broken up, and she did not find much pleasure in boarding-house life; and on her last visit to the North but one, she had felt so lonely that she had longed for the dark faces of her pupils, and had welcomed with pleasure the hour when her task should be resumed.

But for several reasons the school at Patesville was of more importance to Miss Noble at this particular time than it ever had been before. During the last few years her health had not been good. An affection of the heart similar to that from which her mother had died, while not interfering perceptibly with her work, had grown from bad to worse, aggravated by close application to her duties, until it had caused her grave alarm. She did not have perfect confidence in the skill of the Patesville physicians, and to obtain the best medical advice had gone to New York during the summer, remaining there a month under the treatment of an eminent specialist. This, of course, had been expensive and had absorbed the savings of years from a small salary; and when the time came for her to return to Patesville, she was reduced, after paying her traveling expenses, to her last ten-dollar note.

"It is very fortunate," the great man had said at her last visit, "that circumstances permit you to live in the South, for I am afraid you could not endure a Northern winter. You are getting along very well now, and if you will take care of yourself and avoid excitement, you will be better." He said to himself as she went away: "It's only a matter of time, but that is true about us all; and a wise physician does as much good by what he withholds as by what he tells."

Miss Noble had not anticipated any trouble about the school. When she went away the same committee of white men was in charge that had controlled the school since it had become part of the public-school system of the State on the withdrawal of support from the Freedmen's Bureau. While there had been no formal engagement made for the next year, when she had last seen the chairman before she went away, he had remarked that she was looking rather fagged out, had bidden her good-by, and had hoped to see her much improved when she returned. She had left her house in the care of the colored woman who lived with her and did her housework, assuming, of course, that she would take up her work again in autumn.

She was much surprised at first, and later alarmed, to find a rival for her position as teacher of the grammar school. Many of her friends and pupils had called on her since her return, and she had met a number of the people at the colored Methodist church, where she taught in the Sunday-school. She had many friends and supporters, but she soon found out that her opponent had considerable strength. There had been a time when she would have withdrawn and left him a clear field, but at the present moment it was almost a matter of life and death to her—certainly the matter of earning a living—to secure the appointment.

The other candidate was a young man who in former years had been one of Miss Noble's brightest pupils. When he had finished his course in the grammar school, his parents, with considerable sacrifice, had sent him to a college for colored youth. He had studied diligently, had worked industriously during his vacations, sometimes at manual labor, sometimes teaching a country school, and in due time had been graduated from his college with honors. He had come home at the end of his school life, and was very naturally seeking the employment for which he had fitted himself. He was a "bright" mulatto, with straight hair, an intelligent face, and a well-set figure. He had acquired some of the marks of culture, wore a frock-coat and a high collar, parted his hair in the middle, and showed by his manner that he thought a good deal of himself. He was the popular candidate among the progressive element of his people, and rather confidently expected the appointment.

The meeting of the committee was held in the Methodist church, where, in fact, the grammar school was taught, for want of a separate school-house. After the preliminary steps to effect an organization, Mr. Gillespie, who had been elected chairman, took the floor.

"The principal business to be brought befo' the meet'n' this evenin'," he said, "is the selection of a teacher for our grammar school for the ensuin' year. Two candidates have filed applications, which, if there is no objection, I will read to the committee. The first is from Miss Noble, who has been a teacher ever since the grammar school was started."

He then read Miss Noble's letter, in which she called attention to her long years of service, to her need of the position, and to her affection for the pupils, and made formal application for the school for the next year. She did not, from motives of self-respect, make known the extremity of her need, nor did she mention the condition of her health, as it might have been used as an argument against her retention.

Mr. Gillespie then read the application of the other candidate, Andrew J. Williams. Mr. Williams set out in detail his qualifications for the position: his degree from Riddle University; his familiarity with the dead and living languages and the higher mathematics; his views of discipline; and a peroration in which he expressed the desire to devote himself to the elevation of his race and assist the march of progress through the medium of the Patesville grammar school. The letter was well written in a bold, round hand, with many flourishes, and looked very aggressive and overbearing as it lay on the table by the side of the sheet of small note-paper in Miss Noble's faint and somewhat cramped handwriting.

"You have heard the readin' of the applications," said the chairman. "Gentlemen, what is yo' pleasure?"

There being no immmediate response, the chairman continued:

"As this is a matter of consid'able importance, involvin' not only the welfare of our schools, but the progress of our race, an' as our action is liable to be criticized, whatever we decide, perhaps we had better discuss the subjec' befo' we act. If nobody else had anything to obse've, I will make a few remarks."

Mr. Gillespie cleared his throat, and assuming an oratorical attitude, proceeded:

"The time has come in the history of our people when we should stand together. In this age of organization the march of progress requires that we help ourselves, or be left forever behind. Ever since the war we have been sendin' our child'n to school an' educatin' 'em; an' now the time has come when they are leavin' the schools an' colleges, an' are ready to go to work. An' what are they goin' to do? The white people won't hire 'em as clerks in their sto's an' factories an' mills, an' we have no sto's or factories or mills of our own. They can't be lawyers or doctors yet, because we haven't got the money to send 'em to medical colleges an' law schools. We can't elect many of 'em to office, for various reasons. There's just two things they can find to do—to preach in our own pulpits, an' teach in our own schools. If it wasn't for that, they'd have to go on forever waitin' on white folks, like their fo'fathers have done, because they couldn't help it. If we expect our race to progress, we must educate our young men an' women. If we want to encourage 'em to get education, we must find 'em employment when they are educated. We have now an opportunity to do this in the case of our young friend an' fellow citizen, Mr. Williams, whose eloquent an' fine-lookin' letter ought to make us feel proud of him an' of our race.

"Of co'se there are two sides to the question. We have got to consider the claims of Miss Noble. She has been with us a long time an' has done much good for our people, an' we'll never forget her work an' friendship. But, after all, she has been paid for it; she has got her salary regularly an' for a long time, an' she has probably saved somethin', for we all know she hasn't lived high'; an', for all we know, she may have had somethin' left by her parents. An' then again, she's white, an' has got her own people to look after her; they've got all the money an' all the offices an' all the everythin',—all that they've made an' all that we've made for fo'hundred years,—an' they sho'ly would look out for her. If she don't get this school, there's probably a dozen others she can get at the North. An' another thing: she is gettin' rather feeble, an it 'pears to me she's hardly able to stand teachin' so many child'n, an' a long rest might be the best thing in the world for her."

"Now, gentlemen, that's the situation. Shall we keep Miss Noble, or shall we stand by our own people? It seems to me there can hardly be but one answer. Self-preservation is the first law of nature. Are there any other remarks?"

Old Abe was moving restlessly in his seat. He did not say anything, however, and the chairman turned to the other member.

"Brother Cotten, what is yo' opinion of the question befo' the board?"

Mr. Cotten rose with the slowness and dignity becoming a substantial citizen, and observed:

"I think the remarks of the chairman have great weight. We all have nothin' but kind feelin's fer Miss Noble, an' I came here tonight somewhat undecided how to vote on this question. But after listenin' to the just an' forcible arguments of Brother Glaspy, it 'pears to me that, after all, the question befo' us is not a matter of feelin', but of business. As a business man, I am inclined to think Brother Glaspy is right. If we don't help ourselves when we get a chance, who is goin' to help us?"

"That bein' the case," said the chairman, "shall we proceed to a vote? All who favor the election of Brother Williams—"

At this point Old Abe, with much preliminary shuffling, stood up in his place and interrupted the speaker.

"Mr. Chuhman," he said, "I s'pose I has a right ter speak in dis meet'n? I s'pose I is a member er dis committee?"

"Certainly, Brother Johnson, certainly; we shall be glad to hear from you."

"I s'pose I's got a right ter speak my min', ef I is po' an' black, an' don' weah as good clo's as some other members er de committee?"

"Most assuredly, Brother Johnson," answered the chairman, with a barber's suavity, "you have as much right to be heard as any one else. There was no intention of cuttin' you off."

"I s'pose," continued Abe, "dat a man wid fo'teen child'n kin be 'lowed ter hab somethin' ter say 'bout de schools er dis town?"

"I am sorry, Brother Johnson, that you should feel slighted, but there was no intention to igno' yo' rights. The committee will be please' to have you ventilate yo' views."

"Ef it's all be'n an' done reco'nized an' 'cided dat I's got de right ter be heared in dis meet'n, I'll say w'at I has ter say, an' it won't take me long ter say it. Ef I should try ter tell all de things dat Miss Noble has done fer de niggers er dis town, it'd take me till ter-morrer mawnin'. Fer fifteen long yeahs I has watched her incomin's an' her outgoin's. Her daddy was a Yankee kunnel, who died fighting fer ou' freedom. She come heah when we—yas, Mr. Chuhman, when you an' Br'er Cotten—was jest sot free, an' when none er us did n'have a rag ter ou' backs. She come heah, an' she tuk yo' child'n an' my child'n, an she teached 'em sense an' manners an' religion an' book-l'arnin'. When she come heah we didn' hab no chu'ch. Who writ up No'th an' got a preacher sent to us, an' de fun's ter buil' dis same chu'ch-house we're settin' in ternight? Who got de money f'm de Bureau to s'port de school? An' when dat was stop', who got de money f'm de Peabody Fun'? Talk about Miss Noble gittin' a sal'ry! Who paid dat sal'ry up to five years ago? Not one dollah of it come outer ou' pockets!

"An' den, w'at did she git fer de yuther things she done? Who paid fer teachin' de Sunday-school? Who paid her fer de gals she kep' f'm thrown' deyse'ves away? Who paid fer de boys she kep' outer jail? I had a son dat seemed to hab made up his min' ter go straight ter hell. I made him go ter Sunday-school, an' somethin' dat woman said teched his heart, an' he behaved hisse'f, an' I ain' got no reason fer ter be 'shame er 'im. An' I can 'member, Br'er Cotten, when you did n'own fo' houses an' a fahm. An' when yo' fus wife was sick, who sot by her bedside an' read de Good Book ter'er, w'en dey wuz n'nobody else knowed how ter read it, an' comforted her on her way across de col', dahk ribber? An' dat ain' all I kin 'member, Mr. Chuhman! When yo' gal Fanny was a baby, an' sick, an' nobody knowed what was de matter wid'er, who sent fer a doctor, an' paid 'im fer comin', an' who he'ped nuss dat chile, an' tol' yo' wife w'at ter do, an' save' dat chile's life, jes as sho'as de Lawd had save' my soul?

"An' now, aftuh fifteen yeahs o' slavin' fer us, who ain't got no claim on her, aftuh fifteen yeahs dat she has libbed 'mongs' us an' made herse'f one of us, an endyoed havin' her own people look down on her, aftuh she has growed ole an' gray wukkin' fer us an' our child'en, we talk erbout turnin' 'er out like a' ole hoss ter die! It 'pears ter me some folks has po' mem'ries! Whar would we' a' be'n ef her folks at de No'th had n' 'membered us no bettuh? An' we had n' done nothin', fer dem to 'member us fer. De man dat kin fergit w'at Miss Noble has done fer dis town is unworthy de name er nigger! He oughter die an' make room fer some 'spectacle dog!

"Br'er Glaspy says we got a' educated young man, an' we mus' gib him sump'n' ter do. Let him wait; ef I reads de signs right he won't hab ter wait long fer dis job. Let him teach in de primary schools, er in de country; an' ef he can't do dat, let 'im work awhile. It don't hahm a' educated man ter work a little; his fo'fathers has worked fer hund'eds of years, an' we's worked, an' we're heah yet, an' we're free, an' we's gettin' ou' own houses an' lots an' hosses an' cows—an' ou' educated young men. But don't let de fus thing we do as a committee be somethin' we ought ter be 'shamed of as long as we lib. I votes fer Miss Noble, fus, las', an' all de time!"

When Old Abe sat down the chairman's face bore a troubled look. He remembered how his baby girl, the first of his children that he could really call his own, that no master could hold a prior claim upon, lay dying in the arms of his distracted young wife, and how the thin, homely, and short-sighted white teacher had come like an angel into his cabin, and had brought back the little one from the verge of the grave. The child was a young woman now, and Gillespie had well-founded hopes of securing the superior young Williams for a son-in-law; and he realized with something of shame that this later ambition had so dazzled his eyes for a moment as to obscure the memory of earlier days.

Mr. Cotten, too, had not been unmoved, and there were tears in his eyes as he recalled how his first wife, Nancy, who had borne with him the privations of slavery, had passed away, with the teacher's hand in hers, before she had been able to enjoy the fruits of liberty. For they had loved one another much, and her death had been to them both a hard and bitter thing. And, as Old Abe spoke, he could remember, as distinctly as though they had been spoken but an hour before, the words of comfort that the teacher had whispered to Nancy in her dying hour and to him in his bereavement.

"On consideration, Mr. Chairman," he said, with an effort to hide a suspicious tremor in his voice and to speak with the dignity consistent with his character as a substantial citizen, "I wish to record my vote for Miss Noble."

"The chair," said Gillepsie, yielding gracefully to the majority, and greatly relieved that the responsibility of his candidate's defeat lay elsewhere, "will make the vote unanimous, and will appoint Brother Cotten and Brother Johnson a committee to step round the corner to Miss Noble's and notify her of her election."

The two committeemen put on their hats, and, accompanied by several people who had been waiting at the door to hear the result of the meeting, went around the corner to Miss Noble's house, a distance of a block or two away. The house was lighted, so they knew she had not gone to bed. They went in at the gate, and Cotten knocked at the door.

The colored maid opened it.

"Is Miss Noble home?" said Cotten.

"Yes; come in. She's waitin' ter hear from the committee."

The woman showed them into the parlor. Miss Noble rose from her seat by the table, where she had been reading, and came forward to meet them. They did not for a moment observe, as she took a step toward them, that her footsteps wavered. In her agitation she was scarcely aware of it herself.

"Miss Noble," announced Cotten, "we have come to let you know that you have be'n 'lected teacher of the grammar school fer the next year."

"Thank you; oh, thank you so much!" she said. "I am very glad. Mary"—she put her hand to her side suddenly and tottered—"Mary, will you—"

A spasm of pain contracted her face and cut short her speech. She would have fallen had Old Abe not caught her and, with Mary's help, laid her on a couch.

The remedies applied by Mary, and by the physician who was hastily summoned, proved unavailing. The teacher did not regain consciousness.

If it be given to those whose eyes have closed in death to linger regretfully for a while about their earthly tenement, or from some higher vantage-ground to look down upon it, then Henrietta Noble's tolerant spirit must have felt, mingling with its regret, a compensating thrill of pleasure; for not only those for whom she had labored sorrowed for her, but the people of her own race, many of whom, in the blindness of their pride, would not admit during her life that she served them also, saw so much clearer now that they took charge of her poor clay, and did it gentle reverence, and laid it tenderly away amid the dust of their loved and honored dead.

Two weeks after Miss Noble's funeral the other candidate took charge of the grammar school, which went without any further obstacles to the march of progress.

Part II
Questions and Activities

❧ ◆ ☙

1. What do you think motivated Cynthia Bishop and Martha Rogers to teach where they did? What would be the equivalent kind of teaching assignment for a middle-class White woman today? What might motivate such a woman today to accept a difficult assignment like Bishop's and Rogers'?

2. In Charles Chesnutt's "The March of Progress," the school committee votes to offer the job to the elderly, White Miss Noble. Do you agree or disagree with that decision? Think of a contemporary parallel to this situation in a modern urban community. Which candidate would you endorse for the job and why?

3. What, if any, aspects of Bronson Alcott's method still seem appropriate for today's classroom?

4. Compare attitudes toward discipline in the Early Republic with those manifest in the stories in this section. How do you account for the differences? Do any of the common school attitudes toward discipline persist in classrooms today? How and in what ways?

5. Read Part II of Nancy Hoffman's book, *Woman's True Profession*, and compare Charlotte Forten's experiences as a Black woman, teaching freedmen in the South, with the experiences of other White women doing the same work.

6. Elizabeth Palmer Peabody's excerpt about Bronson Alcott's school, and the stories by Whitman and Eggleston all deal with the subject of classroom discipline. Write a "philosophy of classroom discipline" that you think all three of these individuals would agree with and accept.

SUGGESTED READINGS

Hoffman, N. *Woman's "True" Profession: Voices From the History of Teaching* (New York: Feminist Press, 1981).

Kaestle, C. *Pillars of the Republic: Common Schools and American Society, 1780–1860* (New York: Hill and Wang, 1983).

Kaufman, P. W. *Women Teachers on the Frontier* (New Haven: Yale University Press, 1984).

Stevenson, B. (ed.) *The Journals of Charlotte Forten Grimke* (New York: Oxford University Press, 1988).

Tyack, D. B. *The One Best System: A History of American Urban Education* (Boston: Harvard University Press, 1974). See Part Two, "From Village School to Urban System: Bureaucratization in the Nineteenth Century."

Scho ol Boys correcting their Master

FIG. 1. Schoolboys correcting their master in a colonial classroom (1794).
Reprinted courtesy of the American Antiquarian Society.

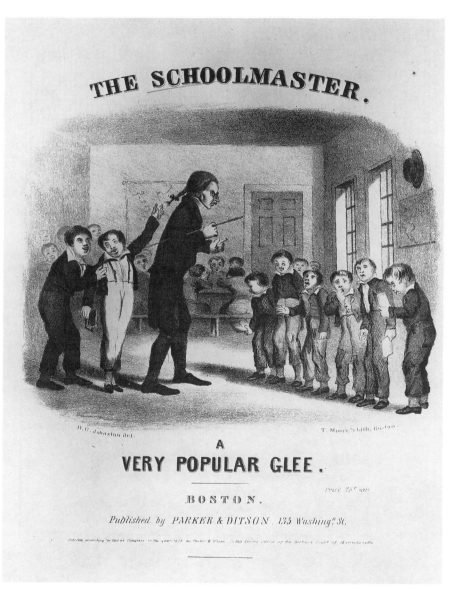

FIG. 2. An early New England schoolroom scene. Lithograph by T. Moore after David Claypoole Johnston (1839). Reprinted courtesy of the American Antiquarian Society.

SEA-ISLAND SCHOOL, No. 1.—ST. HELENA ISLAND. ESTABLISHED APRIL, 1862.

VAN-INGEN—SNYDER

Supported by the Pennsylvania Branch

TEACHERS { MISS LAURA M. TOWNE,
 " ELLEN MURRAY,
 MRS. HARRIOT W. RUGGLES.

FIG. 3. The Sea Island School on St. Helena Island, est. 1862. Artist: Garrison. Taken from the Sophia Smith collection, Smith College, Northampton, MA. Reprinted with permission from Van-Ingen-Snyder; part of the PA Branch of the American Freedman's Union Commission flyer.

FIG. 4. "The Noon Recess," a wood engraving from a sketch by Winslow Homer (1873). Reprinted with permission from the State Historical Society of Wisconsin.

FIG. 5. A late 19th century photograph of the interior of a schoolroom in Whiterock, Iowa. Photo courtesy of the State Historical Society of Iowa—Des Moines.

FIG. 6. The Pleasant Ridge School in Pleasant Ridge, Iowa (circa 1890). Photo courtesy of the State Historical Society of Iowa—Des Moines.

FIG. 7. Anne Sullivan and Helen Keller. Taken from the Sophia Smith collection, Smith College, Northampton, MA.

FIG. 8.   A drawing of Hull-House as it appeared in 1910. Taken from the Sophia Smith collection, Smith College, Northampton, MA. From *Autobiographical Notes Upon Twenty Years at Hull-House* by Jane Addams.

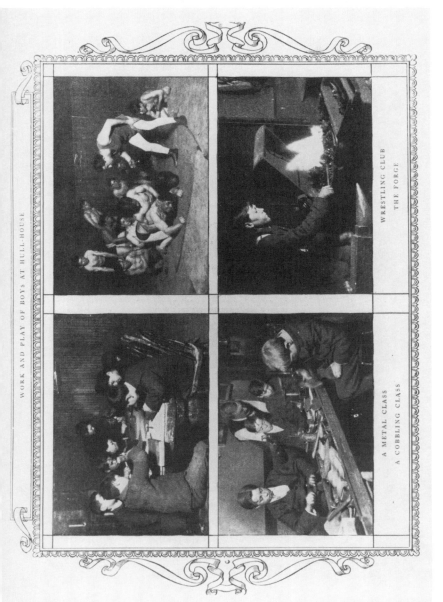

FIG. 9. The Progressive curriculum at Hull-House. Taken from the Sophia Smith collection, Smith College, Northampton, MA. From *Autobiographical Notes Upon Twenty Years at Hull-House* by Jane Addams.

FIG. 10. The American teacher at midcentury. A *Saturday Evening Post* cover by Norman Rockwell (1956). Reprinted with permission of the Norman Rockwell Family Trust. Copyright © 1956 by the Norman Rockwell Trust.

Part III

"The Heart Is the Teacher":
The Teacher in The Progressive Era

The years between 1880 and 1945 marked a period of intense change in American schools. In virtually every respect, public education underwent dramatic evolution: curriculum expanded, methodologies of teaching became more innovative and "scientific," the population within the public schools changed markedly, and the teaching force continued to evolve. No period in American public schooling approaches the Progressive era in the richness and speed of its innovation. Indeed, many believe that the first years of the 20th century represent the high point in America's egalitarian experiment with mass public education.

As Lawrence Cremin pointed out in *The Transformation of the School*, Progressivism itself began as a social movement. The years following the Civil War were characterized by a series of social and cultural changes that necessarily impacted all aspects of American life. In the last decades of the 19th century, urbanization and industrialization brought radical change. As foreign markets expanded and factories proliferated, Americans moved into the cities in unprecedented numbers. By 1900, one in every three Americans lived in a city, and many of those cities were immense. The rate of urban growth was dramatically illustrated by census figures for New York City where, between the years 1860 and 1914, population rose from 850,000 to 4 million. Rural Americans moving into these vast metropolises were confronted with a great range of problems. Traditional family values quickly evaporated in the urban centers. Where small-town America had been homogeneous and stable, city life was mobile, impersonal, and multicultural. Skills that were valued in the rural community were useless in the city. Factory work, as social critics and reformers would point out, was alienating and, in many cases, exploitative.

The problems of city life were compounded by another powerful social phenonemon: Mass immigration in the last years of the 19th century changed the face of the American city as never before. The immigrants who had come to America in earlier decades were from regions of northern and western Europe where customs, languages, and physical traits did not radically differ from those of the founding fathers. Although Irish Catholics arriving in the 1830s and 1840s had resisted religious assimilation, they had worked themselves into the fabric of American culture by the turn of the century, and posed less threat to the Protestant mainstream. The new immigrants, however, were of a wholly different sort. Beginning in 1882, great waves of Russian and eastern European refugees—more than 10 million in all—flooded the American shores. Poles, Bohemians, Rumanians, Greeks, and Hungarians congregated in the cities, forming impoverished communities of their own along city blocks. The new immigrants, sensing the hostility of the native born, resisted assimilation, clinging tenaciously to old-world languages, mores, and political orientations. The response of Protestant Americans was often in the form of prejudice and racism.

As in the Common School period, but with a new ferocity, reformers and politicians turned to the public schools to Americanize the new citizens. Compulsory education laws spread after 1852, when Massachusetts led the nation in requiring some schooling for all children, ages 8 to 14. By 1890, 27 states had compulsory education laws, and by 1918, all states had passed equivalent legislation.

So it was that vast numbers of non-English-speaking children, many poor and hungry, entered the public school system. The mandate for the teacher was to turn this varied, disordered, and ambivalent mass of humanity into a purely American product, a mandate that gained urgency as the numbers of immigrants increased and as philosophers publically considered the consequences of neglecting their education. Social Darwinists like Herbert Spencer and William Torrey Harris exhorted schools to provide an ethics-based, assimilationist curriculum that would, in Harris's words, "estrange" the child from his natural, animal nature. "Education," wrote Harris, "is the process of the adoption of the social order in place of one's mere animal caprice" (Rippa, 1988, p. 176).

A similar attitude prevailed with regard to other marginal groups in the United States, most notably, the Native American and the African American. Toward the end of the 19th century, reformers turned their attention to the "plight" of the American Indian by launching an aggressive campaign to assimilate the remaining tribal youth in White-run schools. Supported by federal funds channeled through the Bureau of Indian Affairs, two kinds of schools were established for this purpose: reservation schools, usually located close to where the Indians resided; and boarding schools, built far away from the tribal communities. Both kinds of institutions repudiated the tribal culture and history, and sought to instill, instead, lessons in American patriotism and White vocational skills, like carpentry and housekeeping. Although sometimes bathed in humanistic rhetoric, the agenda of the agencies that established such schools was clearly to promote the eradication of the American Indian culture.

Black Americans also gained little from the expansion of schooling during the Progressive era. Indeed, the rise of Jim Crow laws after the turn of the century actually set back the cause of Black education for decades to come. Schools for Black youth in the South received little or no state aid, White teachers rarely chose to teach in them, and formally educated Black teachers were hard to find. The physical conditions of many of these schools were utterly abysmal. In the North, de facto segregation again made for sharp discrepancies between Black and White schools. Although record numbers of children, of all ethnicities, were now entering schools and remaining there at least through Grade 6, bureaucrats and administrators did little to acknowledge the differences between them, or respond to their varied needs.

At the same time that conservative voices were pressing for assimilation, however, another strand of Progressivism—more humanistic and liberal—was gaining ground. For individuals like Jane Addams and John Dewey, the new immigrant population required that educators rethink the value of old lessons, and consider ways to make schooling more responsive to the real needs of students. For Addams, that meant the creation of settlement houses—large-scale communities of learning in which all aspects of life were addressed and all ages and nationalities were welcome. Addams' Hull House in Chicago provided a great range of services to newly arrived immigrants and their families. Hull House produced maps and newspapers, it provided the first public playground for children, the first juvenile court, and the first public bath houses. Hull House "clubs" kept immigrant children off the streets. There was a Hull House Museum, a coal purchasing cooperative, an office for investigating public health problems. Perhaps most importantly, however, Addams' program attempted to systematically acknowledge and celebrate the diversity of her clientele. Instead of renouncing the customs and cultures of the many immigrant groups served by the settlement, Addams chose to tap that diversity as a vital component of the Hull House program. Classes in foreign languages ran beside English classes. Workshops in Polish cooking or Ukrainian handicrafts co-existed with practical seminars on how to negotiate with a landlord. Addams' deeply held belief that culture could be democratized without being debased was a cornerstone of the new Progressive approach to education.

Other key aspects of Progressivism could be seen in the alternative methodologies that were developed and disseminated in schools of education. Child-centeredness—a concern for the psychological and developmental needs of individual children—gained popular support in schools as the theories of Francis Parker, John Dewey, and William Heard Kilpatrick were translated into curriculum. With its roots in the teachings of Rousseau and Pestalozzi, the child-centered movement focused on nurturing such character traits as creativity and curiosity. "Learning by doing," the inverse of old-style rote instruction, was combined by the Progressives with a commitment to the teaching of democratic principles and citizenship. The resulting curriculum was a truly modern and multicultural amalgam, an approach to schooling designed to meet the needs of immigrant and native born alike.

The humanistic rhetoric of Progressivism did not extend, however, to the treatment of teachers. Just when curriculum grew more liberal and flexible for students, new contraints were imposed on those who taught them. Small, ungraded schools had given way to large, graded institutions run by increasingly complex bureaucracies, governed by "scientific" laws of organizational behavior. Many of the newly trained school administrators (who, ironically, called themselves "Progressives") became tyrants, wielding the power of "scientifically derived" rules of pedagogy over powerless teachers. Power issues were irritated by the growing gender distinctions between teachers and administrators during these years. By 1880, 57.2% of teachers were female; by 1920, that number had increased to more than 86%. At the same time, newly created principalships, assistant principalships, superintendencies, and other central office positions were assumed almost exclusively by men. Hence, a two-tier system of workers and managers became entrenched in these years—a system that had tied to it sharp distinctions of power, prestige, and income.

The irony embedded in such a two-tier system was not lost on many of the key intellectual figures of the day. John Dewey recognized the unlikely possibility that "the views of the body of teachers, in most cities and towns of the United States, will at the present time have any real, positive, constructive influence in determining the basic educational policy of the schools of their communities..." (Dewey, 1919, p. 428). Activists like Margaret Haley and Ella Flagg Young wondered at the irony of a school system that taught principles of democracy while treating its own employees like victims of a fascist regime. Observations like these led, in the first decades of the 20th century to the formation of unions, and to the first attempts to agitate for teacher pensions, improved working conditions, and equal pay for equal work. Inspired by the abuses of a new system that treated them like children, teachers began to unite, for the first time, as professionals.

The stories in this section of the book consider many aspects of the Progressive Movement in education as they apply to teachers and teaching. Progressive ideas that are illustrated here include a range of tales about immigrant schooling, both in the settlement house and in the public school; the new child-centered methodologies; and the tyranny of teacher supervisors. The memoirs of Anne Sullivan, Helen Keller's brilliant teacher, offer yet another view of both diversity and innovation in education. It is Sullivan's concern for every aspect of her pupil's well-being that marks her as an archetypal Progressive educator.

It should be noted, however, that the focus of Part III is largely on the exceptional aspects of Progressivism—those traits in the movement that have helped to characterize this period as a golden age in American education. Certainly not every teacher was a champion of immigrant children, nor was every school a center for humanistic inquiry. Still, the Progressive period stands as a moment when some of the nation's greatest intellectuals turned their attention to the problems of schooling, and when the work of teachers, for better or worse, became transformed into something close to a genuine profession.

From *"The Letters of Anne Sullivan,"* 1887

ঞ ◆ েঃ

Helen Keller (1880–1968) was 19 months old when a childhood illness claimed both her sight and hearing. Trapped in a dark, silent world, Keller became, in the next 6 years of her life, increasingly wild and unmanageable. When their daughter turned 7, Helen Keller's parents contacted the famous Perkins Institution for the Blind in Boston, requesting a private tutor for the child who clearly longed to communicate with the outside world. "The most important day I remember in all my life," Keller would later write," was the day my teacher, Anne Mansfield Sullivan, came to me." Sullivan not only taught Keller to read braille and to communicate through sign and speech, she became her pupil's lifelong friend and companion. The relationship of teacher and student—both brilliant women, with powerful, independent spirits—comes through vividly in Helen's autobiographies and in Anne Sullivan's letters.

Sullivan began, herself, as a student at the Perkins Institution, after a childhood illness left her almost blind. Earlier in the century, Perkins had gained worldwide fame because of Dr. Samuel Gridley Howe's pioneering work with Laura Bridgman, a girl much like Helen Keller, who made remarkable progress through a combination of lessons in braille and the manual alphabet. During her years at Perkins, Sullivan became familiar with Howe's teaching techniques, and brought those same techniques into the Keller home. Her sensitive methodology and her generous spirit made her an ideal teacher: Helen Keller went on to earn her B. A. at Radcliffe and to spend her long and influential career as a social reformer and crusader for the rights of the disenfranchised. In fact, Keller was an outspoken socialist throughout her adult life, although this aspect of her life is not generally known.

Anne Sullivan's success in teaching her pupil has been immortalized not only in Helen's and Anne's writing, but also in numerous essays and films on the subject. The passages presented here are excerpted from Anne Sullivan's letters to her friend, Sophia C. Hopkins, at Perkins Institute. The letters were first published as a supplement to Helen Keller's autobiography, *The Story of My Life* (1905). They chronicle Sullivan's first meeting with Helen, her efforts to discipline the girl, and the moment of breakthrough

161

when Helen finally understood the relationship between the manual alphabet and the world of things and ideas. The blend here of intense, individualized instruction and high emotion makes the story a compelling example of the Progressive sensibility in action.

FROM *"THE LETTERS OF ANNE SULLIVAN,"* 1887

It was 6:30 when I reached Tuscumbia. I found Mrs. Keller and Mr. James Keller waiting for me. They said somebody had met every train for two days. The drive from the station to the house, a distance of one mile, was very lovely and restful. I was surprised to find Mrs. Keller a very young-looking woman, not much older than myself, I should think. Captain Keller met us in the yard and gave me a cheery welcome and a hearty handshake. My first question was, "Where is Helen?" I tried with all my might to control the eagerness that made me tremble so that I could hardly walk. As we approached the house I saw a child standing in the doorway, and Captain Keller said, "There she is. She has known all day that some one was expected, and she has been wild ever since her mother went to the station for you." I had scarcely put my foot on the steps, when she rushed toward me with such force that she would have thrown me backward if Captain Keller had not been behind me. She felt my face and dress and my bag, which she took out of my hand and tried to open. It did not open easily, and she felt carefully to see if there was a keyhole. Finding that there was, she turned to me, making the sign of turning a key and pointing to the bag. Her mother interfered at this point and showed Helen by signs that she must not touch the bag. Her face flushed, and when her mother attempted to take the bag from her, she grew very angry. I attracted her attention by showing her my watch and letting her hold it in her hand. Instantly the tempest subsided, and we went upstairs together. Here I opened the bag, and she went through it eagerly, probably expecting to find something to eat. Friends had probably brought her candy in their bags, and she expected to find some in mine. I made her understand, by pointing to a trunk in the hall and to myself and nodding my head, that I had a trunk, and then made the sign that she had used for eating, and nodded again. She understood in a flash and ran downstairs to tell her mother, by means of emphatic signs, that there was some candy in a trunk for her. She returned in a few minutes and helped me put away my things. It was too comical to see her put on my bonnet and cock her head first on one side, then on the other, and look in the mirror, just as if she could see. Somehow I had expected to see a pale, delicate child—I suppose I got the idea from Dr. Howe's description of Laura Bridgman when she came to the Institution. But there's nothing pale or delicate about Helen. She is large, strong, and ruddy, and as unrestrained in her movements as a young colt. She has none of those nervous habits that are so noticeable and so distressing in blind children. Her body is well formed and vigorous, and Mrs. Keller says she has not been ill a day since the illness that deprived her of her sight and hearing. She has a fine head, and it is set on her shoulders just right. Her face is hard to describe. It is intelligent, but lacks mobility, or soul, or something. Her mouth is large and finely shaped. You see at a glance that she is blind. One eye is larger than the other, and protrudes noticeably. She rarely smiles; indeed, I have seen her smile only once or twice since I came. She is unresponsive and even impatient of caresses from any one except her mother. She is very quick-tempered and wilful, and nobody, except her brother James, has attempted to control her. The greatest problem I shall have to solve is how to discipline and control her without breaking her spirit. I shall go rather slowly at first and try to win her love. I shall not attempt to conquer her by force alone; but I shall insist on reasonable obedience from the start. One thing that impresses everybody is Helen's tireless activity. She is never still a moment. She is here, there, and everywhere. Her hands are in everything; but nothing holds her attention for long. Dear child, her restless spirit gropes in the dark. Her untaught, unsatisfied hands destroy whatever they touch because they do not know what else to do with things.

She helped me unpack my trunk when it came, and was delighted when she found the doll the little girls sent her. I thought it a good opportunity to teach her her first word. I spelled "d-o-l-l" slowly in her hand and pointed to the doll and nodded my head, which seems to be her sign for possession. Whenever anybody gives her anything, she points to it, then to herself, and nods her head. She looked puzzled and felt my hand, and I repeated the letters. She imitated them very well and pointed to the doll. Then I took the doll, meaning to give it back to her when she had made the letters; but she thought I meant to take it from her, and in an instant she was in a temper, and tried to seize the doll. I shook my head and tried to form the letters with her fingers; but she got more and more angry. I forced her into a chair and held her there until I was nearly exhausted. Then it occurred to me that it was useless to continue the struggle—I must do something to turn the current of her thoughts. I let her go, but refused to give up the doll. I went downstairs and got some cake (she is very fond of sweets). I showed Helen the cake and spelled "c-a-k-e" in her hand, holding the cake toward her. Of course she wanted it and tried to take it; but I spelled the word again and patted her hand. She made the letters rapidly, and I gave her the cake, which she ate in a great hurry, thinking, I suppose, that I might take it from her. Then I showed her the doll and spelled the word again, holding the doll toward her as I held the cake. She made the letters "d-o-l" and I made the other "l" and gave her the doll. She ran downstairs with it and could not be induced to return to my room all day.

Yesterday I gave her a sewing-card to do. I made the first row of vertical lines and let her feel it and notice that there were several rows of little holes. She began to work delightedly and finished the card in a few minutes, and did it very neatly indeed. I thought I would try another word; so I spelled "c-a-r-d." She made the "c-a," then stopped and thought, and making the sign for eating and pointing downward she pushed me toward the door, meaning that I must go downstairs for some cake. The two letters "c-a," you see, had reminded her of Friday's "lesson"—not that she had any idea that cake was the name of the thing, but it was simply a matter of association, I suppose. I finished the word "c-a-k-e" and obeyed her command. She was delighted. Then I spelled "d-o-l-l" and began to hunt for it. She follows with her hands every motion you make, and she knew that I was looking for the doll. She pointed down, meaning that the doll was downstairs. I made the signs that she had used when she wished me to go for the cake, and pushed her toward the door. She started forward, then hesitated a moment, evidently debating within herself whether she would go or not. She decided to send me instead. I shook my head and spelled "d-o-l-l" more emphatically, and opened the door for her; but she obstinately refused to obey. She had not finished the cake she was eating, and I took it away, indicating that if she brought the doll I would give her back the cake. She stood perfectly still for one long moment, her face crimson; then her desire for the cake triumphed, and she ran downstairs and brought the doll, and of course I gave her the cake, but could not persuade her to enter the room again.

She was very troublesome when I began to write this morning. She kept coming up behind me and putting her hand on the paper and into the ink-bottle. These blots are her handiwork. Finally I remembered the kindergarten beads, and set her to work stringing them. First I put on two wooden beads and one glass bead, then made her feel of the string and the two boxes of beads. She nodded and began at once to fill the string with wooden beads. I shook my head and took them all off and made her feel of the two wooden beads and the one glass bead. She examined them thoughtfully and began again. This time she put on the glass bead first and the two wooden ones next. I took them off and showed her that the two wooden ones must go on first, then the glass bead. She had no further trouble and filled the string quickly, too quickly, in fact. She tied the ends together when she had finished the string, and put the beads round her neck. I did not make the knot large enough in the next string, and the beads came off as fast as she put them on; but she solved the difficulty herself by putting the string through a bead and tying it. I thought this very clever. She amused herself with the beads until dinner-time, bringing the strings to me now and then for my approval.

My eyes are very much inflamed. I know this letter is very carelessly written. I had a lot to say, and couldn't stop to think how to express things neatly. Please do not show my letter to any one. If you want to, you may read it to my friends.

Monday P. M.

I had a battle royal with Helen this morning. Although I try very hard not to force issues, I find it very difficult to avoid them.

Helen's table manners are appalling. She puts her hands in our plates and helps herself, and when the dishes are passed, she grabs them and takes out whatever she wants. This morning I would not let her put her hand in my plate.

She persisted, and a contest of wills followed. Naturally the family was much disturbed, and left the room. I locked the dining-room door, and proceeded to eat my breakfast, though the food almost choked me. Helen was lying on the floor, kicking and screaming and trying to pull my chair from under me. She kept this up for half an hour, then she got up to see what I was doing. I let her see that I was eating, but I did not let her put her hand in the plate. She pinched me, and I slapped her every time she did it. Then she went all round the table to see who was there, and finding no one but me, she seemed bewildered. After a few minutes she came back to her place and began to eat her breakfast with her fingers. I gave her a spoon, which she threw on the floor. I forced her out of the chair and made her pick it up. Finally I succeeded in getting her back in her chair again, and held the spoon in her hand, compelling her to take up the food with it and put it in her mouth. In a few minutes she yielded and finished her breakfast peaceably. Then we had another tussle over folding her napkin. When she had finished, she threw it on the floor and ran toward the door. Finding it locked, she began to kick and scream all over again. It was another hour before I succeeded in getting her napkin folded. Then I let her out into the warm sunshine and went up to my room and threw myself on the bed exhausted. I had a good cry and felt better. I suppose I shall many such battles with the little woman before she learns the only two essential things I can teach her, obedience and love.

Good-by, dear. Don't worry; I'll do my best and leave the rest to whatever power manages that which we cannot. I like Mrs. Keller very much.

Tuscumbia, Alabama, March 11, 1887

Since I wrote you, Helen and I have gone to live all by ourselves in a little garden-house about a quarter of a mile from her home, only a short distance from Ivy Green, the Keller homestead. I very soon made up my mind that I could do nothing with Helen in the midst of the family, who have always allowed her to do exactly as she pleased. She has tyrannized over everybody, her mother, her father, the servants, the little darkies who play with her, and nobody had every seriously disputed her will, except occasionally her brother James, until I came; and like all tyrants she holds tenaciously to her divine right to do as she pleases. If she ever failed to get what she wanted, it was because of her inability to make the vassals of her household understand what it was. Every thwarted desire was the signal for a passionate outburst, and as she grew older and stronger, these tempests became more violent. As I began to teach her, I was beset by many difficulties. She wouldn't yield a point without contesting it to the bitter end. I couldn't coax her or compromise with her. To get her to do the simplest thing, such as combing her hair or washing her hands or buttoning her boots, it was necessary to use force, and, of course, a distressing scene followed. The family naturally felt inclined to interfere, especially her father, who cannot bear to see her cry. So they were all willing to give in for the sake of peace. Besides, her past experiences and associations were all against me. I saw clearly that it was useless to try to teach her language or anything else until she learned to obey me. I have thought about it a great deal, and the more I think, the more certain I am that obedience is the gateway through which knowledge, yes, and love, too, enter the mind of the child. As I wrote you, I meant to go slowly at first. I had an idea that I could win the love and confidence of my little pupil by the same means that I should use if she could see and hear. But I soon found that I was cut off from all the usual approaches to the child's heart. She accepted everything I did for her as a matter of course, and refused to be caressed, and there was no way of appealing to her affection or sympathy or childish love of approbation. She would or she wouldn't, and there was an end of it. Thus it is, we study, plan and prepare ourselves for a task, and when the hour for action arrives, we find that the system we have followed with such labour and pride does not fit the occasion; and there's nothing for us to do but rely on something within us, some innate capacity for knowing and doing, which we did not know we possessed until the hour of our great need brought it to light.

I had a good, frank talk with Mrs. Keller, and explained to her how difficult it was going to be to do anything with Helen under the existing circumstances. I told her that in my opinion the child ought to be separated from the family for a few weeks at least—that she must learn to depend on and obey me before I make any headway. After a long time Mrs. Keller said that she would think the matter over and see what Captain Keller thought of sending Helen away with me. Captain Keller fell in with the scheme most readily and suggested that the little garden-house at the "old place" be got ready for us. He said that Helen might recognize the place, as she had often been there; but she would have no idea of her surroundings, and they could come every day to see that all was going well, with the understanding, of course, that she was to know nothing of their visits. I hurried the preparations for our departure as much as possible, and here we are.

The little house is a genuine bit of paradise. It consists of one large square room with a great fireplace, a spacious bay-window, and a small room where our servant, a little negro boy, sleeps. There is a piazza in front, covered with vines that grow so luxuriantly that you have to part them to see the garden beyond. Our meals are brought from the house and we usually eat on the piazza. The little negro boy takes care of the fire when we need one; so I can give my whole attention to Helen.

She was greatly excited at first, and kicked and screamed herself into a sort of stupor; but when supper was brought she ate heartily and seemed brighter, although she refused to let me touch her. She devoted herself to her dolls the first evening, and when it was bedtime she undressed very quietly; but when she felt me get into bed with her, she jumped out on the other side, and nothing that I could do would induce her to get in again. But I was afraid she would take cold, and I insisted that she must go to bed. We had a terrific tussle, I can tell you. The struggle lasted for nearly two hours. I never saw such strength and endurance in a child. But fortunately for us both, I am a little stronger, and quite as obstinate when I set out. I finally succeeded in getting her on the bed and covered her up, and she lay curled up as near the edge of the bed as possible.

The next morning she was very docile, but evidently homesick. She kept going to the door, as if she expected some one, and every now and then she would touch her cheek, which is her sign for her mother, and shake her head sadly. She played with her dolls more than usual, and would have nothing to do with me. It is amusing and pathetic to see Helen with her dolls. I don't think she has any special tenderness for them—I have never seen her caress them; but she dresses and undresses them many times during the day and handles them exactly as she has seen her mother and the nurse handle her baby sister.

This morning Nancy, her favourite doll, seemed to have some difficulty about swallowing the milk that was being administered to her in large spoonfuls; for Helen suddenly put down the cup and began to slap her on the back and turn her over on her knees, trotting her gently and patting her softly all the time. This lasted for several minutes; then this mood passed, and Nancy was thrown ruthlessly on the floor and pushed to one side, while a large, pink-cheeked, fuzzy-haired member of the family received the mother's undivided attention.

Helen knows several words now, but she has no idea how to use them, or that everything has a name. I think, however, she will learn quickly enough by and by. As I have said before, she is wonderfully bright and active and as quick as lightning in her movements.

March 13, 1887.

You will be glad to hear that my experiment is working out finely. I have not had any trouble at all with Helen, either yesterday or to-day. She has learned three new words, and when I give her the objects, the names of which she has learned, she spells them unhesitatingly; but she seems glad when the lesson is over.

We had a good frolic this morning out in the garden. Helen evidently knew where she was as soon as she touched the boxwood hedges, and made many signs which I did not understand. No doubt they were signs for the different members of the family at Ivy Green....

March 20, 1887.

My heart is singing for joy this morning. A miracle has happened! The light of understanding has shone upon my little pupil's mind, and behold, all things are changed!

The wild little creature of two weeks ago has been transformed into a gentle child. She is sitting by me as I write, her face serene and happy, crocheting a long red chain of Scotch wool. She learned the stitch this week, and is very proud of the achievement. When she succeeded in making a chain that would reach across the room, she patted herself on the arm and put the first work of her hands lovingly against her cheek. She lets me kiss her now, and when she is in a particularly gentle mood, she will sit in my lap for a minute or two; but she does not return my caresses. The great step—the step that counts—has been taken. The little savage has learned her first lesson in obedience, and finds the yoke easy. It now remains my pleasant task to direct and mould the beautiful intelligence that is beginning to stir in the child-soul. Already people remark the change in Helen. Her father looks in at us morning and evening as he goes to and from his office, and sees her contentedly stringing her beads or making horizontal lines on her sewing-card, and exclaims, "How quiet she is!" When I came, her movements were so insistent that one always felt there was something unnatural and almost weird about her. I have noticed also that she eats much less, a fact which troubles her father so much that he is anxious to get her home. He says she is homesick. I don't agree with him; but I suppose we shall have to leave our little bower very soon.

Helen has learned several nouns this week. "M-u-g" and "m-i-l-k," have given her more trouble than other words. When she spells "milk," she points to the mug, and when she spells "mug," she makes the sign for pouring or drinking, which shows that she has confused the words. She has no idea yet that everything has a name....

March 28, 1887.

Helen and I came home yesterday. I am sorry they wouldn't let us stay another week; but I think I have made the most I could of the opportunities that were mine the past two weeks, and I don't expect that I shall have any serious trouble with Helen in the future. The back of the greatest obstacle in the path of progress is broken. I think "no" and "yes," conveyed by a shake or a nod of my head, have become facts as apparent to her as hot and cold or as the difference between pain and pleasure. And I don't intend that the lesson she has learned at the cost of so much pain and trouble shall be unlearned. I shall stand between her and the over-indulgence of her parents. I have told Captain and Mrs. Keller that they must not interfere with me in any way. I have done my best to make them see the terrible injustice to Helen of allowing her to have her way in everything, and I have pointed out that the processes of teaching the child that everything cannot be as he wills it, are apt to be painful both to him and to his teacher. They have promised to let me have a free hand and help me as much as possible. The improvement they cannot help seeing in their child has given them more confidence in me. Of course, it is hard for them. I realize that it hurts to see their afflicted little child punished and made to do things against her will. Only a few hours after my talk with Captain and Mrs. Keller (and they had agreed to everything), Helen took a notion that she wouldn't use her napkin at table. I think she wanted to see what would happen. I attempted several times to put the napkin round her neck; but each time she tore it off and threw it on the floor and finally began to kick the table. I took her plate away and started to take her out of the room. Her father objected and said that no child of his should be deprived of his food on any account.

Helen didn't come up to my room after supper, and I didn't see her again until breakfast-time. She was at her place when I came down. She had put the napkin under her chin, instead of pinning it at the back, as was her custom. She called my attention to the new arrangement, and when I did not object she seemed pleased and patted herself. When she left the dining-room, she took my hand and patted it. I wondered if she was trying to "make up." I thought I would try the effect of a little belated discipline. I went back to the dining-room and got a napkin. When Helen came upstairs for her lesson, I arranged the objects on the table as usual, except that the cake, which I always give her in bits as a reward when she spells a word quickly and correctly, was not there. She noticed this at once and made the sign for it. I showed her the napkin and pinned it round her neck, then tore it off and threw it on the floor and shook my head. I repeated this performance several times. I think she understood perfectly well; for she slapped her hand two or three times and shook her head. We began the lesson as usual. I gave her an object, and she spelled the name (she knows twelve now). After spelling half the words, she stopped suddenly, as if a thought had flashed into her mind, and felt for the napkin. She pinned it round her neck and made the sign for cake (it didn't occur to her to spell the word, you see). I took this for a promise that if I gave her some cake she would be a good girl. I gave her a larger piece than usual, and she chuckled and patted herself.

April 3, 1887.

We almost live in the garden, where everything is growing and blooming and glowing. After breakfast we go out and watch the men at work. Helen loves to dig and play in the dirt like any other child. This morning she planted her doll and showed me that she expected her to grow as tall as I. You must see that she is very bright, but you have no idea how cunning she is.

At ten we come in and string beads for a few minutes. She can make a great many combinations now, and often invents new ones herself. Then I let her decide whether she will sew or knit or crochet. She learned to knit very quickly, and is making a wash-cloth for her mother. Last week she made her doll an apron, and it was done as well as any child of her age could do it. But I am always glad when this work is over for the day. Sewing and crocheting are inventions of the devil, I think. I'd rather break stones on the king's highway than hem a handkerchief. At eleven we have gymnastics. She knows all the free-hand movements and the "Anvil Chorus" with the dumb-bells. Her father says he is going to fit up a gymnasium for her in the pump-house; but we both like a good romp better than set exercises. The hour from twelve to one is devoted to the learning of new words. *But you mustn't think this is the only time I spell to Helen; for I spell in her hand everything we do all day long, although she has no idea as yet what the spelling means.* After dinner I rest for an hour, and Helen plays with her dolls or frolics in the yard with the little darkies, who were her constant companions before I came. Later I join them, and we make the rounds of the outhouses. We visit the horses and mules in their stalls and hunt for eggs and feed the turkeys. Often, when the weather is fine, we drive from four to six, or go to see her aunt at Ivy Green or her cousins in the town. Helen's instincts are decidedly social; she likes to have people about her and to visit her friends, partly, I think, because they always have things she likes to eat. After supper we go to my room and do all sorts of things until eight, when I undress the little woman and put her to bed. She sleeps with me now. Mrs. Keller wanted to get a nurse for her; but I concluded I'd rather be her nurse than look after a stupid, lazy negress. Besides, I like to have Helen depend on me for everything, *and I find it much easier to teach her things at odd moments than at set times.*

On March 31st I found that Helen knew eighteen nouns and three verbs. Here is a list of the words. Those with a cross after them are words she asked for herself: *Doll, mug, pin, key, dog, hat, cup, box, water, milk, candy, eye (x), finger (x), toe (x), head (x), cake, baby, mother, sit, stand, walk.* On April 1st she learned the nouns *knife, fork, spoon, saucer, tea, papa, bed,* and the verb *run.*

April 5, 1887.

I must write you a line this morning because something very important has happened. Helen has taken the second great step in her education. She has learned that *everything has a name, and that the manual alphabet is the key to everything she wants to know.*

In a previous letter I think I wrote you that "mug" and "milk" had given Helen more trouble than all the rest. She confused the nouns with the verb "drink." She didn't know the word for "drink," but went through the pantomime of drinking whenever she spelled "mug" or "milk." This morning, while she was washing, she wanted to know the name for "water." When she wants to know the name of anything, she points to it and pats my hand. I spelled "w-a-t-e-r" and thought no more about it until after breakfast. Then it occurred to me that with the help of this new word I might succeed in straightening out the "mug-milk" difficulty. We went out to the pump-house, and I made Helen hold her mug under the spout while I pumped. As the cold water gushed forth, filling the mug, I spelled "w-a-t-e-r" in Helen's free hand. The word coming so close upon the sensation of cold water rushing over her hand seemed to startle her. She dropped the mug and stood as one transfixed. A new light came into her face. She spelled "water" several times. Then she dropped on the ground and asked for its name and pointed to the pump and the trellis, and suddenly turning round she asked for my name. I spelled "Teacher." Just then the nurse brought Helen's little sister into the pump-house, and Helen spelled "baby" and pointed to the nurse. All the way back to the house she was highly excited, and learned the name of every object she touched, so that in a few hours she had added thirty new words to her vocabulary. Here are some of them: *Door, open, shut, give, go, come,* and a great many more.

P. S.—I didn't finish my letter in time to get it posted last night; so I shall add a line. Helen got up this morning like a radiant fairy. She has flitted from object to object, asking the name of everything and kissing me for very gladness. Last night when I got in bed, she stole into my arms of her own accord and kissed me for the first time, and I thought my heart would burst, so full was it of joy.

"The Arts At Hull-House" From *Twenty Years At Hull-House*[1] (c. 1891)

❧ ◆ ☙

Jane Addams, 1910

This excerpt from Addams' *Twenty Years At Hull-House* vividly illustrates the richness of the Hull House curriculum. In addition to a description of art lessons at the settlement house, Addams speaks of the museum and music concerts that were held there. Throughout her discussion, Addams' sensitivity to and appreciation of the immigrants' cultures and interests comes through clearly. An appreciation of the arts, Addams felt, was central to human happiness. But culture needed to be defined more broadly in a newly diverse America. Handicrafts and folk music were seen as legitimate art forms, with a value and appeal of their own. At Hull House, traditional barriers between high and low arts were often blurred.

Jane Addams (1860–1935) began her remarkable life as the daughter of a prominent Illinois statesman. Her first ambition was to become a doctor, but she settled instead for teaching. Growing up motherless, Addams developed a deep attachment to her father, and modeled her intellectual life around his own. After his death, Addams decided to devote her life's energy to social reform. Her work at Hull-House began in 1889 and served as a prototype for similar settlement houses that proliferated in other Midwestern and Eastern cities. In addition to her work at Hull-House, Addams worked on behalf of a range of reform causes including child labor laws, women's suffrage, educational reform, and world peace. She helped to found The Women's International League for Peace and Freedom and served as its president until her death. Although Addams received the Nobel Peace Prize in 1931, her opposition to American involvement in the First World War was seen as a betrayal by many Americans.

---

[1]Reprinted by permission of the Sophia Smith Collection, Smith College.

"THE ARTS AT HULL-HOUSE" FROM
TWENTY YEARS AT HULL-HOUSE
(C. 1891)

Jane Addams, 1910

The first building erected for Hull-House contained an art gallery well lighted for day and evening use and our first exhibit of loaned pictures was opened in June, 1891, by Mr. and Mrs. Barnett of London. It is always pleasant to associate their hearty sympathy with that first exhibit, and thus to connect it with their pioneer efforts at Toynbee Hall to secure for working people the opportunity to know the best art, and with their establishment of the first permanent art gallery in an industrial quarter.

We took pride in the fact that our first exhibit contained some of the best pictures Chicago afforded, and we conscientiously insured them against fire and carefully guarded them by night and day.

We had five of these exhibits during two years, after the gallery was completed: two of oil paintings, one of old engravings and etchings, one of water colors, and one of pictures especially selected for use in the public schools. These exhibits were surprisingly well attended and thousands of votes were cast for the most popular pictures. Their value to the neighborhood of course had to be determined by each one of us according to the value he attached to beauty and the escape it offers from dreary reality into the realm of the imagination. Miss Starr always insisted that the arts should receive adequate recognition at Hull-House and urged that one must always remember "the hungry individual soul which without art will have passed unsolaced and unfed, followed by other souls who lack the impulse his should have given."

The exhibits afforded pathetic evidence that the older immigrants do not expect the solace of art in this country; an Italian expressed great surprise when he found that we, although Americans, still liked pictures, and said quite naively that he didn't know that Americans cared for anything but dollars—that looking at pictures was something people only did in Italy.

The extreme isolation of the Italian colony was demonstrated by the fact that he did not know that there was a public art gallery in the city nor any houses in which pictures were regarded as treasures.

A Greek was much surprised to see a photograph of the Acropolis at Hull-House, because he had lived in Chicago for thirteen years and had never before met any Americans who knew about this foremost glory of the world. Before he left Greece he had imagined that Americans would be most eager to see pictures of Athens, and as he was a graduate of a school of technology, he had prepared a book of colored drawings and had made a collection of photographs which he was sure Americans would enjoy. But although from his fruit stand near one of the large railroad stations he had

conversed with many Americans and had often tried to lead the conversation back to ancient Greece, no one had responded, and he had at last
concluded that "the people of Chicago knew nothing of ancient times."

The loan exhibits were continued until the Chicago Art Institute was
opened free to the public on Sunday afternoons and parties were arranged
at Hull-House and conducted there by a guide. In time even these parties
were discontinued as the galleries became better known in all parts of the
city and the Art Institute management did much to make pictures popular.

From the first a studio was maintained at Hull-House which has developed through the changing years under the direction of Miss Benedict, one
of the residents who is a member of the faculty in the Art Institute. Buildings
on the Hull-House quadrangle furnish studios for artists who find something
of the same spirit in the contiguous Italian colony that the French artist is
traditionally supposed to discover in his beloved Latin Quarter. These artists
uncover something of the picturesque in the foreign colonies, which they
have reproduced in painting, etching, and lithography. They find their
classes filled not only by young people possessing facility and sometimes
talent, but also by older people to whom the studio affords the one opportunity of escape from dreariness; a widow with four children who supplemented a very inadequate income by teaching the piano, for six years never
missed her weekly painting lesson because it was "her one pleasure"; another
woman, whose youth and strength had gone into the care of an invalid
father, poured into her afternoon in the studio once a week all of the longing
for self-expression which she habitually suppressed.

Perhaps the most satisfactory results of the studio have been obtained
through the classes of young men who are engaged in the commercial arts,
and who are glad to have an opportunity to work out their own ideas. This
is true of young engravers and lithographers; of the men who have to do
with posters and illustrations in various ways. The little pile of stones and
the lithographer's handpress in a corner of the studio have been used in
many an experiment, as has a set of beautiful type loaned to Hull-House by
a bibliophile.

The work of the studio almost imperceptibly merged into the crafts, and
well within the first decade a shop was opened at Hull-House under the
direction of several residents who were also members of the Chicago Arts
and Crafts Society. This shop is not merely a school where people are taught
and then sent forth to use their teaching in art according to their individual
initiative and opportunity, but where those who have already been carefully
trained, may express the best they can in wood or metal. The Settlement
soon discovers how difficult it is to put a fringe of art on the end of a day
spent in a factory. We constantly see young people doing overhurried work.
Wrapping bars of soap in pieces of paper might at least give the pleasure of
accuracy and repetition if it could be done at a normal pace, but when paid
for by the piece, speed becomes the sole requirement and the last suggestion

of human interest is taken away. In contrast to this the Hull-House shop affords many examples of the restorative power in the exercise of a genuine craft; a young Russian who, like too many of his countrymen, had made a desperate effort to fit himself for a learned profession, and who had almost finished his course in a night law school, used to watch constantly the work being done in the metal shop at Hull-House. One evening in a moment of sudden resolve, he took off his coat, sat down at one of the benches, and began to work, obviously as a very clever silversmith. He had long concealed his craft because he thought it would hurt his efforts as a lawyer and because he imagined an office more honorable and "more American" than a shop. As he worked on during his two leisure evenings each week, his entire bearing and conversation registered the relief of one who abandons the effort he is not fitted for and becomes a man on his own feet, expressing himself through a familiar and delicate technique.

Miss Starr at length found herself quite impatient with her role of lecturer on the arts, while all the handicraft about her was untouched by beauty and did not even reflect the interest of the workman. She took a training in bookbinding in London under Mr. Cobden-Sanderson and established her bindery at Hull-House in which design and workmanship, beauty and thoroughness, are taught to a small number of apprentices.

From the very first winter, concerts which are still continued were given every Sunday afternoon in the Hull-House drawing room and later, as the audiences increased, in the larger halls. For these we are indebted to musicians from every part of the city. Mr. William Tomlins early trained large choruses of adults as his assistants did of children, and the response to all of these showed that while the number of people in our vicinity caring for the best music was not large, they constituted a steady and appreciative group. It was in connection with these first choruses that a public-spirited citizen of Chicago offered a prize for the best labor song, competition to be open to the entire country. The responses to the offer literally filled three large barrels and speaking at least for myself as one of the bewildered judges, we were more disheartened by their quality than even by their overwhelming bulk. Apparently the workers of America are not yet ready to sing, although I recall a creditable chorus trained at Hull-House for a large meeting in sympathy with the anthracite coal strike in which the swinging lines

> Who was it made the coal?
> Our God as well as theirs.

seemed to relieve the tension of the moment. Miss Eleanor Smith, the head of the Hull-House Music School, who had put the words to music, performed the same office for the "Sweatshop" of the Yiddish poet, the translation of which presents so graphically the bewilderment and tedium of the New York shop that it might be applied to almost any other machinery industry as the first verse indicates—

> "The roaring of the wheels has filled my ears,
>   The clashing and the clamor shut me in,
> Myself, my soul, in chaos disappears,
>   I cannot think or feel amid the din."

It may be that this plaint explains the lack of labor songs in this period of industrial maladjustment when the worker is overmastered by his very tools. In addition to sharing with our neighborhood the best music we could procure, we have conscientiously provided careful musical instruction that at least a few young people might understand those old usages of art; that they might master its trade secrets, for after all it is only through a careful technique that artistic ability can express itself and be preserved.

From the beginning we had classes in music, and the Hull-House Music School, which is housed in quarters of its own in our quieter court, was opened in 1893. The school is designed to give a thorough musical instruction to a limited number of children. From the first lessons they are taught to compose and to reduce to order the musical suggestions which may come to them, and in this wise the school has sometimes been able to recover the songs of the immigrants through their children. Some of these folk songs have never been committed to paper, but have survived through the centuries because of a touch of undying poetry which the world has always cherished; as in the song of a Russian who is digging a post hole and finds his task dull and difficult until he strikes a stratum of red sand, which in addition to making digging easy, reminds him of the red hair of his sweetheart, and all goes merrily as the song lifts into a joyous melody. I recall again the almost hilarious enjoyment of the adult audience to whom it was sung by the children who have revived it, as well as the more sober appreciation of the hymns taken from the lips of the cantor, whose father before him had officiated in the synagogue.

The recitals and concerts given by the school are attended by large and appreciative audiences. On the Sunday before Christmas the program of Christmas songs draws together people of the most diverging faiths. In the deep tones of the memorial organ erected at Hull-House, we realize that music is perhaps the most potent agent for making the universal appeal and inducing men to forget their differences.

Some of the pupils in the music school have developed during the years into trained musicians and are supporting themselves in their chosen profession. On the other hand, we constantly see the most promising musical ability extinguished when the young people enter industries which so sap their vitality that they cannot carry on serious study in the scanty hours outside of factory work. Many cases indisputably illustrate this: a

Bohemian girl, who, in order to earn money for pressing family needs, first ruined her voice in a six months' constant vaudeville engagement, returned to her trade working overtime in a vain effort to continue the vaudeville income; another young girl whom Hull-House had sent to the high school so long as her parents consented, because we realized that a beautiful voice is often unavailable through lack of the informing mind, later extinguished her promise in a tobacco factory; a third girl who had supported her little sisters since she was fourteen, eagerly used her fine voice for earning money at entertainments held late after her day's work, until exposure and fatigue ruined her health as well as a musician's future; a young man whose music-loving family gave him every possible opportunity, and who produced some charming and even joyous songs during the long struggle with tuberculosis which preceded his death, had made a brave beginning, not only as a teacher of music but as a composer. In the little service held at Hull-House in his memory, when the children sang his composition, "How Sweet is the Shepherd's Sweet Lot," it was hard to realize that such an interpretive pastoral could have been produced by one whose childhood had been passed in a crowded city quarter.

Even that bitter experience did not prepare us for the sorrowful year when six promising pupils out of a class of fifteen, developed tuberculosis. It required but little penetration to see that during the eight years the class of fifteen school children had come together to the music school, they had approximately an even chance, but as soon as they reached the legal working age only a scanty moiety of those who became self-supporting could endure the strain of long hours and bad air. Thus the average human youth, "With all the sweetness of the common dawn," is flung into the vortex of industrial life wherein the everyday tragedy escapes us save when one of them becomes conspicuously unfortunate. Twice in one year we were compelled

> "To find the inheritance of this poor child
> His little kingdom of a forced grave."

It has been pointed out many times that Art lives by devouring her own offspring and the world has come to justify even that sacrifice, but we are unfortified and unsolaced when we see the children of Art devoured, not by her, but by the uncouth stranger, Modern Industry, who, needlessly ruthless and brutal to her own children, is quickly fatal to the offspring of the gentler mother. And so schools in art for those who go to work at the age when more fortunate young people are still sheltered and educated constantly epitomize one of the haunting problems of life: why do we permit the waste of this most precious human faculty, this consummate possession of civilization? When we fail to provide the vessel in which it may be treasured, it runs out upon the ground and is irretrievably lost.

The universal desire for the portrayal of life lying quite outside of personal experience evinces itself in many forms. One of the conspicuous features of our neighborhood, as of all industrial quarters, is the persistency with which the entire population attends the theater. The very first day I saw Halsted Street a long line of young men and boys stood outside the gallery entrance of the Bijou Theater, waiting for the Sunday matinée to begin at two o'clock, although it was only high noon. This waiting crowd might have been seen every Sunday afternoon during the twenty years which have elapsed since then. Our first Sunday evening in Hull-House, when a group of small boys sat on our piazza and told us "about things around here," their talk was all of the theater and of the astonishing things they had seen that afternoon.

But quite as it was difficult to discover the habits and purposes of this group of boys because they much are heavy and dull, and that it will take political or philanthropic machinery to change them. This divides a city into rich and poor; into the favored, who express their sense of the social obligation by gifts of money, and into the unfavored, who express it by clamoring for a "share"—both of them actuated by a vague sense of justice. This division of the city would be more justifiable, however, if the people who thus isolate themselves on certain streets and use their social ability for each other gained enough thereby and added sufficient to the sum total of social progress to justify the witholding of the pleasures and results of that progress from so many people who ought to have them. But they cannot accomplish this for the social spirit discharges itself in many forms, and no one form is adequate to its total expression.

"Of the Coming of John" From
The Souls of Black Folk

℘ ◆ ℀

W. E. B. Du Bois, 1903

One of the great intellectual controversies spanning the years of the Progressive movement concerned the education of African Americans. In the decades following the end of the Civil War, both Black and White educators began to develop segregated colleges and training institutes to meet the needs of a growing number of African American youth eager to join the workforce. By the turn of the century, two opposing views of schooling were being debated within the Black community. Those views were represented on the one hand by Booker T. Washington, a former slave, and a "gradualist," who believed the best strategy for gaining acceptance and equality was in a conciliatory stance toward the White status quo. The first few generations of freed Blacks, believed Washington, should receive industrial and practical educations, should become useful laborers within the society, and should gradually garner the respect of the White power structure through this slow movement within the system. Booker T. Washington's model for this ideal industrial education was the Hampton Institute, the school he himself attended, which readied freed Blacks for the trades and other skilled, but menial work. Washington hoped to duplicate Hampton's success at Tuskegee Institute, which he founded in 1881.

On the other side of the argument was W. E. B. Du Bois (1868–1963). Du Bois was Northern born, and Harvard educated. Throughout his long career as a writer and activist, Du Bois rejected the Tuskegee–Hampton approach, believing instead that a significant cohort of Black youth (or what Du Bois called a "talented tenth") should be educated specifically and immediately for leadership. Du Bois believed that the only route to Black equality and respect was through a rigorous, classical education and aggressive political agitation. "The difficulty with Hampton [Institute]," wrote Du Bois, "is that its ideals are low. It is ... deliberately educating a servile class for a servile place" (Aptheker, 1973, p. 216).

Du Bois began his work with the firmly held conviction that if Blacks were formally educated in the great European tradition, Whites would no longer discriminate against them. Only later in his life did he realize that he was incorrect; that racism persists regardless of the education and refinement of those toward whom it is directed.

"The Coming of John" is a powerful testament to the plight of the educated Black man in America. Du Bois' hero begins as a happy, undisciplined farmhand. Education sobers and saddens him; it also renders him dangerous in the eyes of the White, Southern establishment. Although John comes back to his town with "new" ideas, those ideas are ironically no more radical than Booker T. Washington's: He hopes to set up a Black industrial college. Still, he is viewed with suspicion and fear. When it is discovered that he is teaching his Black students about the French Revolution, John's school is closed down. From that point on, we sense, he is a doomed man.

Du Bois' story seems deeply pessimistic. Although it is a relatively early piece of writing, it exposes the seeds of an anger and disappointment that intensified during the writer's long life.

"OF THE COMING OF JOHN" FROM
THE SOULS OF BLACK FOLK

W. E. B. Du Bois, 1903

What bring they 'neath the midnight,
　　Beside the River-sea?
They bring the human heart wherein
　　No nightly calm can be;
That droppeth never with the wind,
　　Nor drieth with the dew;
O calm it, God; thy calm is broad
　　To cover spirits too.
The river floweth on.

MRS. BROWNING.

Carlisle street runs westward from the centre of Johnstown, across a great black bridge, down a hill and up again, by little shops and meat-markets, past single-storied homes, until suddenly it stops against a wide green lawn. It is a broad, restful place, with two large buildings outlined against the west. When at evening the winds come swelling from the east, and the great pall of the city's smoke hangs wearily above the valley, then the red west glows like a dreamland down Carlisle Street, and, at the tolling of the supper-bell, throws the passing forms of students in dark silhouette against the sky. Tall and black, they move slowly by, and seem in the sinister light to flit before the city like dim warning ghosts. Perhaps they are; for this is Wells Institute, and these black students have few dealings with the white city below.

And if you will notice, night after night, there is one dark form that ever hurries last and late toward the twinkling lights of Swain Hall,—for Jones is never on time. A long, straggling fellow he is, brown and hard-haired, who seems to be growing straight out of his clothes, and walks with a half-apologetic roll. He used perpetually to set the quiet dining-room into waves of merriment, as he stole to his place after the bell had tapped for prayers; he seemed so perfectly awkward. And yet one glance at his face made one forgive him much,—that broad, good-natured smile in which lay no bit of art or artifice, but seemed just bubbling good-nature and genuine satisfaction with the world.

He came to us from Altamaha, away down there beneath the gnarled oaks of Southeastern Georgia, where the sea croons to the sands and the sands listen till they sink half drowned beneath the waters, rising only here and there in long, low islands. The white folk of Altamaha voted John a good boy,—fine plough-hand, good in the rice-fields, handy everywhere, and always good-natured and respectful. But they shook their heads when his mother wanted to send him off to school. "It'll spoil him,—ruin him," they said; and they talked as though they knew. But full half the black folk followed him proudly to the station, and carried his queer little trunk and many bundles. And there they shook and shook hands, and the girls kissed him shyly and the boys clapped him on the back. So the train came, and he pinched his little sister lovingly, and put his great arms about his mother's neck, and then was away with a puff and a roar into the great yellow world that flamed and flared about the doubtful pilgrim. Up the coast they hurried, past the squares and palmettos of Savannah, through the cotton-fields and through the weary night, to Millville, and came with the morning to the noise and bustle of Johnstown.

And they that stood behind, that morning in Altamaha, and watched the train as it noisily bore playmate and brother and son away to the world, had thereafter one ever-recurring word,—"When John comes." Then what parties were to be, and what speakings in the churches; what new furniture in the front room,—perhaps even a new front room; and there would be a new schoolhouse, with John as teacher; and then perhaps a big wedding; all this and more—when John comes. But the white people shook their heads.

At first he was coming at Christmas-time,—but the vacation proved too short; and then, the next summer,—but times were hard and schooling costly, and so, instead, he worked in Johnstown. And so it drifted to the next summer, and the next,—till playmates scattered, and mother grew gray, and sister went up to the Judge's kitchen to work. And still the legend lingered,—"When John comes."

Up at the Judge's they rather liked this refrain; for they too had a John—a fair-haired, smooth-faced boy, who had played many a long summer's day to its close with his darker namesake. "Yes, sir! John is at Princeton, sir," said the broad-shouldered gray-haired Judge every morning as he marched down to the postoffice. "Showing the Yankees what a Southern gentleman can do," he added; and strode home again with his letters and papers. Up at the great pillared house they lingered long over the Princeton letter,—the Judge and his frail wife, his sister and growing daughters. "It'll make a man of him," said the Judge, "college is the place." And then he asked the shy little waitress, "Well, Jennie, how's your John?" and added reflectively, "Too bad, too bad your mother sent him off,—it will spoil him." And the waitress wondered.

Thus in the far-away Southern village the world lay waiting, half consciously, the coming of two young men, and dreamed in an inarticulate way of new things that would be done and new thoughts that all would think. And yet it was singular that few thought of two Johns,—for the black folk thought of one John, and he was black; and the white folk thought of another John, and he was white. And neither world thought the other world's thought, save with a vague unrest.

Up in Johnstown, at the Institute, we were long puzzled at the case of John Jones. For a long time the clay seemed unfit for any sort of moulding. He was loud and boisterous, always laughing and singing, and never able to work consecutively at anything. He did not know how to study; he had no idea of thoroughness; and with his tardiness, carelessness, and appalling good-humor, we were sore perplexed. One night we sat in faculty-meeting, worried and serious; for Jones was in trouble again. This last escapade was too much, and so we solemnly voted "that Jones, on account of repeated disorder and inattention to work, be suspended for the rest of the term."

It seemed to us that for the first time life ever struck Jones as a really serious thing was when the Dean told him he must leave school. He stared at the gray-haired man blankly, with great eyes. "Why,—why," he faltered, "but—I haven't graduated!" Then the Dean slowly and clearly explained, reminding him of the tardiness and the carelessness, of the poor lessons and neglected work, of the noise and disorder, until the fellow hung his head in confusion. Then he said quickly, "But you won't tell mammy and sister,—you won't write mammy, now will you? For if you won't I'll go out into the city and work, and come back next term and show you something." So the Dean promised faithfully, and John shouldered his little trunk, giving neither word nor look to the giggling boys, and walked down Carlisle Street to the great city, with sober eyes and a set and serious face.

Perhaps we imagined it, but someway it seemed to us that the serious look that crept over his boyish face that afternoon never left it again. When he came back to us he went to work with all his rugged strength. It was a hard struggle, for things did not come easily to him,—few crowding memories of early life and teaching came to help him on his new way; but all the world toward which he strove was of his own building, and he builded slow and hard. As the light dawned lingeringly on his new creations, he sat rapt and silent before the vision, or wandered alone over the green campus peering through and beyond the world of men into a world of thought. And the thoughts at times puzzled him sorely; he could not see just why the circle was not square, and carried it out fifty-six decimal places one midnight,—would have gone further, indeed, had not the matron rapped for lights out. He caught terrible colds lying on his back in the meadows of nights, trying to think out the solar system; he had grave doubts as to the ethics of the Fall of Rome, and strongly suspected the Germans of being thieves and rascals, despite his text-books; he pondered long over every new Greek word, and wondered why this meant that and why it couldn't mean something else, and how it must have felt to think all things in Greek. So he thought and puzzled along for himself,—pausing perplexed where others skipped merrily, and walking steadily through the difficulties where the rest stopped and surrendered.

Thus he grew in body and soul, and with him his clothes seemed to grow and arrange themselves; coat sleeves got longer, cuffs appeared, and collars got less soiled. Now and then his boots shone, and a new dignity crept into his walk. And we who saw daily a new thoughtfulness growing in his eyes began to expect something of this plodding boy. Thus he passed out of the preparatory school into college, and we who watched him felt four more years of change, which almost transformed the tall, grave man who bowed to us commencement morning. He had left his queer thought-world and come back to a world of motion and of men. He looked now for the first time sharply about him, and wondered he had seen so little before. He grew slowly to feel almost for the first time the Veil that lay between him and the white world; he first noticed now the oppression that had not seemed oppression before, differences that erstwhile seemed natural, restraints and slights that in his boyhood days had gone unnoticed or been greeted with a laugh. He felt angry now when men did not call him "Mister," he clenched his hands at the "Jim Crow" cars, and chafed at the color-line that hemmed in him and his. A tinge of sarcasm crept into his speech, and a vague bitterness into his life; and he sat long hours wondering and planning a way around these crooked things. Daily he found himself shrinking from the choked and narrow life of his native town. And yet he always planned to go back to Altamaha,—always planned to work there. Still, more and more as the day approached he hesitated with a nameless dread; and even the day after graduation he seized with eagerness the offer of the Dean to send him North with the quartette during the summer vacation, to sing for the Institute. A breath of air before the plunge, he said to himself in half apology.

It was a bright September afternoon, and the streets of New York were brilliant with moving men. They reminded John of the sea, as he sat in the square and watched them, so changelessly changing, so bright and dark, so grave and gay. He scanned their rich and faultless clothes, the way they carried their hands, the shape of their hats; he peered into the hurrying carriages. Then, leaning back with a sigh, he said, "This is the World." The notion suddenly seized him to see where the world was going; since many of the richer and brighter seemed hurrying all one way. So when a tall, light-haired young man and a little talkative lady came by, he rose half hesitatingly and followed them. Up the street they went, past stores and gay shops, across a broad square, until with a hundred others they entered the high portal of a great building.

He was pushed toward the ticket-office with the others, and felt in his pocket for the new five-dollar bill he had hoarded. There seemed really no time for hesitation, so he drew it bravely out, passed it to the busy clerk, and received simply a ticket but no change. When at last he realized that he had paid five dollars to enter he knew not what, he stood stockstill amazed. "Be careful," said a low voice behind him: "you must not lynch the colored gentleman simply because he's in your way," and a girl looked up roguishly into the eyes of her fair-haired escort. A shade of annoyance passed over the escort's face. "You *will* not understand us in the South," he said half impatiently, as if continuing an argument. "With all your professions, one never sees in the North so cordial and intimate relations between white and black as are everyday occurrences with us. Why, I remember my closest playfellow in boyhood was a little Negro named after me, and surely two,—*well!*" The man stopped short and flushed to the roots of his hair, for there directly beside his reserved orchestra chairs sat the negro he had stumbled over in the hallway. He hesitated and grew pale with anger, called the usher and gave him his card, with a few peremptory words, and slowly sat down. The lady deftly changed the subject.

All this John did not see, for he sat in a half-maze minding the scene about him; the delicate beauty of the hall, the faint perfume, the moving myriad of men, the rich clothing and low hum of talking seemed all a part of a world so different from his, so strangely more beautiful than anything he had known, that he sat in dreamland, and started when, after a hush, rose high and clear the music of Lohengrin's swan. The infinite beauty of the wail lingered and swept through every muscle of his frame, and put it all a-tune. He closed his eyes and grasped the elbows of the chair, touching unwittingly the lady's arm. And the lady drew away. A deep longing swelled in all his heart to rise with that clear music out of the dirt and dust of that low life that held him prisoned and befouled. If he could only live up in the free air where birds sang and setting suns had no touch of blood! Who had called him to be the slave and butt of all? And if he had called, what right had he to call when a world like this lay open before men?

Then the movement changed, and fuller, mightier harmony swelled away. He looked thoughtfully across the hall, and wondered why the beautiful gray-haired woman looked so listless, and what the little man could be whispering about. He would not like to be listless and idle, he thought, for he felt with the music the movement of power within him. If he but had some master-work, some life-service, hard, —aye, bitter hard, but without the cringing and sickening servility, without the cruel hurt that hardened his heart and soul. When at last a soft sorrow crept across the violins, there came to him the vision of a far-off home,—the great eyes of his sister, and the dark drawn face of his mother. And his heart sank below the waters, even as the sea-sand sinks by the shores of Altamaha, only to be lifted aloft again with that last ethereal wail of the swan that quivered and faded away into the sky.

It left John sitting so silent and rapt that he did not for some time notice the usher tapping him lightly on the shoulder and saying politely, "Will you step this way, please, sir?" A little surprised, he arose quickly at the last tap, and, turning to leave his seat, looked full into the face of the fair-haired young man. For the first time the young man recognized his dark boyhood playmate, and John knew that it was the Judge's son. The White John started, lifted his hand, and then froze into his chair; the black John smiled lightly, then grimly, and followed the usher down the aisle. The manager was sorry, very, very sorry,—but he explained that some mistake had been made in selling the gentleman a seat already disposed of; he would refund the money, of course,—and indeed felt the matter keenly, and so forth, and—before he had finished John was gone, walking hurriedly across the square and down the broad streets, and as he passed the park he buttoned his coat and said, "John Jones, you're a natural-born fool." Then he went to his lodgings and wrote a letter, and tore it up; he wrote another, and threw it in the fire. Then he seized a scrap of paper and wrote: "Dear Mother and Sister—I am coming—John"

"Perhaps," said John, as he settled himself on the train, "perhaps I am to blame myself in struggling against my manifest destiny simply because it looks hard and unpleasant. Here is my duty to Altamaha plain before me; perhaps they'll let me help settle the Negro problems there,—perhaps they won't. 'I will go in to the King which is not according to the law; and if I perish, I perish.'" And then he mused and dreamed, and planned a life-work; and the train flew south.

Down in Altamaha, after seven long years, all the world knew John was coming. The homes were scrubbed and scoured,—above all, one; the gardens and yards had an unwonted trimness, and Jennie bought a new gingham. With some finesse and negotiation, all the dark Methodists and Presbyterians were induced to join in a monster welcome at the Baptist Church; and as the day drew near, warm discussions arose on every corner as to the exact extent and nature of John's accomplishments. It was noontide on a gray and cloudy day when he came. The black town flocked to the depot, with a little of the white at the edges,—a happy throng, with "Good-mawnings" and "Howdys" and laughing and joking and jostling. Mother sat yonder in the window watching; but sister Jennie stood on the platform, nervously fingering her dress, tall and lithe, with soft brown skin and loving eyes peering from out a tangled wilderness of hair. John rose gloomily as the train stopped, for he was thinking of the "Jim Crow" car; he stepped to the platform, and paused: a little dingy station, a black crowd gaudy and dirty, a half-mile of dilapidated shanties along a straggling ditch of mud. An overwhelming sense of the sordidness and narrowness of it all seized him; he looked in vain for his mother, kissed coldly the tall, strange girl who called him brother, spoke a short, dry word here and there; then, lingering neither for handshaking nor gossip, started silently up the street, raising his hat merely to the last eager old aunty, to her open-mouthed astonishment. The people were distinctly bewildered. This silent, cold man,—was this John? Where was his smile and hearty hand-grasp? "'Peared kind o' down in the mouf," said the Methodist preacher thoughtfully. "Seemed monstus stuck up," complained a Baptist sister. But the white postmaster from the edge of the crowd expressed the opinion of his folks plainly. "That damn Nigger," said he, as he shouldered the mail and arranged his tobacco, "has gone North and got plum full o' fool notions; but they won't work in Altamaha." And the crowd melted away.

The meeting of welcome at the Baptist Church was a failure. Rain spoiled the barbecue, and thunder turned the milk in the ice-cream. When the speaking came at night, the house was crowded to overflowing. The three preachers had especially prepared themselves, but somehow John's manner seemed to throw a blanket over everything,—he seemed so cold and preoccupied, and had so strange an air of restraint that the Methodist brother could not warm up to his theme and elicited not a single "Amen"; the Presbyterian prayer was but feebly responded to, and even the Baptist preacher, though he wakened faint enthusiasm, got so mixed up in his favorite sentence that he had to close it by stopping fully fifteen minutes sooner than he meant. The people moved uneasily in their seats as John rose to reply. He spoke slowly and methodically. The age, he said, demanded new ideas; we were far different from those mean of the seventeenth and eighteenth centuries,—with broader ideas of human brotherhood and destiny. Then he spoke of the rise of charity and popular education, and particularly of the spread of wealth and work. The question was, then, he added reflectively, looking at the low discolored ceiling, what part the Negroes of this land would take in the striving of the new century. He sketched in vague outline the new Industrial School that might rise among the pines, he spoke in detail of the charitable and philanthropic work that might be organized, of money that might be saved for banks and business. Finally he urged unity, and deprecated especially religious and denominational bickering. "To-day," he said, with a smile, "the world cares little whether a man be Baptist or Methodist, or indeed a churchman at all, so long as he is good and true. What difference does it make whether a man be baptized in river or washbowl, or not at all? Let's leave all that littleness, and look higher." Then, thinking of nothing else, he slowly sat down. A painful hush seized that crowded mass. Little had they understood of what he said, for he spoke an unknown tongue, save the last word about baptism; that they knew, and they sat very still while the clock ticked. Then at last a low suppressed snarl came from the Amen corner, and an old bent man arose, walked over the seats, and climbed straight up into the pulpit. He was wrinkled and black, with scant gray and tufted hair; his voice and hands shook as with palsy; but on his face lay the intense rapt look of the religious fanatic. He seized the Bible with his rough, huge hands; twice he raised it inarticulate, and then fairly burst into words, with rude and awful eloquence. He quivered, swayed, and bent; then rose aloft in perfect majesty, till the people moaned and wept, wailed and shouted, and a wild shrieking arose from the corners where all the pent-up feeling of the hour gathered itself and rushed into the air. John never knew clearly what the old man said; he only felt himself held up to scorn and scathing denunciation for trampling on the true religion, and he realized with amazement that all unknowingly he had put rough, rude hands on something this little world held sacred. He arose silently, and passed out into the night. Down toward the sea he went, in the fitful starlight, half conscious of the girl who followed timidly after him. When at last he stood upon the bluff, he turned to his little sister and looked upon her sorrowfully, remembering with sudden pain how little thought he had given her. He put his arm about her and let her passion of tears spend itself on his shoulder.

Long they stood together, peering over the gray unresting water.

"John," she said, "does it make every one—unhappy when they study and learn lots of things?"

He paused and smiled. "I am afraid it does," he said.

"And, John, are you glad you studied?"

"Yes," came the answer, slowly but positively.

She watched the flickering lights upon the sea, and said thoughtfully, "I wish I was unhappy,—and—and," putting both her arms about his neck, "I think I am, a little, John."

It was several days later that John walked up to the Judge's house to ask for the privilege of teaching the Negro school. The Judge himself met him at the front door, stared a little hard at him, and said brusquely, "Go 'round to the kitchen door, John, and wait." Sitting on the kitchen steps, John stared at the corn, thoroughly perplexed. What on earth had come over him? Every step he made offended some one. He had come to save his people, and before he left the depot he had hurt them. He sought to teach them at the church, and had outraged their deepest feelings. He had schooled himself to be respectful to the Judge, and then blundered into his front door. And all the time he had meant right,—and yet, and yet, somehow he found it so hard and strange to fit his old surroundings again, to find his place in the world about him. He could not remember that he used to have any difficulty in the past, when life was glad and gay. The world seemed smooth and easy then. Perhaps,—but his sister came to the kitchen door just then and said the Judge awaited him.

The Judge sat in the dining-room amid his morning's mail, and he did not ask John to sit down. He plunged squarely into the business. "You've come for the school, I suppose. Well, John, I want to speak to you plainly. You know I'am a friend to your people. I've helped you and your family, and would have done more if you hadn't got the notion of going off. Now I like the colored people, and sympathize with their reasonable aspirations; but you and I both know, John, that in this country the Negro must remain subordinate, and can never expect to be the equal of white men. In their place, your people can be honest and respectful; and God knows, I'll do what I can to help them. But when they want to reverse nature, and rule white men, and marry white women, and sit in my parlor, then, by God! we'll hold them under if we have to lynch every Nigger in the land. Now, John, the question is, are you, with your education and Northern notions, going to accept the situation and teach the darkies to be faithful servants and laborers as your fathers were,—I knew you father, John, he belonged to my brother, and he was a good Nigger. Well—well, are you going to be like him, or are you going to try to put fool ideas of rising and equality into these folks' heads, and make them discontented and unhappy?"

"I am going to accept the situation, Judge Henderson," answered John, with a brevity that did not escape the keen old man. He hesitated a moment, and then said shortly, "Very well,—we'll try you awhile. Good morning."

It was a full month after the opening of the Negro school that the other John came home, tall, gay, and headstrong. The mother wept, the sisters sang. The whole white town was glad. A proud man was the Judge, and it was a goodly sight to see the two swinging down Main Street together. And yet all did not go smoothly between them, for the younger man could not and did not veil his contempt for the little town, and plainly had his heart set on New York. Now the one cherished ambition of the Judge was to see his son mayor of Altamaha, representative to the legislature, and—who could say?—governor of Georgia. So the argument often waxed hot between them. "Good heavens, father," the younger man would say after dinner, as he lighted a cigar and stood by the fireplace, "you surely don't expect a young fellow like me to settle down permanently in this—this God-forgotten town with nothing but mud and Negroes?" "I did," the Judge would answer laconically; and on this particular day it seemed from the gathering scowl that he was about to add something more emphatic, but neighbors had already begun to drop in to admire his son, and the conversation drifted.

"Heah that John is livenin' things up at the darky school," volunteered the postmaster, after a pause.

"What now?" asked the Judge, sharply.

"Oh, nothin' in particulah,—just his almighty air and uppish ways. B'lieve I did heah somethin' about his givin' talks on the French Revolution, equality, and such like. He's what I call a dangerous Nigger."

"Have you heard him say anything out of the way?"

"Why, no,—but Sally, our girl, told my wife a lot of rot. Then, too, I don't need to heah: a Nigger what won't say 'sir' to a white man, or—"

"Who is this John?" interrupted the son.

"Why, it's little black John, Peggy's son,—your old playfellow."

The young man's face flushed angrily, and then he laughed.

"Oh," said he, "it's the darky that tried to force himself into a seat beside the lady I was escorting—"

But Judge Henderson waited to hear no more. He had been nettled all day, and now at this he rose with a half-smothered oath, took his hat and cane, and walked straight to the schoolhouse.

For John, it had been a long, hard pull to get things started in the rickety old shanty that sheltered his school. The Negroes were rent into factions for and against him, the parents were careless, the children irregular and dirty, and books, pencils, and slates largely missing. Nevertheless, he struggled hopefully on, and seemed to see at last some glimmering of dawn. The attendance was larger and the children were a shade cleaner this week. Even the booby class in reading showed a little comforting progress. So John settled himself with renewed patience this afternoon.

"Now, Mandy," he said cheerfully, "that's better; but you mustn't chop your words up so: 'If—the—man—goes.' Why, your little brother even wouldn't tell a story that way, now would he?"

"Naw, suh, cain't talk."

"All right; now let's try again: 'If the man—'"

"John!"

The whole school started in surprise, and the teacher half arose, as the red, angry face of the Judge appeared in the open doorway.

"John, this school is closed. You children can go home and get to work. The white people of Altamaha are not spending their money on black folks to have their heads crammed with impudence and lies. Clear out! I'll lock the door myself."

Up at the great pillared house the tall young son wandered aimlessly about after his father's abrupt departure. In the house there was little to interest him; the books were old and stale, the local newspaper flat, and the women had retired with headaches and sewing. He tried a nap, but it was too warm. so he sauntered out into the fields, complaining disconsolately, "Good Lord! how long will this imprisonment last!" He was not a bad fellow,—just a little spoiled and self-indulgent, and as headstrong as his proud father. He seemed a young man pleasant to look upon, as he sat on the great black stump at the edge of the pines idly swinging his legs and smoking. "Why, there isn't even a girl worth getting up a respectable flirtation with," he growled. Just then his eye caught a tall, willowy figure hurrying toward him on the narrow path. He looked with interest at first, and then burst into a laugh as he said, "Well, I declare, if it isn't Jennie, the little brown kitchen-maid! Why, I never noticed before what a trim little body she is. Hello, Jennie! Why, you haven't kissed me since I came home," he said gaily. The young girl stared at him in surprise and confusion,—faltered something inarticulate, and attempted to pass. But a willful mood had seized the young idler, and he caught at her arm. Frightened, she slipped by; and half mischievously he turned and ran after her through the tall pines.

Yonder, toward the sea, at the end of the path, came John slowly, with his head down. He had turned wearily homeward from the schoolhouse; then, thinking to shield his mother from the blow, started to meet his sister as she came from work and break the news of his dismissal to her. "I'll go away," he said slowly; "I'll go away and find work, and send for them. I cannot live here longer." And then the fierce, buried anger surged up into his throat. He waved his arms and hurried wildly up the path.

The great brown sea lay silent. The air scarce breathed. The dying day bathed the twisted oaks and mighty pines in black and gold. There came from the wind no warning, not a whisper from the cloudless sky. There was only a black man hurrying on with an ache in his heart, seeing neither sun nor sea, but starting as from a dream at the frightened cry that woke the pines, to see his dark sister struggling in the arms of a tall and fair-haired man.

He said not a word, but, seizing a fallen limb, struck him with all the pent-up hatred of his great black arm; and the body lay white and still beneath the pines, all bathed in sunshine and in blood. John looked at it dreamily, then walked back to the house briskly, and said in a soft voice, "Mammy, I'm going away,—I'm going to be free."

She gazed at him dimly and faltered, "No'th, honey, is yo' gwine No'th agin?"

He looked out where the North Star glistened pale above the waters, and said, "Yes, mammy, I'm going—North."

Then, without another word, he went out into the narrow lane, up by the straight pines to the same winding path and seated himself on the great black stump, looking at the blood where body had lain. Yonder in the gray past he had played with that dead boy, romping together under the solemn trees. The night deepened; he thought of the boys at Johnstown. He wondered how Brown had turned out, and Carey? And Jones,—Jones? Why, he was Jones, and he wondered what they would all say when they knew, when they knew, in that great long dining-room with its hundreds of merry eyes. Then as the sheen of the starlight stole over him, he thought of the gilded ceiling of that vast concert hall, and heard stealing toward him the faint sweet music of the swan. Hark! was it music, or the hurry and shouting of men? Yes, surely! Clear and high the faint sweet melody rose and fluttered like a living thing, so that the very earth trembled as with the tramp of horses and murmur of angry men.

He leaned back and smiled toward the sea, whence rose the strange melody, away from the dark shadows where lay the noise of horses galloping, galloping on. With an effort he roused himself, bent forward, and looked steadily down the pathway, softly humming the " Song of the Bride,"—

"Freudig geführt, ziehet dahin."

Amid the trees in the dim morning twilight he watched their shadows dancing and heard their horses thundering toward him, until at last they came sweeping like a storm, and he saw in from that haggard white-haired man, whose eyes flashed red with fury. Oh, how he pitied him,—pitied him,— and wondered if he had the coiling twisted rope. Then, as the storm burst round him, he rose slowly to his feet and turned his closed eyes toward the Sea.

And the world whistled in his ears.

From
"Morris and the Honourable Tim"

୫ ◆ ଓ

Myra Kelly, 1904

This story, from Myra Kelly's collection of short fiction, *Little Citizens*, depicts life in an urban school from the point of view of a young, well-intended teacher. Constance Bailey's "first-reader" classroom is composed mainly of Jewish immigrant children, whose knowledge of the English language is quite limited. Kelly's depiction of their stuggles and successes, and of their exaggerated vernacular tend toward stereotype, but the work vividly illustrates, nonetheless, many of the difficulties of teaching in turn-of-the-century urban America.

Not only does Constance Bailey contend with a large class of diverse children, all limited in their skills, she is also the victim of a supervisory system that scares and intimidates new and experienced teachers alike. Mr. Timothy O'Shea is an example of the "new manager," the product of Progressive theories on school organization that sought to quantify teaching methodologies into a series of rigid formulas. Supervisors were trained to stalk classrooms, searching for breaches in teaching form and technique. Obviously, this new kind of supervision often degenerated into tyranny. One contemporary account described the Progressive supervisor as a "malignant sphinx," marking down the teacher's every move in his "doomsday book" (Gilbert, 1906, p. 85). Timothy O'Shea is clearly a manager of this same ilk.

Myra Kelly (1875–1910) wrote from firsthand experience. Born into a middle-class family in Dublin, Kelly moved with her parents to New York's Lower East Side, the area of New York in which many of her immigrant subjects lived. After attending Horace Mann High School and Teachers College, Columbia University, Kelly began teaching at P. S. 147. Her years in this school provided material for most of her popular stories about schooling.

FROM "MORRIS AND THE HONOURABLE TIM"

Myra Kelly, 1904

On the first day of school, after the Christmas holidays, Teacher found herself surrounded by a howling mob of little savages in which she had much difficulty in recognizing her cherished First-Reader Class. Isidore Belchatosky's face was so wreathed in smiles and foreign matter as to be beyond identification; Nathan Spiderwitz had placed all his trust in a solitary suspender and two unstable buttons; Eva Kidansky had entirely freed herself from restraining hooks and eyes; Isidore Applebaum had discarded shoe-laces; and Abie Ashnewsky had bartered his only necktie for a yard of "shoe-string" licorice.

Miss Bailey was greatly disheartened by this reversion to the original type. She delivered daily lectures on nail-brushes, hair-ribbons, shoe polish, pins, buttons, elastic, and other means to grace. Her talks on soap and water became almost personal in tone, and her insistence on a close union between such garments as were meant to be united, led to a lively traffic in twisted and disreputable safety-pins. And yet the First-Reader Class, in all other branches of learning so receptive and responsive, made but halting and uncertain progress towards that state of virtue which is next to godliness.

Early in January came the report that "Gum Shoe Tim" was on the war-path and might be expected at any time. Miss Bailey heard the tidings in calm ignorance until Miss Blake, who ruled over the adjoining kingdom, interpreted the warning. A license to teach in the public schools of New York is good for only one year. Its renewal depends upon the reports of the Principal in charge of the school and of the Associate Superintendent in whose district the school chances to be. After three such renewals the license becomes permanent, but Miss Bailey was, as a teacher, barely four months old. The Associate Superintendent for her vicinity was the Honourable Timothy O'Shea, known and dreaded as "Gum Shoe Tim," owing to his engaging way of creeping softly up back stairs and appearing, all unheralded and unwelcome, upon the threshold of his intended victim.

This, Miss Blake explained, was in defiance of all the rules of etiquette governing such visits of inspection. The proper procedure had been that of Mr. O'Shea's predecessor, who had always given timely notice of his coming and a hint as to the subjects in which he intended to examine the children. Some days later he would amble from room to room, accompanied by the amiable Principal, and followed by the gratitude of smiling and unruffled teachers.

This kind old gentleman was now retired and had been succeeded by Mr. O'Shea, who, in addition to his unexpectedness, was adorned by an abominable temper, an overbearing manner, and a sense of cruel humour. He had almost finished his examinations at the nearest school where, during a brisk campaign of eight days, he had caused five dismissals, nine cases of nervous exhaustion, and an epidemic of hysteria.

Day by day nerves grew more tense, tempers more unsure, sleep and appetite more fugitive. Experienced teachers went stolidly on with the ordinary routine while beginners devoted time and energy to the more spectacular portions of the curriculum. But no one knew the Honourable Timothy's pet subjects and so no one could specialize to any great extent.

Miss Bailey was one of the beginners, and Room 18 was made to shine as the sun. Morris Mogilewsky, Monitor of the Gold-Fish Bowl, wrought busily until his charges glowed redly against the water plants in their shining bowl. Creepers crept, plants grew, and ferns waved under the care of Nathan Spiderwitz, Monitor of the Window Boxes. There was such a martial swing and strut in Patrick Brennan's leadership of the line that it informed even the timid heart of Isidore Wishnewsky with a war-like glow and his feet with a spasmodic but well-meant tramp. Sadie Gonorowsky and Eva, her cousin, sat closely side by side, no longer "mad on theirselves," but "mit kind feelings." The work of the preceding term was laid in neat and docketed piles upon the low book-case. The children were enjoined to keep clean and entire. And Teacher, a nervous and unsmiling Teacher, waited dully.

A week passed thus, and then the good-hearted and experienced Miss Blake hurried ponderously across the hall to put Teacher on her guard.

"I've just had a note from one of the grammar teachers," she panted. "'Gum Shoe Tim' is up in Miss Greene's room. He'll take this floor next. Now, see here, child, don't look so frightened. The Principal is with Tim. Of course you're nervous, but try not to show it. And you'll be all right, his lay is discipline and reading. Well, good luck to you!"

Miss Bailey took heart of grace. The children read surprisingly well, were absolutely good, and the enemy under convoy of the friendly Principal would be much less terrifying than the enemy at large and alone. It was, therefore, with a manner almost serene that she turned to greet the kindly concerned Principal and the dreaded "Gum Shoe Tim." The latter she found less ominous of aspect than she had been led to fear, and the Principal's charming little speech of introduction made her flush with quick pleasure. And the anxious eyes of Sadie Gonorowsky, noting the flush, grew calm as Sadie whispered to Eva, her close cousin:

"Say, Teacher has a glad. She's red on the face. It could to be her papa."

"No. It's comp'ny," answered Eva sagely. "It ain't her papa. It's comp'ny the whiles Teacher takes him by the hand."

The children were not in the least disconcerted by the presence of the large man. They always enjoyed visitors and they liked the heavy gold chain which festooned the wide white waistcoat of this guest; and, as they watched him, the Associate Superintendent began to superintend.

He looked at the children all in their clean and smiling rows: he looked at the flowers and the gold fish; at the pictures and the plaster casts: he looked at the work of the last term and he looked at Teacher. As he looked he swayed gently on his rubber heels and decided that he was going to enjoy the coming quarter of an hour. Teacher pleased him from the first. She was neither old nor ill-favoured, and she was most evidently nervous. The combination appealed both to his love of power and his peculiar sense of humour. Settling deliberately in the chair of state, he began:

"Can the children sing, Miss Bailey?"

They could sing very prettily and they did.

"Very nice, indeed," said the voice of visiting authority. "Very nice. Their music is exceptionally good. And are they drilled? Children, will you march for me?"

Again they could and did. Patrick marshaled his line in time and triumph up and down the aisles to the evident interest and approval of the "comp'ny," and then Teacher led the class through some very energetic Swedish movements. While arms and bodies were bending and straightening at Teacher's command and example, the door opened and a breathless boy rushed in. He bore an unfolded note and, as Teacher had no hand to spare, the boy placed the paper on the desk under the softening eyes of the Honourable Timothy, who glanced down idly and then pounced upon the note and read its every word.

"For you, Miss Bailey," he said in the voice before which even the school janitor had been known to quail. "Your friend was thoughtful, though a little late." And poor palpitating Miss Bailey read.

"Watch out!" 'Gum Shoe Tim' is in the building. The Principal caught him on the back stairs and they're going round together. He's as cross as a bear. Greene in dead faint in dressing-room. Says he's going to fire her. Watch out for him, and send the news on. His lay is reading and discipline."

Miss Bailey grew cold with sick and unreasoning fear. As she gazed wide-eyed at the living confirmation of the statement that "Gum Shoe Tim" was "as cross as a bear," the gentle-hearted Principal took the paper from her nerveless grasp.

"It's all right," he assured her. "Mr. O'Shea understands that you had no part in this. It's all right. You are not responsible."

But Teacher had no ears for his soothing. She could only watch with fascinated eyes as the Honourable Timothy reclaimed the note and wrote across its damning face:

"Miss Greene may come to. She is not fired.—T. O'S."

"Here, boy," he called; "take this to your teacher." The puzzled messenger turned to obey, and the Associate Superintendent saw that though his dignity had suffered his power had increased. To the list of those whom he might, if so disposed, devour, he had now added the name of the Principal, who was quick to understand that an unpleasant investigation lay before him. If Miss Bailey could not be held responsible for this system of inter-classroom communication, it was clear that the Principal could.

Every trace of interest had left Mr. O'Shea's voice as he asked:
"Can they read?"

"Oh, yes, they read," responded Teacher, but her spirit was crushed and the children reflected her depression. Still, they were marvellously good and that blundering note had said, "Discipline is his lay." Well, here he had it.

There was one spectator of this drama, who, understanding no word nor incident therein, yet missed no shade of the many emotions which had stirred the light face of his lady. Towards the front of the room sat Morris Mogilewsky, with every nerve tuned to Teacher's, and with an appreciation of the situation in which the other children had no share. On the afternoon of one of those dreary days of waiting for the evil which had now come, Teacher had endeavoured to explain the nature and possible result of this ordeal to her favourite. It was clear to him now that she was troubled, and he held the large and unaccustomed presence of the comp'ny mit whiskers responsible. Countless generations of ancestors had followed and fostered the instinct which now led Morris to propitiate an angry power. Luckily, he was prepared with an offering of a suitable nature. He had meant to enjoy it for yet a few days, and then to give it to Teacher. She was such a sensible person about presents. One might give her one's most cherished possession with a brave and cordial heart, for on each Friday afternoon she returned the gifts she had received during the week. And this with no abatement of gratitude.

Morris rose stealthily, crept forward, and placed a bright blue bromo-selt-zer bottle in the fat hand which hung over the back of the chair of state. The hand closed instinctively as, with dawning curiosity, the Honourable Timothy studied the small figure at his side. It began in a wealth of loosely curling hair which shaded a delicate face, very pointed as to chin and monopolized by a pair of dark eyes, sad and deep and beautiful. A faded blue "jumper" was buttoned tightly across the narrow chest; frayed trousers were precariously attached to the "jumper," and impossible shoes and stockings supplemented the trousers. Glancing from boy to bottle, the "comp'ny mit whiskers" asked:

"What's this for?"

"For you."

"What's in it?"

"A present."

Mr. O'Shea removed the cork and proceeded to draw out incredible quantities of absorbent cotton. When there was no more to come, a faint tinkle sounded within the blue depths, and Mr. O'Shea, reversing the bottle, found himself possessed of a trampled and disfigured sleeve link of most palpable brass.

"It's from gold," Morris assured him. "You puts it in your—'scuse me—shirt. Wish you health to wear it."

"Thank you," said the Honourable Tim, and there was a tiny break in the gloom which had enveloped him. And then, with a quick memory of the note and of his anger:

"Miss Bailey, who is this young man?"

And Teacher, of whose hobbies Morris was one, answered warmly: "That is Morris Mogilewsky, the best of boys. He takes care of the gold-fish, and does all sorts of things for me. Don't you, dear?"

"Teacher, yiss ma'an," Morris answered. "I'm lovin' much mit you. I gives presents on the company over you."

"Ain't he rather big to speak such broken English?" asked Mr. O'Shea. "I hope you remember that it is part of your duty to stamp out the dialect."

"Yes, I know," Miss Bailey answered. "But Morris has been in America for so short a time. Nine months, is it not?"

"Teacher, yiss ma'an. I comes out of Russia," responded Morris, on the verge of tears and with his face buried in Teacher's dress.

Now Mr. O'Shea had his prejudices—strong and deep. He had been given jurisdiction over that particular district because it was his native heath, and the Board of Education considered that he would be more in sympathy with the inhabitants than a stranger. The truth was absolutely the reverse. Because he had spent his early years in a large old house on East Broadway, because he now saw his birthplace changed to a squalid tenement, and the happy hunting grounds of his youth grown ragged and foreign—swarming with strange faces and noisy with strange tongues—Mr. O'Shea bore a sullen grudge against the usurping race.

He resented the caressing air with which Teacher held the little hand placed so confidently within her own and he welcomed the opportunity of gratifying his still ruffled temper and his racial antagonism at the same time. He would take a rise out of this young woman about her little Jew. She would be comforted later on. Mr. O'Shea rather fancied himself in the role of comforter, when the sufferer was neither old nor ill-favoured. And so he set about creating the distress which he would later change to gratitude and joy. Assuredly the Honourable Timothy had a well-developed sense of humour.

"His English is certainly dreadful," remarked the voice of authority, and it was not an English voice, nor is O'Shea distinctively an English name. "Dreadful. And, by the way, I hope you are not spoiling these youngsters. You must remember that you are fitting them for the battle of life. Don't coddle your soldiers. Can you reconcile your present attitude with discipline?"

"With Morris—yes," Teacher answered. "He is gentle and tractable beyond words."

"Well, I hope you're right," grunted Mr. O'Shea, "but don't coddle them."

And so the incident closed. The sleeve link was tucked, before Morris's yearning eyes, into the reluctant pocket of the wide white waistcoat, and

Morris returned to his place. He found his reader and the proper page, and the lesson went on with brisk serenity: real on the children's part, but bravely assumed on Teacher's. Child after child stood up; read; sat down again; and it came to be the duty of Bertha Binderwitz to read the entire page of which the others had each read a line. She began jubilantly, but soon stumbled, hesitated, and wailed:

"Stands a fierce word. I don't know what it is," and Teacher turned to write the puzzling word upon the blackboard.

Morris's heart stopped with a sickening suddenness and then rushed madly on again. He had a new and dreadful duty to perform. All his mother's counsel, all his father's precepts told him that it was his duty. Yet fear held him in his little seat behind his little desk, while his conscience insisted on this unalterable decree of the social code: "So somebody's clothes is wrong it's polite you says 'scuse' und tells it out."

And here was Teacher whom he dearly loved, whose ideals of personal adornment extended to full sets of buttons on jumpers and to laces in both shoes, here was his immaculate lady fair in urgent need of assistance and advice, and all because she had on that day inaugurated a delightfully vigorous exercise for which, architecturally, she was not designed.

There was yet room for hope that some one else would see the breach and brave the danger. But no. The visitor sat stolidly in the chair of state, the Principal sat serenely beside him, the children sat each in his own little place, behind his own little desk, keeping his own little eyes on his own little book. No. Morris's soul cried with Hamlet's:

> *"The time is out of joint;—O cursed spite,*
> *That ever I was born to set it right!"*

Up into the quiet air went his timid hand. Teacher, knowing him in his more garrulous moods, ignored the threatened interruption of Bertha's spirited résumé, but the windmill action of the little arm attracted the Honourable Tim's attention.

"The best of boys wants you," he suggested, and Teacher perforce asked:

"Well, Morris, what is it?"

Not until he was on his feet did the Monitor of the Gold-Fish Bowl, appreciate the enormity of the mission he had undertaken. The other children began to understand, and watched his struggle for words and breath with sympathy or derision, as their natures prompted. But there are no words in which one may politely mention ineffective safety-pins to one's glass of fashion. Morris's knees trembled queerly, his breathing grew difficult, and Teacher seemed a very great way off as she asked again:

"Well, what is it, dear?"

Morris panted a little, smiled weakly, and then sat down. Teacher was evidently puzzled, the "Comp'ny" alert, the Principal uneasy.

"Now, Morris," Teacher remonstrated, "you must tell me what you want."

But Morris had deserted his etiquette and his veracity, and murmured only:

"Nothings."

"Just wanted to be noticed," said the Honourable Tim. "It is easy to spoil them." And he watched the best of boys rather closely, for a habit of interrupting reading lessons, wantonly and without reason, was a trait in the young of which he disapproved.

When this disapprobation manifested itself in Mr. O'Shea's countenance, the loyal heart of Morris interpreted it as a new menace to his sovereign. No later than yesterday she had warned them of the vital importance of coherence. "Every one knows," she had said, "that only common little boys and girls come apart. No one ever likes them," and the big stranger was even now misjudging her.

Again his short arm agitated the quiet air. Again his trembling legs upheld a trembling boy. Again authority urged. Again Teacher asked:

"Well, Morris, what is it, dear?"

All this was as before, but not as before was poor harassed Miss Bailey's swoop down the aisle, her sudden taking of Morris's troubled little face between her soft hands, the quick near meeting with her kind eyes, the note of pleading in her repetition:

"What do you want, Morris?"

He was beginning to answer when it occurred to him that the truth might make her cry. There was an unsteadiness about her upper lip which seemed to indicate the possibility. Suddenly he found that he no longer yearned for words in which to tell her of her disjointment, but for something else—anything else—to say.

His miserable eyes escaped from hers and wandered to the wall in desperate search for conversation. There was no help in the pictures, no inspiration in the plaster casts, but on the blackboard he read, "Tuesday, January twenty-first, 1902." Only the date, but he must make it serve. With Teacher close beside him, with the hostile eye of the Honourable Tim upon him, hedged round about by the frightened or admiring regard of the First-Reader Class, Morris blinked rapidly, swallowed resolutely, and remarked:

"Teacher, this year's Nineteen-hundred-and-two," and knew that all was over.

The caressing clasp of Teacher's hands grew into a grip of anger. The countenance of Mr. O'Shea took on the beatified expression of the prophet who has found honour and verification in his own country.

"The best of boys has his off days and this in one of them," he remarked.

"Morris," said Teacher, "did you stop a reading lesson to tell me that? Do you think I don't know what the year is? I'm ashamed of you."

Never has she spoken thus. If the telling had been difficult to Morris when she was "glad on him," it was impossible now that she was a prey to such evident "mad feelings." And yet he must make some explanation. So he murmured: "Teacher, I tells you 'scuse. I know you knows what year stands, on'y it's polite I tells you something, und I had a fraid."

"And so you bothered your Teacher with that nonsense," said Tim. "You're a nice boy!"

Morris's eyes were hardly more appealing than Teacher's as the two culprits, for so they felt themselves, turned to their judge.

"Morris is a strange boy," Miss Bailey explained. "He can't be managed by ordinary methods—"

"And extraordinary methods don't seem to work to-day," Mr. O'Shea interjected.

"—and I think," Teacher continued, "that it might be better not to press the point."

"Oh, if you have no control over him—" Mr. O'Shea was beginning pleasantly, when the Principal suggested:

"You'd better let us hear what he has to say, Miss Bailey; make him understand that you are master here." And Teacher, with a heart-sick laugh at the irony of this advice in the presence of the Associate Superintendent, turned to obey.

But Morris would utter no words but these, dozens of times repeated: "I have a fraid." Miss Bailey coaxed, bribed, threatened and cajoled; shook him surreptitiously, petted him openly. The result was always the same: "It's polite I tells you something out, on'y I had a fraid."

"But, Morris, dear, of what?" cried Teacher. "Are you afraid of me? Stop crying now and answer. Are you afraid of Miss Bailey?"

"N-o-o-oh m-a-a-an."

"Are you afraid of the Principal?"

"N-o-o-oh m-a-a-an."

"Are you afraid"—with a slight pause, during which a native hue of honesty was foully done to death—"of the kind gentleman we are all so glad to see?"

"N-o-o-oh m-a-a-an."

"Well, then, what is the matter with you? Are you sick? Don't you think you would like to go home to your mother?"

"N-o-o-oh m-a-a-an; I ain't sick. I tells you 'scuse."

The repeated imitation of a sorrowful goat was too much for the Honourable Tim.

"Bring that boy to me," he commanded. "I'll show you how to manage refractory and rebellious children."

With much difficulty and many assurances that the gentleman was not going to hurt him, Miss Bailey succeeded in untwining Morris's legs from the supports of the desk and in half carrying, half leading him up to the chair of state. An ominous silence had settled over the room. Eva Gonorowsky was weeping softly, and the redoubtable Isidore Applebaum was stiffened in a frozen calm.

"Morris," began the Associate Superintendent in his most awful tones, "will you tell me why you raised your hand? Come here, sir."

Teacher urged him gently, and like dog to heel, he went. He halted within a pace or two of Mr. O'Shea, and lifted a beseeching face towards him.

"I couldn't to tell nothing out," said he. "I tells you 'scuse. I'm got a fraid."

The Honourable Tim lunged quickly and caught the terrified boy preparatory to shaking him, but Morris escaped and fled to his haven to safety—his Teacher's arms. When Miss Bailey felt the quick clasp of the thin little hands, the heavy beating of the over-tried heart, and the deep convulsive sobs, she turned on the Honourable Timothy O'Shea and spoke:

"I must ask you to leave this room at once," she announced. The Principal started, and then sat back. Teacher's eyes were dangerous, and the Honourable Tim might profit by a lesson. "You've frightened the child until he can't breathe. I can do nothing with him while you remain. The examination is ended. You may go."

Now Mr. O'Shea saw he gone a little too far in his effort to create the proper dramatic setting for his clemency. He had not expected the young woman to "rise" quite so far and high. His deprecating half-apology, half-eulogy, gave Morris the opportunity he craved.

"Teacher," he panted; "I wants to whisper mit you in the ear."

With a dextrous movement he knelt upon her lap and tore out his solitary safety-pin. He then clasped her tightly and made his explanation. He began in the softest of whispers, which increased in volume as it did in interest, so that he reached the climax at the full power of his boy soprano voice.

"Teacher, Missis Bailey, I know you know what year stands. On'y it's polite I tells you something, und I had a fraid the while the comp'ny mit the whiskers sets and rubbers. But, Teacher, it's like this: your jumper's sticking out und you could take mine safety-pin."

He had understood so little of all that had passed that he was beyond being surprised by the result of this communication. Miss Bailey had gathered him into her arms and had cried in a queer helpless way. And as she cried she had said over and over again: "Morris, how could you? Oh, how could you, dear? How could you?"

The Principal and "the comp'ny mit whiskers" had looked solemnly at one another for a struggling moment, and had then broken into laughter, long and loud, until the visiting authority was limp and moist. The children waited in polite uncertainty, but when Miss Bailey, after some indecision, had contributed a wan smile, which later grew into a shaky laugh, the First-Reader Class went wild.

Then the Honourable Timothy arose to say good-by. He reiterated his praise of the singing and reading, the blackboard work and the moral tone.

An awkward pause ensued, during which the Principal engaged the young Gonorowskys in impromptu conversation. The Honourable Tim crossed over to Miss Bailey's side and steadied himself for a great effort.

"Teacher," he began meekly, "I tells you 'scuse. This sort of thing makes a man feel like a bull in a china shop. Do you think the little fellow will shake hands with me? I was really only joking."

"But surely he will," said Miss Bailey, as she glanced down at the tangle of dark curls resting against her breast. "Morris, dear, aren't you going to say good-by to the gentleman?"

Morris relaxed one hand from its grasp on his lady and bestowed it on Mr. O'Shea.

"Good by," said he gently. "I gives you presents, from gold presents, the while you're friends mit Teacher. I'm loving much mit her too."

At this moment the Principal turned, and Mr. O'Shea, in a desperate attempt to retrieve his dignity, began: "As to class management and discipline—"

But the Principal was not to be deceived.

"Don't you think, Mr. O'Shea," said he, "that you and I had better leave the management of the little ones to the women? You have noticed, perhaps, that this is Nature's method."

A Schoolmaster of the Great City (c. 1898–1907)

ʚ◦ ◆ ◦ʚ

Angelo Patri, 1917

Angelo Patri's autobiographical story of his own first years in the classroom shows the makings of a true Progressive educator. Patri (1877–1965), who spent his career as a teacher and administrator in New York City schools, describes in this account his sense of dismay at the old-fashioned methodologies and subjects that had long been a staple of urban school curriculums. In this excerpt from Patri's book, the new teacher quickly realized that "the whole system of marking and punishments and rewards was wrong...[that it put] the child on the lowest possible plane" (p. 15). Patri comes to the same conclusions as other great Progressive thinkers of his day, when he concludes that the child "must move and not sit still: that he must make mistakes and not merely repeat perfect forms: that he must be himself and not a miniature reproduction of the teacher. The sacredness of the child's individuality," he realizes, "must be the moving passion of the teacher" (p. 15).

Patri's emphasis on movement, discovery, and doing, his stress of individuality and his recognition of the child's "sacred" nature are all key elements of the Progressive ideology. In his own career as an educator, Patri attempted to put these ideas into practice. As a principal in Public Schools 4 and 45 in the Bronx (1908–1944), the author pioneered a range of Progressive methods and subjects. In shop classes, Patri encouraged sewing, writing, working with clay and metal. He organized student orchestras in his schools, allowed students to plant fruit and vegetable gardens, and generally nurtured creativity in the context of the fundamentals. Many of Patri's Progressive notions were probably gleaned from his training at Columbia University at the turn of the century, a period when great liberal educators like William Heard Kilpatrick influenced both teaching and teacher training there.

In addition to his work in schools, Patri wrote a syndicated column called "Our Children" that ran in newspapers across the country. He also authored a number of children's books and self-help books that instructed parents in raising and educating their children.

FROM *A SCHOOLMASTER OF THE GREAT CITY*
(c . 1898–1907)

Angelo Patri, 1917

The principal under whom I did my first teaching was one with whom I had studied as a pupil in the grades. He was opening a new school and welcomed me cordially. Leading me to a classroom he opened the door and pushed me in, saying, "This is your class." Then he vanished.

There were sixty-six children in that room. Their ages ran from eight to fifteen. They had been sitting there daily annoying the substitutes who were sent to the room and driving them out of school. The cordial reception I had been given by the principal held more of relief for himself than of kindness for me.

The first day passed. The last few straggling boys filed out an hour or so after school hours. One of the biggest boys whom I had detained for disorder stopped long enough on his way out to ask, "Coming back to-morrow?"

"Yes, of course I am coming back. Why do you ask?"

"Well, some of them come one day and some come two days. To-morrow will be two days."

This boy did not know me. My strong point was discipline. I knew little of subject matter, pedagogy or psychology, except a number of words that had never become a part of me. I had one notion that was strong—discipline. That was the idea. Had I not been kept after hours to study my lessons, slapped for asking my neighbour for a pencil, made to kneel for hours for absenting myself from school, for defending my rights to the teacher? Had I not been marked, rated, percented all the ten years of my life in school?

Discipline then was the basic idea in teaching. You made pupils do what you wanted; you must be the master. Memory, and those who ought to have known, preached discipline. It was the standard for judging my work as a teacher. My continuance in the profession depended upon discipline.

At least there was no conflict of aim. Since discipline was the thing, I would discipline, and I did. I oppressed; I went to the homes; I sent registered letters. I followed up each infraction of rules relentlessly. There was no getting away from me. I was making sure that the children were punished for their misdeeds.

I followed the truants into their homes because I wanted relief from a principal who sent me a note every time my attendance fell below a certain per cent. I visited the parents to complain of the work the children were doing, because the principal said I must hold their noses to the grindstone.

I seemed to say to the children, in the words of Edmond Holmes, "You are a model yourself, or rather I will model you, on me. What I do, you are to learn to do. What I think, you are to learn to think. What I believe, you are to learn to believe. What I admire, you are to learn to admire. What I aim at, you are to learn to aim at. What I am, you are to learn to be."

At the end of my first month I was an assured success. My discipline of the class and the promptness with which I followed up the absentees gained recognition. I was promoted from teaching a fourth-year class to a fifth-year class. The new class was made for me especially because I was efficient. It was composed of all the children that the other teachers in approximate grades did not want. They were fifty misfits.

The room given me was the corner of an assembly room, shut in by rolling doors. The benches were long affairs and were not screwed to the floor. A writing lesson could be conducted only when the desk which formed part of the seat in front was turned up, so that it became the desk for the seat behind. No hour went by but some boy or girl of the fifty managed to upset one of the desks; then the papers would scatter, and the ink would flow on the new floor. Some of the children would laugh; others would howl, and my best friend in the front seat would stand on his head. This he said was in preparation for the time when he was to become a tumbler at the circus. Judging from the hardness of the bumps his head got he was undergoing rather severe training.

Discipline—my favourite word—why, discipline was failing, failing terribly. If I kept the children after hours they would not come to school the next day until they had made up the time that I had taken from them. If I went to their parents, the parents simply said they could not help it; they knew that these were bad children. They seemed to feel sorry for this mere slip of a boy who used up his afternoons and evenings calling upon them.

Discipline, discipline! It was no use. I tried to say again, "You are to model yourself, or rather I will model you, on me. What I do you are to learn to do, etc." But somehow the words would not come. Discipline, my great stronghold, had failed for I had come into contact with those who defied discipline.

What was I to do? I began to tell over again the stories I faintly remembered having heard in the days when father sat and talked and we listened, not daring to move lest we lose a syllable of what he said. I told them about my own childhood in the mountains of Italy, about midnight expeditions when we loaded the mules with provisions and carried food to our friends, the last of the Bourbon adherents. I told them about a wolf that attacked the sheep at night until my father seized and killed it barehanded.

When I related these stories they listened. They hardly breathed. Each day I would end so that more could be expected. Then I began to bargain with them, trading what they liked for what the schools said they should have. I bribed them with promises of more stories to come if they would be "good" and do the work assigned.

The struggle was between the child and the teacher, and the struggle was over the facts of the curriculum—the children refusing to learn and the teacher insisting that they must. But discipline was restored, and victory won, by bargaining.

Woe to the boy or girl who transgressed and thus prevented the telling of the story. No arithmetic, no story! No silence, no story! The children from other classes asked to be changed. They too wanted stories. I had them by the hundreds, for as soon as I had caught the interest of the children the stories of adventure gave place to the old hero tales.

Discipline once more was my watchword.

Then a new trouble arose. I had been teaching a year when "Methods" became the school watch-word, and everybody set about learning how to teach arithmetic, spelling, history and geography. Each teacher had his own methods and supervisors going from one room to another were puzzled by the variety.

The principal restored order out of chaos. A method book was written. Every subject was treated and the steps of procedure in each were carefully marked out. A programme of the day's work was prescribed and we were expected to follow the stated order. Inspection by the principal and other supervisors was based on these.

I heard the teachers talk of these things as impositions. When I failed to follow directions I was severely criticised. I began asking the reason for it all.

Why should I teach history in the prescribed way?

"Class, open books to page 37. Study the first paragraph."

Two minutes later.

"Close books. Tell me what you learned."

In such instruction there was no stopping, no questioning, no valuation: nothing but deadly, mechanical grind. Every teacher and every class had to do these things in just this way.

The spelling routine was worst. Twenty new words were to be assigned each day for study. The words had to be difficult, too, for through them the children were to train their memories—their minds, as the principal put it. The next day at a signal the children wrote the twenty words in the order in which they had been assigned, from memory, if they could. Papers were exchanged and the children were asked to correct them. If a child failed to discover an error it was a point against him. The names of those who "missed" were written on the board with a check for each mistake. The pupils who failed had to remain after hours and repeat the list from memory, accurately as to its spelling and sequence.

This was a fixed procedure which no teacher dared modify because the supervisor came around and questioned the children as to the accuracy of the records on the boards.

Instead of protesting, the teacher set about acquiring devices which would give the desired results with the minimum of effort on the part of the teacher and pupils. It was no longer a question of teaching. It was simply a question of getting the better of the supervisor.

My method was simple and efficacious. There was no place where I could get twenty new words with so little expenditure of time and effort as in the dictionary. The dictionary arrangement offered a valuable aid in itself. I selected two a's, two b's, etc., until I had the desired twenty.

The advantages of this scheme were apparent to the children. They could more easily remember and check up their list when it was based upon alphabetical arrangement. The per cent of my returns then became high, and the mental strain on the class and teacher was reduced to the minimum.

Still the question arose in my mind—"Why must I do this sort of thing?"

Another year passed before I realised that my fellow teachers were talking about Education, the Science of Education and its principles. It appeared that in the universities were men who could teach a man why he taught and how to do it. There was one thing I had learned and that was the insufficiency of my equipment as a teacher. Discipline, boss standard, was nerve taxing and not altogether productive.

After two years of teaching I found myself nowhere, and was depressed. I questioned the value of my services to the children. The work I did was not its own criticism but was judged by some one else whose standard seemed to be capricious, depending upon his humour and my relation to him. I felt the need of new ideas and convictions, and I decided to go to the university to see what those who were supposed to know had to tell.

I wondered if my return to college with the deliberate purpose of learning what I wanted definitely to know, would prove profitable.

Toward the close of the year's work I summed it up. First one institution and then another! From this professor, and a little later from that, came words, words, words. They were all so far away, so ineffectual, so dead. I was disheartened.

The next year, however, I came upon the thing I needed. This was a course with Dr. McMurry and the text-book used as a basis of discussion, was Dewey's Essay on "Ethical Principles."

Here were strange and new words to use in relation to teaching. Conduct was the way people behaved, and it had little to do with learning, as such. But conduct, not ability to write lessons, was the real test of learning and the sign of culture.

Conduct furnished the key as to whether the child had real social interests and intelligence and power. Conduct meant action, whereas school meant passivity. Conduct meant individual freedom and not blind adherence to formulated dogma. The knowledge gained had to be used immediately and the worth of the knowledge judged by its fitness to the immediate needs of the child.

The greatest fallacy of the child education was the "training-for-the-future" idea. Training for the future meant dying for the present.

Conduct said the child was a being constantly active, rarely silent, never a purely parrot-like creature. Conduct said the teacher must keep his hands off; he must watch and guide; he could not force; he could not drive. He could put the problems but the children themselves must solve them.

The disciplinary habit was a matter of action on the part of the children rather than one of silent obedience; judgment was a matter of applied knowledge and not word juggling.

Social sympathy was the result of close contact, mutual help, common work, common play, judicious leadership. Laughing, talking, dreaming even, were part of school life, the give and take of the group. Conduct always carried the idea of some one else; no isolation, no selfishness.

Then the whole system of marking and punishment and rewards was wrong. It was putting the child on the lowest plane possible. It was preventing him from working in response to an ideal.

I realised then that the child must move and not sit still: that he must make mistakes and not merely repeat perfect forms: that he must be himself and not a miniature reproduction of the teacher. The sacredness of the child's individuality must be the moving passion of the teacher.

These things I learned from my masters. It was a wholesome reaction against my disciplinary idea, and a healthy soul-giving impetus to my daily teaching.

I had come in contact with the personality of a great teacher, fearless, candid, and keen, with nothing dogmatic in his nature. Under this leadership I came in touch with vital ideas and I began to work, not in the spirit of passive obedience, but in one of mental emancipation.

There was a new pleasure and much more freedom in my teaching. I went back to the children ready to challenge their intelligence, keen to see them grapple and solve problems set for them, eager to watch them carry into their daily lives the ideas of the school.

I looked back into my own experiences, analysed them, built them up, and through them interpreted the struggles of the children before me. The God of Discipline was replaced by the God of Watchfulness.

I tried to carry over into classroom practice the results of what I had learned. I tried to teach in the light of the saner point of view. My supervisors objected to the variations I was trying to introduce into the teaching of history, spelling and the rest.

"You'll find those things may be all right in theory but they will not do in practice," they said. But I refused to compromise, to yield to beliefs merely because I was told to do so or because others about me yielded to beliefs and policies.

Just when the feeling came upon me that I was really beginning to enter into the secret of child training the principal came to me and said, "You are wasting your time. You are wasting the children's time. You are totally unfit for this work. If I had a son he should not be put in your class."

His idea was that, unless you ground children down and made them do as you wanted them to, they would have no fear and respect for you. It was the master and the slave idea. When the teacher rebelled the scourge of sarcasm was relentless.

There were times when I felt that he would have been pleased to have lowered my "ratings" to the point where I would have been compelled to retire from the profession, yet he refrained because he too, was compromising with himself.

When I changed from his educational philosophy to mine, his comment was, "Why is it you will not do as I tell you?"

What he did not know was that if he had treated me kindly and asked for co-operation, allowed me some form of self expression, he would have had a wealth of enthusiasm to call upon.

Self respect compelled me to change schools, and I went away, every fibre of my being indignant at his oppression.

The next principal I found lived the doctrine, "I serve children."

Here was a man who actually loved school children; who enjoyed coming into personal contact with them in the classroom, the yards, the streets and their occupations. He helped clothe the poor children and feed them, washed the dirty faces when he found them, and all with the utmost unkindliness and in the belief that such service was a wonderful privilege that had been granted him. All about him was the radiance and glow of progress.

He always told this story with sadness as one of the incidents of his school life. A boy had been brought to him for habitual lateness and without stopping to question him he berated him for his laziness while the child stood silent and patient. When the principal awoke to the situation he asked, "Why were you late, anyway?"

The boy replied that he had to work till three o'clock each morning in order to help the family. The principal apologised and made the boy feel that he understood and sympathised with his struggles.

So he was with the teachers, and with me.

To each of us he seemed to say, "You are tired, brother, come to me and let me hold your quivering hands in my strong, steady ones. Come to me and let me stroke your hot, tired eyes with me cool fingers. I know what makes you tired for I, too, have been tired and worn out.

"Sometimes even now, I get tired when I forget the bigness of the things I want to do. Those faces that you see in the classroom are not set against you, my brother. They are set against the things that bind you and prevent your mind from mingling freely with others.

"You must not think too much of arithmetic, and rules and dates and examinations, for these are not teaching; the children don't grow because of them. They grow because of their contact with you, the best that you know and feel.

"Come with me to the open country and let us live together for awhile. There we will be silent and look into the hearts of children as we do into the heart of nature.

"When we come back the school will be as a new world and you will work with the earnestness of a discoverer patiently awaiting revelations."

The thought of him always makes me feel strong and fresh as a boy who runs shouting through the cool air of a spring morning. I stretch my arms and open wide my eyes and shout the faith that he gave me.

Promotion came and I found myself in another school. There was little of special interest in my experience in this place. Placed in charge of a graduating class, I was supposed to teach science to the boys of the seventh and eighth grades. The only way I could do this was to carry whatever apparatus I needed from room to room. Batteries, tubes, jars, pails, water, gas burners followed me about. As I passed down the stairs and through the halls I looked like a small moving van. In this departmental system the teacher moved, not the children, because the movement of the children would cause too much noise, too much confusion. School was the place for silence!

At the end of two months I moved again. This time it was a graduating class in a school on the lower west side of the city. The building was more than fifty years old. It fitted well with the general neighbourhood picture. It was all run down. There was a miscellaneous sort of population, a mixture of races and colour. The boys lived along the docks, in the rear of factory yards where the men found employment.

The first morning, when I announced to the principal that I was a new teacher, he looked at me doubtfully and said, "Why, this won't do, you don't want to come here. You are only a boy. You are not old enough nor strong enough! The boys in that corner room broke the teacher's eyeglasses and he as a bigger man than you are. They threw the ink wells and the books out of the window. You don't want to come here."

When I saw the assembly a few minutes later I agreed with him. I did not want to be there.

I sat on the platform while the principal conducted the exercises. There was scarcely a child in the room who was not either talking or chewing gum, or slouching in his seat. There was a spirit of unrest throughout the monotonous assembly. There was nothing about the general exercises that could offer the slightest inspiration to either children or teacher. Two or three of the men walked up and down the room eyeing the boys, and the women, each at her place, had their eyes riveted on their classes.

Yet, in spite of all this close supervision, the children were not behaving as if they were happy or as if they liked school. At the end of fifteen minutes they were sent to their rooms and the work of the day began. What work that was no one could appreciate unless he had gone through the halls of the building and felt the struggle that was going on in each room. The very walls seemed to speak of tension and battle.

The antagonism between the children and teachers was far stronger that I had ever seen it before. The antagonism between the school and the neighbourhood was intense. Both came from mutual distrust founded on mutual misunderstanding. The children were afraid of the teachers, and the teachers feared the children.

The neighbourhood was a place from which the teacher escaped, and into which the children burrowed. One never knew as he went through the streets what missile or epithet might greet him. One or the other was certain.

I do not remember a period in my life when I was more silent and soberminded than during the first six months of my career in this school. Day in and day out I sat quietly scarcely saying an unnecessary word and by gestures rather than speech indicating to the children what I wanted done.

I went through the building silent, rarely speaking. I looked out upon the streets, silent. I visited the shops and listened to the talk of the fathers. I visited some of the homes. Here too, I talked little, trying to get people to talk to me.

The school was failing. I was failing and my whole mind was concentrated upon finding the cause and the remedy.

After school hours I would stare out of the windows and look out upon the strange mixture of people with their prejudices, their sensitiveness and their shiftlessness and ponder upon the gulf between them and me.

There was no attempt on the part of the school to understand the problem and to direct the lives of the pupils. In fact, teaching the curriculum was the routine business of the day—no more. There was apparently little affection for the children, and no interest in the parents as co-workers in their education.

When the principal assigned the assembly exercises and the discipline of the school to me, I was glad. I had learned to believe in children. I had begun to analyse my own childhood more carefully. Here was an opportunity to test my knowledge in a larger way than the classroom offered.

I began telling the boys what a fine assembly was like in other schools. Once more I resorted to stories. They never failed. Father had done his share nobly. The big restless crowd settled down and listened. As each day went by, cautiously I put the problem of school discipline before them and they responded by taking over much of the responsibility for it themselves. A sort of council was held in my room each week at which the problems of the school were discussed. From fifty to one hundred of the most responsible boys in the school attended and as there were only about twelve hundred in all, the representatives were fairly adequate to the need.

This experience helped me wonderfully. Through it I gained, increased confidence in the children, in the power of the school, in myself.

From *The Heart Is the Teacher* (c. 1920)[1]

$\mathcal{SO} \quad \blacklozenge \quad \mathcal{CS}$

Leonard Covello, 1958

This excerpt from Leonard Covello's (1887–1982) autobiography chron-
icles the teacher's final victory in a conflict that stands at the heart of
Progressivism and the immigrant experience in the public schools: Covello,
a long-time advocate of Italian culture and language, sought to give Italian
the same academic status in the public schools as French, German, Spanish,
and Latin. For Covello and other immigrant teachers and parents, the fight
for inclusion of their native language in the schools extends far beyond
simple matters of curriculum; it represents the minority groups' struggle for
a full and equal place in the society at large. Set in 1920, the theme of this
excerpt clearly echoes contemporary arguments for bilingual education.

Covello's life and career exemplifies the new balance many immigrants tried
to strike between assimilation and loyalty to their native cultures. Throughout
his life, Covello nurtured and celebrated his Italian roots, even as he moved
successfully through the American system of higher education and a profession
in the public schools. Born in Avigliano, Italy, Covello immigrated with his
family to East Harlem when he was 8 years old. After graduating from Columbia
University, Covello began his career teaching French and Spanish at De Witt
Clinton High School, then established and chaired the Department of Italian
at that school. From DeWitt Clinton, Covello moved on to the principalship
of Benjamin Franklin High School. He completed a PhD at New York University, writing his dissertation on "The Social Background of the Italian-American
School Child," and then went on to teach a series of courses on the immigrant
experience at the university level. Covello's work on behalf of the Italian
American community in New York is legion. He established the Lincoln Club
of Little Italy, worked for the Italian League for Social Service, served as
vice-president of the Italian Teachers Association and was a leader in the Italian

---

[1] An early draft of this essay is found in the Leonard Covello papers, Balch Institute for Ethnic Studies, Philadelphia.

Parents Association, which organized in 1927. His goal, in all these projects, was to gain equality and self-respect for immigrant groups in the city. Although he never used the words, Covello was clearly an early advocate for multiculturalism and diversity.

FROM *THE HEART IS THE TEACHER*

Leonard Covello, 1958

In September, 1920, I again stepped into a classroom and looked into the faces of about twenty-five boys who formed my first class in Italian at De Witt Clinton, perhaps the only Italian class in any public school in the country at that time. Our efforts and struggles prior to the war had succeeded, and there was a deep satisfaction in this achievement. Surely the language and culture of Italy held a place beside that of France, Germany, or Spain. Surely the student from the lower or upper East Side had a right to that spiritual lift that comes from knowing that the achievements of one's people have been recognized.

For this basic belief those of us who espoused this simple cause were often criticized by fellow teachers and by the general public. They argued that we were keeping the boys "foreigners." The boys were in America now and should use English exclusively. I was myself accused of "segregating" my students, and more than once by Italian-Americans themselves. The war had strengthened the idea of conformity. Americanization meant the casting off of everything that was "alien," especially the language and culture of national origin. Yet the amazing paradox lay in the fact that is was perfectly all right for the Italo-American boy to study Latin or French, German or Spanish.

Fortunately, at De Witt Clinton, we had the approval of Dr. Francis H. Paul, the principal, who was sympathetic with our point of view. It was he who had made the *Circolo* possible in the first place and who had later approved the introduction of the teaching of Italian.

Dr. Paul called me into his office one day not long after my return and spoke about the problem of the rapidly increasing number of students of Italian origin now coming to Clinton from all over the city. "These boys are not easy to handle," he said, sitting at the edge of his desk. "To put it bluntly, it will be your job to look after these boys. I will see to it that your schedule is changed so that you will have time to take care of them. In short, Leonard, from now on I want you to be the father-confessor of these East Side boys."

In an out-of-the-way corner of the old De Witt Clinton building, I found a small room that was being used as a stock room. Together with some of my students I spent several Saturdays cleaning and painting and putting it in shape for an office. The room had a very narrow window and just enough space for a desk, a few file cabinets, some chairs, and a mimeographing machine. It wasn't much of an office, but it was good enough for a beginning.

It was good enough for the first office of the first Italian Department in the public schools of New York City.

In this two-by-four office I held conferences, handled disciplinary problems, interviewed parents, and planned our work. For the very first time in my experience as a teacher I began to have a feeling of inner satisfaction which rose from the knowledge that here was a job that I really wanted to do. All my thoughts about a professorship or becoming a medical doctor faded, never to be revived. No longer was I merely teaching a language or a subject. Here I was grappling with *all* the problems affecting the boys coming to me for help.

Often I would be working in my office, late in the afternoon, and a knock would come on the door, hesitant, reluctant, and I would know at once that it was another of my boys coming to me for help or advice. When the knock came during school hours I could almost be sure it had to do with a school problem. But when it sounded out of the stillness of the deserted corridors, I could be equally sure that the problem was a personal one.

At this moment I can still see Joe D'Angelo sitting in the chair near my desk. He was a tall boy, weighing about one hundred and eighty pounds, dressed in a new suit and carrying a derby. To make it easier for him to talk I kept my eyes on the narrow knot of his tie while he fumbled to explain why he had come. He was going to a party. His companions were waiting for him outside the school. "I had to see you first, Mr. Covello. I gotta get this thing off my chest. It's the old man. He keeps hittin' me all the time. No matter what I say or do he's gotta start cloutin' me. He's a big guy and he works on the docks, and it hurts, and I can't stand it no more."

"If he really hurts you...," I started to say.

Joe D'Angelo shook his head. "That's not it." He held out a bony fist across the desk for my observation. "What he don't know is I've been fighting around the Jersey clubs a lot under the name of Kid Angel. I'm pretty good. That's what he don't know. If I hit him I could put him in the hospital. That's what I'm scared of. It's gonna happen and it would kill my mother."

After a silence I said, "How is it you never told them at home about the boxing?"

"Because ever since I was a little kid my mother has been telling everybody that I was going to be a lawyer."

"While you want to be a fighter?"

"No. I want to be a lawyer. But I make a couple of bucks in these club matches. I get a kick out of it, and I don't have to work in a store or a factory after school. Only thing is, I could never make them believe it."

I sent Joe off to his party and told him to spend the night with his uncle who lived in the Bronx. Then I took the subway downtown to the "Little Italy" of Greenwich Village. The D'Angelo family lived in one of those red brick tenements on MacDougal Street. As I entered the downstairs hall and caught the odor of garlic and tomato sauce, I felt right at home. Pappa D'Angelo himself, clad in his undershirt, answered the door. He was short, with heavy shoulders and a gray moustache, and an iron-gray stubble of hair covered his head and became a mattress of gray on his chest. He looked at me, wiped his mouth with a bright, checkered napkin, and was about to slam the door in my face. When he caught the name De Witt Clinton, his manner changed.

"*Perdona!* Scuse me, please. I think you was selling piano or something." He gently took hold of my arm and ushered me inside, directly into the kitchen. "Ninitta," he said to the middle-aged woman seated at the table. "Get up. Get one more plate. Is the teacher from the school where Joe go. Clintona." Suddenly he stopped dead. "Is Joe?" he shouted. "What he do? He do something bad? That why you here? I kill him! I break all the bones in his head!"

The mother started to cover her face with her hands in anticipation of some terrible calamity. I took hold of the father's arm and, wagging my free hand in a characteristic Italian gesture, at the same time speaking in the Neapolitan dialect, said, "Who said anything about Joe being a bad boy? Joe is a good boy. He is a very good student."

When both father and mother got over the staggering fact that I could not only speak Italian but could even speak their dialect, they made me sit down and eat a dish of sausage and peppers. "It is an honor. You will do us a great honor, Signor Maestro," Pappa D'Angelo insisted, in the most flowery language at his command. "Also a glass of wine. A gentle glass of wine made with my own hands. So he is a good student, Giuseppe? And good he should be." He extended a massive paw. "With this instrument I have taught him right from wrong. Respect for his elders. For those who instruct him in school. In the old tradition. In this way he will become educated and become a lawyer and not work on the docks like his father."

"Exactly," I agreed, rolling a mouthful of wine over my tongue. "It is just that I have come to see you about. Giuseppe is getting too big. You have to handle him differently, now."

"I have been telling him this again and again," the mother broke in.

"Quiet," Pappa D'Angelo said. "Where is the harm in a father correcting his son? This is something new. Something American. I have heard of it but I do not understand. Only this very evening I had to give Giuseppe a lesson in economy. A derby! Imagine, a boy buying and wearing a derby. To go to work in a factory!"

"With me," I said, "it was shiny shoes with buttons. Besides it was his own money—money that he earned with his own hands."

"Which changes nothing at all."

"But which makes for impatience and loss of temper. He is getting too old for you to knock him around. He is afraid that one day he is going to forget himself and hurt you. That is what he is afraid of."

It was a joke. Pappa D'Angelo started to laugh. He downed a full glass of wine and heaved his powerful chest. "Ha, ha. Now he thinks he can lick his pappa." He slammed his fist down on the table. "Wait he come home, I show him. I show him who the boss in this house, lilla snotnose!" All of a sudden he was so mad at his son again that he could only talk the language of the docks.

"Wait a minute," I said. "Calm down. Do you know what kind of work your son does when he is not in school? Do you know how he makes the money that he gives you here at home and that paid for the derby?"

I told them as simply as I could that their son was not working in a factory but was making money as a prize fighter.

The father did not get it right away. "A fighter," he asked, "with the hands?"

"With the hands. A boxer. I have been told that even though he is very young, he is good. He would have a future as a fighter. But Joe does not want to be a fighter. He fights so that he can earn money to be a lawyer. But he is afraid when you beat him that someday he is going to forget you are his father."

"*Madonna!*" the mother breathed.

Pappa D'Angelo rocked his head. After a while, as if this were not enough, he scratched it furiously. He looked at me sheepishly. He started to smile. The smile broadened into a grin.

"That lilla sonamangonia!" he said.

That was my encounter with the D'Angelo family. There were so many others in those days that sometimes it seems as if I spent almost as much time in the homes of my students as I did at the school. There was Nick Barone, who didn't show up in class for a couple of days. He worked on an ice wagon after school, and one of the big ice blocks toppled over and smashed his hand, landing him in the hospital. Nick had spoken to me about his parents. They could speak no English at all and both mother and father worked at home doing stitching and needle piece work for the garment industry—the common exploitation of the time. They had little or no contact at all with the outside world.

The Barone family lived in the Italian section around 28th Street and Second Avenue. I went there after school and found the small tenement flat in a state of turmoil—crowded with neighbors, and the mother and father carrying on so that I thought for sure that Nick had passed away. When I was finally able to make them understand who I was, both parents grabbed my hands, imploring me to save Nick before it was too late.

"He will die there," the father lamented. "Everyone knows what goes on in a hospital—the last stage before the grave. A soul could die in a torment of thirst and no one would lift a finger to bring you a glass of water."

"Old superstitions about hospitals," I sought to explain; "stories from the old country when distances were great and knowledge of medicine limited and the patient almost always died before reaching the hospital. It is different now."

"But we could take such wonderful care of him at home here," the mother entreated. "I could cook him a chicken, make him broth and pastina and food to get well. The good Lord knows what they will feed him there, if anything."

After I had managed to calm them somewhat, I had both the mother and father put on their best clothes and I took them to the hospital, where up until now they had not dared to go. We found Nick sitting up in bed, joking with a nurse and having a gay time with his companions in the ward. When one of the interns even spoke to them in Italian, their attitude changed to one of great wonderment.

On the way home from the hospital the father turned to me with an expression of guilt and deep embarrassment. "You must forgive us. There are many things here we know nothing about. It is hard to change old ideas and the way we think even though we see the changes every day in our children."

He shook his head. "If only everybody in the world could speak the same tongue, then perhaps things would not be quite so hard to understand." And the more I came into contact with the family life of my boys, the more I became aware of the vital importance of language in the double orientation—to family and to community—of the immigrant child.

Though Italian was now being taught as a first language in De Witt Clinton, it was not being taught as a first language in other high schools. A student could study Italian only after he had had a year of Latin, French, or Spanish. We determined to do what was necessary—have the Board of Education of New York City pass a by-law placing Italian on an equal footing with the other languages.

The campaign to accomplish this involved civic leaders, interested citizens, and members of the Italian Teachers Association, particularly Professor Mario E. Cosenza of City College, who was president of this association for many years.

We invited parents to entertainments at which our students put on plays in Italian, we publicized the campaign in the Italian newspapers, and we had conferences at the Board of Education. The most effective part of the campaign was the home visits that we made—speaking to the individual parents about signing petitions to introduce Italian in a particular school.

How many homes I entered at this period where I had to guide a trembling hand in the signing of an "X"! How many cups of coffee I drank, jet black with just a speck of sugar, while explaining our purpose. The parents were usually astonished that they should be consulted in the matter of what was to be taught to their children. They couldn't believe the schools were really interested in their opinion.

"Signor Maestro, we are people who never had any education. In Italy we worked in the fields from when the sun came up in the morning until it went down at night. In America we work, but we hope that with our children it will be different. That is why we came to America. But do not ask us to decide things we know nothing about."

Our visits usually turned into lessons in democracy, trying to make the immigrant understand his rights and privileges. "Would you prefer your son to study Italian, or some other foreign language?"

"What a question! Naturally, we prefer him to study our own language. But *real* Italian. Italian as you speak it, Signor Maestro—the Italian of our great men, of Garibaldi."

In May, 1922, through our work and the help of Salvatore Cotillo, New York State Senator elected by the East Harlem community, the Board of Education placed Italian on an equal footing with other languages in the schools of New York City.

I had longed for the day when I would have just one class in Italian to teach. Never did I imagine that in the space of a few years there would be hundreds of boys studying Italian at Clinton—and that there would be five teachers in the Italian Department.

"Children of Loneliness"[1]

❧ ◆ ☙

Anzia Yezierska, 1923

Although much has been written about the plight of the immigrant student in urban schools, far less attention has been paid to the life and world of the immigrant teacher. Whereas the vast majority of teachers in the 19th century were native born, that trend began to shift during the Progressive period. In the first decades of the century, immigrants and the children of immigrants entered the profession in unprecedented numbers. As early as 1900, 27,000 foreign born teachers worked in American schools, a figure that represented more than 6% of all teachers nationwide (U.S. Bureau of Census, 1900, p. 489). The vast majority of those teachers were women.

Anzia Yezierska's heroine in this powerful short story shows us the immigrant teacher's struggle to find her place in the new world. Torn between the assimilationist values she admires and the ties of the old world, as they are represented by her parents, Rachel Ravinsky is truly alone. She is comfortable in neither world; and neither her family nor her new American friends have the will or desire to attend to her dilemma. Like thousands of other immigrant teachers in the first decades of the century, Rachel will have to suppress her own sense of alienation and isolation to effectively Americanize her students.

Anzia Yezierska (1885–1970) had a difficult but fascinating life. Born in a mud hut in Plinsk, on the Russian–Polish border, she immigrated at 15 to New York's Lower East Side. There, Yezierska joined the ranks of other immigrants in the ghetto sweatshops, attending night school to learn to read and write. Only 3 years after arriving, she won a scholarship to study "domestic science" at Columbia University, and then went on to teach briefly in city schools. With the publication of her first story, in 1915, Yezierska became a full-time and highly successful writer. So popular was her work that the movie producer Samuel Goldwyn purchased the rights to one of her novels and brought her to Hollywood, accompanied by much fanfare. Dubbed "The Queen of the Ghetto" and "The Immigrant Cinderella," Yezierska quickly developed an aversion to the Hollywood culture, returning within a year. She could not write, she discovered, when separated from the Lower East Side of her youth.

One of the more interesting aspects of Yezierska's life was her relationship with John Dewey. After making his acquaintance in 1917, Anzia audited his famous seminar in social and political thought at Columbia. During the course of the year, they became romantically involved. The relationship evidently meant a great deal to both the 32-year-old student and the 58-year-old teacher, because both wrote about it in their own work; he, in poetry and she, in a novel entitled *All I Could Never Be* (1932). Yezierska's most famous book, *Bread Givers* (1925) was reissued in 1975. This autobiographical novel about a young woman's efforts to escape from the oppressive tenement world and the suffocating religious values of her father led to a renewed interest in her work.

"CHILDREN OF LONELINESS"

Anzia Yezierska, 1923

"Oh, Mother, can't you use a fork?" exclaimed Rachel as Mrs. Ravinsky took the shell of the baked potato in her fingers and raised it to her watering mouth.

"Here, *Teacherin* mine, you want me to learn in my old age how to put the bite in my mouth?" The mother dropped the potato back into her plate, too wounded to eat. Wiping her hands on her blue-checked apron, she turned her glance to her husband, at the opposite side of the table.

"Yankev," she said bitterly, "stick your bone on a fork. Our *teacherin* said she dassn't touch no eatings with the hands."

"All my teachers died already in the old country," retorted the old man. "I ain't going to learn nothing new no more from my American daughter." He continued to suck the marrow out of the bone with that noisy relish that was so exasperating to Rachel.

"It's no use," stormed the girl, jumping up from the table in disgust; "I'll never be able to stand it here with you people."

"'You people?' What do you mean by 'you people?'" shouted the old man, lashed into fury by his daughter's words. "You think you got a different skin from us because you went to college?"

"It drives me wild to hear you crunching bones like savages. If you people won't change, I shall have to move and live by myself."

Yankev Ravinsky threw the half-gnawed bone upon the table with such vehemence that a plate broke into fragments.

"You witch you!" he cried in a hoarse voice tense with rage. "Move by yourself! We lived without you while you was away in college, and we can get on without you further. God ain't going to turn his nose on us because we ain't got table manners from America. A hell she made from this house since she got home."

"*Shah!* Yankev *leben*," pleaded the mother, "the neighbors are opening the windows to listen to our hollering. Let us have a little quiet for a while till the eating is over."

But the accumulated hurts and insults that the old man had borne in the one week since his daughter's return from college had reached the breaking-point. His face was convulsed, his eyes flashed, and his lips were flecked with froth as he burst out in a volley of scorn:

"You think you can put our necks in a chain and learn us new tricks? You think you can make us over for Americans? We got through till fifty years of our lives eating in our own way—"

"Wo is me, Yankev *leben*!" entreated his wife. "Why can't we choke ourselves with our troubles? Why must the whole world know how we are tearing ourselves by the heads? In all Essex Street, in all New York, there ain't such fights like by us."

Her pleadings were in vain. There was no stopping Yankev Ravinsky once his wrath was roused. His daughter's insistence upon the use of a knife and fork spelled apostasy, Anti-Semitism, and the aping of the Gentiles.

Like a prophet of old condemning unrighteousness, he ran the gamut of denunciation, rising to heights of fury that were sublime and godlike, and sinking from sheer exhaustion to abusive bitterness.

"*Pfui* on all your American colleges! *Pfui* on the morals of America! No respect for old age. No fear for God. Stepping with your feet on all the laws of the holy Torah. A fire should burn out the whole new generation. They should sink into the earth, like Korah."

"Look at him cursing and burning! Just because I insist on their changing their terrible table manners. One would think I was killing them."

"Do you got to use a gun to kill?" cried the old man, little red threads darting out of the whites of his eyes.

"Who is doing the killing? Aren't you choking the life out of me? Aren't you dragging me by the hair to the darkness of past ages every minute of the day? I'd die of shame if one of my college friends should open the door while you people are eating."

"You—you—"

The old man was on the point of striking his daughter when his wife seized the hand he raised.

"*Mincha!* Yankeve, you forgot *Mincha!*"

This reminder was a flash of inspiration on Mrs. Ravinsky's part, the only thing that could have ended the quarreling instantly. *Mincha* was the prayer just before sunset of the orthodox Jews. This religious rite was so automatic with the old man that at his wife's mention of *Mincha* everything was immediately shut out, and Yankev Ravinsky rushed off to a corner of the room to pray.

"*Ashrai Yoishwai Waisahuh!*"

"Happy are they who dwell in Thy house. Ever shall I praise Thee. *Selah!* Great is the Lord, and exceedingly to be praised; and His greatness is unsearchable. On the majesty and glory of Thy splendor, and on Thy marvelous deeds, will I mediate."

The shelter from the storms of life that the artist finds in his art, Yankev Ravinsky found in his prescribed communion with God. All the despair caused by his daughter's apostasy, the insults and disappointments he suffered, were in his sobbing voice. But as he entered into the spirit of his prayer, he felt the man of flesh drop away in the outflow of God around him. His voice mellowed, the rigid wrinkles of his face softened, the hard glitter of anger and condemnation in his eyes was transmuted into the light of love as he went on:

"The Lord is gracious and merciful; slow to anger and of great loving-kindness. To all that call upon Him in truth He will hear their cry and save them."

Oblivious to the passing and repassing of his wife as she warmed anew the unfinished dinner, he continued:

"Put not your trust in princes, in the son of man in whom there is no help." Here Reb Ravinsky paused long enough to make a silent confession for the sin of having placed his hope on his daughter instead of on God. His whole body bowed with the sense of guilt. Then in a moment his humility was transfigured into exaltation. Sorrow for sin dissolved in joy as he became more deeply aware of God's unfailing protection.

"Happy is he who hath the God of Jacob for his help, whose hope is in the Lord his God. He healeth the broken in heart, and bindeth up their wounds."

A healing balm filled his soul as he returned to the table, where the steaming hot food awaited him. Rachel sat near the window pretending to read a book. Her mother did not urge her to join them at the table, fearing another outbreak, and the meal continued in silence.

The girl's thoughts surged hotly as she glanced from her father to her mother. A chasm of four centuries could not have separated her more completely from them than her four years at Cornell.

"To think that I was born one of these creatures! It's an insult to my soul. What kinship have I with these two lumps of ignorance and superstition? They're ugly and gross and stupid. I'm all sensitive nerves. They want to wallow in dirt."

She closed her eyes to shut out the sight of her parents as they silently ate together, unmindful of the dirt and confusion.

"How is it possible that I lived with them and like them only four years ago? What is it in me that so quickly gets accustomed to the best? Beauty and cleanliness are as natural to me as if I'd been born on Fifth Avenue instead of the dirt of Essex Street."

A vision of Frank Baker passed before her. Her last long talk with him out under the trees in college still lingered in her heart. She felt that she had only to be with him again to carry forward the beautiful friendship that had sprung up between them. He had promised to come shortly to New York. How could she possibly introduce such a born and bred American to her low, ignorant, dirty parents?

"I might as well tear the thought of Frank Baker out of my heart," she told herself. "If he just once sees the pigsty of a home I come from, if he just sees the table manners of my father and mother, he'll fly through the ceiling."

Timidly, Mrs. Ravinsky turned to her daughter.

"Ain't you going to give a taste the eating?"

No answer.

"I fried the *lotkes* special' for you—"

"I can't stand your fried, greasy stuff."

"Ain't even my cooking good no more either?" Her gnarled, hard-worked hands clutched at her breast. "God from the world, for what do I need yet any more my life? Nothing I do for my child is no use no more."

Her head sank; her whole body seemed to shrivel and grow old with the sense of her own futility.

"How I was hurrying to run by the butcher before everybody else, so as to pick out the grandest, fattest piece of brust!" she wailed, tears streaming down her face. "And I put my hand away from my heart and put a whole fresh egg into the lotkes, and I stuffed the stove full of coal like a millionaire so as to get the *lotkes* fried so nice and brown; and now you give a kick on everything I done—"

"Fool woman," shouted her husband, "stop laying yourself on the ground for your daughter to step on you! What more can you expect from a child raised up in America? What more can you expect but that she should spit in your face and make dirt from you?" His eyes, hot and dry under their lids, flashed from his wife to his daughter. "The old Jewish eating is poison to her; she must have *trefa* ham—only forbidden food."

Bitter laughter shook him.

"Woman, how you patted yourself with pride before all the neighbors, boasting of our great American daughter coming home from college! This is our daughter, our pride, our hope, our pillow for our old age that we were dreaming about! This is our American *teacherin*! A Jew-hater, an Anti-Semite we brought into the world, a betrayer of our race who hates her own father and mother like the Russian Czar once hated a Jew. She makes herself so refined, she can't stand it when we use the knife or fork the wrong way;

but her heart is that of a brutal Cossack, and she spills her own father's and mother's blood like water."

Every word he uttered seared Rachel's soul like burning acid. She felt herself becoming a witch, a she-devil, under the spell of his accusations.

"You want me to love you yet?" She turned upon her father like an avenging fury. "If there's any evil hatred in my soul, you have roused it with your cursed preaching."

"*Oi-i-i!* Highest One! pity Yourself on us!" Mrs. Ravinsky wrung her hands. "Rachel, Yankev, let there be an end to this knife-stabbing! Gottuniu! my flesh is torn to pieces!"

Unheeding her mother's pleading, Rachel rushed to the closet where she kept her things.

"I was a crazy idiot to think that I could live with you people under one roof." She flung on her hat and coat and bolted for the door.

Mrs. Ravinsky seized Rachel's arm in a passionate entreaty.

"My child, my heart, my life, what do you mean? Where are you going?"

"I mean to get out of this hell of a home this very minute," she said, tearing loose from her mother's clutching hands.

"Wo is me! My child! We'll be to shame and to laughter by the whole world. What will people say?"

"Let them say! My life is my own; I'll live as I please." She slammed the door in her mother's face.

"They want me to love them yet," ran the mad thoughts in Rachel's brain as she hurried through the streets, not knowing where she was going, not caring. "Vampires, bloodsuckers fastened on my flesh! Black shadow blighting every ray of light that ever came my way! Other parents scheme and plan and wear themselves out to give their child a chance, but they put dead stones in front of every chance I made for myself."

With the cruelty of youth to everything not youth, Rachel reasoned:

"They have no rights, no claims over me like other parents who do things for their children. It was my own brains, my own courage, my own iron will that forced my way out of the sweatshop to my present position in the public schools. I owe them nothing, nothing, nothing."

Two weeks already away from home. Rachel looked about her room. It was spotlessly clean. She had often said to herself while at home with her parents: "All I want is an empty room, with a bed, a table, and a chair. As long as it is clean and away from them, I'll be happy." But was she happy?

A distant door closed, followed by the retreating sound of descending footsteps. Then all was still, the stifling stillness of a rooming-house. The white, empty walls pressed in upon her, suffocated her. She listened acutely for any stir of life, but the continued silence was unbroken save for the insistent ticking of her watch.

"I ran away from home burning for life," she mused, "and all I've found is the loneliness that's death." A wave of self-pity weakened her almost to the point of tears. "I'm alone! I'm alone!" she moaned, crumpling into a heap.

"Must it always be with me like this," her soul cried in terror, "either to live among those who drag me down or in the awful isolation of a hall bedroom? Oh, I'll die of loneliness among these frozen, each-shut-in-himself Americans! It's one thing to break away, but, oh, the strength to go on alone! How can I ever do it? The love instinct is so strong in me; I can not live without love, without people."

The thought of a letter from Frank Baker suddenly lightened her spirits. That very evening she was to meet him for dinner. Here was hope—more than hope. Just seeing him again would surely bring the certainty.

This new rush of light upon her dark horizon so softened her heart that she could almost tolerate her superfluous parents.

"If I could only have love and my own life, I could almost forgive them for bringing me into the world. I don't really hate them; I only hate them when they stand between me and the new America that I'm to conquer."

Answering her impulse, her feet led her to the familiar Ghetto streets. On the corner of the block where her parents lived she paused, torn between the desire to see her people and the fear of their nagging reproaches. The old Jewish proverb came to her mind: "The wolf is not afraid of the dog, but he hates his bark." "I'm not afraid of their black curses for sin. It's nothing to me if they accuse me of being an Anti-Semite or a murderer, and yet why does it hurt me so?"

Rachel had prepared herself to face the usual hail-storm of reproaches and accusations, but as she entered the dark hallway of the tenement, she heard her father's voice chanting the old familiar Hebrew psalm of "The Race of Sorrows":

"Hear my prayer, O Lord, and let my cry come unto Thee.

"For my days are consumed like smoke, and my bones are burned as an hearth.

"I am like a pelican of the wilderness.

"I am like an owl of the desert.

"I have eaten ashes like bread and mingled my drink with weeping."

A faintness came over her. The sobbing strains of the lyric song melted into her veins like a magic sap, making her warm and human again. All her strength seemed to flow out of her in pity for her people. She longed to throw herself on the dirty, ill-smelling tenement stairs and weep: "Nothing is real but love—love. Nothing so false as ambition."

Since her early childhood she remembered often waking up in the middle of the night and hearing her father chant this age-old song of woe. There flashed before her a vivid picture of him, huddled in the corner beside the table piled high with Hebrew books, swaying to the rhythm of his Jeremiad, the sputtering light of the candle stuck in a bottle throwing uncanny shadows over his gaunt face. The skull cap, the side-locks, and the long gray beard made him seem like some mystic stranger from a far-off world and not a father. The father of the daylight who ate with a knife, spat on the floor, and who was forever denouncing America and Americans was different from this mystic spirit who could thrill with such impassioned rapture.

Thousands of years of exile, thousands of years of hunger, loneliness, and want swept over her as she listened to her father's voice. Something seemed to be crying out to her to run in and seize her father and mother in her arms and hold them close.

"Love, love—nothing is true between us but love," she thought.

But why couldn't she do what she longed to do? Why, with all her passionate sympathy for them, should any actual contact with her people seem so impossible? No, she couldn't go in just yet. Instead, she ran up on the roof, where she could be alone. She stationed herself at the air-shaft opposite their kitchen window, where for the first time since she had left in a rage she could see her old home.

Ach! what sickening disorder! In the sink were the dirty dishes stacked high, untouched, it looked, for days. The table still held the remains of the last meal. Clothes were strewn about the chairs. The bureau drawers were open, and their contents brimmed over in mad confusion.

"I couldn't endure it, this terrible dirt!" Her nails dug into her palms, shaking with the futility of her visit. "It would be worse than death to go back to them. It would mean giving up order, cleanliness, sanity, everything that I've striven all these years to attain. It would mean giving up the hope of the new world—the hope of Frank Baker."

The sound of the creaking door reached her where she crouched against the air-shaft. She looked again into the murky depths of the room. Her mother had entered. With arms full of paper bags of provisions, the old woman paused on the threshold, her eyes dwelling on the dim figure of her husband. A look of pathetic tenderness illumined her wrinkled features.

"I'll make you something good to eat for you, yes?"

Reb Ravinsky only dropped his head on his breast. His eyes were red and dry, sandy with sorrow that could find no release in tears. Good God! never had Rachel seen such profound despair. For the first time she noticed the grooved tracings of withering age knotted on his face and the growing hump on her mother's back.

"Already the shadow of death hangs over them," she thought as she watched them. "They're already with one foot in the grave. Why can't I be human to them before they're dead? Why can't I?"

Rachel blotted away the picture of the sordid room with both hands over her eyes.

"To death with my soul! I wish I were a plain human being with a heart instead of a monster of selfishness with a soul."

But the pity she felt for her parents began now to be swept away in a wave of pity for herself.

"How every step in advance costs me my heart's blood! My greatest tragedy in life is that I always see the two opposite sides at the same time. What seems to me right one day seems all wrong the next. Not only that, but many things seem right and wrong at the same time. I feel I have a right to my own life, and yet I feel just as strongly that I owe my father and mother something. Even if I don't love them, I have no right to step over them. I'm drawn to them by something more compelling than love. It is the cry of their dumb, wasted lives."

Again Rachel looked into the dimly lighted room below. Her mother placed food upon the table. With a self-effacing stoop of humility, she entreated, "Eat only while it is hot yet."

With his eyes fixed almost unknowingly, Reb Ravinsky sat down. Her mother took the chair opposite him, but she only pretended to eat the slender portion of the food she had given herself.

Rachel's heart swelled. Yes, it had always been like that. Her mother had taken the smallest portion of everything for herself. Complaints, reproaches, upbraidings, abuse, yes, all these had been heaped by her upon her mother; but always the juiciest piece of meat was placed on her plate, the thickest slice of bread; the warmest covering was given to her, while her mother shivered through the night.

"Ah, I don't want to abandon them!" she thought; "I only want to get to the place where I belong. I only want to get to the mountain-tops and view the world from the heights, and then I'll give them everything I've achieved."

Her thoughts were sharply broken in upon by the loud sound of her father's eating. Bent over the table, he chewed with noisy gulps a piece of herring, his temples working to the motion of his jaws. With each audible swallow and smacking of the lips, Rachel's heart tightened with loathing.

"Their dirty ways turn all my pity into hate." She felt her toes and her fingers curl inward with disgust. "I'll never amount to anything if I'm not strong enough to break away from them once and for all." Hypnotizing herself into her line of self-defense, her thoughts raced on: "I'm only cruel to be kind. If I went back to them now, it would not be out of love, but because of weakness—because of doubt and unfaith in myself."

Rachel bluntly turned her back. Her head lifted. There was iron will in her jaws.

"If I haven't the strength to tear free from the old, I can never conquer the new. Every new step a man makes is tearing away from those clinging to him. I must get tight and hard as rock inside of me if I'm ever to do the things I set out to do. I must learn to suffer and suffer, walk through blood and fire, and not bend from my course."

For the last time she looked at her parents. The terrible loneliness of their abandoned old age, their sorrowful eyes, the wrung-dry weariness on their faces, the whole black picture of her ruined, desolate home, burned into her flesh. She knew all the pain of one unjustly condemned, and the guilt of one with the spilt blood of helpless lives upon his hands. Then came tears, blinding, wrenching tears that tore at her heart until it seemed that they would rend her body into shreds.

"God! God!" she sobbed as she turned her head away from them, "if all this suffering were at least for something worth while, for something outside myself. But to have to break them and crush them merely because I have a fastidious soul that can't stomach their table manners, merely because I can't strangle my aching ambitions to rise in the world!"

She could no longer sustain the conflict which raged within her higher and higher at every moment. With a sudden tension of all her nerves she pulled herself together and stumbled blindly down stairs and out of the house. And she felt as if she had torn away from the flesh and blood of her own body.

Out in the street she struggled to get hold of herself again. Despite the tumult and upheaval that racked her soul, an intoxicating lure still held her up—the hope of seeing Frank Baker that evening. She was indeed a storm-racked ship, but within sight of shore. She need but throw out the signal, and help was nigh. She need but confide to Frank Baker of her break with her people, and all the dormant sympathy between them would surge up. His understanding would widen and deepen because of her great need for his understanding. He would love her the more because of her great need for his love.

Forcing back her tears, stepping over her heart-break, she hurried to the hotel where she was to meet him. Her father's impassioned rapture when he chanted the Psalms of David lit up the visionary face of the young Jewess.

"After all, love is the beginning of the real life," she thought as Frank Baker's dark, handsome face flashed before her. "With him to hold on to, I'll begin my new world."

Borne higher and higher by the intoxicating illusion of her great destiny, she cried:

"A person all alone is but a futile cry in an unheeding wilderness. One alone is but a shadow, an echo of reality. It takes two together to create reality. Two together can pioneer a new world."

With a vision of herself and Frank Baker marching side by side to the conquest of her heart's desire, she added:

"No wonder a man's love means so little to the American woman. They belong to the world in which they are born. They belong to their fathers and mothers; they belong to their relatives and friends. They are human even without a man's love. I don't belong; I'm not human. Only a man's love can save me and make me human again."

It was the busy dinner-hour at the fashionable restaurant. Pausing at the doorway with searching eyes and lips eagerly parted, Rachel's swift glance circled the lobby. Those seated in the dining-room beyond who were not too absorbed in one another, noticed a slim, vivid figure of ardent youth; but with dark, age-old eyes that told of the restless seeking of her homeless race.

With nervous little movements of anxiety, Rachel sat down, got up, then started across the lobby. Half-way, she stopped, and her breath caught.

"Mr. Baker," she murmured, her hands fluttering toward him with famished eagerness. His smooth, athletic figure had a cock-sureness that to the girl's worshipping gaze seemed the perfection of male strength.

"You must be doing wonderful things," came from her admiringly, "you look so happy, so shining with life."

"Yes,"—he shook her hand vigorously,—"I've been living for the first time since I was a kid. I'm full of such interesting experiences. I'm actually working in an East Side settlement."

Dazed by his glamourous success, Rachel stammered soft phrases of congratulation as he led her to a table. But seated opposite him, the face of this untried youth, flushed with the health and happiness of another world than that of the poverty-crushed Gehtto [sic], struck her almost as an insincerity.

"You in an East Side settlement?" she interrupted sharply. "What reality can there be in that work for you?"

"Oh," he cried, his shoulders squaring with the assurance of his master's degree in sociology, "it's great to get under the surface and see how the other half live. It's so picturesque! My conception of these people has greatly changed since I've been visiting their homes." He launched into a glowing account of the East Side as seen by a twenty-five-year-old college graduate.

"I thought them mostly immersed in hard labor, digging subways or slaving in sweatshops," he went on. "But think of the poetry which the immigrant is daily living!"

"But they're so sunk in the dirt of poverty, what poetry do you see there?"

"It's their beautiful home life, the poetic devotion between parents and children, the sacrifices they make for one another—"

"Beautiful home life? Sacrifices? Why, all I know of is the battle to the knife between parents and children. It's black tragedy that boils there, not the pretty sentiments that you imagine."

"My dear child,"—he waved aside her objection,—"you're too close to judge dispassionately. This very afternoon, on one of my friendly visits, I came upon a dear old man who peered up at me through horn-rimmed glasses behind his pile of Hebrew books. He was hardly able to speak English, but I found him a great scholar."

"Yes, a lazy old do-nothing, a bloodsucker on his wife and children."

Too shocked for remonstrance, Frank Baker stared at her.

"How else could he have time in the middle of the afternoon to pore over his books?" Rachel's voice was hard with bitterness. "Did you see his wife? I'll bet she was slaving for him in the kitchen. And his children slaving for him in the sweat-shop."

"Even so, think of the fine devotion that the women and children show in making the lives of your Hebrew scholars possible. It's a fine contribution to America, where our tendency is to forget idealism."

"Give me better a plain American man who supports his wife and children and I'll give you all those dreamers of the Talmud."

He smiled tolerantly at her vehemence.

"Nevertheless," he insisted, "I've found wonderful material for my new book in all this. I think I've got a new angle on the social types of your East Side."

An icy band tightened about her heart. "Social types," her lips formed. How could she possibly confide to this man of the terrible tragedy that she had been through that very day? Instead of the understanding and sympathy that she had hoped to find, there were only smooth platitudes, the sightseer's surface interest in curious "social types."

Frank Baker talked on. Rachel seemed to be listening, but her eyes had a far-off, abstracted look. She was quiet as a spinning-top is quiet, her thoughts and emotions revolving within her at high speed.

"That man in love with me? Why, he doesn't see me or feel me. I don't exist to him. He's only stuck on himself, blowing his own horn. Will he never stop with his 'I,''I,''I'? Why, I was a crazy lunatic to think that just because we took the same courses in college, he would understand me out in the real world."

All the fire suddenly went out of her eyes. She looked a thousand years old as she sank back wearily in her chair.

"Oh, but I'm boring you with all my heavy talk on sociology." Frank Baker's words seemed to come to her from afar. "I have tickets for a fine musical comedy that will cheer you up, Miss Ravinsky—"

"Thanks, thanks," she cut in hurriedly. Spend a whole evening sitting beside him in a theater when her heart was breaking? No. All she wanted was to get away—away where she could be alone. "I have work to do," she heard herself say. "I've got to get home."

Frank Baker murmured words of polite disappointment and escorted her back to her door. She watched the sure swing of his athletic figure as he strode away down the street, then she rushed up-stairs.

Back in her little room, stunned, bewildered, blinded with her disillusion, she sat staring at her four empty walls.

Hours passed, but she made no move, she uttered no sound. Doubled fists thrust between her knees, she sat there, staring blindly at her empty walls.

"I can't live with the old world, and I'm yet too green for the new. I don't belong to those who gave me birth or to those with whom I was educated."

Was this to be the end of all her struggles to rise in America, she asked herself, this crushing daze of loneliness? Her driving thirst for an education, her desperate battle for a little cleanliness, for a breath of beauty, the tearing away from her own flesh and blood to free herself from the yoke of her parents—what was it all worth now? Where did it lead to? Was loneliness to be the fruit of it all?

Night was melting away like a fog; through the open window the first lights of dawn were appearing. Rachel felt the sudden touch of the sun upon her face, which was bathed in tears. Overcome by her sorrow, she shuddered and put her hand over her eyes as tho to shut out the unwelcome contact. But the light shone through her fingers.

Despite her weariness, the renewing breath of the fresh morning entered her heart like a sunbeam. A mad longing for life filled her veins.

"I want to live," her youth cried. "I want to live, even at the worst."

Live how? Live for what? She did not know. She only felt she must struggle against her loneliness and weariness as she had once struggled against dirt, against the squalor and ugliness of her Ghetto home.

Turning from the window, she concentrated her mind, her poor tired mind, on one idea.

"I have broken away from the old world; I'm through with it. It's already behind me. I must face this loneliness till I get to the new world. Frank Baker can't help me; I must hope for no help from the outside. I'm alone; I'm alone till I get there.

"But am I really alone in my seeking? I'm one of the millions of immigrant children, children of loneliness, wandering between worlds that are at once too old and too new to live in."

"Split Cherry Tree"[1]

ဆ ◆ ဗ

Jesse Stuart, 1939

Progressive education is traditionally associated with the city school and
the immigrant experience. But the principles of Progressive thought also
affected more rural sections of America, often imported there by teachers
trained in large urban colleges and universities. Hands-on learning and the
introduction of new subjects and methodologies came later to rural America, but it eventually changed these schools as well.

The impact of the "new education" on small-town America is the subject
of Jesse Stuart's famous story, "Split Cherry Tree." Stuart's hero is a young,
enlightened teacher who has clearly imbibed the spirit of John Dewey and
Francis Parker. His students learn biology by exploring outdoors. His classroom is equipped with microscopes, and his approach to discipline is clearly
calculated to teach rather than to shame. Professor Herbert's conflict with
the parent of one of his students underscores the distance between the old
way of teaching and the new. His approach threatens and confounds the
parent, whose ambivalence about public schooling in general is reminiscent
of the feelings of urban immigrants, who were also wary of the influence of
outsiders. The resolution to this story may strike some modern readers as a
bit naive, but it underscores the idealism associated with the Progressive
reform movement, and the spirit of equality and compromise that many of
the liberal Progressives believed in so deeply.

Jesse Stuart himself was a great advocate of public schools. Born in a log
cabin in Green-up, Kentucky, he spent many years as a teacher, a principal, and
a superintendent of schools. In his autobiography, *The Thread that Runs So True*,
Stuart wrote of his own education and of his deep and abiding commitment to
the profession. The National Education Association called the book "The Most
Important Book of 1949." Jesse Stuart's subject was farm life in America. His
is a regional voice, which conjures up a world that has mostly vanished.

"SPLIT CHERRY TREE"

Jesse Stuart, 1939

"I don't mind staying after school," I says to Professor Herbert, "but I'd rather you'd whip me with a switch and let me go home early. Pa will whip me anyway for getting home two hours late."

"You are too big to whip," says Professor Herbert, "and I have to punish you for climbing that cherry tree. You boys knew better than that! The other five boys have paid their dollar each. You have been the only one who has not helped pay for the tree. Can't you borrow a dollar?"

"I can't," I says. "I'll have to take the punishment. I wish it would be quicker punishment. I wouldn't mind."

Professor Herbert stood and looked at me. He was a big man. He wore a gray suit of clothes. The suit matched his gray hair.

"You don't know my father," I says to Professor Herbert. "He might be called a little old-fashioned. He makes us mind him until we're twenty-one years old. He believes: 'If you spare the rod you spoil the child.' I'll never be able to make him understand about the cherry tree. I'm the first of my people to go to high school."

"You must take the punishment," says Professor Herbert. "You must stay two hours after school today and two hours after school tomorrow. I am allowing you twenty-five cents an hour. That is good money for a high school student. You can sweep the school-house floor, wash the blackboards and clean windows. I'll pay the dollar for you."

I couldn't ask Professor Herbert to loan me a dollar. He never offered to loan it to me. I had to stay and help the janitor and work out my fine at a quarter an hour.

I thought as I swept the floor: "What will Pa do to me? What lie can I tell him when I go home? Why did we ever climb that cherry tree and break it down for anyway? Why did we run crazy over the hills away from the crowd? Why did we do all of this! Six of us climbed up in a little cherry tree after one little lizard! Why did the tree split and fall with us? It should have been a stronger tree! Why did Eif Crabtree just happen to be below us plowing and catch us in his cherry tree? Why wasn't he a better man than to charge us six dollars for the tree?"

It was six o'clock when I left the schoolhouse. I had six miles to walk home. It would be after seven when I got home. I had all my work to do when I got home. It took Pa and me both to do the work. Seven cows to milk. Nineteen head of cattle to feed, four mules, twenty-five hogs, firewood and stovewood to cut and water to draw from the well. He would be doing it when I got home. He would be mad and wondering what was keeping me!

I hurried home. I would run under the dark leafless trees. I would walk fast uphill. I would run down the hill. The ground was freezing. I had to hurry. I had to run and reached the long ridge that led to our cow pasture. I ran along this ridge. The wind dried the sweat on my face. I ran across the pasture to the house.

I threw down my books in the chipyard, I ran to the barn to spread fodder on the ground for the cattle. I didn't take time to change my clean school clothes for my old work clothes. I ran out to the barn. I saw Pa spreading fodder on the ground to the cattle. That was my job. I ran to the fence. I says: "Leave that for me, Pa. I'll do it. I'm just a little late."

"I see you are," says Pa. He turned and looked at me. His eyes danced fire. "What in th' world has kept you so. Why ain't you been here to help me with this work? Make a gentleman out'n one boy in th' family and this is what you get! Send you to high school and you get too onery fer th' buzzards to smell!"

I never said anything. I didn't want to tell why I was late from school. Pa stopped scattering the bundles of fodder. He looked at me. He says: "Why are you gettin' in here this time o' night? You tell me or I'll take a hickory withe to you right here on th' spot."

I says: "Our Biology Class went on a field trip today. Six of us boys broke down a cherry tree. We had to give a dollar apiece to pay for the tree. I didn't have the dollar. Professor Herbert is making me work out my dollar. He gives me twenty-five cents an hour. I had to stay in this afternoon. I'll have to stay in tomorrow afternoon!"

"Are you telling me th' truth?" says Pa.

"I'm telling the truth," I says. "Go and see for yourself."

"That's just I'll do in th' morning," says Pa. "Jist whose cherry tree did you break down?"

"Eif Crabtree's cherry tree!"

"My God," says Pa, "what was you doing clear out in Eif Crabtree's place? He lives four miles from th' County High School. Don't they teach you no books at that high school? Do they jist let you get out and gad over th' hillsides? If that's all they do I'll keep you at home, Dave. I've got work here fer you to do!"

"Pa," I says, "spring is just getting here. We take a subject in school where we have to have bugs, snakes, flowers, lizards, frogs and plants. It is Biology. It was a pretty day today. We went out to find a few of these. Six of us boys saw a lizard at the same time sunning on a cherry tree. We all went up the tree to get it. We broke the tree down. It split at the forks. Eif Crabtree was plowing down below us. He ran up the hill and got our names. The other boys gave their dollars apiece. I didn't have mine. Professor Herbert put mine in for me. I have to work it out at school."

"Poor man's son, huh," says Pa. "I'll attend to that myself in th' mornin'. I'll take keer o' 'im. He ain't from this county nohow. I'll go down there in th' mornin' and see 'im. Lettin' you leave your books and galavant all over th' hills. What kind of damn school is it nohow! Didn't do that, my son, when I's a little shaver in school. All fared alike too."

"Pa please don't go down there," I says. "Just let me have fifty cents and pay the rest of my fine! I don't want you to go down there! I don't want you to start anything with Professor Herbert!"

"Ashamed of your old Pap are you, Dave," says Pa, "after th' way I've worked to raise you! Tryin' to send you to school so you can make a better livin' than I've made.

"I'll straighten this thing out myself! I'll take keer o' Professor Herbert myself! He ain't got no right to keep you in and let the other boys off jist because they've got th' money! I'm a poor man. A bullet will go in a Professor same as it will any man. It will go in a rich man same as it will a poor man. Now you get into this work before I take one o' these withes and cut the shirt off'n your back!"

I thought once I'd run through the woods above the barn just as hard as I could go. I thought I'd leave high school and home forever! Pa could not catch me! I'd get away! I couldn't go back to school with him. He'd have a gun and maybe he'd shoot Professor Herbert. It was hard to tell what he would do. I could tell Pa that school had changed in the hills from the way it was when he was a boy but he wouldn't understand. I could tell him we studied frogs, birds, snakes, lizards, flowers, insects. But Pa wouldn't understand. If I did run away from home it wouldn't matter to Pa. He would see Professor Herbert anyway. He would think that high school and Professor Herbert had run me away from home. There was no need to run away. I'd just have to stay, finish foddering the cattle and go to school with Pa the next morning.

I would take a bundle of fodder, remove the hickory witheband from around it and scatter it on rocks, clumps of greenbriars and brush so the cattle wouldn't trample it under their feet. I would lean it up against the oak trees and the rocks in the pasture just above our pigpen on the hill. The fodder was cold and frosty where it had set out in the stacks. I would carry bundles of the fodder from the stack until I had spread out a bundle of each steer. Pa went to the barn to feed the mules and throw corn in the pen to the hogs.

The moon shone bright in the cold March sky. I finished my work by moonlight. Professor Herbert really didn't know how much work I had to do at home. If he had known he would not have kept me after school. He would have loaned me a dollar to have paid my part on the cherry tree. He had never lived in the hills. He didn't know the way the hill boys had to work so that they could go to school. Now he was teaching in a County High School where all the boys who attended were from hill farms.

After I'd finished doing my work I went to the house and ate my supper. Pa and Mom had eaten. My supper was getting cold. I heard Pa and Ma talking in the front room. Pa was telling Mom about me staying after school.

"I had to do all th' milkin' tonight, chop th' wood myself. It's too hard on me after I've turned ground all day. I'm goin' to take a day off tomorrow and see if I can't remedy things a little. I'll go down to that high school tomorrow. I won't be a very good scholar fer Professor Herbert nohow. He won't keep me in atter school. I'll take a different kind of lesson down there and make 'im acquainted with it."

"Now Luster," says Mom, "you jist stay away from there. Don't cause a lot o' trouble. You can be jailed fer a trick like that. You'll get th' Law atter you. You'll jist do down there and show off and plague your own boy Dave to death in front o' all th' scholars!"

"Plague or no plague," says Pa, "he don't take into consideration what all I haf to do here, does he? I'll show 'im it ain't right to keep one boy in and let the rest go scot-free. My boy is good as th' rest, ain't he? A bullet will make a hole in a schoolteacher same as it will anybody else. He can't do me that way and get by with it. I'll plug 'im first. I aim to go down there bright and early in the mornin' and get all this straight! I aim to see about bug larnin' and this runnin' all over God's creation huntin' snakes, lizards, and frogs. Ransackin' th' country and goin' through cherry orchards and breakin' th' trees down atter lizards! Old Eif Crabtree ought to a-poured th' hot lead to 'em instead o' chargin' six dollar fer th' tree! He ought to a-got old Herbert th' first one!"

I ate my supper. I slipped upstairs and lit the lamp. I tried to forget the whole thing. I studied plane geometry. Then I studied my biology lesson. I could hardly study for thinking about Pa. "He'll go to school with me in the morning. He'll take a gun for Professor Herbert! What will Professor Herbert think of me! I'll tell him when Pa leaves that I couldn't help it. But Pa might shoot him. I hate to go with Pa. Maybe he'll cool off about it tonight and not go in the morning."

Pa got up at four o'clock. He built a fire in the stove. Then he built a fire in the fireplace. He got Mom up to get breakfast. Then he got me up to help feed and milk. By the time we had our work done at the barn, Mom had breakfast ready for us. We ate our breakfast. Daylight came and we could see the bare oak trees covering white with frost. The hills were white with frost. A cold wind was blowing. The sky was clear. The sun would soon come out and melt the frost. The afternoon would be warm with sunshine and the frozen ground would thaw. There would be mud on the hills again. Muddy water would then run down the little ditches on the hills.

"Now Dave," says Pa, "Let's get ready fer school. I aim to go with you this mornin' and look into bug larnin', frog larnin', lizard and snake larnin' and breakin' down cherry trees! I don't like no sicha foolish way o' larnin' myself!"

Pa hadn't forgot. I'd have to take him to school with me. He would take me to school with him. We were going early. I was glad we were going early.

If Pa pulled a gun on Professor Herbert there wouldn't be so many of my classmates there to see him.

I knew that Pa wouldn't be at home in the high school. He wore overalls, big boots, a blue shirt and a sheepskin coat and a slouched black hat gone to seed at the top. He put his gun in its holster. We started trudging toward the high school across the hill.

It was early when we got to the County High School. Professor Herbert had just got there. I just thought as we walked up the steps into the schoolhouse: "Maybe Pa will find out Profesor Herbert is a good man. He just doesn't know him. Just like I felt toward the Lambert boys across the hill. I didn't like them until I'd seen them and talked to them. After I went to school with them and talked to them, I liked them and we were friends. It's a lot in knowing the other fellow."

"You're th' Professor here, ain't you?" says Pa.

"Yes," says Professor Herbert, "and you're Dave's father."

"Yes," says Pa, pulling out his gun and laying it on the seat in Professor Herbert's office. Professor Herbert's eyes got big behind his black-rimmed glasses when he saw Pa's gun. Color came into his pale cheeks.

"Jist a few things about this school I want to know," says Pa. "I'm tryin' to make a scholar out'n Dave. He's the only one out'n eleven youngins I've sent to high school. Here he comes in late and leaves me all th, work to do! He said you's all out bug huntin' yesterday and broke a cherry tree down. He had to stay two hours after school yesterday and work out money to pay on that cherry tree! Is that right?"

"Wwwwy," said Professor Herbert, "I guess it is."

He looked at Pa's gun.

"Well," says Pa, "this ain't no high school. It's a damn bug school, a lizard school, a snake school! It ain't no damn school nohow!"

"Why did you bring that gun," says Professor Herbert to Pa.

"You see that little hole," says Pa as he picked up the long blue forty-four and put his finger on the end of the barrel, "a bullet can come out'n that hole that will kill a schoolteacher same as it will kill any other man. It will kill a rich man same as a poor man. It will kill a man. But atter I come in and saw you, I know'd I wouldn't need it. This maul o' mine could do you up in a few minutes."

Pa stood there, big, hard, brown-skinned and mighty beside of Professor Herbert. I didn't know Pa was so much bigger and harder. I'd never seen Pa in a schoolhouse before. I'd seen Professor Herbert. He always looked big before to me. He didn't look big standing beside of Pa.

"I was only doing my duty," says Professor Herbert, "Mr. Sexton, and following the course of study the state provided us with."

"Course o' study," says Pa, "what study, bug study? Varmit study? Takin' youngins to th' woods. Boys and girls all out there together a-galavantin' in the brush and kickin' up their heels and their poor old Ma's and Pa's at home a-slavin' to keep 'em in school and give 'em a education! You know that's dangerous too puttin' a lot o' boys and girls out together like that! Some o' us Paps is liable to add a few to our families!"

Students are coming into the schoolhouse now.

Professor Herbert says: "Close the door, Dave, so others won't hear."

I walked over and closed the door. I was shaking like a leaf in the wind. I thought Pa was going to hit Professor Herbert every minute. He was doing all the talking. His face was getting red. The red color was coming through the brown weather-beaten skin on Pa's face.

"I was right with these students," says Professor Herbert. "I know what they got into and what they didn't. I didn't send one of the other teachers with them on this field trip. I went myself. Yes, I took the boys and girls together. Why not?"

"It jist don't look good to me," says Pa, "a-takin' all this swarm of youngins out to pilage th' whole deestrict. Breakin' down cherry trees. Keepin' boys in atter school."

"What else could I have done with Dave, Mr. Sexton?" says Professor Herbert. "The boys didn't have any business all climbing that cherry tree after one lizard. One boy could have gone up in the tree and got it. The farmer charged us six dollars. It was a little steep I think but we had it to pay. Must I make five boys pay and let your boys off? He said he didn't have the dollar and couldn't get it. So I put it in for him. I'm letting him work it out. He's not working for me. He's working for the school!"

"I jist don't know what you could a-done with 'im," says Pa, "only a-larruped 'im with a withe! That's what he needed!"

"He's too big to whip," says Professor Herbert pointing to me. "He's a man in size."

"He's not too big fer me to whip," says Pa. "They ain't too big until they're over twenty-one! It jist don't look fair to me! Work one and let th' rest out because they got th' money. I don't see what bugs has got to do with a high school! It don't look good to me nohow!"

Pa picked up his gun and put it back in his holster. The red color left Professor Herbert's face. He talked more to Pa. Pa softened a little. It looked funny to see Pa in the high school building. It was the first time he'd ever been there.

"We were not only hunting snakes, toads, flowers, butterflies, lizards," says Professor Herbert, "but, Mr. Sexton, I was hunting dry timothy grass to put in an incubator and raise some protozoa."

"I don't know what that is," says Pa. "Th' incubator is th' new-fangled way o' cheatin' th' hens and raisin' chickens. I ain't so sure about th' breed o' chickens you mentioned."

"You've heard of germs, Mr. Sexton, haven't you," says Professor Herbert.

"Jist call me Luster if you don't mind," says Pa, very casual like.

"All right, Luster, you've heard of germs, haven't you?"

"Yes," says Pa, "but I don't believe in germs. I'm sixty-five years old and I ain't seen one yet!"

"You can't see them with your naked eye," says Professor Herbert. "Just keep that gun in the holster and stay with me in the high school today. I have a few things I want to show you. That scum on your teeth has germs on it."

"What," says Pa, "you means to tell me I've got germs on my teeth!"

"Yes," says Professor Herbert. "The same kind as we might be able to find in a living black snake if we dissect it!"

"I don't mean to dispute your word," says Pa, "but damned if I believe it. I don't believe I have germs on my teeth!"

"Stay with me today and I'll show you. I want to take you through the school anyway! School has changed a lot in the hills since you went to school. I don't guess we had high schools in this county when you went to school!"

"No," says Pa, "jist readin', writin' and cipherin'. We didn't have all this bug larnin', frog larnin' and findin' germs on your teeth and in the middle o' black snakes! Th' world's changin'."

"It is," says Professor Herbert, "and we all hope for the better. Boys like your own there are going to help change it. He's your boy. He knows all of what I've told you. You stay with me today."

"I'll shore stay with you," says Pa. "I want to see th' germs off'n my teeth. I jist want to see a germ. I've never seen one in my life. 'Seein' is believin', 'Pap allus told me."

Pa walks out of the office with Professor Herbert. I just hoped Professor Herbert didn't have Pa arrested for pulling his gun. Pa's gun has always been a friend to him when he goes to settle disputes.

The bell rang. School took up. I saw the students when they marched in the schoolhouse look at Pa. They would grin and punch each other. Pa just stood there and watched them pass in at the schoolhouse door. Two long lines marched in the house. The boys and girls were clean and well-dressed. Pa stood over in the school yard under a leafless elm, in his sheepskin coat, his big boots laced in front with buckskin and his heavy socks stuck above his boot tops. Pa's overalls legs were baggy and wrinkled between his coat and boot tops. His blue work shirt showed at the collar. His big black hat showed his gray-streaked black hair. His face was hard and weather-tanned to the color of ripe fodder blade. His hands were big and gnarled like the roots of the elm tree he stood beside.

When I went to my first class I saw Pa and Professor Herbert going around the schoolhouse. Professor Herbert and Pa just quietly came in and sat down for awhile. I heard Fred Wurts whisper to Glenn Armstrong: "Who is that old man? Lord, he's a rough looking scamp." Glenn whispered back: "I think's he's Dave's Pap." The students in geometry looked at Pa. They must have wondered what he was doing in school. Before the class was over, Pa and Professor Herbert got up and went out. I saw them together down on the playground. Professor Herbert was explaining to Pa. I could see the prints of Pa's gun under his coat when he's walk around.

At noon in the high school cafeteria Pa and Professor Herbert sat together at the little table where Professor Herbert always ate by himself. They ate together. The students watched the way Pa ate. He ate with his knife instead of his fork. A lot of the students felt sorry for me after they found out he was my father. They didn't have to feel sorry for me. I wasn't ashamed of Pa after I found out he wasn't going to shoot Professor Herbert. I was glad they had made friends. I wasn't ashamed of Pa. I wouldn't be as long as he behaved. He would find out about the high school as I had found out about the Lambert boys across the hill.

In the afternoon when to biology Pa was in the class. He was sitting on one of the high stools beside the microscope. We went ahead with our work just as if Pa wasn't in the class. I saw Pa take his knife and scrape tartar from one of his teeth. Professor Herbert put it on the lens and adjusted the microscope for Pa. He adjusted it and worked awhile. Then he says: "Now Luster, look! Put your eye right down to the light. Squint the other eye!"

Pa put his head down and did as Professor Herbert said: "I see 'im," says Pa. "I'll be damned. Who'd a ever thought that? Right on a body's teeth! Right in a body's mouth. You're right certain they ain't no fake to this, Professor Herbert?"

"No, Luster," says Professor Herbert. "It's there. That's the germ. Germs live in a world we cannot see with the naked eye. We must use the microscope. There are millions of them in our bodies. Some are harmful. Others are helpful."

Pa holds his face down and looks through the microscope. We stop and watch Pa. He sits upon the tall stool. His knees are against the table. His legs are long. His coat slips up behind when he bends over. The handle of his gun shows. Professor Herbert pulls his coat down quickly:

"Oh, yes," says Pa. He gets up and pulls his coat down. Pa's face gets a little red. He knows about his gun and he knows he doesn't have any use for it in high school.

"We have a big black snake over here we caught yesterday," says Professor Herbert. "We'll chloroform him and dissect him and show you he has germs in his body too."

"Don't do it," says Pa. "I'll believe you. I jist don't want to see you kill the black snake. I never kill one. They are good mousers and a lot o' help to us on the farm. I like black snakes. I jist hate to see people kill 'em. I don't allow 'em killed on my place."

The students look at Pa. They seem to like him better after he said that. Pa with a gun in his pocket but a tender heart beneath his ribs for snakes, but not for man! Pa won't whip a mule at home. He won't whip his cattle.

"Man can defend hisself," says Pa, "but cattle and mules can't. We have the drop on 'em. Ain't nothin' to a man that'll beat a good pullin' mule. He ain't got th' right kind o' a heart!"

Professor Herbert took Pa through the laboratory. He showed him the different kinds of work we were doing. He showed him our equipment. They stood and talked while we worked. Then they walked out together. They talked louder when they got out in the hall.

When our biology class was over I walked out ot the room. It was our last class for the day. I would have to take my broom and sweep two hours to finish paying for the split cherry tree. I just wondered if Pa would want me to stay. He was standing in the hallway watching the students march out.

He looked lost among us. He looked like a leaf turned brown on the tree among the treetop filled with growing leaves.

I got my broom and started to sweep. Professor Herbert walked up and says: "I'm going to let you do that some other time. You can go home with your father. He is waiting out there."

I laid my broom down, got my books, and went down the steps.

Pa says: "Ain't you got two hours o' sweepin' yet to do?"

I says: "Professor Herbert said I could do it some other time. He said for me to go home with you."

"No," says Pa. "You are goin' to do as he says. He's a good man. School has changed from my day and time. I'm a dead leaf, Dave. I'm behind. I don't belong here. If he'll let me I'll get a broom and we'll both sweep one hour. That pays your debt. I'll hep you pay it. I'll ast 'im and see if he won't let me hep you."

"I'm going to cancel the debt," says Professor Herbert. "I just wanted you to understand, Luster."

"I understand," says Pa, "and since I understand he must pay his debt fer th' tree and I'm goin' to hep 'im."

"Don't do that," says Professor Herbert. "It's all on me."

"We don't do things like that," says Pa. "We're just and honest people. We don't want somethin' fer nothin'. Professor Herbert, you're wrong now and I'm right. You'll haf to listen to me. I've larned a lot from you. My boy must go on. Th' world has left me. It changed while I've raised my family and plowed th' hills. I'm a just and honest man. I don't skip debts. I ain't larned 'em to do that. I ain't got much larnin' myself but I do know right from wrong atter I see through a thing."

Professor Herbert went home. Pa and I stayed and swept one hour. It looked funny to see Pa use a broom. He never used one at home. Mom used the broom. Pa used the plow. Pa did hard work. Pa says: "I can't sweep. Durned if I can. Look at th's streaks o' dirt I leave on th' floor! Seems like no work a-tall fer me. Brooms is too light 'r somethin'. I'll jist do the best I can, Dave. I've been wrong about th' school."

I says: "Did you know Professor Herbert can get a warrant out for you for bringing your pistol to school and showing it in his office! They can railroad you for that!"

"That's all right," says Pa. "I've made that right. Professor Herbert ain't goin' to take it to court. He likes me. I like 'im. We jist had to get together. He had the remedies. He showed me. You must go on to school. I am as strong a man as ever come out'n th' hills fer my years and th' hard work I've done. But I'm behind, Dave. I'm a little man. You're hands will be softer than mine. Your clothes will be better. You'll allus look cleaner than your old Pap. Jist remember, Dave, to pay your debts and be honest. Jist be kind to animals and don't bother th' snakes. That's all I got agin' th' school. Puttin' black snakes to sleep and cuttin' 'em open."

It was late when we got home. Stars were in the sky. The moon was up. The ground was frozen. Pa took his time going home. I couldn't run like I did the night before. It was ten o'clock before we got the work finished, our suppers eaten. Pa sat before the fire and told Mom he was going to take her and show her a germ some time. Mom hadn't seen one either. Pa told her about the high school and the fine man Professor Herbert was. He told Mom about the strange school across the hill and how different it was from the school in their day and time.

Part III
Questions and Activities

$\mathcal{SO}$ ◆ $\mathcal{CB}$

1. Many of the stories in this section describe the experiences of immigrant teachers during the Progressive period. What similar kinds of problems and issues are manifest in the writings of Leonard Covello, Angelo Patri, and Anzia Yezierska?

2. Jesse Stuart's story "Split Cherry Tree" alludes throughout to the real-life story of George Washington cutting down a cherry tree. What do you think is the significance of the allusion? If we see this story as a parable of George Washington's experience, what role does the teacher, Professor Herbert, play in that parable?

3. How does Jane Addams' voice, as a native-born educator, differ from the voices of her immigrant counterparts?

4. Compare the character of John in, W. E. B. Du Bois' story with the other African American teachers you have read about in Parts I and II (Daniel Alexander Payne, Charlotte Forten, and Charles Chesnutt's Mr. Williams). How is his experience different and why? What might account for the shift in tone and theme in Du Bois's work?

5. What are the differences (if any) between the experiences of immigrant public school children today and those of children in the Progressive period?

6. Research the strategies used today to educate children who are both blind and deaf.

7. Write a dialogue, set in a contemporary school, between an immigrant child and his or her teacher in which the child describes the fears and difficulties he or she experiences in the school and the community.

8. Create a plan for a contemporary equivalent of Jane Addams' Hull House. What kinds of services, resources, programs, and so on would be particularly useful and pertinent for the immigrants of today?

SUGGESTED READINGS

Anderson, J. D. *The Education of Blacks in the South, 1860–1935* (Chapel Hill: University of North Carolina Press, 1988).

Cremin, L. A. *The Transformation of the School: Progressivism, 1876–1957* (New York: Vintage Books, 1964).

Curti, M. *The Social Ideas of American Educators* (New York: Charles Scribner's Sons, 1935). Chapter 9 deals with William Torrey Harris and chapter 11 deals with Francis Wayland Parker; these are two key progressive thinkers.

Dworkin, M. S. *Dewey on Education* (New York: Teachers College Press, 1959).

Graber, K. (Ed.) *Sister to the Sioux: The Memoirs of Elaine Goodale Eastman 1885–1891* (Lincoln: University of Nebraska Press, 1978).

Warren, D. (Ed.). *American Teachers: Histories of a Profession At Work.* (New York: MacMillian Publishing Co., 1989).

Part IV

"Tell Him the House Is Falling In":
The Teacher, 1945–1994

The stories in this section depict the world of the teacher in the 50 years since the end of World War II. For the teaching profession, as for the country as a whole, it was a period of tremendous social change and upheaval. The antiwar and Civil Rights movements of the 1960s and 1970s, as well as the ongoing Women's Movement, brought major changes not only to schools, but also to those who taught in them. The feminized teaching force of the 1950s began to evolve in the face of shifting social patterns. Gains made by teachers' unions in the 1960s altered the look and appeal of the profession. New requirements for certification, beginning in the late 1970s, affected who could teach and when. Finally, the increased diversity of the public school population in the 1980s and 1990s brought new challenges to those who entered the field.

In the decade following WWII, many of the child-centered ideas associated with Progressivism came under attack. Postwar prosperity, a spirit of patriotism, and a rising anticommunist sentiment turned politicians and intellectuals alike against the educational ideas that had dominated schools since the turn of the century. A series of reports and studies by Arthur Bestor, Hyman Rickover, and other reputable scientists and social critics publicly renounced the goals of the Progressives, and called for a back-to-basics curriculum that stressed foreign languages and the sciences. The launching of Sputnik, in 1957, was the coup de grace for child-centeredness. For almost a decade afterward, both federal and corporate funding poured into school programs designed to nurture the gifted and talented, and to boost American competitiveness in the sciences. For the teacher, the late 1950s and early 1960s was a period of relative conformity and strict hierarchies, not unlike those of the previous decades. The buoyant postwar economy had opened the job market for men, luring many remaining male teachers into other professions. Teaching had come to be seen, by the mid-20th century, as women's work—calling on maternal rather than intellectual skills. Teachers were required to become certified, but methods courses tended to script their work through rigid rules of pedagogy, rather than develop in them reflective and problem-solving skills. Although much innovative curriculum work followed after the Sputnik scare, virtually none of it sought the input of practitioners. The New Math and other such programs were designed by scholars quite apart from real teachers and real schools. Indeed, the ultimate failure of such programs was later attributed to lack of practitioner's input, and an unrealistic view of what teachers could achieve in real classrooms.

For African Americans and other people of color, the 1950s and early 1960s brought little opportunity in the teaching profession. According to the federal census in 1950, 7% of American teachers were Black, a number that clearly fell below the Black enrollment in public schools. Most of those teachers taught in segregated schools in the South. The postwar baby boom had created a significant teacher shortage that allowed White teachers some freedom to choose where they worked. Few chose Black schools. This fact, combined with the Jim Crow laws, afforded Black teachers—many of them trained in Black normal schools—at least one predictable source of employment in southern states.

The spirit of conservatism and consensus that characterized the 1950s and early 1960s gave way to its opposite in the period that followed. From the mid-1960s to the end of the 1970s, schools became centers of radical experimentation and creativity. The impact of the Civil Rights movement and a change in political administrations shifted federal priorities in terms of school funding. President Johnson's vision of the Great Society brought the nation's attention to an underclass that had been neglected in the postwar period. The passing of the Elementary and Secondary Schools Act in 1965 represented a sea change in national priorities in education. The $1 billion allocated in Title One of that Act provided assistance in the form of grants to programs designed to meet the needs of the "educationally deprived." Title One's Head Start, and the many other programs and projects that grew out of these liberal policies in the late 1960s brought on a kind of neo-Progressivism in schools. Open schools and alternative schools sought to recognize individual needs in a way that was quite out of vogue in the previous decade. The failure of conventional public schools to respond to the real and varied interests and abilities of students was a subject of national debate. Spurred on by the antigovernment feeling that accompanied the Vietnam War, intellectuals attacked the schools as instruments of socialization and conformity—traits once venerated and now vilified. Some intellectuals, like Ivan Illich and Paul Goodman, called for the disbanding of public education altogether. The "deschooling movement," supported by these people, sought to replace conventional schools and textbooks with a kind of apprenticeship or guild system in which students could move from one experience in the real world to another, gathering skills in practice.

Several stories in this section illustrate quite vividly why schools were so mercilessly attacked. The failure of the curriculum to engage the increasingly diverse student body, and the general failure of schools to acknowledge the difficult lives of poor, urban children brought disorder to many classrooms. The traditional forms of authority that had held children in check in the past—even when they were unhappy, bored, or otherwise unengaged—no longer held sway. Norms of free speech and student power replaced earlier norms of quiet obedience.

The Civil Rights, antiwar, and feminist movements had a strong impact on the teaching force as well. In the late 1960s, young men entered the field in larger numbers in order to avoid the draft. Educated women, for whom teaching was once the only viable professional option, now found the job market opening wide for them, as the women's movement broke down traditional barriers in the workplace. National legislation providing scholarship assistance opened higher education to Blacks and other minorities, and affirmative action mandates brought more teachers of color into integrated schools in both the North and South. By 1980, nearly 10% of the national teaching force was Black, although that figure continued to lag behind the growing percentages of African American students in the public schools. Throughout the 1980s, the numbers of minority teachers continued to climb, never keeping pace, however, with the rising enrollments of non-White students.

The White teacher working in a non-White school was the subject of a number of widely read stories during the late 1960s and early 1970s. Novels, memoirs, and short stories by Vivien Paley (1979), James Herndon (1965), Jonathan Kozol, and others documented the social and cultural gap between the establishment, represented by the teacher or school, and the counterculture—often depicted as an alienated underclass, unwilling or unable to play by the old rules. Much of this literature was intended as social criticism, and was successful in developing public support for compensatory educational programs for the poor.

Although great gains made by the teachers' unions in the mid-1960s improved working conditions for teachers, many of the stories in this section show that teaching remains a tremendously difficult job into the present decade. The widespread violence and drugs in public schools creates a frightening and hostile environment for student and teacher alike. Budget cuts undermine the quality of instruction and demoralize the rank and file of teachers, who find themselves continually compromising their standards. Dan Lortie's seminal sociology of the profession, *Schoolteacher*, published in the mid-1970s, gave statistical support to truths that come through powerfully in these stories and memoirs: For the most part, teachers remain isolated, overworked, and unappreciated. Their work is defined in increasingly broad terms, but their compensation and working conditions continue to lag far behind other professional fields. Many recent narratives on and by teachers, including several in this section, underscore the extent to which even the best teachers continue to feel alienated and overwhelmed. Lily Chin, a formidable teacher of Hispanic students in San Antonio, seems to personify the feelings of many when she begs her daughter not to consider teaching as a career. These modern teachers' complaints echo in uncanny and unsettling ways the complaints of America's very first teachers in the 18th century. It certain ways, it seems, surprisingly little has changed.

"A Wreath For Miss Totten"[1]

ဆ ◆ ဗ

Hortense Calisher, 1950

Hortense Calisher was born in New York City in 1911, and grew up in a middle-class Jewish family. Her father was originally from Richmond, Virginia and her mother was a German immigrant. A product of the city schools, Calisher graduated from Barnard College as a philosophy major. After her marriage and a brief stint as a social worker, Calisher left New York and spent most of the next two decades raising two children and working for various liberal causes. It was not until 1948 that she grew tired of suburban domesticity and began to write seriously. In that same year, her short story "The Ginger Box" appeared in *The New Yorker*. With the 1951 publication of her first collection, *The Absence of Angels*, Calisher established herself as a talent. "A Wreath for Miss Totten" was included in that volume, which was followed by numerous novels and other collections of short fiction, including the much praised *Collected Stories of Hortense Calisher*, which was published in 1975.

"A Wreath for Miss Totten" deals with a learning disabled student and her devoted teacher. The story is told retrospectively from the point of view of another child in Miss Totten's class. In a number of ways, Calisher's teacher is the embodiment of the 1950s popular ideal: a woman of extraordinary devotion and skill with young children, who gives selflessly, and seems to ask nothing in return. Miss Totten has no "other" life besides the one she lives in the classroom. With her old-fashioned dress and strict, old-world ways, she seems untouched by the outside world or the changing times.

Totten's work with Mooley, an African American child with a severe speech impediment, offers insight into the treatment of learning disabled students in the decades before legislation mandated special programs for such children. Before encountering the wise Miss Totten, Mooley had been mistakenly diagnosed as mentally retarded. Totten receives no support or training in how to draw out the child, but works intuitively to integrate her

---

into a large, heterogeneous classroom. Through her own hard work—most of it after school—Totten succeeds in helping Mooley, and even in improving her speech. In doing so, the lonely teacher emerges as an archetype of decency for her student and for the reader.

"A WREATH FOR MISS TOTTEN"

Hortense Calisher, 1950

Children growing up in the country take their images of integrity from the land. The land, with its changes, is always about them, a pervasive truth, and their midget foregrounds are crisscrossed with minute dramas which are the animalcules of a larger vision. But children who grow in a city where there is nothing greater than the people brimming up out of subways, rivuleting in the streets—these children must take their archetypes where and if they find them.

In P.S. 146, between periods, when the upper grades were shunted through the halls in that important procedure known as "departmental," although most of the teachers stood about chatting relievedly in couples, Miss Totten always stood at the door of her "home room," watching us straightforwardly, alone. As, straggling and muffled, we lined past the other teachers, we often caught snatches of upstairs gossip which we later perverted and enlarged; passing before Miss Totten we deflected only that austere look, bent solely on us.

Perhaps, with the teachers, as with us, she was neither admired nor loathed but simply ignored. Certainly none of us ever fawned on her as we did on the harshly blond and blue-eyed Miss Steele, who never wooed us with a smile but slanged us delightfully in the gym, giving out the exercises in a voice like scuffed gravel. Neither did she obsess us in the way of the Misses Comstock, two liverish, stunted women who could have had nothing so vivid about them as our hatred for them, and though all of us had a raffish hunger for metaphor, we never dubbed Miss Totten with a nickname.

Miss Totten's figure, as she sat tall at her desk or strode angularly in front of us rolling down the long maps over the blackboard, had that instantaneous clarity, one metallic step removed from the real, of the daguerreotype. Her clothes partook of this period too—long, saturnine waists and skirts of a stuff identical with that in a good family umbrella. There was one like it in the umbrella-stand at home—a high black one with a seamed ivory head. The waists enclosed a vestee of dim, but steadfast lace; the skirts grazed narrow boots of that etiolated black leather, venerable with creases, which I knew to be a sign both of respectability and foot trouble. But except for the vestee, all of Miss Totten, too, folded neatly to the dark point of her shoes, and separated from these by her truly extraordinary length, her face presided above, a lined, ocher ellipse. Sometimes, as I watched it on drowsy afternoons, her face floated away altogether and came to rest on the stand at home. Perhaps it was because of this guilty image that I was the only one who noticed Miss Totten's strange preoccupation with "Mooley" Davis.

Most of us in Miss Totten's room had been together as a group since first grade, but we had not seen Mooley since down in second grade, under the elder and more frightening of the two Comstocks. I had forgotten Mooley completely, but when she reappeared I remembered clearly the incident which had given her her name.

That morning, very early in the new term, back in Miss Comstock's, we had lined up on two sides of the classroom for a spelling bee. These were usually a relief to good and bad spellers alike, since it was the only part of our work which resembled a game, and even when one had to miss and sit down, there was kind of dreamy catharsis in watching the tenseness of those still standing. Miss Comstock always rose for these occasions and came forward between the two lines, standing there in an oppressive close-up in which we could watch the terrifying action of the cords in her spindling gray neck and her slight smile as a boy or a girl was spelled down. As the number of those standing was reduced, the smile grew, exposing the oversize slabs of her teeth, through which the words issued in a voice increasingly unctuous and soft.

On this day the forty of us still shone with the first fall neatness of new clothes, still basked in that delightful anonymity in which neither our names nor our capacities were already part of the dreary foreknowledge of the teacher. The smart and quick had yet to assert themselves with their flying, staccato hands; the uneasy dull, not yet forced into recitations which would make their status clear, still preserved in the small, sinking corners of their hearts a lorn, factitious hope. Both teams were still intact when the word "mule" fell to the lot of a thin colored girl across the room from me, in clothes perky only with starch, her rusty fuzz of hair drawn back in braids so tightly sectioned that her eyes seemed permanently widened.

"Mule," said Miss Comstock, giving out the word. The ranks were still full. She had not yet begun to smile.

The girl looked back at Miss Comstock, soundlessly. All her face seemed drawn backward from the silent, working mouth, as if a strong, pulling hand had taken hold of the braids.

My turn, I calculated, was next. The procedure was to say the word, spell it out, and say it again. I repeated it in my mind: "Mule. M-u-l-e. Mule."

Miss Comstock waited quite a long time. Then she looked around the class, as if asking them to mark well and early this first malfeasance and her handling of it.

"What's your name?" she said.

"Ull-ee." The word came out in a glottal, molasses voice, hardly articulate, the *l*'s scarcely pronounced.

"Lilly?"

The girl nodded.

"Lilly what?"

"Duh-avis."

"Oh. Lilly Davis. Mmmm. Well, spell 'mule,' Lilly." Miss Comstock trilled out her name beautifully.

The tense brown bladder of the girl's face swelled desperately, then broke at the mouth. "Mool," she said, and stopped. "Mmmm -oo-"

The room tittered. Miss Comstock stepped closer.

"*Mule!*"

The girl struggled again. "Mool."

This time we were too near Miss Comstock to dare laughter.

Miss Comstock turned to our side. "Who's next?"

I half raised my hand.

"Go on." She wheeled around on Lilly, who was sinking into her seat. "No. Don't sit down."

I lowered my eyelids, hiding Lilly from my sight. "Mule," I said. "M-u-l-e. Mule."

The game continued, words crossing the room uneventfully. Some children survived. Others settled, abashed, into their seats, craning around to watch us. Again the turn came around to Lilly.

Miss Comstock cleared her throat. She had begun to smile.

"Spell it now, Lilly," she said. "Mule."

The long-chinned brown face swung from side to side in an odd writhing movement. Lilly's eyeballs rolled. Then the thick sound from her mouth was lost in the hooting, uncontrollable laughter of the whole class. For there was no doubt about it: the long, coffee-colored face, the whitish glint of the eyeballs, the bucking motion of the head suggested it to us all—a small brown quadruped, horse or mule, crazily stubborn, or at bay.

"Quiet!" said Miss Comstock. And we hushed, although she had not spoken loudly. For the word had smirked out from a wide, flat smile and on the stringy neck beneath there was a creeping, pleasurable flush which made it pink as a young girl's.

That was how Mooley Davis got her name, although we had a chance to use it only for a few weeks, in a taunting singsong when she hung up her coat in the morning, or as she flicked past the little dust-bin of a store where we shed our pennies for nigger-babies and tasteless, mottoed hearts. For after a few weeks, when it became clear that her cringing, mucoused talk was getting worse, she was transferred to the "ungraded" class. This group, made up of the mute, the shambling, and the oddly tall, some of whom were delivered by bus, was housed in a basement part of the school, with a separate entrance which was forbidden us not only by rule but by a lurking distaste of our own.

The year Mooley reappeared in Miss Totten's room, a dispute in the school system had disbanded all the ungraded classes in the city. Here and there, now, in the back seat of a class, there would be some grown-size boy who read haltingly from a primer, fingering the stubble of his slack jaw. Down in 4-A there was a shiny, petted doll of a girl, all crackling hairbow and nimble wheelchair, over whom the teachers shook their heads feelingly, saying: "Bright as a dollar! Imagine!" as if there were something sinister in the fact that useless legs had not impaired the musculature of a mind. And in our class, in harshly clean, faded dresses which were always a little too infantile for her, her spraying ginger hair cut short now and held by a round comb which circled the back of her head like a snaggle-toothed tiara which had slipped, there was this bony, bug-eyed wraith of a girl who raised her hand instead of saying "Present!" when Miss Totten said "Lilly Davis?" at roll call, and never spoke at all.

It was Juliet Hoffman, the pace-setter among the girls in the class, who spoke Mooley's nickname first. A jeweller's daughter, Juliet had achieved an eminence even beyond that due her curly profile, embroidered dresses, and prancing, leading-lady ways when, the Christmas before, she had brought as her present to teacher a real diamond ring. It had been a modest diamond, to be sure, but undoubtedly real, and set in real gold. Juliet had heralded it for weeks before and we had all seen it—it and the peculiar look on the face of the teacher, a young substitute whom we hardly knew—when she had lifted it from the pile of hankies and fancy notepaper on her desk. The teacher, over the syrupy protests of Mrs. Hoffman, had returned the ring, but its sparkle lingered on, iridescent around Juliet's head.

On our way out at three o'clock that first day with Miss Totten, Juliet nudged at me to wait. Obediently, I waited behind her. Twiddling her bunny muff, she minced over to the clothes closet and confronted the new girl.

"I know you," she said. "Mooley Davis, that's who you are!" A couple of the other children hung back to watch.

"Aren't you? Aren't you Mooley Davis?"

I remember just how Mooley stood there because of the coat she wore. She just stood there holding her coat against her stomach with both hands. It was a coat of some pale, vague tweed, cut the same length as mine. But it wrapped the wrong way over for a girl and the revers, wide ones, came all the way down and ended way below the pressing hands.

"Where you been?" Juliet flipped us all a knowing grin. "You been in ungraded?"

One of Mooley's shoulders inched up so that it almost touched her ear, but beyond that, she did not seem able to move. Her eyes looked at us, wide and fixed. I had the feeling that all of her had retreated far, far back behind the eyes which—large and light, and purposefully empty—had been forced to stay.

My back was to the room, but on the suddenly wooden faces of the others I saw Miss Totten's shadow. Then she loomed thinly over Juliet, her arms, which were crossed at her chest, hiding the one V of white in her garments, so that she looked like an umbrella which had been tightly furled.

"What's *your* name?" she asked, addressing not so much Juliet as the white muff which, I noticed now, was slightly soiled.

"Jooly-ette."

"Hmm. Oh, yes. Juliet Hoffman."

"Jooly-ette, it is." She pouted creamily up at Miss Totten, her glance narrow with the assurance of finger rings to come.

Something flickered in the nexus of yellow wrinkles around Miss Totten's lips. Poking out a bony forefinger, she held it against the muff. "You tell your mother," she said slowly, "that the way she spells it, it's *Juliet*."

Then she dismissed the rest of us but put a delaying hand on Mooley. Turning back to look, I saw that she had knelt down painfully, her skirt-hem graying in the floor dust, and staring absently over Mooley's head she was buttoning up the queerly shaped coat.

After a short, avid flurry of speculation we soon lost interest in Mooley, and in the routine Miss Totten devised for her. At first, during any kind of oral work, Mooley took her place at the black-board and wrote down her answers, but later, Miss Totten sat her in the front row and gave her a small slate. She grew very quick at answering, particularly in "mental arithmetic" and in the card drills, when Miss Totten held up large Manila cards with significant locations and dates inscribed in her Palmer script, and we went down the rows, snapping back the answers.

Also, Mooley had acquired a protector in Ruby Green, the other Negro girl in the class—a huge, black girl with an arm-flailing, hee-haw way of talking and a rich, contralto singing voice which we had often heard in solo at Assembly. Ruby, boasting of her singing in night clubs on Saturday nights, of a father who had done time, cowed us all with these pungent inklings of the world on the other side of the dividing line of Amsterdam Avenue—that deep, velvet murk of Harlem which she lit for us with the flash of razors, the honky-tonk beat of the "numbahs," and the plangent wails of the mugged. Once, hearing David Hecker, a doctor's son, declare "Mooley has a cleft palate, that's what," Ruby wheeled and put a large hand on his shoulder, holding it there in menacing caress.

"She ain' got no cleff palate, see? She talk sometime, 'roun' home." She glared at us each in turn with such a pug-scowl that we flinched, thinking she was going to spit. Ruby giggled.

"She got no cause to talk, 'roun' here. She just don' need to bother." She lifted her hand from David, spinning him backward, and joined arms with the silent Mooley. "Me neither!" she added, and walked Mooley away, flinging back at us her gaudy, syncopated laugh.

Then one day, lolloping home after three, I suddenly remembered my books and tam, and above all my homework assignment, left in the pocket of my desk at school. I raced back there. The janitor, grumbling, unlocked the side door at which he had been sweeping and let me in. In the mauve, settling light the long maw of the gym held a rank, uneasy stillness. I walked up the spiral metal stairs feeling that I had thieved on some part of the school's existence not intended for me. Outside the ambushed quiet of Miss Totten's room I stopped, gathering breath. Then I heard voices, one of them surely Miss Totten's dark, firm tones, the other no more than an arrested gurgle and pause.

I opened the door slowly. Miss Totten and Mooley raised their heads. It was odd, but although Miss Totten sat as usual at her desk, her hands clasped to one side of her hat, lunch-box, and the crinkly boa she wore all spring, and although Mooley was at her own desk in front of a spread copy of our thick reader, I felt the distinct, startled guilt of someone who interrupts an embrace.

"Yes?" said Miss Totten. Her eyes had the drugged look of eyes raised suddenly from close work. I fancied that she had reddened slightly, like someone accused.

"I left my books."

Miss Totten nodded, and sat waiting. I walked down the row to my desk and bent over, fumbling for my things, my haunches awkward under the watchfulness behind me. At the door, with my arms full, I stopped, parroting the formula of dismissal.

"Good afternoon, Miss Totten."

"Good afternoon."

I walked home slowly. Miss Totten, when I spoke to her, had seemed to be watching my mouth, almost with enmity. And in front of Mooley there had been no slate.

In class the next morning, as I collected the homework in my capacity as monitor, I lingered a minute at Mooley's desk, expecting some change, perhaps in her notice of me, but there was none. Her paper was the same as usual, written in a neat script quite legible in itself, but in a spidery backhand which just faintly silvered the page, like a communiqué issued out of necessity, but begrudged.

Once more I had a glimpse of Miss Totten and Mooley together, on a day when I had joined the slangy, athletic Miss Steele who was striding capably along in her Ground Grippers on the route I usually took home. Almost at once I had known I was unwelcome, but I trotted desperately in her wake, not knowing how to relieve her of my company. At last a stitch in my side forced me to stop, in front of a corner fishmongers'.

"Folks who want to walk home with me have to step on it!" said Miss Steele. She allotted me one measuring, stone-blue glance, and moved on.

Disposed on the bald white window-stall of the fish store there was a rigidly mounted eel which looked as if only its stuffing prevented it from growing onward, sinuously, from either impersonal end. Beside it were several tawny shells. A finger would have to avoid the spines on them before being able to touch their rosy, pursed throats. As the pain in my side lessened, I raised my head and saw my own face in the window, egg-shaped and sad. I turned away. Miss Totten and Mooley stood on the corner, their backs to me, waiting to cross. A trolley clanged by, then the street was clear, and Miss Totten, looking down, nodded gently into the black boa and took Mooley by the hand. As they passed down the hill to St. Nicholas Avenue and disappeared, Mooley's face, smoothed out and grave, seemed to me, enviably, like the serene, guided faces of the children I had seen walking securely under the restful duennaship of nuns.

Then came the first day of Visiting Week, during which, according to convention, the normal school day would be on display, but for which we had actually been fortified with rapid-fire recitations which were supposed to erupt from us in sequence, like the somersaults which climax acrobatic acts. On this morning, just before we were called to order, Dr. Piatt, the principal, walked in. He was a gentle man, keeping to his office like a snail, and we had never succeeded in making a bogey of him, although we tried. Today he shepherded a group of mothers and two men, officiously dignified, all of whom he seated on some chairs up front at Miss Totten's left. Then he sat down too, looking upon us benignly, his head cocked a little to one side in a way he had, as if he hearkened to some unseen arbiter who whispered constantly to him of how bad children could be, but he benevolently, insistently, continued to disagree.

Miss Totten, alone among the teachers, was usually immune to visitors, but today she strode restlessly in front of us and as she pulled down the maps one of them slipped from her hand and snapped back up with a loud, flapping roar. Fumbling for the roll-book, she sat down and began to call the roll from it, something she usually did without looking at the book and favoring each of us, instead, with a warming nod.

"Arnold Ames?"

"Pres-unt!"

"Mary Bates?"

"Pres-unt!"

"Wanda Becovic?"

"Pres-unt!"

"Sidney Cohen?"

"Pres-unt!"

"L—Lilly Davis?"

It took us a minute to realize that Mooley had not raised her hand. A light, impatient groan rippled over the class. But Mooley, her face uplifted in a blank stare, was looking at Miss Totten. Miss Totten's own lips moved.

There seemed to be a cord between her lips and Mooley's. Mooley's lips moved, opened.

"Pres-unt!"

The class caught its breath, then righted itself under the sweet, absent smile of the visitors. With flushed, lowered lids, but in a rich full voice, Miss Totten finished calling the roll. Then she rose and came forward with the Manila cards. Each time, she held up the name of a state and we answered with its capital city.

Pennsylvania.

"Harrisburg!" said Arnold Ames.

Illinois.

"Springfield!" said Mary Bates.

Arkansas.

"Little Rock!" said Wanda Becovic.

North Dakota.

"Bismarck!" said Sidney Cohen.

Idaho.

We were afraid to turn our heads.

"Buh...Boise!" said Mooley Davis.

After this, we could hardly wait for the turn to come around to Mooley. When Miss Totten, using a pointer against the map, indicated that Mooley was to "bound" the state of North Carolina, we focused on one spot with such attention that the visitors, grinning at each other, shook their heads at such zest. But Dr. Piatt was looking straight at Miss Totten, his lips parted, his head no longer to one side.

"N-north Cal...Callina." Just as the deaf gaze at the speaking, Mooley's eyes never left Miss Totten's. Her voice issued, burred here, choked there, but unmistakably a voice. "Bounded by Viginia on the north...Tennessee on the west...South Callina on the south...and on the east...and on the east..." She bent her head and gripped her desk with her hands. I gripped my own desk, until I saw that she suffered only from the common failing—she had only forgotten. She raised her head.

"And on the east," she said joyously, "and on the east by the Atlannic Ocean."

Later that term Miss Totten died. She had been forty years in the school system, we heard in the eulogy at Assembly. There was no immediate family, and any of us who cared to might pay our respects at the chapel. After this, Mr. Moloney, who usually chose *Whispering* for the dismissal march, played something slow and thrumming which forced us to drag our feet until we reached the door.

Of course none of us went to the chapel, nor did any of us bother to wonder whether Mooley went. Probably she did not. For now that the girl withdrawn for so long behind those rigidly empty eyes had stepped forward into them, they flicked about quite normally, as captious as anyone's.

Once or twice in the days that followed we mentioned Miss Totten, but it was really death that we honored, clicking our tongues like our elders. Passing the umbrella-stand at home, I sometimes thought of Miss Totten, furled forever in her coffin. Then I forgot her too, along with the rest of the class. After all this was only reasonable in a class which had achieved Miss Steele.

But memory, after a time, dispenses its own emphasis, making a *feuilleton* of what we once thought most ponderable, laying its wreath on what we never thought to recall. In the country, the children stumble upon the griffin mask of the mangled pheasant, and they learn; they come upon the murderous love-knot of the mantis, and they surmise. But in the city, although no man looms very large against the sky, he is silhouetted all the more sharply against his fellows. And sometimes the children there, who know so little about the natural world, stumble still upon that unsolicited good which is perhaps only a dislocation in the insensitive rhythm of the natural world. And if they are lucky, memory holds it in waiting. For what they have stumbled upon is their own humanity—their aberration, and their glory. That must be why I find myself wanting to say aloud to someone: "I remember…a Miss Elizabeth Totten."

"Doctor Jack-o'-lantern"[1]

ଖ ◆ ଓ

Richard Yates, 1954

Although written in 1954, this story of a poor, inner city child relocated to an affluent suburban school is vividly contemporary in theme and tone. Vincent Sabella is clearly a troubled child, whose presence in Miss Price's classroom is confusing both to the reader and the teacher. We know that he has grown up in "some kind of orphanage" and that he is presently living in foster care. But the details of his situation remain elusive, as they might well be in a real school system uninterested in the problems of its less fortunate students. This story, however, is not Vincent's but Miss Price's. Her efforts to reach the child, efforts that are invariably unsuccessful and "off the mark," underscore the difficulties of bridging cultural and class differences in the classroom. Even with the best of intentions, this teacher ultimately makes things worse rather than better for her unhappy pupil.

"Doctor Jack-o'-lantern" was originally published as part of a volume of short stories entitled *Eleven Kinds of Loneliness*. Yates' first novel was entitled *Revolutionary Road*. The book brought him national attention, and continues to be his most widely read work. Like the story included here, *Revolutionary Road* takes place in suburbia. Yates' characters are often ordinary people whose careers and relationships are thwarted by both their personal failures and the intrinsic difficulties of life itself. His work explores, in Yates' words, "the spectre of personal isolation that haunts everyone."

Born in Yonkers, New York, Richard Yates (1926–1992) taught writing on the college level, both at Columbia University and at the University of Iowa. He also worked for the United Press Association and as a special assistant in the Attorney General's Office.

---

[1]Reprinted with permission.

"DOCTOR JACK-O'-LANTERN"

Richard Yates, 1954

All Miss Price had been told about the new boy was that he'd spent most of his life in some kind of orphanage, and that the gray-haired "aunt and uncle" with whom he now lived were really foster parents, paid by the Welfare Department of the City of New York. A less dedicated or less imaginative teacher might have pressed for more details, but Miss Price was content with the rough outline. It was enough, in fact, to fill her with a sense of mission that shone from her eyes, as plain as love, from the first morning he joined the fourth grade.

He arrived early and sat in the back row—his spine very straight, his ankles crossed precisely under the desk and his hands folded on the very center of its top, as if symmetry might make him less conspicuous—and while the other children were filing in and settling down, he received a long, expressionless stare from each of them.

"We have a new classmate this morning," Miss Price said, laboring the obvious in a way that made everybody want to giggle. "His name is Vincent Sabella and he comes from New York City. I know we'll all do our best to make him feel at home."

This time they all swung around to stare at once, which caused him to duck his head slightly and shift his weight from one buttock to the other. Ordinarily, the fact of someone's coming from New York might have held a certain prestige, for to most of the children the city was an awesome, adult place that swallowed up their fathers every day, and which they themselves were permitted to visit only rarely, in their best clothes, as a treat. But anyone could see at a glance that Vincent Sabella had nothing whatever to do with skyscrapers. Even if you could ignore his tangled black hair and gray skin, his clothes would have given him away: absurdly new corduroys, absurdly old sneakers and a yellow sweatshirt, much too small, with the shredded remains of a Mickey Mouse design stamped on its chest. Clearly, he was from the part of New York that you had to pass through on the train to Grand Central—the part where people hung bedding over their windowsills and leaned out on it all day in a trance of boredom, and where you got vistas of straight, deep streets, one after another, all alike in the clutter of their sidewalks and all swarming with gray boys at play in some desperate kind of ball game.

The girls decided that he wasn't very nice and turned away, but the boys lingered in their scrutiny, looking him up and down with faint smiles. This was the kind of kid they were accustomed to thinking of as "tough," the kind whose stares had made all of them uncomfortable at one time or another in unfamiliar neighborhoods; here was a unique chance for retaliation.

"What would you like us to call you, Vincent?" Miss Price inquired. "I mean do you prefer Vincent, or Vince, or—or what?" (It was purely an academic question; even Miss Price knew that the boys would call him "Sabella" and that the girls wouldn't call him anything at all.)

"Vinny's okay," he said in a strange, croaking voice that had evidently yelled itself hoarse down the ugly streets of his home.

"I'm afraid I didn't hear you," she said, craning her pretty head forward and to one side so that a heavy lock of hair swung free of one shoulder. "Did you say 'Vince'?"

"Vinny, I said," he said again, squirming.

"Vincent, is it? All right, then, Vincent." A few of the class giggled, but nobody bothered to correct her; it would be more fun to let the mistake continue.

"I won't take the time to introduce you to everyone by name, Vincent," Miss Price went on, "because I think it would be simpler just to let you learn the names as we go along, don't you? Now, we won't expect you to take any real part in the work for the first day or so; just take your time, and if there's anything you don't understand, why, don't be afraid to ask."

He made an unintelligible croak and smiled fleetingly, just enough to show that the roots of his teeth were green.

"Now then," Miss Price said, getting down to business. "This is Monday morning, and so the first thing on the program is reports. Who'd like to start off?"

Vincent Sabella was momentarily forgotten as six or seven hands went up, and Miss Price drew back in mock confusion. "Goodness, we do have a lot of reports this morning," she said. The idea of the reports—a fifteen-minute period every Monday in which the children were encouraged to relate their experiences over the weekend—was Miss Price's own, and she took a pardonable pride in it. The principal had commended her on it at a recent staff meeting, pointing out that it made a splendid bridge between the worlds of school and home, and that it was a fine way for children to learn poise and assurance. It called for intelligent supervision—the shy children had to be drawn out and the show-offs curbed—but in general, as Miss Price had assured the principal, it was fun for everyone. She particularly hoped it would be fun today, to help put Vincent Sabella at ease, and that was why she chose Nancy Parker to start off; there was nobody like Nancy for holding an audience.

The others fell silent as Nancy moved gracefully to the head of the room; even the two or three girls who secretly despised her had to feign enthrallment when she spoke (she was that popular), and every boy in the class, who at recess liked nothing better than to push her shrieking into the mud, was unable to watch her without an idiotically tremulous smile.

"Well—" she began, and then she clapped a hand over her mouth while everyone laughed.

"Oh, *Nancy*," Miss Price said. "You know the rule about starting a report with 'well.'"

Nancy knew the rule; she had only broken it to get the laugh. Now she let her fit of giggles subside, ran her fragile forefingers down the side seams of her skirt, and began again in the proper way. "On Friday my whole family went for a ride in my brother's new car. My brother bought this new Pontiac last week, and he wanted to take us all for a ride—you know, to try it out and everything? So we went into White Plains and had dinner in a restaurant there, and then we all wanted to go see this movie, 'Doctor Jekyll and Mr. Hyde,' but my brother said it was too horrible and everything, and I wasn't old enough to enjoy it—oh, he made me so mad! And then, let's see. On Saturday I stayed home all day and helped my mother make my sister's wedding dress. My sister's engaged to be married, you see, and my mother's making this wedding dress for her? So we did that, and then on Sunday this friend of my brother's came over for dinner, and then they both had to get back to college that night, and I was allowed to stay up late and say goodbye to them and everything, and I guess that's all." She always had a sure instinct for keeping her performance brief—or rather, for making it seem briefer than it really was.

"Very good, Nancy," Miss Price said. "Now, who's next?"

Warren Berg was next, elaborately hitching up his pants as he made his way down the aisle. "On Saturday I went over to Bill Stringer's house for lunch," he began in his direct, man-to-man style, and Bill Stringer wriggled bashfully in the front row. Warren Berg and Bill Stringer were great friends, and their reports often overlapped. "And then after lunch we went into White Plains, on our bikes. Only we saw 'Doctor Jekyll and Mr. Hyde.'" Here he nodded his head in Nancy's direction, and Nancy got another laugh by making a little whimper of envy. "It was real good, too," he went on, with mounting excitement. "It's all about this guy who—"

"About *a man* who," Miss Price corrected.

"About a man who mixes up this chemical, like, that he drinks? And whenever he drinks this chemical, he changes into this real monster, like? You see him drink this chemical, and then you see his hands start to get all scales all over them, like a reptile and everything, and then you see his face start to change into this real horrible-looking face—with fangs and all? Sticking out of his mouth?"

All the girls shuddered in pleasure. "Well," Miss Price said, "I think Nancy's brother was probably wise in not wanting her to see it. What did you do *after* the movie, Warren?"

There was a general "Aw-w-w!" of disappointment—everyone wanted to hear more about the scales and fangs—but Miss Price never liked to let the reports degenerate into accounts of movies. Warren continued without much enthusiasm: all they had done after the movie was fool around Bill Stringer's yard until suppertime. "And then on Sunday," he said, brightening again, "Bill Stringer came over to *my* house, and my dad helped us rig up this old tire on this long rope? From a tree? There's this steep hill down behind my house, you see—this ravine, like?—and we hung this tire so that what you do is, you take the tire and run a little ways and then lift your feet, and you go swinging way, way out over the ravine and back again."

"That sounds like fun," Miss Price said, glancing at her watch.

"Oh, it's *fun*, all right," Warren conceded. But then he hitched up his pants again and added, with a puckering of his forehead, "'Course it's pretty dangerous. You let go of that tire or anything, you'd get a bad fall. Hit a rock or anything, you'd probably break your leg, or your spine. But my dad said he trusted us both to look out for our own safety."

"Well, I'm afraid that's all we'll have time for, Warren," Miss Price said. "Now, there's just time for one more report. Who's ready? Arthur Cross?"

There was a soft groan, because Arthur Cross was the biggest dope in class and his reports were always a bore. This time it turned out to be something tedious about going to visit his uncle on Long Island. At one point he made a slip—he said "botormoat" instead of "motorboat"—and everyone laughed with the particular edge of scorn they reserved for Arthur Cross. But the laughter died abruptly when it was joined by a harsh, dry croaking from the back of the room. Vincent Sabella was laughing too, green teeth and all, and they all had to glare at him until he stopped.

When the reports were over, everyone settled down for school. It was recess time before any of the children thought much about Vincent Sabella again, and then they thought of him only to make sure that he was left out of everything. He wasn't in the group of boys that clustered around the horizontal bar to take turns at skinning-the-cat, or the group that whispered in a far corner of the playground, hatching a plot to push Nancy Parker in the mud. Nor was he in the larger group, of which even Arthur Cross was a member, that chased itself in circles in a frantic variation of the game of tag. He couldn't join the girls, of course, or the boys from the other classes, and so he joined nobody. He stayed on the apron of the playground, close to school, and for the first part of the recess he pretended to be very busy with the laces of his sneakers. He would squat to undo and retie them, straighten up and take a few experimental steps in a springy, athletic way, and then get down and go to work on them again. After five minutes of this he gave it up, picked up a handful of pebbles and began shying them at an invisible target several yards away. That was good for another five minutes, but then there were still five minutes left, and he could think of nothing to do but stand there, first with his hands in his pockets, then with his hands on his hips, and then with his arms folded in a manly way across his chest.

Miss Price stood watching all this from the doorway, and she spent the full recess wondering if she ought to go out and do something about it. She guessed it would be better not to.

She managed to control the same impulse at recess the next day, and every other day that week, though every day it grew more difficult. But one thing she could not control was a tendency to let her anxiety show in class. All Vincent Sabella's errors in schoolwork were publicly excused, even those having nothing to do with his newness, and all his accomplishments were singled out for special mention. Her campaign to build him up was painfully obvious, and never more so than when she tried to make it subtle; once, for instance, in explaining an arithmetic problem, she said, "Now, suppose Warren Berg and Vincent Sabella went to the store with fifteen cents each, and candy bars cost ten cents. How many candy bars would each boy have?" By the end of the week he was well on the way to becoming the worst possible kind of teacher's pet, a victim of the teacher's pity.

On Friday she decided the best thing to do would be to speak to him privately, and try to draw him out. She could say something about the pictures he had painted in art class—that would do for an opening—and she decided to do it at lunchtime.

The only trouble was that lunchtime, next to recess, was the most trying part of Vincent Sabella's day. Instead of going home for an hour as the other children did, he brought his lunch to school in a wrinkled paper bag and ate it in the classroom, which always made for a certain amount of awkwardness. The last children to leave would see him still seated apologetically at his desk, holding his paper bag, and anyone who happened to straggle back later for a forgotten hat or sweater would surprise him in the middle of his meal—perhaps shielding a hard-boiled egg from view or wiping mayonnaise from his mouth with a furtive hand. It was a situation that Miss Price did not improve by walking up to him while the room was still half full of children and sitting prettily on the edge of the desk beside his, making it clear that she was cutting her own lunch hour short in order to be with him.

"Vincent," she began, "I've been meaning to tell you how much I enjoyed those pictures of yours. They're really very good."

He mumbled something and shifted his eyes to the cluster of departing children at the door. She went right on talking and smiling, elaborating on her praise of the pictures; and finally, after the door had closed behind the last child, he was able to give her his attention. He did so tentatively at first; but the more she talked the more he seemed to relax, until she realized she was putting him at ease. It was as simple and as gratifying as stroking a cat. She had finished with the pictures now and moved on, triumphantly, to broader fields of praise. "It's never easy," she was saying, "to come to a new school and adjust yourself to the—well, the new work, and new working methods, and I think you've done a splendid job so far. I really do. But tell me, do you think you're going to like it here?"

He looked at the floor just long enough to make his reply—"It's awright"—and then his eyes stared into hers again.

"I'm so glad. Please don't let me interfere with your lunch, Vincent. Do go ahead and eat, that is, if you don't mind my sitting here with you." But it was now abundantly clear that he didn't mind at all, and he began to unwrap a bologna sandwich with what she felt sure was the best appetite he'd had all week. It wouldn't even have mattered very much now if someone from the class had come in and watched, though it was probably just as well that no one did.

Miss Price sat back more comfortably on the desk top, crossed her legs and allowed one slim stockinged foot to slip part of the way out of its moccasin. "Of course," she went on, "it always does take a little time to sort of get your bearings in a new school. For one thing, well, it's never too easy for the new member of the class to make friends with the other members. What I mean is, you mustn't mind if the others seem a little rude to you at first. Actually, they're just as anxious to make friends as you are, but they're shy. All it takes is a little time, and a little effort on your part as well as theirs. Not too much, of course, but a little. Now for instance, these reports we have Monday mornings—they're a fine way for people to get to know one another. A person never feels he has to make a report; it's just a thing he can do if he wants to. And that's only one way of helping others to know the kind of person you are; there are lots and lots of ways. The main thing to remember is that making friends is the most natural thing in the world, and it's only a question of time until you have all the friends you want. And in the meantime, Vincent, I hope you'll consider *me* your friend, and feel free to call on me for whatever advice or anything you might need. Will you do that?"

He nodded, swallowing.

"Good." She stood up and smoothed her skirt over her long thighs. "Now I must go or I'll be late for *my* lunch. But I'm glad we had this little talk, Vincent, and I hope we'll have others."

It was probably a lucky thing that she stood up when she did, for if she'd stayed on that desk a minute longer Vincent Sabella would have thrown his arms around her and buried his face in the warm gray flannel of her lap, and that might have been enough to confuse the most dedicated and imaginative of teachers.

At report time on Monday morning, nobody was more surprised than Miss Price when Vincent Sabella's smudged hand was among the first and most eager to rise. Apprehensively she considered letting someone else start off, but then, for fear of hurting his feelings, she said, "All right, Vincent," in as matter-of-fact a way as she could manage.

There was a suggestion of muffled titters from the class as he walked confidently to the head of the room and turned to face his audience. He looked, if anything, too confident: there were signs, in the way he held his shoulder and the way his eyes shone, of the terrible poise of panic.

"Saturday I seen that pitcha," he announced.

"Saw, Vincent," Miss Price corrected gently.

"That's what I mean," he said; "I sore that pitcha. 'Doctor Jack-o'-lantern and Mr. Hide.'"

There was a burst of wild, delighted laughter and a chorus of correction: "Doctor *Jekyll!*"

He was unable to speak over the noise. Miss Price was on her feet, furious. "It's a *perfectly natural mistake!*" she was saying. "There's no reason for any of you to be so rude. Go on, Vincent, and please excuse this very silly interruption." The laughter subsided, but the class continued to shake their heads derisively from side to side. It hadn't, of course, been a perfectly natural mistake at all; for one thing it proved that he was a hopeless dope, and for another it proved that he was lying.

"That's what I mean," he continued. "'Doctor Jackal and Mr. Hide.' I got it a little mixed up. Anyways, I seen all about where his teet' start comin' outa his mout' and all like that, and I thought it was very good. And then on Sunday my mudda and fodda come out to see me in this car they got. This Buick. My fodda siz, 'Vinny, wanna go for a little ride?' I siz, 'Sure, where yiz goin'?' He siz, 'Anyplace ya like.' So I siz, 'Let's go out in the country a ways, get on one of them big roads and make some time.' So we go out—oh, I guess fifty, sixty miles—and we're cruisin' along this highway, when this cop starts tailin' us? My fodda siz, 'Don't worry, we'll shake him,' and he steps on it, see? My mudda's gettin' pretty scared, but my fodda siz, 'Don't worry, dear.' He's tryin' to make this turn, see, so he can get off the highway and shake the cop? But just when he's makin' the turn, the cop opens up and starts shootin', see?"

By this time the few members of the class who could bear to look at him at all were doing so with heads on one side and mouths partly open, the way you look at a broken arm or a circus freak.

"We just barely made it," Vincent went on, his eyes gleaming, "and this one bullet got my fodda in the shoulder. Didn't hurt him bad—just grazed him, like—so my mudda bandaged it up for him and all, but he couldn't do no more drivin' after that, and we had to get him to a doctor, see? So my fodda siz, 'Vinny, think you can drive a ways?' I siz, 'Sure, if you show me how.' So he showed me how to work the gas and the brake, and all like that, and I drove to the doctor. My mudda siz, 'I'm prouda you, Vinny, drivin' all by yourself.' So anyways, we got to the doctor, got my fodda fixed up and all, and then he drove us back home." He was breathless. After an uncertain pause he said, "And that's all." Then he walked quickly back to his desk, his stiff new corduroy pants whistling faintly with each step.

"Well, that was very—entertaining, Vincent," Miss Price said, trying to act as if nothing had happened. "Now, who's next?" But nobody raised a hand.

Recess was worse than usual for him that day; at least it was until he found a place to hide—a narrow concrete alley, blind except for several closed fire-exit doors, that cut between two sections of the school building. It was reassuringly dismal and cool in there—he could stand with his back to the wall and his eyes guarding the entrance, and the noises of recess were as remote as the sunshine. But when the bell rang he had to go back to class, and in another hour it was lunchtime.

Miss Price left him alone until her own meal was finished. Then, after standing with one hand on the doorknob for a full minute to gather courage, she went in and sat beside him for another little talk, just as he was trying to swallow the last of a pimento-cheese sandwich.

"Vincent," she began, "we all enjoyed your report this morning, but I think we would have enjoyed it more—a great deal more—if you'd told us something about your real life instead. I mean," she hurried on, "for instance, I noticed you were wearing a nice new windbreaker this morning. It is new, isn't it? And did your aunt buy it for you over the weekend?"

He did not deny it.

"Well then, why couldn't you have told me about going to the store with your aunt, and buying the windbreaker, and whatever you did afterwards. That would have made a perfectly good report." She paused, and for the first time looked steadily into his eyes. "You do understand what I'm trying to say, don't you, Vincent?"

He wiped crumbs of bread from his lips, looked at the floor, and nodded.

"And you'll remember next time, won't you?"

He nodded again. "Please may I be excused, Miss Price?"

"Of course you may."

He went to the boys' lavatory and vomited. Afterwards he washed his face and drank a little water, and then he returned to the classroom. Miss Price was busy at her desk now, and didn't look up. To avoid getting involved with her again, he wandered out to the cloakroom and sat on one of the long benches, where he picked up someone's discarded overshoe and turned it over and over in his hands. In a little while he heard the chatter of returning children, and to avoid being discovered there, he got up and went to the fire-exit door. Pushing it open, he found that it gave onto the alley he had hidden in that morning, and he slipped outside. For a minute or two he just stood there, looking at the blankness of the concrete wall; then he found a piece of chalk in his pocket and wrote out all the dirty words he could think of, in block letters a foot high. He had put down four words and was trying to remember a fifth when he heard a shuffling at the door behind him. Arthur Cross was there, holding the door open and reading the words with wide eyes. "Boy," he said in an awed half-whisper. "Boy, you're gonna get it. You're really gonna *get* it."

Startled, and then suddenly calm, Vincent Sabella palmed his chalk, hooked his thumbs in his belt and turned on Arthur Cross with a menacing look. "Yeah?" he inquired. "Who's gonna squeal on me?"

"Well, nobody's gonna squeal on you," Arthur Cross said uneasily, "but you shouldn't go around writing—"

"Arright," Vincent said, advancing a step. His shoulders were slumped, his head thrust forward and his eyes narrowed, like Edward G. Robinson. "Arright. That's all I wanna know. I don't like squealers, unnastand?"

While he was saying this, Warren Berg and Bill Stringer appeared in the doorway—just in time to hear it and to see the words on the wall before Vincent turned on them. "And that goes fa you too, unnastand?" he said. "Both a yiz."

And the remarkable thing was that both their faces fell into the same foolish, defensive smile that Arthur Cross was wearing. It wasn't until they had glanced at each other that they were able to meet his eyes with the proper degree of contempt, and by then it was too late. "Think you're pretty smart, don'tcha, Sabella?" Bill Stringer said.

"Never mind what I think," Vincent told him. "You heard what I said. Now let's get back inside."

And they could do nothing but move aside to make way for him, and follow him dumfounded into the cloakroom.

It was Nancy Parker who squealed—although, of course, with someone like Nancy Parker you didn't think of it as squealing. She had heard everything from the cloakroom; as soon as the boys came in she peeked into the alley, saw the words and, setting her face in a prim frown, went straight to Miss Price. Miss Price was just about to call the class to order for the afternoon when Nancy came up and whispered in her ear. They both disappeared into the cloakroom—from which, after a moment, came the sound of the fire-exit door being abruptly slammed—and when they returned to class Nancy was flushed with righteousness, Miss Price very pale. No announcement was made. Classes proceeded in the ordinary way all afternoon, though it was clear that Miss Price was upset, and it wasn't until she was dismissing the children at three o'clock that she brought the thing into the open. "Will Vincent Sabella please remain seated?" She nodded at the rest of the class. "That's all."

While the room was clearing out she sat at her desk, closed her eyes and massaged the frail bridge of her nose with thumb and forefinger, sorting out half-remembered fragments of a book she had once read on the subject of seriously disturbed children. Perhaps, after all, she should never have undertaken the responsibility of Vincent Sabella's loneliness. Perhaps the whole thing called for the attention of a specialist. She took a deep breath.

"Come over here and sit beside me, Vincent," she said, and when he had settled himself, she looked at him. "I want you to tell me the truth. Did you write those words on the wall outside?"

He stared at the floor.

"Look at me," she said, and he looked at her. She had never looked prettier: her cheeks slightly flushed, her eyes shining and her sweet mouth pressed into a self-conscious frown. "First of all," she said, handing him a small enameled basin streaked with poster paint, "I want you to take this to the boys' room and fill it with hot water and soap."

He did as he was told, and when he came back, carrying the basin carefully to keep the suds from spilling, she was sorting out some old rags in the bottom drawer of her desk. "Here," she said, selecting one and shutting the drawer in a businesslike way. "This will do. Soak this up." She led him back to the fire exit and stood in the alley watching him, silently, while he washed off all the words.

When the job had been done, and the rag and basin put away, they sat down at Miss Price's desk again. "I suppose you think I'm angry with you, Vincent," she said. "Well, I'm not. I almost wish I could be angry—that would make it much easier—but instead I'm hurt. I've tried to be a good friend to you, and I thought you wanted to be my friend too. But this kind of thing—well, it's very hard to be friendly with a person who'd do a thing like that."

She saw, gratefully, that there were tears in his eyes. "Vincent, perhaps I understand some things better than you think. Perhaps I understand that sometimes, when a person does a thing like that, it isn't really because he wants to hurt anyone, but only because he's unhappy. He knows it isn't a good thing to do, and he even knows it isn't going to make him any happier afterwards, but he goes ahead and does it anyway. Then when he finds he's lost a friend, he's terribly sorry, but it's too late. The thing is done."

She allowed this somber note to reverberate in the silence of the room for a little while before she spoke again. "I won't be able to forget this, Vincent. But perhaps, just this once, we can still be friends—as long as I understand that you didn't mean to hurt me. But you must promise me that you won't forget it either. Never forget that when you do a thing like that, you're going to hurt people who want very much to like you, and in that way you're going to hurt yourself. Will you promise me to remember that, dear?"

The "dear" was as involuntary as the slender hand that reached out and held the shoulder of his sweatshirt; both made his head hang lower than before.

"All right," she said. "You may go now."

He got his windbreaker out of the cloakroom and left, avoiding the tired uncertainty of her eyes. The corridors were deserted, and dead silent except for the hollow, rhythmic knocking of a janitor's push-broom against some distant wall. His own rubber-soled tread only added to the silence; so did the lonely little noise made by the zipping-up of his windbreaker, and so did the faint mechanical sigh of the heavy front door. The silence made it all the more startling when he found, several yards down the concrete walk outside, that two boys were walking beside him: Warren Berg and Bill Stringer. The were both smiling at him in an eager, almost friendly way.

"What'd she do to ya, anyway?" Bill Stringer asked.

Caught off guard, Vincent barely managed to put on his Edward G. Robinson face in time. "Nunnya business," he said, and walked faster.

"No, listen—wait up, hey," Warren Berg said, as they trotted to keep up with him. "What'd she do, anyway? She bawl ya out, or what? Wait up, hey, Vinny."

The name made him tremble all over. He had to jam his hands in his windbreaker and force himself to keep on walking; he had to force his voice to be steady when he said "Nunnya *business*, I told ya. Lea' me alone."

But they were right in step with him now. "Boy, she must of given you the works," Warren Berg persisted. "What'd she say, anyway? C'mon, tell us, Vinny."

This time the name was too much for him. It overwhelmed his resistance and made his softening knees slow down to a slack, conversational stroll. "She din say nothin'" he said at last; and then after a dramatic pause he added, "She let the ruler do her talkin' for her."

"The *ruler*? Ya mean she used a *ruler* on ya?" Their faces were stunned, either with disbelief or admiration, and it began to look more and more like admiration as they listened.

"On the knuckles," Vincent said through tightening lips. "Five times on each hand. She siz, 'Make a fist. Lay it out here on the desk.' Then she takes the ruler and *Whop! Whop! Whop!* Five times. Ya think that don't hurt, you're crazy."

Miss Price, buttoning her polo coat as the front door whispered shut behind her, could scarcely believe her eyes. This couldn't be Vincent Sabella—this perfectly normal, perfectly happy boy on the sidewalk ahead of her, flanked by attentive friends. But it was, and the scene made her want to laugh aloud with pleasure and relief. He was going to be all right, after all. For all her well-intentioned groping in the shadows she could never have predicted a scene like this, and certainly could never have caused it to happen. But it was happening, and it just proved, once again, that she would never understand the ways of children.

She quickened her graceful stride and overtook them, turning to smile down at them as she passed. "Goodnight, boys," she called, intending it as a kind of cheerful benediction; and then, embarrassed by their three startled faces, she smiled even wider and said, "Goodness, it *is* getting colder, isn't it? That windbreaker of yours looks nice and warm, Vincent. I envy you." Finally they nodded bashfully at her; she called goodnight again, turned, and continued on her way to the bus stop.

She left a profound silence in her wake. Staring after her, Warren Berg and Bill Stringer waited until she had disappeared around the corner before they turned on Vincent Sabella.

"Ruler, my eye!" Bill Stringer said. "Ruler, my eye!" He gave Vincent a disgusted shove that sent him stumbling against Warren Berg, who shoved him back.

"Jeez, you lie about *everything*, don'tcha, Sabella? You lie about *everything!*"

Jostled off balance, keeping his hands tight in the windbreaker pockets, Vincent tried in vain to retain his dignity. "Think I care if yiz believe me?" he said, and then because he couldn't think of anything else to say, he said it again. "Think I care if yiz believe me?"

But he was walking alone. Warren Berg and Bill Stringer were drifting away across the street, walking backwards in order to look back on him with furious contempt. "Just like the lies you told about the policeman shooting your father," Bill Stringer called.

"Even *movies* he lies about," Warren Berg put in; and suddenly doubling up with artificial laughter he cupped both hands to his mouth and yelled, "Hey, Doctor Jack-o'-lantern!"

It wasn't a very good nickname, but it had an authentic ring to it—the kind of a name that might spread around, catch on quickly, and stick. Nudging each other, they both took up the cry:

"What's the matter, Doctor Jack-o'-lantern?"

"Why don'tcha run on home with Miss Price, Doctor Jack-o'-lantern?"

"So long, Doctor Jack-o'-lantern!"

Vincent Sabella went on walking, ignoring them, waiting until they were out of sight. Then he turned and retraced his steps all the way back to school, around through the playground and back to the alley, where the wall was still dark in spots from the circular scrubbing of his wet rag.

Choosing a dry place, he got out his chalk and began to draw a head with great care, in profile, making the hair long and rich and taking his time over the face, erasing it with moist fingers and reworking it until it was the most beautiful face he had ever drawn: a delicate nose, slightly parted lips, an eye with lashes that curved as gracefully as a bird's wing. He paused to admire it with a lover's solemnity; then from the lips he drew a line that connected with a big speech balloon, and in the balloon he wrote, so angrily that the chalk kept breaking in his fingers, every one of the words he had written that noon. Returning to the head, he gave it a slender neck and gently sloping shoulders, and then, with bold strikes, he gave it the body of a naked woman: great breasts with hard little nipples, a trim waist, a dot for a navel, wide hips and thighs that flared around a triangle of fiercely scribble pubic hair. Beneath the picture he printed its title: "Miss Price."

He stood there looking at it for a little while, breathing hard, and then he went home.

From *Death At an Early Age: The Destruction of the Hearts and Minds of Negro Children in the Boston Public Schools*[1]

⁍ ◆ ⁃

Jonathan Kozol, 1967

This excerpt from Jonathan Kozol's first nonfiction book relates the author's experience teaching fourth grade in a Boston ghetto school during the mid-1960s. The passage presents the reader with a vivid picture of the repressive methods and the irrelevant materials used in a school system that Kozol sees as fundamentally racist. As an idealistic and politically sensitive young teacher, Kozol rebeled against the status quo. Hoping to inspire interest and engagement, he introduced to his students a work of literature by an African American poet that is not part of the prescribed curriculum. The piece excerpted here shows the consequences, for an untenured teacher, of that kind of rebellion. *Death At an Early Age* documents a period when public school busing had not yet been mandated in Boston. Tensions concerning issues of integration and the fair distribution of resources, however, can still be felt powerfully in Kozol's book.

Jonathan Kozol has spent his career writing about homelessness, inadequate public education and other injustices experienced by poor people in America. The product of a privileged education himself, including a B. A., from Harvard and a Rhodes Scholarship stint at Oxford, Kozol chose public school teaching in the inner city over other occupations that were open to him. His many nonfiction works recount his experiences teaching elementary-age children, running a free school, and working in adult illiteracy programs. *Death at an Early Age* received the National Book Award in 1968. His most recent writing, including *Savage Inequalities: Children In America's Schools* (1991) revisited the themes of his earlier works. It received the New England Book Award and other citations.

---

[1]Reproduced with permission.

FROM *DEATH AT AN EARLY AGE:*
THE DESTRUCTION OF THE HEARTS
AND MINDS OF NEGRO CHILDREN
IN THE BOSTON PUBLIC SCHOOLS

Jonathan Kozol, 1967

The room in which I taught my Fourth Grade was not a room at all, but the corner of an auditorium. The first time I approached that corner, I noticed only a huge torn stage curtain, a couple of broken windows, a badly listing blackboard and about thirty-five bewildered-looking children, most of whom were Negro. White was overcome in black among them, but white and black together were overcome in chaos. They had desks and a teacher, but they did not really have a class. What they had was about one quarter of the auditorium. Three or four blackboards, two of them broken, made them seem a little bit set apart. Over at the other end of the auditorium there was another Fourth Grade class. Not much was happening at the other side at that minute so that for the moment the noise did not seem so bad. But it became a real nightmare of conflicting noises a little later on. Generally it was not until ten o'clock that the bad crossfire started. By ten-thirty it would have attained such a crescendo that the children in the back rows of my section often couldn't hear my questions and I could not hear their answers. There were no carpetings or sound-absorbers of any kind. The room, being large, and echoing, and wooden, added resonance to every sound. Sometimes the other teacher and I would stagger the lessons in which our classes would have to speak aloud, but this was a makeshift method and it also meant that our classes had to be induced to maintain an unnatural and otherwise unnecessary rule of silence during the rest of the time. We couldn't always do it anyway, and usually the only way out was to try to outshout each other so that both of us often left school hoarse or wheezing. While her class was reciting in unison you could not hear very much in mine. When she was talking alone I could be heard above her but the trouble then was that little bits of her talk got overheard by my class. Suddenly in the middle of our geography you could hear her saying:

"AFTER YOU COMPARE, YOU HAVE GOT TO BRING DOWN."
Or "PLEASE GIVE THAT PENCIL BACK TO HENRIETTA!!"

Neither my class nor I could help but be distracted for a moment of sudden curiosity about exactly what was going on. Hours were lost in this way. Yet that was not the worst. More troublesome still was the fact that we did not ever *feel* apart. We were tucked in the corner and anybody who wanted could peek in or walk in or walk past. I never minded an intruder or observer, but to notice and to stare at any casual passer-by grew to be an irresistible temptation for the class. On repeated occasions I had to say to the children: "The class is still going. Let them have their discussion. Let them walk by if they have to. You should still be paying attention over here."

Soon after I came into that auditorium, I discovered that it was not only our two Fourth Grades that were going to have their classes here. We were to share the space also with the glee club, with play rehearsals, special reading, special arithmetic, and also at certain times a Third or Fourth Grade phonics class. I began to make head-counts of numbers of pupils and I started jotting them down:

Seventy children from the two regular Fourth Grades before the invasion. Then ninety one day with the glee club and remedial arithmetic.

One hundred and seven with the play rehearsal.

One day the sewing class came in with their sewing machines and then that seemed to become a regular practice in the hall. Once I counted one hundred and twenty people. All in the one room. All talking, singing, yelling, laughing, reciting—and all at the same time. Before the Christmas break it became apocalyptic. Not more than one half of the classroom lessons I had planned took place throughout that time.

"Mr. Kozol—I can't hear you."

"Mr. Kozol—what's going on out there?"

"Mr. Kozol—couldn't we sing with them?"

One day something happened to dramatize to me, even more powerfully than anything yet, just what a desperate situation we were really in. What happened was that a window whose frame had rotted was blown right out of its sashes by a strong gust of wind and began to fall into the auditorium, just above my children's heads. I had noticed that window several times before and I had seen that its frame was rotting, but there were so many other things equally rotted or broken in the school building that it didn't occur to me to say anything about it. The feeling I had was that the Principal and custodians and Reading Teacher and other people had been in that building for a long time before me and they must have seen the condition of the windows. If anything could be done, if there were any way to get it corrected, I assumed they would have done it by this time. Thus, by not complaining and by not pointing it out to anyone, in a sense I went along with the rest of them and accepted it as something inevitable. One of the most grim things about teaching in such a school and such a system is that you do not like to be an incessant barb and irritation to everybody else, so you come under a rather strong compulsion to keep quiet. But after you have been quiet for a while there is an equally strong temptation to begin to accept the conditions of your work or of the children's plight as natural. This, in a sense, is what had happened to me during that period and that, I suppose, is why I didn't say anything about the rotting window. Now one day it caved in.

First there was a cracking sound, then a burst of icy air. The next thing I knew, a child was saying: "Mr. Kozol—look at the window! I turned and looked and saw that it was starting to fall in. It was maybe four or five feet tall and it came straight inward out of its sashes toward the heads of the children. I was standing, by coincidence, only about four or five feet off and was able to catch it with my hand. But the wind was so strong that it nearly blew right out of my hands. A couple of seconds of good luck—for it was a matter of chance that I was standing there—kept glass from the desks of six or seven children and very possibly preserved the original shape of half a dozen of their heads. The ones who had been under the glass were terrified but the thing that I noticed with most wonder was that they tried very hard to hide their fear in order to help me get over my own sense of embarrassment and guilt. I soon realized I was not going to be able to hold the thing up by myself and I was obliged to ask one of the stronger boys in the class to come over and give me a hand. Meanwhile, as the children beneath us shivered with the icy wind and as the two of us now shivered also since it was a day when the mercury was hovering all morning close to freezing, I asked one of the children in the front row to run down and fetch the janitor.

When he asked me what he should tell him, I said: "Tell him the house is falling in." The children laughed. It was the first time I had ever come out and said anything like that when the children could hear me. I am sure my reluctance to speak out like that more often must seem odd to many readers, for at this perspective it seems odd to me as well. Certainly there were plenty of things wrong within that school building and there was enough we could have joked about. The truth, however, is that I did not often talk like that, nor did many of the other teachers, and there was a practical reason for this. Unless you were ready to buck the system utterly, it would become far too difficult to teach in an atmosphere of that kind of honesty. It generally seemed a great deal easier to pretend as well as you could that everything was normal and okay. Some teachers carried out this posture with so much eagerness, in fact, that their defense of the school ended up as something like a hymn of praise and adoration. "You children should thank God and feel blessed with good luck for all you've got. There are so many little children in the world who have been given so much less." The books are junk, the paint peels, the cellar stinks, the teachers call you nigger, and the windows fall in on your heads. "Thank God that you don't live in Russia or Africa! Thank God for all the blessings that you've got!" Once, finally, the day after the window blew in, I said to a friend of mine in the evening after school: "I guess that the building I teach in is not in very good condition." But to state a condition of dilapidation and ugliness and physical danger in words as mild and indirect as those is almost worse than not saying anything at all. I had a hard time with that problem—the problem of being honest and of confronting openly the extent to which I was compromised by going along with things that were abhorrent and by accepting as moderately reasonable or unavoidably troublesome things which, if they were inflicted on children of my own, I would have condemned savagely.

After the window blew in on us that time, the janitor finally came up and hammered it shut with nails so that it would not fall in again but also so that it could not open. It was a month before anything was done about the large gap left by a missing pane. Children shivered a few feet away from it. The Principal walked by frequently and saw us. So did supervisors from the School Department. So of course did the various lady experts who traveled all day from room to room within our school. No one can say that dozens of people did not know that children were sitting within the range of freezing air. At last one day the janitor came up with a piece of cardboard or pasteboard and covered over about a quarter of that lower window so that there was no more wind coming in but just that much less sunshine too. I remember wondering what a piece of glass could cost in Boston and I had the idea of going out and buying some and trying to put it in myself. That rectangle of cardboard over our nailed-shut window was not removed for a quarter of the year. When it was removed, it was only because a television station was going to come and visit in the building and the School Department wanted to make the room look more attractive. But it was winter when the window broke, and the repairs did not take place until the middle of the spring.

In case a reader imagines that my school may have been unusual and that some of the other schools in Roxbury must have been in better shape, I think it's worthwhile to point out that the exact opposite seems to have been the case. The conditions in my school were said by many people to be considerably better than those in several of the other ghetto schools.

Perhaps a reader would like to know what it is like to go into a new classroom in the same way that I did and to see before you suddenly, and in terms you cannot avoid recognizing, the dreadful consequences of a year's wastage of real lives.

You walk into a narrow and old wood-smelling classroom and you see before you thirty-five curious, cautious and untrusting children, aged eight to thirteen, of whom about two-thirds are Negro. Three of the children are designated to you as special students. Thirty per cent of the class is reading at the Second grade level in a year and in a month in which they should be reading at the height of Fourth Grade performance or at the beginning of the Fifth. Seven children out of the class are up to par. Ten substitutes or teacher changes. Or twelve changes. Or eight. Or eleven. Nobody seems to know how many teachers they have had. Seven of their lifetime records are missing: symptomatic and emblematic at once of the chaos that has been with them all year long. Many more lives than just seven have already been wasted but the seven missing records become an embittering symbol of the lives behind them which, equally, have been lost or mislaid. (You have to spend the first three nights staying up until dawn trying to reconstruct these records out of notes and scraps.) On the first math test you give, the class average comes out to 36. The children tell you with embarrassment that it has been like that since fall.

You check around the classroom. Of forty desks, five have tops with no hinges. You lift a desk-top to fetch a paper and you find that the top has fallen off. There are three windows. One cannot be opened. A sign on it written in the messy scribble of a hurried teacher or some custodial person warns you: DO NOT UNLOCK THIS WINDOW IT IS BROKEN. The general look of the room is as of a bleak-light photograph of a mental hospital. Above the one poor blackboard, gray rather than really black, and hard to write on, hangs from one tack, lopsided, a motto attributed to Benjamin Franklin: "*Well begun is half done.*" Everything, or almost everything like that, seems a mockery of itself.

Into this grim scenario, drawing on your own pleasures and memories, you do what you can to bring some kind of life. You bring in some cheerful and colorful paintings by Joan Miró and Paul Klee. While the Miró do not arouse much interest, the ones by Klee become an instantaneous success. One picture in particular, a watercolor titled "Bird Garden," catches the fascination of the entire class. You slip it out of the book and tack it up on the wall beside the doorway and it creates a traffic jam every time the children have to file in or file out. You discuss with your students some of the reasons why Klee may have painted the way he did and you talk about the things that can be accomplished in a painting which could not be accomplished in a photograph. None of this seems to be above the children's heads. Despite this, you are advised flatly by the Art Teacher that your naïveté has gotten the best of you and that the children cannot possibly appreciate this. Klee is too difficult. Children will not enjoy it. You are unable to escape the idea that the Art Teacher means herself instead.

For poetry, in place of the recommended memory gems, going back again into your own college days, you make up your mind to introduce a poem of William Butler Yeats. It is about a lake isle called Innisfree, about birds that have the funny name of "linnets" and about a "bee-loud glade." The children do not all go crazy about it but a number of them seem to like it as much as you do and you tell them how once, three years before, you were living in England and you helped a man in the country to make his home from wattles and clay. The children become intrigued. They pay good attention and many of them grow more curious about the poem than they appeared at first. Here again, however, you are advised by older teachers that you are making a mistake: Yeats is too difficult for children. They can't enjoy it, won't appreciate it, wouldn't like it. You are aiming way above their heads....Another idea comes to mind and you decide to try out an easy and rather well-known and not very complicated poem of Robert Frost. The poem is called "Stopping By Woods on a Snowy Evening." This time, your supervisor happens to drop in from the School Department. He looks over the mimeograph, agrees with you that it's a nice poem, then points out to you—tolerantly, but strictly—that you have made another mistake. "Stopping By Woods" is scheduled for Sixth Grade. It is not "a Fourth Grade poem," and it is not to be read or looked at during the Fourth Grade. Bewildered as you are by what appears to be a kind of idiocy, you still feel reproved and criticized and muted and set back and you feel that you have been caught in the commission of a serious mistake.

On a series of other occasions, the situation is repeated. The children are offered something new and something lively. They respond to it energetically and they are attentive and their attention does not waver. For the first time in a long while perhaps there is actually some real excitement and some growing and some thinking going on within that one small room. In each case, however, you are advised sooner or later that you are making a mistake. Your mistake, in fact, is to have impinged upon the standardized condescension on which the entire administration of the school is based. To hand Paul Klee's pictures to the children of this classroom, and particularly in a twenty-dollar volume, constitutes a threat to the school system. It is not different from sending a little girl from the Negro ghetto into an art class near Harvard Yard. Transcending the field of familiarity of the administration, you are endangering its authority and casting a blow at its self-confidence. The way the threat is handled is by a continual and standardized underrating of the children: They can't do it, couldn't do it, wouldn't like it, don't deserve it....In such a manner, many children are tragically and unjustifiably held back from a great many of the good things that they might come to like or admire and are pinned down instead to books the teacher knows and to easy tastes that she can handle. This includes, above all, of course, the kind of material that is contained in the Course of Study.

Try to imagine, for a child, how great the gap between the outside world and the world conveyed within this kind of school must seem: A little girl, maybe Negro, comes in from a street that is lined with car-carcasses. Old purple Hudsons and one-wheel-missing Cadillacs represent her horizon and mark the edges of her dreams. In the kitchen of her house roaches creep and large rats crawl. On the way to school a wino totters. Some teenage white boys slow down their car to insult her, and speed on. At school, she stands frozen for fifteen minutes in a yard of cracked cement that overlooks a hillside on which trash has been unloaded and at the bottom of which the New York, New Haven and Hartford Railroad rumbles past. In the basement, she sits upon broken or splintery seats in filthy toilets and she is yelled at in the halls. Upstairs, when something has been stolen, she is told that she is the one who stole it and is called a liar and forced abjectly to apologize before a teacher who has not the slightest idea in the world of who the culprit truly was. The same teacher, behind the child's back, ponders audibly with imagined compassion: "What can you do with this kind of material? How can you begin to teach this kind of child?"

Gradually going crazy, the child is sent after two years of misery to a pupil adjustment counselor who arranges for her to have some tests and considers the entire situation and discusses it with the teacher and finally files a long report. She is, some months later, put onto a waiting-list some place for once-a-week therapy but another year passes before she has gotten anywhere near to the front of a long line. By now she is fourteen, has lost whatever innocence she still had in the back seat of the old Cadillac and, within two additional years, she will be ready and eager for dropping out of school.

Once at school, when she was eight or nine, she drew a picture of a rich-looking lady in an evening gown with a handsome man bowing before her but she was told by an insensate and wild-eyed teacher that what she had done was junk and garbage and the picture was torn up and thrown away before her eyes. The rock and roll music that she hears on the Negro station is considered "primitive" by her teachers but she prefers its insistent rhythms to the dreary monotony of school. Once, in Fourth Grade, she got excited at school about some writing she had never heard about before. A handsome green book, brand new, was held up before her and then put into her hands. Out of this book her teacher read a poem. The poem was about a Negro—a woman who was a maid in the house of a white person—and she liked it. It remained in her memory. Somehow without meaning to, she found that she had done the impossible for her: she had memorized that poem. Perhaps, horribly, in the heart of her already she was aware that it was telling about her future: fifty dollars a week to scrub floors and bathe little white babies in the suburbs after an hour's street-car ride. The poem made her want to cry. The white lady, the lady for whom the maid was working, told the maid she loved her. But the maid in the poem wasn't going to tell any lies in return. She knew she didn't feel any love for the white lady and she told the lady so. The poem was shocking to her, but it seemed bitter, strong and true. Another poem in the same green book was about a little boy on a merry-go-round. She laughed with the class at the question he asked about a Jim Crow section on a merry-go-round, but she also was old enough to know that it was not a funny poem really and it made her, valuably, sad. She wanted to know how she could get hold of that poem, and maybe that whole book. The poems were moving to her....

This was a child in my class. Details are changed somewhat but it is essentially one child. The girl was one of the three unplaced special students in that Fourth Grade room. She was not an easy girl to teach and it was hard even to keep her at her seat on many mornings, but I do not remember that there was any difficulty at all in gaining and holding onto her attention on the day that I brought in that green book of Langston Hughes.

Of all the poems of Langston Hughes that I read to my Fourth Graders, the one that the children liked most was a poem that has the title "Ballad of the Landlord."....This poem may not satisfy the taste of every critic, and I am not making any claims to immortality for a poem just because I happen to like it a great deal. But the reason this poem did have so much value and meaning for me and, I believe, for many of my students, is that it not only seems moving in an obvious and immediate human way but that it *finds* its emotion in something ordinary. It is a poem which really does allow both heroism and pathos to poor people, sees strength in awkwardness and attributes to a poor person standing on the stoop of his slum house every bit as much significance as William Wordsworth saw in daffodils, waterfalls and clouds. At the request of the children later on I mimeographed that poem and, although nobody in the classroom was asked to do this, several of the children took it home and memorized it on their own. I did not assign it for memory, because I do not think memorizing a poem has any special value. Some of the children just came in and asked if they could recite it. Before long, almost every child in the room had asked to have a turn.

All of the poems that you read to Negro children obviously are not going to be by or about Negro people. Nor would anyone expect that all poems which are read to a class of poor children ought to be grim or gloomy or heart-breaking or sad. But when, among the works of many different authors, you do have the will to read children a poem by a man so highly renowned as Langston Hughes, then I think it is important not to try to pick a poem that is innocuous, being like any other poet's kind of poem, but I think you ought to choose a poem that is genuinely representative and then try to make it real to the children in front of you in the way that I tried. I also think it ought to be taken seriously by a teacher when a group of young children come in to him one morning and announce that they have liked something so much that they have memorized it voluntarily. It surprised me and impressed me when that happened. It was all I needed to know to confirm for me the value of reading that poem and the value of reading many other poems to children which will build upon and not attempt to break down, the most important observation and very deepest foundations of their lives.

BOSTON PUBLIC SCHOOLS
SCHOOL COMMITTEE
15 BEACON STREET, BOSTON 8, MASSACHUSETTS

ATTORNEY
THOMAS S. EISENSTADT
MEMBER

A careful investigation of the facts pertaining to the discharge of Mr. Jonathan Kozol reveal that the administration of the Boston Public Schools were fully justified in terminating his service.

Contrary to publicized reports, I have found that the poem incident was not the sole reason for Mr. Kozol's discharge. Rather, this particular incident was merely the climax to a series of incidents involving this teacher. On numerous occasions during his six months of service....Mr. Kozol was advised and counseled by his Principal, Miss —, and his Supervisor, Mr. —, to restrict his reading and reference materials to the list of approved publications. These admonitions were brought about by Mr. Kozol's continual deviation from the 4th grade course of study.

It has been established as a fact that Mr. Kozol taught the poem, "Ballad of the Landlord" to his class and later distributed mimeographed copies of it to his pupils for home memorization. It is also true that a parent of one of his pupils registered a strong objection to the poem to the school principal. Miss _____, properly carrying out her responsibility to all of the pupils and to their parents, admonished the neophyte teacher for his persistent deviation from the course of study. She further suggested that the poem "Ballad of the Landlord" was unsuitable for 4th graders since it could be interpreted as advocating defiance of authority. At this point Mr. Kozol became rude and told Miss_____ that he was a better judge of good literature than she.

The confirmation of the above facts is adequate justification for the discharge of a temporary teacher hired on a day-to-day trial basis. It has been stated quite adequately that the curriculum of this particular school, which is saturated with compensatory programs in an effort to specially assist disadvantaged pupils, does allow for innovation and creative teaching. However, this flexibility does not and should not allow for a teacher to implant in the minds of young children any and all ideas. Obviously, a measure of control over the course of study is essential to protect the 94,000 Boston school children from ideologies and concepts not acceptable to our way of life. Without any restrictions, what guarantees would parents have that their children were not being taught that Adolf Hitler and Nazism were right for Germany and beneficial to mankind?

It should be understood that the fact of the poem's author [sic] happened to be a Negro had no bearing on this matter whatsoever. As a matter of fact, Mr. Kozol was asked by the school principal why other works of Langston Hughes, non-controversial in nature, were not selected for study. In fact, a reference source suggested in the course of study recommends use of the book entitled, "Time for Poetry," published by Foresman which contains six of Langston Hughes' poems; and the Administrative Library contains the book, "More Silver Pennies," by MacMillian [sic] which includes more of Langston Hughes' poems, and also poems by the Negro poet Countee Cullen.

When Miss _____ reported the incident to Deputy Superintendent Sullivan and requested Mr. Kozol's removal from the teaching staff of the _____ School, it climaxed a series of complaints made to Miss Sullivan's office concerning this particular teacher. Superintendent Ohrenberger's decision after carefully weighing the facts of the case was to relieve Mr. Kozol from further service in the Boston Public Schools.

It should be understood that many temporary teachers are released from service every year by the administration of the Boston Public Schools. They are released for a variety of reasons. The overwhelming majority of such cases are discharged because in the opinion of the administrators and supervisors the certain temporary teachers are found unsuitable in training, personality, or character. Mr. Kozol, or anyone else who lacks the personal discipline to abide by rules and regulations, as we all must in our civilized society, is obviously unsuited for the highly responsible profession of teaching.

In conclusion, I must add that Mr. Kozol did bring to his pupils an enthusiasic spirit, a high degree of initiative, and other fine qualities found in the best teachers. It is my hope that Mr. Kozol will develop his latent talents and concomitantly develop an understanding and respect for the value of working within the acceptable codes of behavior.

"Teacher"

৪১ ◆ ৩৪

Richard Dokey, 1982

The subject of teacher burnout has been a much studied phenomenon in the field of education. In looking at the particular kind of malaise that afflicts many veteran teachers, researchers have wondered what factors most contribute to that condition, and what good teachers might be able to do to avoid succumbing to it. Richard Dokey's story offers an answer to those questions in the powerful portrait of Mr. Sexton, a lonely, cynical English teacher forced into an uncomfortable personal relationship with one of his students. Dokey's teacher, who has succeeded in spending many years emotionally separated from his daily work in the classroom, is suddenly forced by the problems of his student to consider the meaning of his life, its impact on his work, and the power inherent in his own position as teacher. "Teacher" shows us how closely connected are the teacher's interior life and the teacher's work, and the consequences of both withholding and revealing those connections.

Richard Dokey has spent his career as a teacher and writer in Southern California. He has published novels, short story collections, and plays, some of which include *August Heat* (1982), *Grandfather's Woman* (1982), *Birthright, Stories of the San Joaquin* (1981), *Sanchez and Other Stories* (1980), and *Two Beer Sun* (1979). Dokey's stories continue to appear in journals and quarterlies, and to be widely anthologized.

"TEACHER" [1]

Richard Dokey, 1982

There was an English teacher who lived alone in the small upstairs apartment above Miller's garage. After school each day he slowly climbed the wooden steps that led to the tiny rooms, his worn briefcase in his hand,

---

[1] This story first appeared in *Southwest Review*. Reprinted with permission.

opened the door (it was never locked—who would want to steal what he owned?), and padded to the single bedroom to remove his clothes. Always, on these lengthening days, hot days that crawled like snails toward summer, he returned from school full of oil and sweat, the underarms of his shirt exuding a pale, musty odor, like dead geraniums. Beside himself with discomfort, he performed the ritual of a long hot bath, his fat white body filling the porcelain tub like sausage. The water pounded from the faucet, crept over his legs as he lay there, made a high, round island of his stomach, and then covered it with a wispy swirl of drowning gray hair. He turned the handles with his feet and rested quietly in the water for twenty minutes, a tired old man in the afternoon.

Later, clean and scented, he sat near the front window, a glass of iced tea in his hand and a bowl of Ritz crackers and cheese on the small stand beside him, and waited for the street to come to life. He read or corrected themes, filling the lined pages with red circles, terse abbreviations, and harsh, angry arrows that struck misplaced modifiers and dangling participles with olympian scorn. The sun fell across the blue sky, the children came out to play, erupting up and down the street, and the boys from the high school ground their violent engines about the neighborhood, hunting for girls. At six the noise disappeared and he walked over to the smorgasbord for dinner. When he returned an hour later, he watched television until ten and went to bed, praying he would not waken in the morning dark. One day after the smorgasbord he was startled to find a boy sitting on the narrow steps.

"'Lo, Mr. Sexton," the boy said, standing. He had enormous blue eyes set deep into a pink, healthy face, a full lower lip, like a girl's, and straw-colored hair. His smooth brow was wrinkled by a frown.

"George," the old man said, "what's wrong?"

The boy shook his head quickly and the hair flopped about, shining in the failing light.

"Stand still, George," the teacher said. "What is it now?"

"I—I wanted to talk to you, Mr. Sexton."

"You're shaking, George," he said. "Is anything wrong?"

The boy tried to hold himself very still, but this only resulted in more severe shaking.

The old man was embarrassed. His face reddened and he put a hand to his mouth, a gesture that had become second nature since he got his false teeth.

"Here, now," he said, "are you hurt? Do you want me to call your parents?"

"Oh, no, no," the boy pleaded, seizing his arm and then dropping it self-consciously. "I'll talk to you, just to you. Please."

He stared at the boy. How the young face looked like all the other young faces. Over the years there had been hundreds and he could not tell them apart. He only just managed to memorize their names each term before they were gone, submerging into the well of his heart like round, smooth stones.

"Well, now," the old teacher said, "let's see here."

"Please, Mr. Sexton."

The boy's hand came out and brushed the old man's sleeve. An odd current passed through his arm and he drew back. He weighed over twice as much as the boy and was head and shoulders taller, yet the touch embarrassed him, like a caress.

"I guess you could come up for a bit," he said, "upstairs here, where I live."

George nodded quickly and for a moment the two of them raised their heads and looked at the green wall of the apartment.

They climbed the stairs and the old man opened the door. Inside, the air was sweetly scented, for each night, before leaving for dinner, he sprayed the room with pine freshener. How he hated the stale, burnt smells of spring: ashes in a fireplace, dust along the edges of books, the open pores of unswept furniture, warmed by the passionless sun.

"Would you care for a drink?" the teacher asked. "I have tea. Or you could have ice water. Maybe I have some orange juice from this morning."

The boy shook his head. Now that he was in the forbidden sanctum, there was a menacing, ominous certainty about things, as though he had no more time to use, as though his life were unraveling toward an immutable, obscure end.

The old man was totally unnerved. He moved about the small room, arranging magazines, straightening cushions, brushing the backs of chairs, stacking his papers neatly on the coffee table, picking up the crumbs off the floor.

"So school is almost over for you, George," he said, sitting heavily in his chair. What else was there to say? "What are you going to be doing, after the summer I mean?"

George sat on the edge of the sofa, facing sideways toward him. He held his hands together between his knees. "Well, I guess I'll go to junior college and then sell insurance, like my dad."

"Insurance," Sexton said. "Yes, that would be nice." A pale image arose in his imagination, some kingly ghost in an old play about kings, moaning, "Remember me, remember me," and then dying away in the sullen fog beyond the castle wall. How they had murdered *him* over the years with their smooth-faced, impenitent silence, making of him a pale, striding specter who haunted classroom after classroom, year after year, in a cheerless longing for sleep.

The young man wrung his hands. "Mr. Sexton," he said.

The teacher turned his watery eyes toward him.

"Mr. Sexton, I'm in trouble, I'm in terrible trouble."

"All right, George," he said.

"I wanted to ask you," George said. "You talk about all that grammar stuff and you know where to put all those marks and how to write things and you know all those stories and what they mean. You know all that kinda stuff. I can't figure any of it out, but you know. Gosh, you know all that stuff, see? You have to be smart to know all that. And I can't ask my folks or tell my friends or anything like that. I'm scared, Mr. Sexton, I'm scared."

George began to cry. It was not easy crying, but harsh, bitter, helpless crying. The old man looked away and covered his mouth with his hand. The room seemed to grow even smaller, pressing the air from his lungs. Then, after a while, George was quiet.

"You know Marla," the boy said, "in my literature class? She sits next to me in the back row."

The picture of a slim, long-haired girl, a plain-faced girl, came to his mind and he nodded.

"We've been going together," George said, "and, anyway"—his lips trembled and bubbles of water appeared in his eyes—"well, she's my girl friend and now she's pregnant. I'm scared, Mr. Sexton, I'm real scared." The boy bent toward him, full of pleading and confusion.

The teacher stood and moved about the room. He wanted to flee down the steps into the cool night. The confession, like a wave of thick hot air, was drowning him.

"Mr. Sexton," the boy said.

"George," he said.

"Mr. Sexton, I don't know what to do."

"George, I'm sorry," the old man said. He felt like a dwarf.

"What do I do?" the boy sobbed. "What do Marla and I do? Our folks will kill us."

"George," he said again. The name hung in his head like a sign blowing in the wind, like the name of a place, but there were no directions about how to get there, not even an arrow pointing the way.

"I—I know you can't tell me what to do. I know that. I just thought you could say something, that's all. I wanted Marla to come but she was too embarrassed. Mr. Sexton?"

"George," he said.

"What should I do?"

The old man stood facing the window. Outside, the grey light was turning to black. The street lamps were on. He tried to focus his mind and realized he was frightened too.

"I—I can't say," he said.

The boy stood. The old man felt him come up behind him.

"Mr. Sexton, the kids kinda laugh at you a lot, you know. They do their homework in your class. But I always thought you knew a lot. You talk about all those grammar things and all those writers and all." The boy came closer. The old man could hardly breathe. "Gee, I'm scared," George said.

"Tomorrow," the teacher said after a pause. "Come and see me tomorrow."

The boy stepped around him. "You mean at school?"

The old man nodded. "Let me think," he said, "let me think. I can't say anything now."

George nodded. "Think," he repeated. "Yeah, think."

"I'll think," said the old man.

"Gee, thanks, Mr. Sexton, thanks a lot."

"Good night, George," he said.

"Well, good night." The boy went to the door, opened it, and backed slowly out.

The old man stood facing the window. He saw George go down the steps and then cross the street to his car. The car roared to life and sped away. He sat down in the chair to think.

He slept little that night and met the dawn awake and frightened, as far away from the boy as winter from spring. He finished his breakfast of dry cereal and milk and went to school. The English faculty were seated at their desks in the small department office, getting ready for class.

"Hey, what's happening, Papa Sex?" Dick Barkley, the modish department head, laughed. Barkley was forty and dressed like one of the kids. Being relevant, he called it.

"Good morning," he returned, setting his briefcase on his desk and picking up his coffee cup. He filled it at the pot and then sat down. He turned his back to the room, which was an unwritten signal that he wanted to work. He sipped his coffee and tried to think.

George and Marla were in his second class and neither of them appeared. He sighed. Maybe they had just decided and that was that, but when the bell rang he found George waiting for him outside the classroom door.

"'Lo, Mr. Sexton," he said.

"George."

"Sorry about class. Marla was pretty upset so we decided to cut. She's in the parking lot waiting for me. Did you think of anything."

The teacher looked down at the boy, whose lonely, helpless face made him seem older. "No," he said, "I haven't. I wish I could tell you something. There aren't too many choices and I know you've thought of them all. I'm sorry."

The boy nodded and stared at his feet. "I guess we'll just have to tell our folks and then go from there." He looked up. "Mr. Sexton?"

"Yes, George."

"I've thought of something terrible, you know." A wild glance came to the boy's eyes. "It might hurt Marla. I wouldn't want to hurt Marla."

The old man felt a peculiar compulsion. He raised his arm and found his hand resting on the boy's shoulder. "George," he said, and drops of perspiration stood out on his forehead. "George, why don't you and Marla come to the smorgie tonight with me for dinner?"

"Go to dinner with you?"

"Yes, let me treat you. I want to very much. Then I'll tell you something. Maybe then I can tell you something." The palms of the old man's hands were damp.

"Okay," George said.

"You think it will be alright? Your folks won't mind?"

"No," George said.

"Fine, then, fine. Come to my place at six."

"Okay," George said.

"Okay," said the old man, showing his teeth.

The boy walked away.

The rest of the day passed quickly. He felt light-headed and apprehensive at the same time. He was being moved forward, almost in spite of himself, as though the waters had stirred deep within him and lifted him to the crest of a curling wave. When he got to the tiny apartment that afternoon, he busied himself cleaning the small rooms and dusting the furniture. Somehow everything had to be right, but he wasn't quite sure for what. Then he bathed and shaved again and sat down in his chair next to the window to wait.

At six George arrived alone.

"Marla couldn't come," the boy said.

"You mean she didn't want to."

"Yeah," the boy nodded. "She gets more scared all the time and I don't know what to tell her."

"I understand," the old man said. They stood in the silence for a moment. "Well, let's go to the smorgie."

They went to eat. George filled his plate three times and then had two helpings of dessert. He drank two glasses of milk. The old man smiled.

"I—I haven't had this much to eat for awhile," George said.

"Eat all you want," the old man said, warmed by the boy's vigor.

"Mom, she's been pretty sick lately. And Pop, well, he doesn't pay too much attention."

"I understand," said the old man.

"Mr. Sexton," George said, "why is it people who live together so long can get to be so lousy with each other?"

The old man reddened. "I don't know," he said. "I guess lives have a hard"—he choked a little, swallowed from the glass of water—"well, a hard time living together." He sat forward in the booth. "George, I want to tell you something—about myself."

"You do?"

"Yes, but not here. You finish up and we'll go back to my place and then I'll tell you. I'll tell you everything you want to know."

The boy cocked his head at the old man and finished his dessert.

Back in the apartment the teacher sat down in the chair by the window and George sat on the sofa. The old man put his hands together.

"George?"

"Yessir."

"I was married, you know. I was married twice." His eyes lifted and turned about the room, half expecting that the cramped silence would echo him and give him reassurance. It only lay back against the walls in mute indifference. "I was married twice in fact," he said.

The boy turned his head a little and regarded him curiously.

"I want to tell you about my first wife. Her name was Meredith and she was beautiful, George, truly beautiful. She was pregnant when we were married." He stopped himself. Pictures of her formed in his brain—slender, dark haired, the hair long and curled about the shoulders. "George, I tried to love her correctly. Well, that's a manner of speaking, you see." He looked at the boy. The smooth, shining face looked back like a stone at the bottom of a pond. The images began to spin in his mind and he remembered everything, all of it, the years and faces and joys and agonies, he remembered what he had tried to forget. "I worshipped her, George. You understand that word worship?"

The boy nodded. "Yessir, I think so."

The old man put his head in his hand. "And then one day there was somebody else."

The boy wiped his mouth and swallowed. He was so embarrassed that his shirt began to grow damp under the arms.

"I cried in my wife's arms. 'You've killed me,' I said, 'you've killed me.' And then I went out and fired a bullet through the window of the man's home. You see, I wanted to fight him, to hurt him, but I knew that was nonsense. I just felt guilty about my wife."

"Yessir," the boy said.

"Well, then it was like a sheet of glass between us. I could see her, but everything was cold and empty. Then we separated and it was over. Six months after the divorce I married Janet."

He raised his head and looked at the boy. George's eyes were distant and strange and old again.

"I brought her presents," the teacher said. "I gave her gifts. I took her places. We traveled and went to concerts. We did so many things." He paused and lowered his head again. "But she died and I never loved her. I just felt guilty about my first wife." He cried softly, his great shoulders rolling and turning. "You see, I never loved my first wife either. And I don't know why. I don't know why."

"Gee, Mr Sexton," George said, staring at him.

The old man lifted his red, watery eyes and looked deep into the boy's. "Life happens. There isn't any right or wrong of it. We just have to decide what to do, that's all. I've been afraid a long time, and so I do the same thing over and over again. And here I am, George."

"Gee," the boy said.

"And that's all I can tell you, George, that's all I have to tell."

They both sat very still for a long time, and he looked at the boy and the boy looked at him and at that moment there just wasn't any life anywhere else in the world, and a terrible thing moved inside him.

"I'm sorry, Mr. Sexton."

The old man nodded. "A long time ago," he said, "a long time."

George stood up. "I guess we'll get married," he said. "I mean we talked it over and we decided, even before I came here tonight, Mr. Sexton. We're gonna get married." The boy's voice was flat and even.

"Oh, George," the old man said.

"We'll do that," he said. "There's the operation, you know, the abortion? But, well—" The boy's eyes flared to life again. "Mr. Sexton, I don't wanna get married. I don't." They stood there a moment and George put out his hand. "Thanks for the dinner," he said.

The old man nodded. They rose and he opened the door. George stepped through and turned about. He looked at the boy. He knew him. He knew him as well as he knew himself. They were the same, boy and old man. They shared fate helplessly, like things preyed upon beneath the sea. George would marry the girl and sell insurance and find oblivion in policies and premiums, and he would fail a few more years, haunt a few more classrooms, and then disappear into the sullen fog. It all came down to this, this lonely bottom of the heart. And in the dry place, the place of stone, there was no hope or joy, no beginning, but only the passionless emptying of life and the understanding. Obscure ends and tombstones tilted in the summer grass.

Then he became angry. The anger flickered up from the ashes of his despair. Over the years he had pitied himself and hidden from himself, but now the anger burned and lit the darkness of his heart. He understood that all he had ever had to offer was his own story, but instead he had given punctuation and grammar and disguised himself from the world; and, except for the boy, he was still disguising himself, still hiding. The anger, lighting the waste and emptiness, became a terrible thing within him, but it gave him back what he had lost.

"Love, George," he said.

"What?" the boy said, standing in the dark beyond the threshold.

The old man reached out and pulled him back into the light. "I'll pay for it or whatever. Whatever it takes, I'll take care of it."

"Mr. Sexton?" George said.

"George, kill the child," the teacher said. "Kill the child."

The boy stared at him in mute affirmation.

From *Socrates, Plato, and Guys Like Me: Confessions of a Gay Schoolteacher*[1]

ᴇᴏ ◆ ᴄ

Eric Rofes, 1985

The subject of the gay schoolteacher has entered the literature on teaching only recently, within the last 15 to 20 years, long after other minority groups had successfully appealed for equal rights within the profession. Even today, teachers whose lifestyles are openly homosexual confront prejudice in many communities in America. Although no statistics exist on the subject, public resistence to gay and lesbian teachers almost certainly has caused qualified homosexual applicants for teaching positions to be turned away or terminated before tenure.

The tension between community values and the homosexual teacher is the subject of this excerpt from Eric Rofes' memoir. The excerpt presents the dramatic confrontation between a high school teacher and a Board of Trustees that has been apprised of his sexual orientation. The "compromise" that is proffered by the Chairman of the Board—that Mr. Rofes can continue to work in the school system if he keeps his homosexuality secret—presents a painful moral dilemma to the protagonist.

Eric Edward Rofes was born in 1954 in Manhasset, New York, and graduated from Harvard University. Of his career as a writer, Rofes says, "I am engaged in two major areas of writing: books for children, which I write in collaboration with children, and books about a broad range of political issues, gay liberation, feminism, and progressive politics." Besides teaching and writing, Rofes has devoted his career to advocacy work, as founder of the Boston Area Gay and Lesbian Schoolworkers, as a member of the Massachusetts Committee for Children and Youth, and as a member of the

---

[1] Excerpt from *Socrates, Plato, and Guys Like Me*, by Eric E. Rofes. Copyright © 1985 by Eric Rofes. Reprinted by permission of Alyson Publications, Inc.

White House Conference on Families. His published works include, *Reviving the Tribe: Regenerating Gay Men's Sexuality and Culture in the Ongoing Epidemic (1995)*, *The Kids Book About Parents* (1984), and *The Kids Book of Death and Dying* (1985).

FROM *SOCRATES, PLATO, AND GUYS LIKE ME: CONFESSIONS OF A GAY SCHOOLTEACHER*

Eric Rofes, 1985

I stood waiting by the front door for Alice and Marie to arrive and escort me to the board meeting. Aware that I'd be a wreck inside despite a composed public appearance, I had arranged to have friends accompany me this evening. Alice served as the faculty representative to the board, so she was expected to attend in any case. Marie had been granted special permission to be present at the meeting and lend silent support to her friend on trial. Thus I stood at the door, gazing out at dusk settling onto the streets of Somerville, waiting for my ride to Shawmut Hills, feeling like a convict about to walk his final mile.

Holly came bounding down the stairway with her hand behind her back. Arriving at the front door, she drew out a small bouquet of spring flowers and pressed it into my hand. "Here, honey," she said smiling. "My best wishes go with you. I really wish I could be there to watch this performance. You'll do all of us proud, I'm sure."

I smelled the flowers and my spring allergies brought tears to my eyes. "Do I look all right?" I asked. "This is a difficult occasion to dress for. None of the fashion books give any indication of what to wear to an execution. I spent about an hour going through the closet and trying to decide what I could wear that would give me some degree of integrity, but not seem too blatant."

Holly looked me over from head to toe. "You look like the perfect preppie schoolteacher. The khakis, the oxford shirt and those loafers are strictly prepster. No one could challenge you tonight. The only thing that's missing is this," she said, reaching into her pocket and pulling out a metallic button which she pinned to my shirt. I looked down and saw the bright pink "Gay and Proud" button against my white shirt. Instinctively, I reached down to take it off, but Holly's hand caught mine.

"No," she said quietly. "Leave it on, at least till you arrive at school. It'll be comforting to know that it's there and you can be sure that—even in the madness of the night—you won't leave it on when you walk into the judge's chambers."

The phone rang and Holly rushed into the kitchen to answer it. I peered out the window, glanced nervously at my watch, and began to pace.

"It's for you," she called to me from the other room.

I directed my pacing toward the phone and grabbed it from Holly. "Hello?" I said, my voice cracking for the first time in years.

"It's just me, Eric." I heard Paul's voice at the other end of the line. "Just calling to send you best wishes for a pleasant evening on Firing Line."

"Thanks, I need all the support I can get."

"Remember, no matter what happens, you have the satisfaction of knowing you've handled this whole thing with a great deal of integrity."

"That's not going to keep me employed, Paul."

"No, it's not. And you might lose your job tonight, although I think they'd be crazy to let you go. But I think you've got to keep in mind that—no matter what happens—you've handled a difficult situation with a great deal of pride and dignity. This could have been a real mess for you and for the school. You've done the responsible thing."

I heard a car honking for me out front. "They're here!" I exclaimed. "I've got to go, Paul. Thanks for calling and call me at midnight and I'll let you know what happened!"

I dropped the phone onto the receiver, kissed Holly good-bye, grabbed my sweater and dashed down the walkway to the car.

The school library had always seemed to be one of the warmer, homier rooms of the school. Located in the center of the building and accessible to every classroom, it easily had become a reflection of Alice's personality over the last dozen years. Stacks of books and periodicals made it clear that this was a room that saw heavy use on a daily basis. The brightly colored finger paintings by first-grade children gave the room a down-to-earth feeling and the wood-stained panels added to the sense of formality and tradition that served to remind the viewer that this was—despite the warmth—an institution of learning.

Tonight as I entered the library, the formality of the wood-stained panels loomed large. The room took on a new feeling, a feeling of conservatism and seriousness. Only Miss Clarkson had arrived and she was carefully arranging the library chairs into a circle in the center of the room.

"Good evening," she said in an unusually awkward tone. "We're all a bit early for the meeting."

Alice and Marie took off their coats and tossed them onto one of the library tables. Plates of Fig Newtons sat on one of the desks, and a coffee machine was beginning to perk. I looked quickly around the room, wondering where I would be sitting when my final judgment was pronounced—by a jury that was distinctly *not* comprised of my peers.

Before I had a chance to ask, Miss Clarkson answered my question. "I think it's best for you to sit over there, Eric," she said, indicating a chair at the edge of the circle. "And Alice and Marie may sit wherever they'd like."

Marie came up beside me. "I'd like to sit next to you," she said, trying to sound cheery. "Is that okay?"

"It sure is," I responded.

"Are you sure you want to keep that button on all night?" she asked, indicating the pink button that I'd forgotten to remove.

I became flustered and took it off quickly, and we settled into our seats just as the clock struck eight. The trustees slowly entered, one-by-one, and greeted us. Several of them were unfamiliar to me, and they introduced themselves and shook my hand. One of them—Peter Larkin—was the man responsible for connecting me to Shawmut Hills just two years earlier. He was one of my professors at Harvard, my thesis advisor, and a friend whom I'd never told about this side of my life. He greeted me and smiled in a way that seemed to express a shared sense of naughtiness—as if Peter and I had together sprung this controversy on the school. The smile was encouraging—the formality and seriousness of the other board members was beginning to feel unduly fatalistic.

When all twelve trustees had taken their seats, Doug Cabot began the meeting. "You all know why we're here tonight," he began, "and I thank you very much for arranging your schedules so that this meeting could take place on such short notice. I know that the last few weeks have been difficult for Eric, as they have been difficult for all of us who are in a situation that is unique and troublesome. As I've told all of you on the telephone, Eric, Miss Clarkson and I met last week and discussed a letter he'd written and enclosed with his contract for next year. In the letter, he explained that, not only is he gay, but he is a political activist and a writer. I think what we're here to discuss tonight is whether or not there is a future for Eric at Shawmut Hills knowing these additional pieces of information."

He paused here and I looked up from the floor where my eyes had been riveted since Mr. Cabot began to speak. I looked from one trustee to another. Serious faces all. One woman, a teacher of anthropology at a nearby high school, seemed troubled to the point of facial contortion. Her son Arthur had been my student during my first year in the school, and I always found her to be supportive and friendly. Her roles as a mother, board member and thinking person seemed to conflict in this situation.

Another trustee, a noted psychiatrist at Massachusetts General Hospital and the father of two young students at the school, seemed to be attempting to maintain a non-judgmental look on his face. Showing no reaction to Doug Cabot's statements, nor any semblance of emotion, he sat through the initial statement with a studied, earnest look on his face.

My eyes glanced from one trustee to another. Only Alice was able to shoot me an occasional smile or wink, and I worked to control my own reaction.

"What I want to make clear from the start of this discussion," Cabot continued, "is that we're not here to judge Mr. Rofes as a teacher. The offer of a contract for a third year at our school indicates that Miss Clarkson finds him to be a commendable teacher and, indeed, most of us have heard very positive feedback from parents and students since his arrival at the school. His ability to challenge the students, as well as maintain strict discipline in the classroom, are what we've wanted to have at the sixth grade level for a long time. There is no doubt in my mind that we'd like to keep Eric at the school and what this meeting is trying to determine is if it is possible for him to continue with us, despite these recent revelations."

Cabot laid out the ground rules for the evening. It would be strictly question and answer for an hour or so, and then I would be asked to leave while the trustees discussed the matter and voted on my continued presence in the school. I was to receive a phone call from Cabot probably late that evening to inform me of their decision.

The discussion began with a question from Doug Cabot. "Why don't you tell us about how you arrived at the point where you decided to send this letter to Miss Clarkson," he suggested.

This seemed like an innocuous starting point, I thought to myself. "I sent the letter after two years of soul-searching," I began. "During my first two years at the school, I have had a lot of conflicting feelings about parts of my life. While I've been developing my abilities to teach children and have been enjoying my teaching experiences, I have also been feeling more and more comfortable as a gay person. I've started to become involved in gay community activities, including some political work. Thus I've found myself torn between two lives that seem incompatible. I'm trying to find a way to survive with them both as comfortably as possible."

"Have you deliberately kept these lives separate up until this point?" Cabot asked.

"Until now," I continued, "I was able to do my work as an activist under a pseudonym. I'd write articles under a fake name, stay out of pictures when the newspapers or television cameras covered an event in which I was involved, and I'd tell lies to people in the gay community about the work I did professionally.

"Even in this school, I'd allow parents and other staff members to attempt to set me up on blind dates with women, permit my students to have the impression that every woman I was seen with was my girlfriend, and I'd even find myself lying about my life to other teachers. I don't want to do these things anymore. I don't want to live with the lies and the deception and I don't want to feel split into two directions. I need to come clean with everyone and live an honest life."

I had spoken this speech in an unusually quiet tone of voice, attempting to keep my remarks free from the strident tones for which I had a tendency. While several trustees nodded, indicating their understanding of my predicament, others looked puzzled or disturbed. The psychiatrist was the only one eager to ask a question.

"Are there other teachers anywhere who are open about this kind of thing?" he asked. "If there are, I haven't heard about it."

"At this point, there are not any openly gay teachers in this part of the country below the college level," I answered. "However, in other parts of the country, teachers of young children, as well as junior high and high school teachers, are openly gay. In some cities teachers are actually protected in their contracts from losing their jobs because they're gay. There aren't hundreds of teachers who are open about this, but there are quite a few and most of them maintain that they simply address questions from their students when and if they come up and then they go about their teaching. It doesn't seem to have such a dramatic effect on the school or on their teaching as one would expect."

Arthur's mother had her hand raised and seemed to be troubled by something I'd said. "I guess what I'm most concerned with," she said, "are the ramifications of this matter for the children. I think all of us are aware of the possible influence this could have on the children's sexual orientation."

I was annoyed at this concern but I tried to keep my perspective. "What influence do you think this will have on the children?" I asked quietly.

"You are teaching children at a very formative age, Eric. Early adolescence is an important time for the kids. I'm concerned with the way this might influence them. Now, you have chosen to be this way yourself and that's your right and your business. But when you go public about it, you influence other people and this concerns me."

"Are you asking me if I think my talking to the children about my sexual orientation will influence them and encourage them to be gay?"

The woman thought for a moment. "I suppose that's what I'm afraid of. I've been told that you work with a group called Committee for Gay Youth, and it seems to me that you're encouraging our young people to be this way. I'm not comfortable with that at all."

"I appreciate your expressing your concern," I said, attempting to appear in control of the matter while, in fact, I was enraged inside at the assumptions she was making. "Committee for Gay Youth does not encourage children or teenagers to have any particular sexual orientation."

Doug Cabot jumped in. "What does this group do, Eric?" he asked.

"We support kids when they choose to identify themselves as gay. We're not rigid at all and we support teens who evolve from one sexual orientation to another. While some adolescents seem to experience a great deal of confusion concerning their sexual orientations, I think it's important to acknowledge that some of them don't. We work primarily with those rare kids who are fifteen or sixteen years old and able to say to themselves 'I'm gay and I need to find some other kids like me.' Otherwise they would probably end up on the streets, without money, in some fairly desperate situations."

Arthur's mother wanted to pursue some points. "What you haven't answered in a way that satisfies me, is whether your coming out, as you call it, would influence our children later in life."

"Most of the studies I've read over the past few years seem to agree that sexual identity is formed during the first few years of life," I said, sounding like a schoolteacher. "By the time a child is in the sixth grade, his or her orientation is pretty well-formed. I think having a gay teacher would allow students who are gay to feel more comfortable with themselves, but I don't think it will cause students to have gay feelings if they wouldn't have had them otherwise."

"But what about these other students?" another woman asked quickly. I'd never before met her, but I knew that she was the director of a nearby hospital and the parent of a fourth-grade girl. She dressed conservatively and seemed a bit older than the other trustees. I had been warned that she might be hostile. "If your other students are primarily heterosexually oriented, in the normal fashion, shouldn't they be able to feel some support? If you tell them that you're homosexual, this might make them feel wrong or out of place."

"I'm sorry," I said, "but I feel there's already a lot of support within this school and within our society for kids who are heterosexual. From the wedding rings we see on teachers' fingers, to the ads we see on television, to most kids' parents, I feel that heterosexual teenagers receive a lot of support and validation."

I wasn't going to get off easy. She continued her hostile line of questioning. "I think this is clearly a question of values," she said in a serious tone. "The question for me is, do the parents of children at Shawmut Hills School want their children to be told that is okay to choose to be a homosexual? Because that's what we'd be doing if we condone this kind of activity on the part of our teachers."

I looked at Alice, needing a supportive face in my line of vision at the moment. Alice was peering over her spectacles, staring with angry eyes at the woman, but she managed to sit quietly without letting her anger erupt. I decided to follow suit and let the bigotry speak for itself while I awaited the next rational question.

Doug Cabot sensed the tension in the room and changed the focus of the discussion. "I was wondering," he said, "whether it would be possible for you to continue doing your political work, as well as working with that youth project, and not let people know that you're a school teacher. You wouldn't necessarily have to tell people that you teach school, and I certainly think it would be fairly easy for you to keep the name of the school private. Would that be possible, Eric?"

While his suggestion was certainly possible, I wondered what he was getting at. If Cabot hoped to keep me at the school by having me hide my professional identity, it was a compromise that I could probably try to make.

I told him so and then added, "I think it's highly unlikely that some people will not connect the gay activist Eric Rofes with the schoolteacher Eric Rofes. If I had a name like 'Doug Cabot', or any name more common than my own, I could see people not assuming they were the same person. But with my name, it seems likely that someone could connect the employee of this school to the activist quoted in the *Globe*.

It was my former professor, Peter Larkin's turn for a question. "What kinds of things can you foresee doing over the next year that would get your name into the *Boston Globe?*" he asked.

"I'm not sure that my name will end up in papers like that," I answered, "But it might. This summer and this fall I'll be doing some organizing work related to gay teachers, especially around the Briggs Initiative in California. That initiative is going to be on the ballot in November throughout the state of California, and would mandate that schools fire any employee who is supportive of gay rights. In my opinion, this is a very frightening thing and we've formed a committee here in Boston to do support work for the people organizing against it in California."

"What kind of work will you be doing?" Larkin continued.

"I'll be doing some public speaking on the issue, possibly as a gay schoolteacher. I don't think I have to announce where I teach school, but I think it's important for teachers around the country to speak out publicly against this initiative."

"Do you mean to say that any schoolteacher in California who speaks positively about gays would be fired under this law?" The question came from a trustee I hadn't noticed before who was sitting in the back of the room, puffing on his pipe. "I find that incredible."

"Yes, it would cause such firings," I answered. "I think this helps you to realize why it's important for me to get involved. This kind of think is pretty dangerous. Any teacher—gay or straight—who simply said it was okay for gays to have rights, could legally lose their jobs."

"If you were allowed to continue to teach here," interjected Doug Cabot, "how would you deal with the subject with the children? Would you allow the issue to come up in the classroom?"

"The subject comes up anyway," I said. "I'm afraid that many of you don't realize that, with sixth graders, at least, homosexuality comes up all the time. When I walked into the classroom two years ago, I vowed never to raise the subject. It came out of the kids all the time. Whether it's questions in health class, current event articles brought in about Anita Bryant, taunts on the playing field, or books in the classroom, homosexuality has found its way into the classroom. Any teacher could tell you that."

Alice spoke up. "What do you mean by books in the classroom?" she asked curiously.

I'd never talked with Alice about this, but I supposed now was as good a time as any for her to find out. "When I began teaching here, I took home copies of all the reading books we had for sixth graders in multiple copies. One of them is a wonderful book called *The Man Without a Face*, which has won all kinds of awards. It's a moving story about a boy from a troubled family and the man who befriends him and becomes his tutor.

"Well, the climax of the book involves the two of them sleeping together in quite an ambiguous manner that leaves the boy confused and disturbed. Now I've never had my students read the book, but I assume that if we have 22 copies of it in my classroom, some teacher has. I raise this issue only to let you know that whether or not I'm teaching this class, homosexuality is a subject that will be dealt with in one way or another. It was here before I got to this school, and it will be here long after I'm gone."

Doug Cabot still seemed concerned. "That is helpful for us to know, Eric, but you didn't answer my question. How would you discuss the matter with the children?"

I paused for a moment while I thought about my response. "I would have to do a little research before I talked to the kids about being gay. Just off the top of my head, I think I'd want to explain to them that I was gay and tell them what it meant. I'd make sure to explain it in more than sexual terms, since too often kids see relationships between adults purely in terms of sex. I'd explain that being gay means that my deepest feelings go toward other men. Then I'd ask them if they had any questions. It would probably be a good idea to break into smaller groups at this time and have the groups develop questions. Then we'd come back and hear their questions."

"What would you tell them about sex, if they asked about it?" the psychiatrist asked.

"I suppose I'd want to make sure that they realized that sex was more than just genital contact, that it involved hugging and kissing and touching."

"Then you'd answer their questions about sex," he continued incredulously.

I knew it was the wrong thing to say but I took a deep breath, glanced at Marie, and answered, "Yes. I believe that children's questions about sex should be answered honestly."

I think it was at this point that several of the trustees made up their mind that I was a lost cause. Both the psychiatrist and the hospital director grew silent for the next forty minutes while the other trustees shifted into discussions about homosexuality and children which ranged from discussing the stereotypes about child molestation to the current far-fetched sociobiological theory that nature created homosexuals to care for children of other people while the parents were busy reaping harvests or killing dinosaurs. I was asked quite personal questions about when I'd come out, my relationship with my parents, and whether or not I had a "partner."

I felt many of the trustees were sincerely struggling to grasp the issues and I was pleased with the range of questions asked. I had a difficult time stomaching some of the off-the-cuff comments from the committee's liberals (one even worked into the conversation the line, "Some of my best friends are ..."), but I felt that they served to balance the hostile looks and well-timed guffaws of the administrator.

After about two hours, the discussion began to wane. I remained keyed up, ready for anything, although the intensity of the discussion had drained me somewhat. "It's getting rather late," Doug Cabot said, glancing at his watch. "I'd like to start bringing this discussion to a close and allow Eric to get home before dawn. Are there any final questions?"

I glanced around the room. There were a few somber faces, a few smiles. Then the hospital administrator raised her voice again.

"I have one final question for Mr. Rofes," she said. "Have you seen a psychiatrist about your problem?"

I was caught a little off guard. As I caught my breath and began to formulate a response, I noticed that many of the other trustees were obviously put off by her question.

"I don't believe I have a problem," I said. "I did see a psychiatrist while I was in college who helped me adjust to being gay, but currently I do not see one."

"Then my follow-up question is," she continued her hostile line of questioning. "Why are you doing this to us?"

Before I could answer, Doug Cabot jumped in. "I don't believe that this question merits a response from Eric. I apologize for —"

I cut him off. "Excuse me, Mr. Cabot," I said, "but I would like a moment to respond to the question. I am not *doing* anything to you or to the school. I could have returned next year, written my gay articles under my own name, and have a major scandal come over the school without any preparation on the part of Miss Clarkson or the trustees. Or I could have walked away from education, robbing the school of another teacher simply because I didn't have the courage to discuss this difficult issue with all of you. I believe that I've chosen an honorable process by which to pursue the matter. I care about this school and I've tried to respond professionally and with sensitivity to everyone involved. I came here tonight prepared to answer questions as best as I could, however difficult and personal they might be. I also came here to be honest with you and not to cover up my political involvement or deceive you about my true thoughts on these matters.

"However, I did not come here to be insulted and I thank the rest of the trustees for their kindness and consideration this evening. It is one thing to find oneself in honest disagreement with others. It is quite another matter to find oneself insulted and I shall not accept any more of your questions."

With that off my chest, I sat there, red-faced, drained, angry and exhausted. I missed Doug Cabot's closing remarks as he summarized the evening's discussion and explained that I would now leave and the trustees would remain and discuss the issue. Since Alice was a part of the discussion,

I would leave with Marie. I found myself shaking hands with my judges and being whisked by Marie out the door and into the cool night air.

Marie drove me home and came in to join me for a cup of coffee while I waited for the phone call from the school. Holly had a fresh pot of coffee ready for us when we walked in the door and she eagerly listened to Marie and me recount our tales of the inquisition.

"That hospital director sure sounds like the Anita Bryant of Shawmut Hills," Holly said. "I suppose there's going to be one in every crowd, but I'm glad you spoke your mind at the end."

"She was just terrible," Marie said shaking her head, "just terrible. I could tell that you were sitting there, trying to be polite, holding your feelings in and sitting on your temper. I don't know how you controlled yourself for as long as you did. You deserve some kind of medal for that performance, sweetie."

"So what are the odds that they'll keep you?" Holly asked. "I know it's hard to tell, especially since the phone might ring at any moment, but what's your prediction?"

I hesitated for a moment. "I think I made it crystal clear that this boy is going to be out—loud and proud—if he continues as a schoolteacher. The question will be whether they're willing to take the risk for the school. The way I see it, they need to weigh having a popular teacher who has somehow managed to earn a pretty decent reputation for academic competence against the fears that the conservative Shawmut Hills establishment might stop sending their kids to the school because a fag is on the faculty."

"What odds do you give me that they'll never find the chutzpah to keep you?" Holly asked. "I mean Shawmut Hills School just doesn't have a reputation for innovation and integrity."

"I don't know," Marie said slowly. "I think they might surprise us. I mean, I'm surprised that they're even considering the question, aren't you, Eric?"

"I guess deep inside me, I am. It really is a big step for the school to even allow the topic into the forum for discussion. And the fact that they're taking it seriously, considering the possibilities, is certainly a step, even if they decide against me."

"I'll bet they're just doing that because they're afraid you'll sue their assess off," Holly said, pouring coffee into our half-empty mugs.

"I'm not so sure of that," I responded quickly. "I give them more credit than that … but you might be right."

"It's difficult to call this one, Holly," Marie said. "Clearly there were some pretty cool characters at the meeting tonight who wouldn't care a bit about a homosexual teaching their kids. But there were some pretty hostile folks as well. In my mind, Cabot's going to be the swing vote. He's a pretty cagey guy and I don't think he showed his cards at all throughout the meeting."

Just then the telephone rang. I rushed to the front foyer and grabbed it before the third ring.

"Hello," I whispered into the receiver, clearly out of breath.

"Hello, is this Eric?"

"Yes it is. Who's calling please?" I asked in my most courteous tone of voice.

"This is Doug Cabot. We've just concluded our meeting and I've been asked to call you and let you know the decision of the committee."

His voice was calm, quiet, and I couldn't sense whether he was about to transmit good news or bad.

"We discussed the matter for about an hour. First of all, everyone was very appreciative of your willingness to answer our questions. We found the discussion to be quite informative. We thought that you conducted yourself in a mature and responsible manner throughout the evening."

He paused here. Get to the point, I thought, my mind racing madly.

"Thank you," I responded. "Did the committee reach a decision?"

"I'm getting to that," Cabot said slowly. "We would very much like to see you return to Shawmut Hills. Everyone feels that you're an excellent teacher and that we should do everything within our power to keep you here. We do feel, however, that—while it would be fine for you to be open about these things within our school community—we really couldn't allow you to use your real name in your writings, nor could we allow you to be photographed at gay events. We'd want you to keep your political activism low-key and away from controversy."

Again he paused, waiting for my reaction. I held my silence this time, forcing him to continue.

"You see, Eric, this school really couldn't stand the public attention that would come if word got out that we had a homosexual teacher. People would withdraw their children and our enrollment would fall. The entire financial stability of the school would be undermined. It's a risk that we could not take and still be a responsible board of trustees, even if we support you in principle.

"Thus we're hoping that you will return to the school next year, but without the same degree of activism."

I didn't know what to say. Yes, the school had made a major step by allowing me to return next year as a gay man, even if they were unwilling to allow me to be a public gay activist. On the other hand, the specific issues which I'd raised—leaving the pseudonyms behind, ending my enforced schizophrenia, feeling comfortable with media exposure—had been circumvented.

"It sounds as if you'd want me to come back, but on your own terms, not on mine," I said quietly.

"We prefer to think of it as, not in our terms or your terms, but in terms that have the best interests of the children in mind."

He was beginning to sound patronizing. "We don't want you to feel that you have to decide about this overnight. Take some time to think about it, maybe discuss it with your friends. But do let us know within the week."

I needed to clarify what he'd told me. This was all happening too quickly and my heart was pounding a mile a minute in my chest.

"If I return to Shawmut Hills," I asked, "what you're saying is that I still have to maintain two separate identifies."

"You might choose to see it that way," Cabot acknowledged. "Your activist activities would have to be kept fully separate from your teaching."

"I'd still have to avoid photos and use a fake name?"

"I think you're correct in saying that," Cabot responded formally.

"Then what you're saying is that you don't want me to return next year, since I have made it very clear to you—both in my letter to Miss Clarkson and in the meeting this evening—that I intend to write under my own name next year."

"That's your decision, Eric."

"But it's *not* my decision. You're trying to absolve yourself and your board of trustees from this decision. You want me to be the one who decided not to return to the school. You don't even have the courage to tell me about your decision directly." I was beginning to shout.

"Now wait a minute, Eric. That's unfair —"

"No, you wait a minute, Mr. Cabot. I want you to answer me one question, and this time you listen carefully. I, Eric Rofes, am going to be an openly gay person next year, in my writing, in my political work, and in my teaching. Am I welcome to return to Shawmut Hills School next year, Mr. Cabot?"

There was a silence at the end of the line. I allowed him a moment to make the decision.

"Under those conditions, Eric, you would not be welcome back," he said slowly and quietly. Then he added, "But take a few days and think about it. We don't need your decision tonight."

"Thank you," I said. "I'm afraid I need to get off the phone now. I appreciate your call."

With that comment, I hung up the receiver, walked directly up the flight of stairs, went into my bedroom, and started to cry.

"Lily Chin" From *A Lifetime of Teaching: Portraits of Five Veteran High School Teachers*

  ↻ ◆ ↾

Rosetta Marantz Cohen, 1991

One of the few Asian American teachers in the San Antonio school system, Lily Chin's reputation as a teacher and administrator was legion in her largely Hispanic community. This portrait, from *A Lifetime of Teaching: Portraits of Five Veteran High School Teachers*, was one of series of "life studies" of teachers who had spent at least 25 years working in public schools throughout the country. Lily's story, like the others, considers the question of why certain individuals manage to remain committed to and enthusiastic about teaching over the course of so many years…especially when the attrition rate in the profession is so high. The portrait is built on interviews with family, colleagues, former students, and of course, with Lily herself. Chin emerges as a person with exceptional energy and an abiding love for her subject, biology. But she is also a product of her times: Lily chose teaching out of default, knowing of no other career option open to her as a woman and a minority. Her thoughts on her Hispanic pupils, on the way the profession has changed, and on teacher education are both sobering and instructive. That Lily would not have chosen this profession had she had access to other options suggests much about the future of teacher recruitment—especially in schools like Brackenridge High School, where salaries and working conditions are less appealing than elsewhere.

 Rosetta Cohen (1955–) composed the portraits of exceptional veterans in the classroom in part to provide role models to preservice teachers. As a new high school teacher, she herself found the stories of experienced professionals far more useful and interesting than the traditional research in her methods courses. Since writing these portraits, a considerable literature on teacher case studies and stories has emerged in the field.

"LILY CHIN" FROM *A LIFETIME OF TEACHING: PORTRAITS OF FIVE VETERAN HIGH SCHOOL TEACHERS*

Rosetta Marantz Cohen, 1991[1]

Brackenridge High School in San Antonio, Texas, is located just south of the center of town, where tourists stroll along the riverbanks or ride barges past the facades of quaint, Mexican-style hotels and restaurants. A river-front room at the new Marriot Hotel rents for over $200 a night, and a small silver bracelet, which might sell for $30 across the Mexican border, goes for an easy $300 in the fashionable shops of River Center Mall.

Though it is only 5 minutes away, the world of Brackenridge High School is very far away from all of this. Just beyond the sports arena and the symphony hall, the streets become narrow and poorly paved. Tall hotels are replaced by single-level garages, open markets, and boarded-up billiard parlors. Across from the school is a sprawling, shabby subdivision, The Courts, where each small house has a metal fence and rusty window grilles.

The high school itself has the clean, severe lines of schools built in the early 1970s, when designs reflected the prevailing notion of the school-as-prison. It is a huge, windowless building that stretches for almost a city block and is unlandscaped outside. Inside, one enters to find a giant mall area, which functions as lunchroom, auditorium, and social center. The administration offices front this mall to the left, receding into dozens of tiny cubicles behind the plate-glass window of the main office.

When I arrive on a late-spring morning, first period has already begun. There are no students around, except for a silent line of young people who lean against the wall outside a room marked CLINIC. They are mostly girls, in tight capri pants and bangs moussed straight up. One boy, in a football jersey, rolls his head back and forth against the cinderblock.

Lily Chin's classroom is on the second floor in the science wing, across from the science office. When I peer into the room for the first time, it takes me over a minute to pick her out from among the multitude of lounging and sauntering ninth graders. She is the shortest person in the room, less than 5 feet tall, and she is wearing the kind of bright, cotton sundress—with a flounce on the bottom and ruffles around the bib—that young girls wear. When I look closer, however, I realize that Lily Chin is not cute or girlish. Instead, there is a certain tense, impacted dynamism—a serious energy about her—that suggests a presence very much to be reckoned with.

Lily extricates herself from a group of students who have been watching a delicate ribbon snake wind around her hand. "Okay, guys," she says,

---

holding her hand and the snake in the air, "it's time to get started. Today, you'll be working on your Picassos."

"What's a Picasso?" asks a boy who continues to lean against Lily's desk.

"A deformed picture!" calls out a girl to his left.

"Okay, a deformed picture," laughs Lily. "He's not my favorite artist, either. But *you* guys are going to be making some great art today. Now, pencils, paste, boards, and scissors are in the center of the room, reference books are in the back." Everyone scatters.

"What's the assignment?" I ask a girl already at work, dribbling paste on a piece of poster board.

"We're supposed to make collages out of monocots, dicots, and insects. Then identify the genus and the species." She reads this information from off the board in a slightly exasperated tone, then shows me a small plastic bag filled with dry grass, a dead grasshopper, and several flourescent bugs, also dead.

All around the room—between lab sinks, on top of cabinets, in corners on the floor—are cages, terrariums, and aquariums filled with Lily's menagerie of gerbils, white mice, fish, crabs, poisonous and nonpoisonous snakes. An enormous albino rabbit roams freely underfoot, ignored by the students. Above the front blackboard hangs a large, hand-printed sign:

PROCESS SKILLS
1. Observing
2. Classifying
3. Communicating
4. Measuring
5. Informing and predicting
6. Defining
7. Controlling variables

Mobiles of birds and bats hang from the ceiling, and from the walls, map-sized pictures of cross-sectioned fish, grasshoppers, and earthworms. Earth is Home to Us All, reads one poster of a lion, Share the Responsibility. Between the ninth graders, the small mammals, the insects, and the fish, the room is teeming with life, a kind of Noah's Ark with desks.

"No bug nabbing!" calls out Lily. She is making her way from desk to desk. "Someone over here said she got a bug nabbed from her bag! Manners, ladies and gentlemen!" The activity in the room has grown more intense. From all corners, imploring voices call out to Lily for her opinion. "Miss, is this good?" "Miss, what should I do now?" "Miss!" "Miss!" Lily remains unperturbed. She neither quickens her pace nor attempts to quiet the hubbub that swells around us. Moving about with her, I feel as if I am swimming in rough but invigorating waters.

***

Lily Chin's real name is Fung May, or Beautiful Fairy. Chinese is the language of Lily's parents and of the country to which she still feels deep ties. Lilly explains her temperament, her values, her decision to go into teaching, and her interest in biology all in terms of her psychic affinity to a place where she has never been. There is something about her that is at once very American and very Chinese. It is the kind of double identity peculiar to those who have assiduously worked to assimilate, yet are too proud to give up a cultural heritage they privately feel is superior to the one they have adopted.

Lily's father arrived in the United States in the early 1920s from a small village in Canton, in the southern part of China. He had heard of a growing Chinese community in south Texas, a community originally built from the offspring of Chinese cooks brought up from Mexico by General Pershing. Forming a partnership with several other Chinese immigrants, Lily's father opened a grocery store on the west side of San Antonio, close to where the Mexican markets now stand. After the death of his first wife, Lily's father returned to China with his five children and remarried almost at once. He then made his way back to the United States, where five more children were born in rapid succession. Lily was number 8.

With other Chinese grocers, Lily's parents formed a merchants' organization that enabled them to receive credit from wholesale dealers, an arrangement that ensured plentiful food on the table and adequate clothes. "We lived in a suite of rooms on the third floor of an old hotel—multiple bodies to a bed," says Lily, "but I never felt poor. We weren't poor, because my parents really knew how to save. My parents worked incredibly hard all their lives, every day, even Sundays; they never had a day off. There was a powerful work ethic there."

Relations with the Anglo community were cordial, but always tenuous. Lily grew up with a keen awareness of public opinion and of the importance of maintaining a good reputation in the community. "We didn't want to look bad to others. That was very important. That was often discussed. We had to be extra good, and we had to be extra careful. And actually," says Lily, still with pride, "the word got around that Orientals always pay their bills. You never had to worry if an Oriental owed you money. It's part of the Chinese custom: You pay all your bills before New Year's. So people knew—the Orientals would be good for their word."

This same pride and self-consciousness extended to schooling, where Lily was always expected to excel, if only, she says, to prove that Chinese people were good and responsible students. "This was the time, of course, when there was terrible discrimination against blacks here in the South. They rode in the backs of buses; they couldn't go into white restaurants. It was never like that for the Chinese. The discrimination, when it happened, was much more subtle. But it was there, and we learned to be very circumspect."

Even now, as we sit and speak day after day in the cluttered science office at Brackenridge, there is a tense self-consciousness about Lily, a sense that words must be chosen with great care to protect, she says, "not only myself, but my family." Again and again, after telling an anecdote that to my ears seems anything but indiscreet, she says, "Don't print that. You didn't hear me say that."

Lily says that her career was essentially decided for her by a high school guidance counselor. "'You're a smart girl,' she says, mimicking the coun-selor's southern drawl. 'You'll make a good teacher.' I really hadn't thought about anything else, partly because there were so few options for women at that time, Oriental women, especially. I just thought, 'Well, why not teach then?' Teachers in China were highly respected people. They were consid-ered extremely important members of the society. That, too, must have been in the back of my mind."

Lily traces her special interest in science back to her Chinese roots—to the grocery store and to Oriental ingenuity and thrift. "In my father's grocery," she explains, "we had octopus and squid and sea cucumbers. He had fish that other people are not interested in using for food. He had all kinds of wonderful and unusual plants that Chinese people eat and use for medicine. And I was exposed to all these things. They interested me from a very young age, because eating was interesting to me. I found everything delicious. Being exposed to all these strange and wonderful things built up a curiosity in me about the world and the way things live and function." When it came time for Lily to select an area of concentration, biology seemed a natural choice.

Having won a substantial teaching scholarship from a local funding organization, Lily chose to attend a small Catholic college in town. The choice turned out to be a good one because the teachers were kind, intelligent, and empathetic. "What I found, I think, by watching those nuns," Lily recalls, "was that a teacher could get the same results from being nice as they could from being demanding; the same results from setting up a comfortable environment as from a tense environment." Ironically, the worst courses, taught by the worst teachers, were the ones required for teacher certification. To this day, Lily resents the inadequate preparation she received and the boredom and waste of those days. "They would give us books to buy, and I thought, 'What a waste of money!' because we didn't ever use the books. We'd use maybe one or two chapters, and that would be it. Absolutely worthless. The only course I remember enjoying was adoles-cent psychology, where the big, central insight of the course was that teenagers think of clothes as the most important thing in their lives. That was the only piece of information I found useful in my 32 years in the classroom."

Lily's initial interview at Brackenridge High School exposed her to a kind of overt prejudice that she had never experienced before, either in the insulated world of her home or at college. The subtle but pervasive bias that marked the questions she was asked remain etched in her mind. "'Why don't you have an accent?' the administrator asked me, when it was perfectly plain from my resumé that I was born in San Antonio. This guy, this bureaucrat from central office couldn't conceive of the fact that, given how I looked, I could possibly be an American." But Lily swallowed her pride and accepted the $3,000 a year job, joining a science department that had on its staff the only other Chinese teacher in the city of San Antonio.

"The first year was very, very hard," Lily remembers. "I had been given a section of physics to teach, even though I wasn't certified in physics and had had only eight credits of physics in college. I had no experience; I had very little maturity. I had never had any real responsibilities before, and of course, no adequate teacher training. If not for the help I received from my Chinese colleague and from my husband, I would have been in serious trouble." As it turned out, Lily more than rose to the occasion. Within 5 years, she was promoted to department chair.

***

In second-period honors biology, students mill around briefly before the bell, then make their way to their assigned seats the moment it sounds. All of Lily's classes seem remarkably homogenous. They are all composed of ninth-grade honors students, almost all Hispanic. In this class, Lily's largest, 26 students sit in a large semicircle at small lab tables, leaving an open stage area around which Lily paces and meanders.

Even before the bell rings, students are shushing one another for quiet, patting the air to signal that the class should settle down to work. This call for silence from a group of ninth graders is an unlikely phenomenon to behold. "We've got a new critter today," says Lily, coming forward with a low-key nonchalance. A big, black, ugly-looking bug is wending its way across her hand. "Look at this, guys," she says, "a hissing cockroach!" Several girls recoil, screwing up their faces and screeching. Others lean forward wide-eyed, straining over the lab tables for a closer look. "Listen," she says, with an exaggerated look of suspense. "One, two, three." She clicks the top of the beetle's shell with her finger, and a long hissing sound is heard, like gas through a hose. For a moment the class is perfectly silent. "Now," she says, shaking the bug into a jar, "let's review chapter 16 for the exam." Even as the students open their textbooks to the page, the spell is not yet entirely broken.

The chapter is entitled Arthropods, Econoderms, and Cordata. It looks very dull. "On the test, you'll be required to know the words at the end of the chapter," Lily says. "Why don't we turn it into a game. I'll act out the word, and you try to guess what it is. Number one," she begins, putting her hands up to cheeks and flapping them back and forth.

"Swimmerets?" someone calls out.

"Swimmerets way up at the head?" says Lily with feigned outrage.

"Operculum!" yells someone else.

"Right! Operculum! What's an operculum?"

"A gill cover."

"All right!" says Lily, and everyone applauds. "Number two," she says, contorting her shoulders back and forth in a spasm.

"Throwing up!" yells a boy in the back.

"That's not a term on your list," yells Lily.

"Molting?" asks a girl.

"All right!" says Lily. And the game goes on.

Everything Lily says in class, every anecdote and piece of information, is perfectly attuned to the ninth-grade sensibility—its squeamishness, its fascination with disease and the grotesque, and with sex and violence. "Our crab molted last night," she tells the class. "Now we can eat it, head and all!"

"Eeyew!" groans the class.

"Arthropods," she says, "have crunchy shells. When you step on an arthropod, it crunches, like cereal."

"Eeyew!" groans the class again.

"Don't ever step on a dead scorpion," she says in as suspenseful voice. "The poison is still in the tail.... The scorpion kills her mate right after she's mated. But Mr. Scorpion gets revenge, because the babies ride around on mama's back and kill her!"

"Eeyew!" yells the class. They can't get enough of it.

***

Lily says that the secret of her success in the classroom is a mixture of the right temperament and a capacity to adapt over time. "I was born under the sign of the rabbit," she says. "Rabbits make good teachers." I must have smirked at this piece of information, because Lily gets up and begins rummaging through a large box of paraphernalia—Bunsen burners, torn posters, beakers—and extracts a rumpled chart depicting the Chinese astrological signs. "Here," she says. "Rabbits are successful. Rabbits like to show off. Rabbits attract respect and attention. As a scientist, I used to not believe in horoscopes. But I do now. Like I believe in acupuncture. I believe in it because it works. And I believe in horoscopes because they're so often right.

"I also believe that change is imperative," she goes on. "People change, life-styles change, education needs to change. So I never do the same thing twice in the classroom…even though I teach five sections of ninth-grade biology. Every one of them is different, every day. Every year I make up new experiments for the course. I do swap shops with other teachers in the department. I'll always try something new at least once, since even the mistakes, I've found, are often worthwhile."

Over the years, Lily has experimented with a great range of programs, especially those that focus on the technique of discovery learning. This is a strategy she always favored, even before it came into vogue. "Biology is a hands-on science, an open-ended science in which there are many variables. In chemistry and physics there are formulas for things, numerical bases for things. Not in biology."

***

Given her fascination with the new, the unusual, and the peculiar, it is not surprising that Lily's great hobby is collecting. She is the queen of the flea market, the original back-lot scavenger. Receiving almost no money from the school for supplies, Lily has come to rely on garage and warehouse clearance sales for teaching resources. Using small grants and out-of-pocket money, she has purchased a veritable warehouse of junk over the years, most of which is stored in the science office at Brackenridge. This room is filled with the fruits of her weekend forays, from cloth-covered room dividers, to an incubator, to a hulking refrigerator. "From Texas Surplus Supplies," she tells me, "I've gotten the most amazing things: 300 bowling pins at three cents apiece; 300 hardhats, $18 for the whole lot!; $3 for all the chairs in the resource room; $12 for a centrifuge." Lily's greatest find, which she proudly points out, is a large amount of diving equipment, consisting of 22 pairs of shoes, plus hoses, tanks, socks, and ropes—"$35,000 worth of equipment for $150!" I can imagine tiny Lily, in her flouncy cotton dress, backing her truck up to the Texas Surplus loading dock to pick up hundreds of pounds of aquatic gear.

"What will you use this stuff for?" I ask.

"You never know when you'll need a diving tank," she says.

***

Lily got started doing district in-services when her reputation as a collector (a "resource person," as the principal calls her) started to spread. Though she began with lectures on how to use the seemingly unusable, she soon moved on to topics like classroom management and organization. "I share with the teachers all the tricks I've learned over the years—my numbering system, for example; the way I've learned to number everything I pass out. If I pass things out in order, I can tell which student got which test, and avoid theft. I also tell them how to do different versions of the same test, so that no two students sitting beside each other have the same copy." Sometimes, Lily tells the teachers, she has to write three or four tests. Cheating is rampant in the school, and students have been known to work out elaborate systems for memorizing test questions, which they sell to later classes. "I lecture the students over and over: Scientists have to be honest; there's no science if there's no honesty. But they still cheat constantly. It's a losing battle."

Part of the problem, says Lily, is that students have changed so much. "Years ago, when I started teaching, most families were intact, even families in the Courts apartments. There was less alcoholism, no drugs. Today, few kids go to church. Few kids learn values at home. They have no social skills except what they get from television. And then, of course, the schools no longer teach civics or ethics like they used to. It's hands-off for the schools when it comes to those subjects. No wonder kids destroy property. No wonder they're rude. No wonder they cheat and steal."

Lily opens her first period class with a cautionary tale. The San Antonio school system holds an aluminum drive each year in which scrap metal and cans are collected to raise money. Last weekend, says Lily, someone stole a dozen alumninum seats from the school's auditorium. Several students snicker at this, and Lily gives them the evil eye. Aluminum was also stolen off a local bridge, making the structure too rickety for use. "One of you could have been killed on that bridge," she says. "Or your mother, or your sister." There is a moment of silence, and then she turns to the work of the day.

It may be that no teacher at Brackenridge High School knows his or her students as well as Lily Chin knows hers, not only because she has been at the school for so many years, but also because she has made a career out of merging traditional classroom activities with the extracurricular. When you take your students on trips, when you sponsor clubs and wash cars with them on Saturdays to raise money, you come to know them in a different way. "When I first started teaching, I mimicked, of course, the way I was taught, by frontal lecture. But soon it was clear that with this population, you need to use other incentives—labs and hands-on stuff."

Realizing this, and yet constrained by time and curricular restrictions, Lily started the Lily Chin Science Club, which has evolved over the years into a large, popular, and successful organization. It has been a breeding ground for aspiring engineers, and a refuge for other students who want a friendly place to hang out after school. It is here in the Science Club (recently renamed the Engineering Club) that Lily exerts her greatest influence, instilling values, manners, and discipline taught in the most inconspicuous way. "I get the students as freshmen," says Lily, "so I can sort of sniff out the ones with potential…and also the ones who are most at risk. And I say to them, 'You really ought to check out this neat club we've got. We go on trips to NASA. We visit colleges. We enter contests.' Once the kids start coming, I can indoctrinate them. I say, 'Colleges and employers want well-rounded people. Well-rounded people have the advantages, even over MAs and PhDs.'"

In the science corridor, across from Lily's room, a display case features some of the inventions of the Engineering Club. This month it contains a flying machine that placed first in a recent state round of the Physics Olympics, and a collection of sea fossils retrieved en route to New Braunfels, Texas. As Lily explains the origin of each piece behind the glass, three or four students shuffle over to survey the artifacts. What I'm observing, I suddenly realize, is a very subtle effort at persuasion.

"I take these ninth graders," Lily tells me later, "and I work with them continuously in the club over 4 years. And some of them—some of them—end up at Rice or MIT or the University of Texas at Austin."

One of Lily's success stories is Sergio, who drops in one afternoon during the last week of the school. He is a freshman at Rice, hoping to become an engineer after graduation. Sergio was one of the special students chosen by Lily to act as a lab assistant, a coveted position whose only tangible reward is the right to include it in one's college application.

"Mrs. Chin," Sergio tells me, "is successful with Hispanic students because she shows them she cares. Many of these kids are apathetic and lazy and uninvolved. She gets them motivated; she gets them moving." I ask him what he remembers best about Lily Chin's class. Incubating eggs and then decorating them, is his reply. Collecting bugs. "She has a gift," says Sergio, "for figuring out entertaining things to do."

What Sergio also tells me is that he wishes his high school preparation had been more rigorous. He has had to work terribly hard at Rice, harder than anyone he knows, to keep on top of things. This would probably not surprise Lily, who has been watching her own expectations change over the years, as students seem less and less willing to meet her even halfway. "Recently," she says, "even my best programs aren't working as they once did." Though Lily received special training several years ago to teach Advanced Placement Biology, the students have shown no interest in such a course. And Lily, perhaps sensing the limits of the possible, has not actively encouraged them. It is enough, she says, to get the students to pass, to help them improve their startlingly poor test-taking skills.

***

On the last day of the grading period, Lily is averaging semester scores while her students work quietly at their desks. "Tell me if you want your grade read aloud," she says. To my surprise, nobody requests that his or her score remain private, nor does anyone express shock or dismay when the grades—51, 43, 48, 70—are read. Even with the automatic 10% that Lily adds to every grade, there are still an extraordinary number of failures.

"It's a terribly frustrating situation," Lily says. "To some extent, the book is to blame. It doesn't target the population well. And the objective tests that go with the text are poor. Their idea of objective questions is different from mine." Next year, Lily and the department will use the text only as an occasional resource. They will make up their own tests and their own experiments, and hope for better results.

The other problem, according to Lily, is that classes are too large to offer the kind of private attention needed to motivate these students. "What's more, we're losing two teachers next year. We're losing them because of a mistake on my part. I saw that we were getting ninth-grade biology students who couldn't read and write at grade level. I went to the middle school and said, 'Don't sign them up for biology after eigth grade. Give them another year to mature.' As a result, the numbers are way down and we're forced to lose one of our very best people. It's a tragedy, and there is nothing I can do about it."

Lily has been department chair at Brackenridge for over 20 years. Though she is a woman, tiny and decidedly low-key in style, her power base in the department has never been threatened. She is also remarkably effective, though nobody can quite define the strategies she uses to create harmony. One physical science teacher refers to her magnetic personality but isn't able to elaborate. Another says only that she is "supportive." Mostly, they tell me anecdotes they know about Lily's classroom teaching, her successes with the Engineering Club, how she parks cars on Friday nights to raise money for school trips, and how she will lend anyone anything she owns, from tests and work sheets to whole curricula. And I realize then that her secret is simply to be a good teacher, a good friend, and to work very, very hard. To be respected for these things is to get your way in others.

Since the passage in 1984 of legislation (House Bill 72) intended to salvage Texas's foundering school system, Lily's role as chair has taken on a new, exasperating dimension. The bill, like most top-down reforms, has served to create large quantities of mostly meaningless paperwork, while intimidating teachers with restrictive mandates concerning performance and evaluations. "In the new evaluation system," Lily explains, "we have outside evaluators coming in—evaluators who have no understanding of what we're doing. These people are making judgments—uninformed judgments—that actually affect salary. This year is a good example: I had an elementary school teacher coming in to evaluate my freshman biology class. She had no understanding of cooperative learning. Her conception of being on task was entirely different from mine."

Another casualty of House Bill 72 is the school club. New mandates stipulate that teachers will not be compensated for club sponsorship. "What this means, of course," says Lily, "is the end of clubs, the end of after-school tutoring. The end of all those things that build rapport between faculty and students, things that help kids get social skills, that give them a chance to be a leader." Though Lily intends to continue the Engineering Club without compensation, she is clearly resentful. "It's just too bad," she says.

***

Lily's husband Bob is a policeman in San Antonio. Like her, he is one of a few Chinese to have entered and succeeded in what has traditionally been an Anglo occupation. He is also a Shriner and member of a Masonic lodge. Lily shows me a photo of her family standing together in their dressiest clothes. They look like the American dream family. Her children are very handsome. As Lily enumerates them, she tells me their Chinese names: Linette, 20, is Snow Cloud; Michelle, 18, is Plum Flower; Brent, the baby, is Han Kew, which means Ask Permission of the Heavens.

According to Lily, much of the credit of her relatively easy life, the seamless merging of career and child care, belongs to Bob. He is, she says, "supportive, wonderful, always right. Sometimes I sit around with women of my generation, and we talk about our husbands and how they always know the answer, how to fix things, who to call, and what to say. Bob is very strong; there's nothing he can't do. He was born under the sign of the ox." Bob's talents also extend, it seems, to child care. Himself the product of a large family, he shared equally in the rearing of the Chin children. "Like an ox," Lily says, "he's a workaholic." Still, one difficulty the family has known is money. "With our salaries, it's not always easy to pay the bills. Every time a kid gets sick it's $50. Every time a major expense comes up, it's a crisis."

It is money that is worrying Lily now. Her middle daughter, Michele (honors student, high school valedictorian, and debating champion), has decided to enter Trinity University's five-year teacher education program. When Lily expresses dismay over this,—"Why couldn't she be a lawyer?" she asks—I assume at first that she is joking. What teacher, lauded by her colleagues, revered by the community, loved by her students, would not want her own child to experience the same rewards? But Lily is too practical and unsentimental to think in those terms. "I went myself to the head of the Education Department at Trinity," she says. "I begged him, 'Please don't encourage my daughter to come to Trinity.' He had basically recruited her. She had had no intention of becoming a teacher until he got hold of her. 'Please,' I said, 'at least give her some scholarship money. Help us out. We're just on that fine line of poverty where we're not eligible for any aid.' And he listened, and smiled, and didn't do anything." Lily sighs. "All that money. And for what? For education courses!"

***

When I watch Lily teach, I can understand why she feels as she does about education courses. There is nothing in her style, in the easy clamor of her classroom and its purposeful disarray, that bears any relation to what is taught in conventional education courses, at least those she experienced years ago. Everything here seems to derive from an intuitive sense of what is interesting, and an instinctive capacity to balance work and pleasure, restrictions and freedom.

Today she is teaching the respiratory system. Out of 3-liter Coke bottles, tubes, balloons, and rubber bands she has created models of the lung, one per student. "What's the rubber on the bottom represent?" asks Lily, making a slow turn around the stage of the classroom.

"A diaphragm?"

"Yes, a diaphragm. Have you ever seen a diaphragm?" asks Lily. "This is a diaphragm." She pulls from the clutter of her desk a large tray covered with plastic. Underneath is a half-dissected cat, whose conveniently large diaphragm is intact. The students abandon their lung models and rush to the center of the room. "Eeyew!" "Is that cholesterol in those veins?" "That's the liver! Isn't that the liver?" "That cat had kittens, right?" "Can you eat a cat?" Lily laughs, and answers every question.

Eventually, after poking one another in the diaphragm, and seeing who can hold his breath the longest, and telling stories from the *National Enquirer* about people who sold their lungs to buy bedroom furniture, the students return to their lung models. When the bell rings, they gather their books together reluctantly. "This is an excellent class," says a young man in a matter-of-fact way, as he walks past me. "Write this down," he says. "Mrs. Lily Chin is the best biology teacher in the country." And he is out the door.

Part IV
Questions and Activities

፠ ◆ ஜ

1. Several of the stories in this section depict teachers working with students of different ethnic or socioeconomic backgrounds from themselves. What are some of the inherent difficulties of teaching students whose color and culture is different from your own? How do the teachers here attempt to bridge race and class differences? In what ways are they successful or unsuccessful?

2. Why does the teacher in Richard Yates' story fail to reach Vincent Sabella? Whose fault is it? What should a teacher do in this situation to help herself work better with Vincent?

3. Do you believe that the sexual orientation of a teacher should be made known to his or her students? Why or why not?

4. How does the image of the teacher that emerges in these stories differ from the image in Part III of this book? Part II? Part I? What (if anything) seems to remain constant over time?

5. Richard Dokey presents a powerful portrait of teacher "burnout" in his story, "Teacher." Explain the nature of Mr. Sexton's revelation about himself at the end of the story. How does that revelation relate to his teaching? How does it relate to the "advice" he gives the boy?

6. Write a lesson plan that you think would work well in Lily Chin's ninth grade Biology class.

SUGGESTED READINGS

Grant, G. *The World We Created at Hamilton High* (Boston: Harvard University Press, 1988).

Hill, R. E. *The Black Women Oral History Project* (Westport, CT: Meckler, 1991).

Jennings, K. (Ed.). *One Teacher in 10: Gay and Lesbian Educators Tell Their Stories* (Boston: Alyson Publications, Inc., 1994).

Kidder, T. *Among Schoolchildren* (Boston: Houghton Mifflin, 1989).

Kozol, J. *Savage Inequalities* (New York: Crown, 1991).

Lortie, D. C. *Schoolteacher: A Sociological Study* (Chicago: University of Chicago Press, 1975).

Mathews, J. *Escalante: The Best Teacher in America* (New York: Holt, 1988).

Palonsky, S. B. *900 Shows a Year: A Look at Teaching from the Teacher's Side of the Desk* (New York: Random House, 1986).

Spring, J. *American Education* (New York: McGraw Hill, 1994).

References

⁎   ◆   ⁏

Addams, Jane. *Twenty Years at Hull House*. New York: The Macmillan Company, 1910.

Anderson, James D. *The Education of Blacks in the South, 1860–1935*. Chapel Hill: The University of North Carolina Press, 1988.

Aptheker, Herbert, ed. *The Correspondence of W. E. B. Du Bois* (v. I). "Selections, 1877–1934." Amherst, MA: University of Massachusetts Press, 1973.

Best, John Hardin, ed. *Benjamin Franklin on Education*. New York: Teachers College, 1967.

Burroughs, John. *My Boyhood*. New York: Doubleday & Co., 1922.

Burton, Warren. *The District School As It Was, Scenery Showings and Other Writings*. Boston: T. R. Marvin, 1852.

Calisher, Hortense. *The Collected Stories of Hortense Calisher*. Arbor House Publishing Company, Inc., 1975.

Carter, Kathy. "The Place of Story in the Study of Teaching and Teacher Education." *Educational Researcher*, 22:1 (Jan–Feb 1993), pp. 5–12,18.

Chesnutt, Charles W. "The March of Progress." *The Century Illustrated Monthly Magazine*, Volume 39 (11/1900-4/1901), 422–428.

Clandinin, D. Jean and F. Michael Connelly. "Teacher as Currriculum Marker." *Handbook of Research on Curriculum: A Project of the American Educational Research Association*. Ed. Philip W. Jackson. New York: Macmillan Publishing Co., 1992.

Cohen, Rosetta. *A Lifetime of Teaching: Portraits of Five Veteran High School Teachers*. New York: Teachers College Press, 1991.

Coles, Robert. *The Call of Stories: Teaching and the Moral Imagination*. Boston: Houghton Mifflin Company, 1989.

Covello, Leonard with Guido D'Agostino. *The Heart is the Teacher*: New York: McGraw-Hill Book Company, Inc.,1958.

Cremin, Lawrence A. *American Education: The National Experience 1783–1876*. New York: Harper Colophon Books,1980.

Cremin, Lawrence A. ed. *The Republic and the School: Horace Mann on The Education of Free Men*. New York: Bureau of Publications, Teachers College, Columbia University, 1957.

Cremin, Lawrence A. *The Transformation of the School: Progressivism, 1876/1957*. New York: Vintage Books, 1964.

Curti, Merle. *The Social Ideas of American Education*. New York: Charles Scribner's Sons, 1935.

Dewey, J. "The Professional Organization of Teachers," in *Journal of Education*. Oct.30, 1919.

Dokey, Richard. *August Heat*. Chicago: Story Press, 1982.

Du Bois, W. E. B. *The Souls of Black Folk*. Chicago: A.C. McClurg, 1904.

Dworkin, Martin S. *Dewey on Education*. New York: Teachers College Press, 1959.

Eggleston, Edward. *The Hoosier Schoolmaster: A Story of Backwoods Life in Indiana*. New York: Grosset & Dunlap, 1899.

Forten, Charlotte. "Life on the Sea Islands: Part I." *Atlantic Monthly*, Volume XIII, No. LXXIX and LXXX (May–June, 1864).

Freneau, Philip. *The Prose of Philip Freneau*. Philip Marsch, ed. New Brunswick: Scarecrow Press, 1955.

Gilbert, C. B. *The School and Its Life*. New York: Silver Burdett, 1906.

Graber, Kay, ed. *Sister to the Sioux: The Memoirs of Elaine Goodale Eastman 1885–91*. Lincoln: University of Nebraska Press, 1978.

Grant, Gerald. *The World We Created At Hamilton High*. Boston: Harvard University Press, 1988.

Greene, Maxine. *Landscapes of Learning*. New York: Teachers College Press, 1978.

Hale, Edward Everett. *A New England Boyhood*. Boston: Little, Brown, and Company, 1927.

Herndon, James. *The Way It Spozed To Be*. New York: Simon and Schuster, 1965.

Hoffman, Nancy. *Women's "True" Profession: Voices From the History of Teaching*. New York: Feminist Press, 1981.

Irving, Washington. *The Sketch Book of Geoffrey Crayon, Gent*. New York, The New American Library. 1981.

Jennings, Kevin, ed. *One Teacher in 10: Gay and Lesbian Educators Tell Their Stories*. Boston: Alyson Publications, Inc., 1994.

Kaestle, Carl F. *Pillars of the Republic: Common Schools and American Society 1780–1860*. New York: Hill and Wang, 1983.

Kaufman, Polly Welts. *Women Teachers on the Frontier*. New Haven: Yale University Press, 1984.

Keller, Helen. *The Story of My life*. New York: Doubleday, Page and Company, 1905.

Kelly, Myra. *Little Citizens*. New York: Grosset and Dunlap,1904.

Kidder, T. *Among Schoolchildren*. Boston: Houghton Mifflin, 1989.

Kozol, Jonathan. *Death at an Early Age: The Destruction of the Hearts and Minds of Negro Children in the Boston Public Schools*. Boston: Houghton Mifflin Company, 1967.

Leary, Lewis. *That Rascal Freneau: A Study in Literary Failure*. New Brunswick, NJ: Rutgers University Press, 1941.

Lester, Julius, ed. *The Seventh Son: The Thought and Writings of W. E. B. Du Bois*. New York: Random House, 1971.

Linn, James Weber. *Jane Addams: A Biography*. New York: D. Appleton-Century Company Incorporated, 1935.

Lortie, Daniel C. *Schoolteacher: A Sociological Study*. Chicago: University of Chicago Press, 1975.

Lutz, Alma. *Emma Willard: Daughter of Democracy*. Boston: Houghton Mifflin Company, 1929.

Lutz, Alma. *Emma Willard: Pioneer Educator of American Women*. Boston: Beacon Press, 1964.

Mann, H. "Fifth Annual Report (1841)" as quoted in Cremin, L. A. (Ed.) *The Republic and the School: Horace Mann on the Education of Free Men*. New York: Bureau of Publication, Teachers College, 1957.

Mathews, J. *Escalante: The Best Teacher in America*. New York: Holt, 1988.

McCuskey, Dorothy. *Bronson Alcott, Teacher*. New York: The Macmillan Company, 1940.

Paley, Vivian Gussin. *White Teacher*. Cambridge, MA: Harvard University Press, 1979.

Palonsky, Stuart B. *900 Shows a Year: A Look at Teaching from A Teacher's Side of the Desk*. New York: McGraw-Hill, 1986.

Patri, Angelo. *A Schoolmaster of the Great City*. New York: The Macmillan Company, 1917.

Payne, Daniel Alexander. *Recollections of Seventy Years*. New York: Arnold Press, 1968.

Peabody, Elizabeth Palmer. *Record of a School Exemplifying the General Principles of Spiritual Culture*. Boston: James Munroe and Company,1835.

Rippa, S. Alexander. *Education in a Free Society: An American History*. New York: Longman Inc., 1988.

Rofes, Eric. *Socrates Plato, and Guys like Me*. Boston: Alyson Publications, Inc., 1985.

Rudolph, Frederick, ed. *Essays on Education in the Early Republic*. Cambridge, MA: Belknap Press of Harvard University, 1965.

Spring, Joel. *American Education*. New York: McGraw Hill, 1994.

Stevenson, B. ed. *The Journals of Charlotte Forten Grimke*. New York: Oxford Univeristy Press, 1988.

Stovall, Floyd, ed. *Prose Works of Walt Whitman* (2 volumes). New York: New York University Press, 1963.

Stuart, Jesse. *Best Loved Stories of Jesse Stuart*. E. H. Richardson, ed. New York: McGraw Hill, 1982.

Thompson, Daniel Pierce. *Locke Amsden, or The Schoolmaster: A Tale*. Boston: Benjamin B. Mussey and Co.,1852.

Trumbull, John. *The Satiric Poems of John Trumbull*. Edwin T. Bowden, ed. Austin: University of Texas Press, 1962.

Tyack, D. *The One Best System: A History of American Urban Education*. Cambridge, MA: Harvard University Press, 1974.

Tyler, Royall. *The Algerine Captive*. Gainesville, FL: Scholars' Facsimile and Reprints, 1967.

United States Bureau of Census, *Population, 1900*, "Teachers."

Warren, Donald, ed. *American Teachers: Histories of a Profession at Work*. New York: Macmillan Publishing Co., 1989.

Whitman, Walt. *Walt Whitman: The Early Poems and the Fiction*. Thomas L. Brasher, ed. New York: New York University Press, 1963.

Willard, Emma Hart. *Educational Biographies, Memoirs of Teachers,Educators,and Promoters and Benefactors of Education, Literature, and Science, Part I: Teachers and Educators* (2nd ed.). New York: F. C. Brownell, 1861.

Winslow, Ola Elizabeth, ed. *Harper's Literary Museum: A Compendium of Instructive, Entertaining and Amusing Matter Selected from Early American Writings.* New York: Harper & Brothers Publishers, 1927.

Yates, Richard. *Eleven Kinds of Loneliness.* New York: Dell Publishing Co., Inc., 1957

Yezierska, Anzia. *Children of Loneliness.* New York: Funk and Wagnalls Co., 1923.

Author Index

❧ ◆ ☙

Subject Index

క్ర ◆ ౮ి